Am I Dreaming

Ozzie Vargas

Copyright © 2014 Ozzie Vargas

All rights reserved.

ISBN-10:0692287558
ISBN-13:9780692287552

DEDICATION

This book is dedicated to the girl of my life, Abigail Vargas.

You will always be my little girl.

To Dad, Axisa, Jenelle, Christian and Justin. Love you all.

Thanks to Nancy for putting up with me for many years.

Special thanks to Ritzi Uranus for her help with editing

And

To Justin Andrades for the book cover and art work.

To my sister Sarita, thank you for helping me get out.

Thanks to G. Who stood by my side. You know who you are. -------

In dying he taught me more about living than I could have ever taught him.

Ozzie Vargas

CONTENTS

PROLOG

Truth is Stranger than Fiction. For the first time in his life Ozzie finds himself confined within the penal system. There he embarks on a quest for answers; Disturbing answers that are rooted much deeper than they appear on the surface. His quest serves two purposes. One is to escape a demon that haunts and torments him. A demon conjured by the death of a loved one, for whom he is responsible for. To his horror there's no place he can hide. How can he run when there's nowhere to escape?

Due to a confrontation, he now finds himself entangled with a bounty on his head. How he can survive… when his assassin is aware of his every move. For protection he forms a volatile alliance with three notorious gang members. Harold is the ring leader of the Latin Kings and Edwin is the top dog of the NETA. Both are brutal but yet well organized gangs. Prince's allure, AKA the Prince of Pentium, is a share in a six million dollar heist. Ozzie conspires and helps all three gang members escape. Each has a devious and conniving reason to do so. Harold's goal is to avenge his brutal beating against a crooked Hollywood police officer. Edwin, a Freemason makes certain assertions and revelation to Ozzie. Those revelations and new discoveries profoundly altered his Destiny. For Ozzie is now confronted with a new set of problems. Stumbling upon a fork in a road, he must now choose a path. Death from different directions confronts him. Are his friends powerful enough to help him survive?

At first a profoundly honest man, influenced by a lack of love, "AM I DREAMING" is a story of love, loss, heroism, honor, cunning, survival and ultimately, hope. Hope that he can somehow influence an outcome of a devious plan set in motion by an elite group.

Shantel Powders, chief editor for Michelle Whitedove books writes, Am I Dreaming is nothing short of phenomenal, Electrifying and mesmerizing . . . The fully realized characters and vivid prose show that Ozzie Vargas is a supremely talented author.

1 INTRODUCTION

Am I dreaming? Is this a rhetorical question? Perhaps! At the very least it's an intriguing one. As I rest on this mattress only 2 inches thick and 22 inches wide, I stare at the bunk above and ponder this question. It's 1:30 am and most of the 55 inmates in my unit are asleep. It is not my turn yet; not my time. That's because of the sleeping cycle that I have developed over the last few years. A cycle brought upon by an event which would cause the sky to darken everywhere I went, and everywhere I looked; even on the most beautiful Florida sunny day. It was a tragic event that no one should be made to experience. Its membership is small. Only a few know that which I feel. It's analogous to experience labor pains; no one can truly know the feeling until they go through it themselves. So at least for the next hour, I will put my thought to paper and see how much I can squeeze in before I get up to serve breakfast. In jail, breakfast is served at 3:30 am, by the inmates. It's actually a wonderful job; that is, if you are confined in jail as I have been for the past five months. During this time I have withered away; going from 228 pounds of solid muscles with a 9% body fat to 199 pounds. It's been 30 years since I remember myself this slim. Anyway, after breakfast I sit down with two fellow inmates and eat as much as I can. I then return to my bunk with extra food which I distribute to a few who don't have the privilege or means for commissary. As of late I've managed to add a few pounds due to serving breakfast.

After breakfast, sleep comes quickly and easily for me. For most inmates, morning comes at 7:00 am. The unit fills with chatter from inmates talking as they sweep and mop their room. Each cell has an open front with no doors to close, no curtains to hide behind, and no privacy at all. With the passage of time, I've become accustomed to sleep through this part of the day. It is not till 10:30 am that I get up. 10:30 am is lunch time. I used to call it breakfast, but it is lunch. By 11:00 am, it's done and I am back to sleep until 1:00 pm. That is my cycle here, at the Paul Rein Detention Facility in Broward County, Florida. It will be 4:00 am the next day before I sleep again. So what are these thoughts I have today? I ask myself, when did it all begin? Was it before I was born? Was it growing up in the south Bronx with an abusive mother? Was it September 9th, 2006? Was it the day Jackie called? I do remember telling her one day, while in the shower as I washed her hair, that she did not choose her profession, but instead it was her profession that chose her. Going on this premise, is it my destiny to be here? Who knows? I guess each person will have a different opinion. Well, it is almost 2:30 am and I have to go and wake three diabetic patients; for the nurse is on the way to administer insulin shots to each. Mr. Stevenson an 80 year old black male is 1st on the list. He spent 45 years in jail for the murder of his wife. I will again attempt to find the answer I seek, in about 20 hours from now.

2 THE CATCH

By Floridian standards, The South Florida weather was still cool. It's taken me 18 years to finally get use to it. Used to the summer heat and used to the shift in finding 70° cool. By northern standards or shall we say, snow birds standards, that is still warm. I now find myself comfortably standing in front of the dealership in Pompano Beach, enjoying the ocean breeze which flows from east to west during the day and shifts from west to east at night. As the beach is only one block away you can periodically taste the salt as the air blows it by. Helena a pretty Brazilian woman stands beside me. She tells me of her experience working with Sergio doing road sales. She was a good sales person and had the Pompano Brazilian market wrapped up. Pompano Beach has one of Florida's biggest Brazilian populations. Despite her being a really good sales person, she often would ask for a flying T.O. (that is car lingo for a customer that suddenly wants to leave). Before the customer realized what was going on I would have them at the table agreeing to purchase the car. That was my job; finance and closer. Hours there were very long and management was very slow in delivering to me what was promised. Sure they sent me to finance school in Texas, and promised me the world, but those promises did not come. It's the reason Sergio left. One evening, after speaking to Helena for several minutes I decided to call him. Before I knew it, I was away doing Road sales; Traveling from New York to Florida and all states in between. I managed to sign up with three different firms. That gave me the flexibility to choose when and where I wanted to work.

A typical sale lasted six days. Selling on the road requires a different approach than selling in one location. The product is the same and doesn't change. What do change are the location and the brand of vehicles. The product does not change, I say, because the product is you. Selling the metal is the easy part. At the dealership, you sell yourself first, then the dealership, and then the auto. The added dimension is that during the road sales, you also sell the sale. That is, you stress the urgency of buying now, during the event, as the deal will never get better.

It's was March 2012 when I found myself in Michigan. Having been removed from cold places for so long has made me forget those feelings of numbness in my hands and feet. As I struggle with the discomfort brought by the weather, I gazed at a well dressed salesperson walking by. That gaze turned into a stare. This tall, thin, fit Anglo was different than the rest. He reminded me of myself. At 6'2", 228 pounds, with broad shoulders and 36 inch waist, I too was a presence wherever I went. The Anglo's name is Dustin. He was the closer and did finance for the outfit. Immediately we took to each other, and shared stories of past experience in the car business. By the end of the week, Dustin had invited me to work full time with his firm. I did not agree to the terms 100%, but I did manage to change my plans to accommodate a partial offer. In this business, closers and team leaders can earn $150,000 to $200,000 a year. However a great salesperson can make as much with half the stress.

My scheduled trip to Turkey with Jackie was about seven weeks away. She called to remind me that I needed to obtain my passport. So I rushed to Florida and got my Jackie fix, along with all her wonderful smells. After I visited the passport office I headed out to a new sale in Missouri, or misery I should say. Having been used to quick witted, suspicious people, always on the go, it appeared to me that this was a different breed. Everyone looked the same. It's as if inbreeding was rampant. Who knows? What I did know was; I wanted out of there.

Two weeks have passed since my passport visit. Jackie received a letter from them. I asked her to read it to me. Disappointing news was an understatement. My passport was denied for past child support. Jackie was furious as she had already purchased the tickets; the bill was over $5000. My blood money was already dried, and my bills were many. She therefore asked for me to never call her again. The following day I called the Department of revenue to see what they were referring to. I know that my support payments for Jenelle and Ozzie were over with and there were no arrears. Christian however who had turned 21 was due $710. So paying over 21 years, a deficit of $710 was all that was standing in the way between Turkey – Jackie and I. At least on the surface, that's what it looked like. However, there was a roadblock. There was just not enough time to pay, reapply, and have a passport issued. It was not meant to be, it was not in my cards. Things went spiraling downwards immediately and Jackie and I headed for Splitsville once again.

Dustin and I had taken a liking to each other. He was a part owner of an escort service in Cincinnati Ohio. Yet he lived on the border of Kentucky. He expressed an interest in setting up shop in Miami, and presented me a business proposal entailing 50%

ownership. At first I paid very little attention, as having been raised in New York, I looked at everything with suspicion. Weeks turned into months. During a sale in Pompano Beach, Dustin decided to scout out a location for the business. It was then I realized his sincerity. By then I was spending much time with a wealthy real estate broker. She had an office in Coral Springs as well as a huge 7000 ft.[2] home. Apart from her two poodles, she was the only living thing there. Many nights I found myself kicking them off my feet. This lady asked me to be a part of her life. She had a lot to offer, and I contemplated the idea. What more can a man ask for? Liz and I took Dustin to see a few locations for our new venture but no specific one was agreed upon. That Monday I left Dustin at the airport and spent the day with Liz. Follow by the evening with Abby, my beautiful daughter.

During that following week, Dustin put me on a conference call with his lawyer, and a business plan was laid out. Two more weeks passed by when Dustin called again. He had a peculiar request. It was rather strange. A request was made that took me off guard. As I sit in the here and now, I ask myself again, "when did it all begin?" Was it here? Was this the turning point I often seek an answer to?

- Ø Hi Art! It's been a few months since we have spoken. How are your lovely daughters?
- Ø Just fine, as well as my granddaughters. How is Abby?
- Ø At 14, she is tall and beautiful, like her mom and Dad; The product of two beautiful Puerto Rican people.

Art and I had known each other for eight years as we work at a dealership together. He had a home in Miami Lakes and rented a room to me from July 2009 through January 2010. It was during this time that I owned an amusement arcade, (casino) in Hialeah, Fl. The Casino being in Miami/Dade County, consisted mostly of a Cuban population. It was a nice business that allowed me much time to do what I wanted. Cameras there allowed me to view it from any place in the world. I sold it within a year and a half, as six other casinos opened shop within a 10 mile radius. It was a business I purchase with my blood money, and I was not about to lose it all.

Ø Art, I am trying to make a connection for a friend and future business partner.

I confided to Art, Dustin's request, as well as our escort service business that was taking place. I knew Art had a few run-ins with the law and thought he might be able to help. However he was not sure he could do so. That same day I called James. James was my brother in law. At 5'10", 190 pounds you would never believe he had a past for collecting money for an organized crime family in the Bronx. James grew up in the hood, although he came from a family of means. He is one of a few people that I admired; for he had a wife and daughters that meant everything in the world to him. Although he appeared as a docile non-threatening individual, when he spoke, you knew he was not a man to play with. You can't work collecting debts for the mob, for many years, if you are inefficient. The only thing that stopped him from rising high in rank was his birthplace; for he was from Trinidad. His skin was tan colored, almost reddish. He looked as if he was always in the sun. After the formalities, I asked James for help with a matter. His first reaction was,

- Ozzie, it's a different world. Don't get involved as there are a great number of snitches out there.
- And that is why I come to you James.

A few days passed when James called. He said he has some Mexicans that will do it, but first they needed to check out credentials; all they needed was a full government name and date of birth. As the day went by, Dustin called me every six hours or so. Just like the kid in the back seat, "are we there yet?" On the third day, I received a call from James. He said he was meeting with his guys on my behalf. Stuff like that takes place face-to-face. A hand shake seals the deal.

A few more days went by when James called again. The report on Dustin was that he was twice a felon and that he was a stickup kid. Those were his exact words. I thought that was credible behavior for Dustin's request. However and more important, James people decide to pull out because Dustin's records show no more information.

- "And what is wrong with that?"
- Well Ozzie, when you history is sealed, it's a possible indication of a government deal, otherwise known as an informant.

After thinking for a few hours about the entire situation, I called Dustin and told him the news. He assured me he was not an informant. I put the whole thing to bed and continued with my road sales. All the time I thought about my girl Jackie and how I could win her back. Being in her presence was good enough for me. She was my medicine, my cured to those dark cloudy days I experienced every day. I figured if I had a business again, I could keep up with her lifestyle; for she was an anesthesiologist. A $260,000 yearly salary allowed her spending freedom, not known to the average wage earner. Before I knew it, my blood money was gone. Not that she took it, but I spent it subconsciously to mask my sleepless nights; my inner demons. She lifted the cloud over my head, and for the first time in a few years, I saw the sun again. I could finally sleep. After boom-boom, as she called it, I would wrap my left arm around her and weave my left leg around hers. Being with her was like being in paradise. I sniffed her every night before I slept. It was the sweetest odor I have ever known on a human. And take my word; I was an expert on woman and odors.

Before I knew it several weeks had gone by. In that time I saw a few locations to set up shop for my new business venture with Dustin. The plan was to restore my wealth and acquire my girl. That was my mission and it seemed I was on target.

- Ø High Art, it's been a month since we spoke.
- Ø Ozzie,
- Ø Yes.
- Ø Are you still interested in that which you spoke off?
- Ø Well Art, I don't know. I would have to make a phone call.

It was now June 3. After a call to Dustin, and with his approval, I called Art and confirmed that the deal was good. From there on everything happened immediately; that morning I was in Illinois, and in the afternoon I was sitting in Dustin's house in Kentucky. He had his buddy and accomplice pick me up in the Cincinnati airport, just 45 minute drive from his house. His buddy and longtime friend, Derek, was a short, stocky black American. I had met him once in Florida during a road sale. Although there was a stark contrast between the two, there were two things they had in common. They dressed well and loved to smoke weed. As I sat in the living room, discussing the plan, I could not help myself from being fixed on the view. The house was on a cul-de-sac. The backyard overlooked the Ohio River, with an elevation of about 300 feet. Boat lights faded as they distanced themselves from where I sat. After discussing a plan with both, I quickly retired.

The next morning I awoke and found myself in a strange house; walking among people I barely knew. If I were a serial killer, I could have massacred seven. Wow, what a thought. Why would I even have a thought like that? Had I suddenly changed and become sinister or was it in my genes? Derek was downstairs in the kitchen. He was the only one awake.

"I'm hungry" I said, and so we took to the nearest Waffle House. During the short ride we exchange stories of our past. Once there we quickly ate and headed back to the house. As the afternoon approached I gathered my bag and loaded the truck for my airport departure. As I neared the airport scanner I thought about the $9,000.00 in my left pocket. Dustin assured me that there would be no questions asked. I emptied my pocket, place the money in an open envelope and then on the gray plastic tray. My heart raced a little fast. Not because of the money, but because of what it was for. I was not afraid of any questions for I had committed no crime, and having money was not illegal. However, in my mind; well that was different. I was up to no good. No one could see it, but I could. The few seconds through the scanner therefore felt like an eternity. In an instance I was all cleared. I picked up my belongings, place the envelope back in my pocket and put my shoes and belt on.

Maggie picked me up in Florida. She was a beautiful, sexy Dominican woman. She was in love with me, but knew she could not have my heart. That beating thing belonged to only one girl and Maggie knew who that was. She had a lot to offer, and like me, loved sex. She was a trooper in bed and she was hot. Nothing was off limit. The ride from Fort Lauderdale airport to the hotel in Coral Springs took about 20 minutes. Shortly upon entering the room I found myself in the shower. I barely got to lather-up when the curtain was pulled to the side. She paused before she entered. There she was, a beautiful, tall, woman, standing naked. Her long dark hair covered her left breast. Her nipples were erect and seeking for my attention. Her Hispanic hips and curvy ass was accentuated by her slim waist. She proceeded to insert her finger within herself, and then placed it in my mouth. What a wonderful scent. I slowly licked her finger. With her, there was no need for foreplay. She was always ready, as was I. Maggie stepped into the shower and backed up onto me. She then bent over forwards. As far as she was concerned, every opening in her body was made for pleasure, and pleasure is surely what I liked. I grabbed her by the hips and pulled her into me. She clearly enjoyed the position. After several minutes she pulled forwards a little and then guided me into her anus. That was her favorite. Who was I to say no? Several more minutes of thrusting past and we then headed to the bed. One hour and numerous orgasms would pass before we succumbed. We ended the evening holding each other and falling asleep without discussing anything.

The next morning was the big day. The day Dustin had put in place. Maggie dropped me off at Liz's house, and proceeded to drive to work in Boca Raton. Liz had left the door open and I quietly entered. I was greeted by her poodles, the ones I often kicked off the bed. Liz was sleeping. As I pulled the sheet back, I could not help but to admire her golden, naked ass. She knew where I spent the night. One thing about me is that, I am brutally honest. I was always a proud, happy man. I loved and took good care of myself; and I feared no man in this world. For that mattered I feared nothing at all. This was a trait I passed on to my son. In reality it was a dangerous trait; one that would have a lasting impact in my life as well as his. Liz also knew my dark secret: about my blood money, and about Jackie. I don't know what was on her mind, but she knew that which she also sought, just as it was for Maggie was off-limits to her as well; that being my heart. That did not stop her from enjoying me, enjoying the moment, enjoying my manhood. Every day I rewarded her with my big stiffness, and this morning was no different. Although I loved woman, respected them and treated each one special, there was one term I would never use. That was the term "make love". It's a tragic story with roots in my mother's abuse of power and authority. Quietly I undressed and slid myself info bed. Liz turned over and kissed me. She pressed her breast onto my chest and reached down for me. She found what she was looking for. With that her lips moved down my chest and continued to my cock. After getting a mouthful she sat on me and moved around until she reached orgasm. However, I was not done. I moved her to my side and entered her from behind. We were both now in the fetal position and I was inside of her. It was 11 AM by the time I awoke again; Liz had taken off to work. I was once again erect, and could smell the scent of both women's juices on me. I showered, had breakfast and proceeded to call Dustin. Today was Thursday, the day to fulfill his request. I checked my bank account for the balance of the required money. The $4000 had not yet hit. Was there a problem? An error, or had I been found out, and the plan foiled. The call to Dustin revealed his inability to execute or should I say implement his desire. Time was now of essence. This was going down today without Plan B. There was no time now for a wire transfer. Dustin banked at Chase Bank and asked if I had access to anyone with an account there. Lo and behold, Maggie came to the mind. I remember her going to a Chase bank in Coral Springs several months ago. So I called her at work and asked her for a favor. She knew I was up to something, but did not know what; she seemed to not care either. It seems she would do whatever I asked. So for now the plan was back in place, however she could not retrieve the money until she left work at 5:30. The branch in Coral Springs was the only one open till 6 PM, and her commute from Boca Raton was about 30 minutes. As she set off from work she dialed the bank to make her appearance known. The branch manager told her there was an issue with the transfer and that they were trying to resolve it. With that she proceeded to the branch, texting me and talking while driving; Informing me every minute of her whereabouts. In turn I was relaying the info to Dustin.

It was a minute or two after six. She witnessed the parking lights go out as she pulled to the front of the bank. Banging her keys on the glass alerted the manager of her presence. He quickly asked her name and escorted her in. People were still conducting business at the branch. Maggie entered and was told to wait for about 10 minutes. All the while, she continued texting me. Again I wondered if the police had been notified. Had I been discovered? Several minutes later she exited the bank and jumped in her car. I followed as she drove to the far corner of the parking lot. Once there she exited her car, and jumped into my passenger seat. She turned towards me with a rather strange look in her eyes. One I have never seen before. She reached for the back of my head with her right arm and pulled me towards her as she moved into my space. Before I knew it, her tongue was in my mouth. She released my head but not my tongue. Her right hand now made its way to my manhood. I responded with an erection. All this took place within seconds. I had to reposition myself for comfort. Without saying one word she reached in her bag and pulled out an envelope. In it was $4000 in new crisp clean $100 bills. As she opened the door and stepped out she uttered seven words. "Love you, -be careful-, call me tonight". Once again I could not help myself but notice her sexy ass, as she walked away. Why was I not her boyfriend, I thought. Surely she was desirable. Oh, Yes I remember. There is someone else for me.

With that, I made two phone calls; One to Dustin and one to Paco. Paco was not his government name. But it's all I had to go by. He was the man I was introduced to by Art; The one who was collecting $13,000. Paco gave me instructions to meet him in one hour in Hollywood Beach Florida. Driving South on I-95, I decided to get a quick bite, as I still had some time to kill. I had passed my meeting place by one exit to acquire food, and so after eating I turned back north on I-95. After the exit I was to turn left, pass the train tracks, and turn left again. I overshot my turn and proceeded to make an illegal U-turn by the tracks. Before I completed the turn I saw the lights, it was coming from the car behind me, for some reason it seemed brighter than normal. Red-blue, red-blue, red-blue. Oh Fuck! I told myself. I knew I was in big trouble. There I was, driving on a suspended license for failure to pay a ticket, with $13,000 cash in an envelope on the front seat. Before I could roll down the window, this tall Broward Sherriff Officer was tapping on it. All he said was,

- Ø "Driver's license and insurance card"

I fumbled through the glove compartment but could not find the insurance card. I then wondered what the end date of the policy was. Had it past, or was it to be renewed any day? I gave the license to the officer along with the registration and proceeded to call Paco.

- Ø Paco, I'm going to be arrested as a BSO officer just pulled me over.

To my surprise, the officer walked over, handed me my documents and said, "Ozzie today is your lucky day." He quickly hopped in his car and sped off with the lights flashing. Paco had not hung up and the phone line was still open.

- Ø You're not going to believe this I said, but I've just been spared.

I looked at the passenger seat as I spoke and fixed my eyes on the envelope. I told Paco I will meet him in 10 minutes as I wanted to be sure I was not being followed. He agreed. For a moment as I slowly drove off, I asked myself, if indeed it was my lucky day. Was I being followed by detectives and the BSO officer was called off? Or was he part of their plan to capture me. I had taken this too far to turn back now. Destiny was taking its course. Before I knew it, I was in too deep. I had not bothered to think this through. Not once was I aware of the penalties for my transgressions or of the consequences. All I thought about was winning my girl back.

Having made my way to the Bass fishing shop in Hollywood I noticed Paco by the front door. He instructed me to pull into a parking spot and walked over. He leaned his head through the front passenger door and asked to see the money. I pointed to the envelope in the front seat and he told me to jump in his Hummer. As I walked towards the rear of my car he said, "Bring a bag". I popped the trunk, which he gazed into and said, "That one will do". It was my gray gym bag. I removed most of the items, and threw the bag over my shoulder. That's when fear struck. "Where is my gun?" Was it in the car? Had I removed it from my bag the day before? Or was it in the trunk? Nothing I could do at this point. I closed the trunk lid, walked to the Hummer and sat in the passenger seat. Art had assured me Paco was okay, and so I did not worry too much about the gun. It took Paco a few minutes to count $13,000. He was rather nervous and I wondered why. I reached to grab the money and call the whole thing off, but again, destiny beckoned and prevailed. After Paco finish counting, he grabbed an item from under the backseat and placed it in my bag. I took a quick look at it, closed the bag, and exited. The distance to my car was less than 20 steps. Halfway between both vehicles I got tunnel vision. As I lifted my eyes from the ground I noticed a Glock pointed at me. "Oh shit"-Ozzie you are fucked. There was some commotion to my side and behind. I was fixed at the lady pointing at me. I could see her finger on the trigger. It was clear I was going to be shot. From my left came a fist which struck my jaw. However it did not move me. It was followed by a push from behind, and I could now make out the yelling. "Drop to the ground. This is the police." As I laid there with my right cheek pressed against the pavement, I said to myself, "Ozzie your life has forever changed." The next thought was where is my gun? The only worst thing that could happen at this point is to find a handgun in my gym bag along the half a kilo of cocaine I just purchased.

The parking lot was now swarming with police. "Where the hell did so many offices come from"? Lights were flashing all over. My cheek was red and inflamed from rubbing against the ground I was now laying on. One officer had his knee on my back exerting pressure. My $200 jeans had a rip at the left knee and blood was pouring out from it.

"Had I been shot?" Was this all a dream? Among all the noise one voice stood out.- "Do you have any weapons on you"? All I could do was say, "No". As I was helped up, hands cuffed behind my back, I looked towards the direction where the lady with the gun was. Just as quickly as she appeared she vanished. However there were still many guns pointing at me.

The front passenger door of a black suburban was opened for me. I was instructed to sit. I did so with my hands cuffed behind my back. A medium build, clean-cut detective, sat in the driver seat. His bright blue eyes caught my attention.

Ø Hello Ozzie. My name is Jerry, What is your full government name?
Ø Ozzie Vargas.
Ø We have been watching you for two weeks. You are looking at a charge with a minimum mandatory sentence of 15 years.

I was surprised; for I had not a clue nor did I ever sit and think about the penalties. Jerry asked if I wanted to cooperate. I was in shock and confused. He said I had solicited an informant who turned me to the detective Paco. I know knew that Art was the informant. Prior to that, I had confided to him many of the details about the person I was trying to connect.

Jerry knew this was my one and only purchase of any illegal drugs. He asked if I wanted to deliver the drugs to Dustin, who was now also under surveillance. I gave Jerry information about Dustin that I had already shared with Art. In reality, I was acting as if I was cooperating, but that's only because they already knew what I was telling them. During my interrogation, Dustin had text me several times. What had started in the parking lot at sunset was drawn till about 9:30. I told Jerry I could not cooperate with delivering the goods to Dustin, and with that I was taken to Fort Lauderdale Main Jail for booking.

It must have been a busy evening in Broward, for the holding cells were full to capacity. There was only standing room in the holding cell I was placed in. Bond was set at $1,000,000. I was photographed, fingerprinted and sent to the third floor. It was 3 AM by the time I was given a mat on the floor to sleep on.

3 WITHIN BARS AND FOUR WALLS

The sun has risen three times since I put my thoughts to paper. Looking at the present and into the future has me scared. Events in the past few months in jail, has set me on a course where death is highly possible. I ask myself a new set of questions. Is it worth it? Will there be more deaths? Will Abby be okay? Once again destiny has called. Things have been set in motion which I can't seem to put a lid on. My daringness, boldness, my lack of fear, my ability to talk my way out of bad situations, all part of my genetic makeup, bestowed upon me by my father, and I in turn upon my son, is now taking me into an underground world. A world of liars, cheats, murderers and drug dealers. How do I stop it? Can I stop it? Is it my inner demon, (which keeps me up all night), that is responsible for where I am headed? Am I still trying to escape from the events which led to the blood money? Will there be more blood money? Fiction and reality are becoming blurred. Harold, who I have now befriended and struck an accord with, has me worried. It's not his physical presence that scares me. It's who he is. It's his connections, his ties, and his people. Any wrong step, any wrong move, any wrong word, can get you dead-finished, kaput. Can I stop myself? I don't know. I don't know. I don't know. Can I fight destiny or should I just go along for the ride and see how it plays out? One set of circumstances followed by another, has brought me here. Frankly, there appears to be an adventurous side to this, just like there was in Ozzie Junior. To see how this all plays out, is adventurous. This journey is going to be rough. Will I be dead soon, or will I live to 82 with Jackie by my side? For I promised her I would do so. I don't know! I don't know! I don't know!

Broward's main jail is an old, dirty jail. Eight floors in all and the higher up you go, the greater the security. Floors seven and eight hold the black and white striped jumpsuits. Red jumpsuits are strictly on the eighth floor. The most serious offenders are found there. The jumpsuit is the only indication of the severity of the crime. There are people there that look outright dangerous, and then there are those who look like they couldn't hurt a fly.

Ages range from 17 to as long as one can live. The third floor, where I was housed, is a transit unit. You spend a few days there and then get bussed to one of three other jails in Pompano Beach.

On the third floor, one pod or unit consist of 15 two-man cells. The jail is not set for comfort. The only place to sit is on a metal seat. It's bolted to the ground and attached to the table. It is difficult to sit for more than 15 minutes. Plastic portable beds about 11 inches high off the ground are scattered in this area; usually about 10. So in total you have about 40 frantic people in a unit, all competing for four phone lines as they try to get and give info to their friends and family.

Because the Broward County jail system is a business, phone calls are each $2.50. It requires the recipients of your call to set up an account with a special phone company. Within the first few days of incarceration, new inmates are on edge. Twice during my stay I yanked the phone from the person in front of me, for making a second or third call in a row.

For the first few days and nights, all I did was replayed my arrest over and over. How could I have allowed this to happen? Will I ever get out? Most of the time is spent wondering how to get out. You think of everyone you know that might help you. The list has those that you are sure will help and those that possibly will. I for sure thought I would be out in a matter of days. On my fourth day I was in front of the magistrate and my bond was reduced to $100,000. I instructed my brother to sell some of my things for bail money as well as to acquire an attorney. With my charges, the going rate for a lawyer was about $20,000. My priority was getting out first, so I decided to stick with the public defender, and then switch to a good attorney.

I quickly found out how easily people turned their backs on you when you need them the most. My nature is a loving, caring and giving one. While I never gave a damn about anyone, I was true and loyal to the handful of people I knew and loved. This included my brother Ismael, who I thought would be the best person to help me out. In life we were one year apart; we were buddies and we were close friends. For many years, we played chess for hours on end. Often we would literally eat, drink and sleep with a chess board between us. At the age of 16 I pressured him to move out with me and so we rented a one bedroom apartment. By then, I had had enough of my abusive mother. Talk about mothers, I knew better than to ask her for help. Ismael was so ashamed of what I did decide to play the judge, the jury and the executioner, as well as God. Sure, he put some money up, and set up a phone account, for which he later build me. He also called a lawyer friend of mine on my behalf. This attorney was not a criminal lawyer, but I used him and paid him $1000 to file a motion for a bond reduction. Two weeks into jail I managed to once again have my bond reduced; this time to $75,000. The prosecutor, who reminded me of my mother, argued I was facing 15 to 30 years and requested I wear and ankle monitor. She also requested Nebbia proceedings. With the Nebbia proceedings one is required to prove that funds being used for bail were not obtained illegally. By this time, the damage had been done. Having played judge and jury, Ismael persuaded friends and family not to help me out. He decided I should be punished and that I was getting what I deserved. Instead of finding a way to help get me out, he decided to keep me in. It was very easy for others to turn their back on me. Even the girl I considered my best friend, the girl I loved, turned her back on me. For Jackie had instructed Ishmael that I never call her again. As I sit here and write at 12:45 AM, I wonder if she could really have said that or was it my brothers doing. I'm afraid to think about it.

I quickly found out how easily people turned their backs on you when you need them the most. My nature is a loving, caring and giving one. While I never gave a damn about anyone, I was true and loyal to the handful of people I knew and loved. This included my brother Ismael, who I thought would be the best person to help me out. In life we were one year apart; we were buddies and we were close friends. For many years, we played chess for hours on end. Often we would literally eat, drink and sleep with a chess board between us. At the age of 16 I pressured him to move out with me and so we rented a one bedroom apartment. By then, I had had enough of my abusive mother. Talk about mothers, I knew better than to ask her for help. Ismael, having been so ashamed of what I did, decided to play the judge, the jury and the executioner as well as God. Sure, he put some money up, and set up a phone account, for which he later build me. He also called a lawyer friend of mine on my behalf. This attorney was not a criminal lawyer, but I used him and paid him $1000 to file a motion for a bond reduction. Two weeks into jail I managed to once again have my bond reduced; this time to $75,000. The prosecutor, who reminded me of my mother, argued I was facing 15 to 30 years and requested I wear and ankle monitor. She also requested Nebbia proceedings. With the Nebbia proceedings one is required to prove that funds being used for bail were not obtained illegally. By this time, the damage had been done. Having played judge and jury, Ismael persuaded friends and family not to help me out. He decided I should be punished and that I was getting what I deserved. Instead of finding a way to help get me out, he decided to keep me in. It was very easy for others to turn their back on me. Even the girl I considered my best friend, the girl I loved, turned her back on me. For Jackie had instructed Ishmael that I never call her again. As I sit here and write at 12:45 AM, I wonder if she could really have said that or was it my brothers doing. I'm afraid to think about it.

Several more weeks past before my bond was issued and posted. Finally, I was going home. But where was home? For the two months before my arrest, I was staying with Jackie as my lease on the condo I occupied expired. My furniture was in storage and my clothing was, of all places at my mothers. Because I had a prior agreement to work six out of the next eight weeks away doing road sales, I figured I stay with her (mom). Hate for my mother was not the right word. Love for my mother, well I never knew what that was like. Indifference for my mother, ah-yes, that's the right word. I didn't love her, I didn't hate her, I just did not care. One good thing I could say about her was she never let me go hungry. After I moved out at 16, she allowed me dinner any time I needed. She also made sure I got a good education: as I went to a Catholic grammar school, a Catholic high school, and went on to New York University.

One of the things I learned in grammar school, during religion class, was that, there are three ways to feel towards a person. One, you could love someone: Two, you could hate someone, and three which is the worst of all; you can be indifferent about someone. When you love someone, you know them and understand them. When you hate someone, what you are really saying is, I have some type of feeling towards you but I am upset at your behavior. But to be indifferent, means, you just don't care and/ or, that person is not worth your time and effort. In other words that person is insignificant. I did not choose to feel this way. It was a natural effect of my relationship with my mother.

Vargas, pack it up. That was the call. The one I've been waiting for. I was going home. My items consisted of a dark blue uniform, two towels, one shirt and one blanket. All of which I was to return. They let me keep my underwear. White cotton boxes with the words "property of Broward County" clearly stamped along the back.

It was 11 AM when the call came. I was taken to the intake unit for departure. There, I was handed my ring, driver's license, sandals, shirt and a pair of jeans that now sported a rip on the left knee. To say the least, I changed in the about 30 seconds. From there I rushed to the next station for exiting. The guard had opened the jail exit door that led outside; I was only two steps away from leaving.

- "Hold it" said the lady behind the counter.

She was short and the counter was high, so you could barely see her. But the words were clear and unmistakable. "One more thing", oh yes I thought, the ankle monitor. The door that was in front of me was now to my back as I had pivoted towards the voice. I proceeded to walk towards it.

- "I don't see the judge's signature on your release".

Well I'm fucked again. So now what? A few more hours? Perhaps one more day? With that I changed to the blue uniform and was taken back to the cell. What I thought would take a day or so, turned into two weeks as the judge was on vacation. Upon her arrival and close examination of the documents presented by the bondsman, both she and the prosecutor, decided not to sign off as of yet. Ismael now needed to provide me more papers and so the lawyer requested a new hearing on the same motion. It was now three weeks since my bond was posted and the state had refused to let me go. The prosecutor argued that the bond was issued on a signature and no collateral was actually posted. So I was set off one more week. Up to this point I have not heard from the Phantom Public defender. Although rumor had it that he was a very good attorney, I wondered, what difference that made, since he was not accessible.

On the fourth week after posting my bond, Tony, the bondsman, appears in court. He argued that 80% of bonds issued, are done with properties that are under water. Meaning, the house has a mortgage greater than its value and therefore no collateral. The prosecutor had argued that since my mother nor would my brother not put up either house, that that was an indication that I was a possible flight risk. Little did she know about my relationship with my mother and how I was raised. To say the least, it was a dysfunctional family. How unfair I thought, for her to make such an assumption. The judge agreed with the prosecutor and now I found myself with a posted, but rejected bond. This whole matter was at the discretion of the judge. And in this case fate was against me. Or was it really? I say faith was against me, but that would be a pessimist point of view. Being an optimist, I say when given lemons make lemonade. So it's not that fate was against me, it's that my fate was destined to go in a different direction.

On the sixth week, after having my posted and rejected bail, I was banded. That is, I was made a trustee. The red band indicates one is medically cleared to serve food. The green one signifies you can work. I was moved to another pod or unit on the third floor. It's a little more relaxed as most of the inmates there are also trustees. For some reason, trustees seem to be an inappropriate term, as they are the ones that move the contraband. However, they have nonviolent charges and on not a major threat to the guards. Having become a trustee I was allowed to shave for the very first time. I guess I was a non-trusted trustee as they always checked upon return, that the blade was attached to the razor. Miller, a trustee, took sick one day, and asked me to serve breakfasts for him. For that I was rewarded with coffee, which the deputies would get from the vending machines. We were also given several breakfast trays to eat. During the entire stay, I would not, could not, fall asleep until after breakfasts; for my demon continued tormenting me for the past six years. Night times were especially hard as the lights were always on. My pod was a loud unit, with many young transient inmates, and it wasn't until about 1 AM when things would quiet down.

While in jail, one of the things I miss most was working out. There were no weights, no machines, nada. In the summer of my 14th year, I discovered a bench set and weights in a house my mother had purchased. I took to it like a fish to water. There was no explanation. Since that time, all the way through now, I have not had more than two weeks straight without working out. That I could not do so now was cruel and unusual punishment. As I think about this, it just dawned on me that Ozzie Jr., and Christian both started lifting weights during the summer of their 14th birthday. Like me they both were intelligent, assured and daring. Could it be in the blood? Ozzie was the only person in the world that would dare to mess up my hair. He knew it bothered me, but all I could do was laugh. One day he went as far as messing up my hair and then stuck a bean in my ear as I lay on my side. It took me about two hours to get that bean out.

4 JESUS

Jesus, not the historical one, but instead, Jesus Costa, a Cuban male about 27 years of age is assigned to my cell. First thing you notice is his swelled forehead sporting 5 inches of stitches. His cousin Ruben who was brought in with him is about four cells down from me. Ruben would come to my cell to figure out how he and Jesus could find a way out of their predicament. That first evening, Jesus went on and on about his life. Frankly, I could care less. He talked about different people he robed as well as burglaries he had committed. (A robbery is committed upon a person and a burglary is stealing property.)

The following day, Ruben joined Jesus in my cell and they started talking about the armed robbery they were now charged with. These two kids did not know how to shut up. This time however I was intrigued as they recalled the events.

Ruben was driving an old standard transmission Honda Accord, which in today's world is not the standard. Let's say manual transmission instead. Jesus was on the back passenger side, accompanied by a female. She sold a 9 mm pistol to Ruben which she previously owned. Ruben had the gun between the seat and his thigh. A man, who became the victim, entered the vehicle and sat in the front passenger side. His intention was to purchase some illegal pills. Instead of selling the contraband, Jesus reached over and put a chock hold on the victim, as Ruben pulled out the gun and pointed it to victims' head. The man did not resist. Instead he reached into his pocket and retrieved his money. Jesus and Ruben relieve the victim of $180.00. The girl in the back seat pocketed the money and the victim was released, storming out of the car. As Ruben tried to start the car for his getaway he handed the gun to the girl. The car stalled and would not start. In a panic they exited the car and she threw the gun away. She then ran to a city bus, which she quickly and quietly boarded. The two cousins ran away from the car, in opposite direction. After about 20 minutes, thinking the cost was cleared, Jesus and Ruben return to the vehicle and were apprehended by the police as they sat in the car. The gun that belonged to Ruben was on the ground several feet away from the car. It was taken in as evidence. Ruben fingerprints were all over it. What they said next would have a lasting effect on my life. It changed my course of action, and put me on a new journey. Not a journey I chose but one that chose me. It was my new destiny. This was now a turn in the road.

As both tried to find a solution, Ruben remembered he had previously beaten a domestic violence case. In that particular case he asked the court for a speedy trial. That is, for all you innocent people, – a trial within sixty days. For he knew the victim would not show up and also that the state might not be ready. His motto became, "no victim – no case". He applied that reasoning to this case and proceeded to tell Jesus that if they were able to eliminate the victim, then there will be no case. With that reasoning they began to plot the murder of the victim while in my presence. The plan was to have the girl who sat in the back seat lure the victim with the promise of returning the $180.00. She was to be followed by someone who would do the murder. This was to go into action within a few days. My heart started racing and I became furious at what I heard. How can I be responsible for another death? I knew all too well the pain and anguish suffered by the loved ones.

As soon as I could, I rushed to the phone and called Ismael. He demanded I keep my mouth shut. "Not your business he said." I agreed and hung up. During dinner I was tormented, although I knew it was not my business. How could I allow an innocent man to die? As I toiled with my dilemma, Mr. Silverstein an elderly Jewish white male asked what was wrong. We often spoke and because I needing a voice to hear, I told of my dilemma. Just as there are three ways to feel towards someone, there are three ways to make a decision; positively, negatively and by default. By "default", in choosing not to choose, one has chosen.

I can't say this dilemma did not allow me to sleep that night, because I rarely sleep at night. For hours on end I was consumed with deciding how to proceed. It wasn't until after breakfast, 4am that I finally succumbed and fell asleep. Early the following morning, Jesus and Ruben were called out, among many others, to be bused to one of the other jails. On my floor people come and go every few days. I was an exception, as a trustee I was needed to work. Work performed by trustees saves the county millions of dollars in labor. In turn all we get is an extra tray of food. I was glad to see the cousins go. Those guys were bad; they reminded me of my mother for some reason.

Ismael also came to mind, for he often told me throughout life that I had a heart of stone. I did grow up a tough kid, albeit quiet and reserved. I think growing up I only loved my father and my two brothers. As much as I loved a woman's companionship, I never let one get remotely close to my heart. Well, there once was one and only one. It's too bad I never let her know.

Shortly after dinner, which takes place about 5:30 or 6:00 pm, I was summoned by a deputy. I exited the unit, was handcuffed and taken to the attorney/client room. There I was asked about my involvement in this murder for hire plot. Turns out Mr. Silverstein sent a message through the kiosk in our unit; I think he was looking for some reward. The kiosk is an enclosed screen where we can place our commissary orders as well as send messages and make request to the office. I told the deputy that I had nothing to say to them and that I was not an accomplice, but that if I was going to say anything, it would only be to Jerry, my arresting officer. Jerry had given me his direct number. The deputies called him at the number I gave them and within 40minutes he and I were alone discussing the matter. Jerry was a high ranking B.S.O. detective whom worked hand in hand with ATF, FBI and DEA as well as the local police department. He was a soft spoken man; one could not help but look at his light blue eyes; He was a salesperson, a persuader; and thus, persuaded me to help. His stated that if I helped out in this, "murder for hire plot", the judge would consider my cooperation favorably, when it came time for my sentence. One thing I like about Jerry was he got straight to the point and made no false promises. He also pitched to me the substantial assistance program. That's a euphemism for a snitch, and/or informant. In the program, the return for cooperating with the police is a greatly reduced sentence. For a few days I thought about this program, but in reality I had already made a decision.

5 ZAMOR

The universe must be speaking to me, trying to tell me of my fate and trying to show me how to get out. For Richard, a young Colombian kid, tells me as we play a game of chess, about his cousin who is a member of the DEA. He spoke of how this cousin was going to get him off his charges. "If so, why are you still here?" I wondered. Turns out things are always a little bit more complicated than what we see on the surface. He continues talking about her and mentions two things that struck me. Richards's crime was grand theft auto. Although it was his first arrest he had numerous robberies under his belt. At 21 he was already a certified mechanic. I don't know which he loved most; stealing cars or fixing them.

His DEA cousin had purchased an impounded vehicle for a nominal fee. The car was valued at over $80,000. It was a confiscated vehicle that was auctioned off by the tow truck company which had impounded it. Having connections pays off. She would be tipped when a high value car was going to go on the auction block. All that was required was to pay the towing and storage fees for the month. His story seemed credible. The second, but more important of the two things he mentioned, was that in being a DEA agent she had power to put inmates into a program; in an undercover capacity, working as a C.I. (confidential informant). So far this was the third time I've hear that. I continued playing chess with Richard although he was not a good player. It was just a way of passing time. However I did note his story.

That same afternoon Mr. Silverstein was moved out of the unit. Not sure as to why, perhaps it was to keep him away from the others, but from whom? When inmates fight or threaten each other they are put on a special list, called the "keep separate" list. A list I would also be a part off. I wondered why Mr. Silverstein was moved, for he was a trustee. Perhaps he requested it on the kiosk, as he often did make special request. Most of which were ignored. Seems he made a complaint about every little thing he thought was unfair. To him everything in jail was unfair. Perhaps he wanted to stay away from Zamor?

Zamor was a Haitian who was not your typical brown skin guy. This guy was literally black; you could not make out the difference between his skin and his hair. Zamor was evil at the core. He was a pathological liar and made it his mission every day to bother Mr. Silverstein. Purposely he would be first to the newspaper and rip out the crossword puzzle so that Mr. Silverstein could not use it. Every morning was a race to the paper between the two. I acquired a dislike for Zamor, but I minded my business. It was not my battle. I've been in a bunch of them when I had a grocery store in N.Y. Truth be told; I've knocked out many people for stealing from the store. Knocking people out was an adrenaline high that became addictive. One day I longed for someone to steal and I realized I needed to leave N.Y.

During that time I had the store, I learned that as tough as many people projected themselves to be, when it came to one on one hand combat the heart was not there, in other worlds no balls. For many it was all a front, analogous to a barking dog. There was something to be said about knocking out someone cold with only one punch. You have to land it right with enough force. Whenever I went to hit someone in my store I would not look at him directly. Instead, I would quietly walk up and land the punch before he could react to it. Bang! Despite this behavior, I was not the violent type. I never bullied anyone; for I despised bullies. For that matter I would not even bother people. I was a laid back, quiet, docile individual; however, I would not tolerate someone stealing from me, or messing with me or my family. I would not let situations escalate. I would immediately put an end to any threat I perceived. If it's one thing I had it was heart, will and balls.

It's been a week now since I met with Jerry and I now find myself in an uncomfortable situation. Zamor who now worked on the 8th floor serving breakfast encountered two individuals. Their names escaped him, but I knew who they were. It was lunch time when he labeled me as "the police". In jail terms, that is a snitch. He tells all the inmates in my unit, how two young Cubans were brought back from one of the Pompano jail to face new charges of attempted murder. Zamor described one of the individuals as having had a big cut on his forehead. That confirmed my suspicion. I knew it was Jesus and his cousin. There was nothing I could do but denied what he was saying. I kept my cool about the situation. "Now that Mr. Silverstein has left you think you can fuck with me?" I told him "Be careful with what you say. Everyone here knows you as a liar and trouble maker. If you say something stupid like that again I promise I will break your jaw." It was clear that I meant what I said. My size and demeanor had intimidated him. There was doubt among the inmates as to Zamor's story. Luckily I had his reputation working against him and so for the moment I contained the situation.

Two days later during lunch another trustee mentioned to me that he saw the Cuban guy on the 8th floor that morning. Zamor took that as an invitation to jump in "see, I told you, you are the police" as I stood up to approach Zamor who was sitting at another table, I could see his nervousness. While still sitting on the metal seat, he leaned to one side ready to spring up and get away. In an instance I contained myself and invited him to my cell, once again I promised to break his jaw.

The penalty for fighting in jail and being the aggressor is 30 days in confinement. There you spend 22 hours of the day locked up. You are not allowed phone calls, radios, commissary or cards. A red jump suit becomes your new attire and the 8th floor your new home. Broward County will now bring battery charges against you, and the worst part is that if you have a court date schedule for your case, you will be sporting the red jump suit. Your judge has you now labeled as a violent person. The last thing I wanted was an add charge of battery to go along with my trafficking charge. Because of all this, most inmates refrained from fighting. Jail is different from prison in this aspect, as people in prison have already been sentenced; 15 years or more is common and so many inmates in prison don't mind an extra 30 days. Sometimes a fight is even warranted. Zamor was aware of all of this. Everyone knew he was all mouth.

At this jail, cells consist of two occupants and no one is supposed to be in someone else's cell. Deputies would often overlook friends from different cells playing cards together in a room. Fights were encouraged among antagonist in the cells as there are no cameras. The inside of the cells were almost entirely out of sight from the deputies. If fight occurred there, the deputies were spared from having to write a report. Despite the tension in the air, Zamor and I resumed our lunch. That tension would escalate as the days went by. For the next few days Zamor greeted many of the new inmates, with a warning that I was the police. Rumor was that a Spanish trustee was responsible for informing the Spanish speaking arrivals and Zamor responsible for informing all others.

Knowing that I was responsible for Jesus being brought back and charged with a new crime, had left a bad taste in my mouth. It now appeared that inmates were staying away from me; not that I really cared, as for the most part I was a loner. The slow witted Florida population seemed to lack common sense. Here in Florida, common sense was not that common. Things are much slower than in the north. People are also slower. Slower in their movements and slower in thought process. I was easily bored with most people and did not care for conversations. So it was easy for me to keep to myself. For the most part my attitude was "fuck-them".

A few more days have passed. A Brazilian named Balbi, in his late 50's was brought to my pod. His picture had made the front page of the local newspaper. Turns out he had a chiropractor's office on Sample Road in Pompano Beach. Arrested with him was the chiropractor that ran the office. They were very careful of what they said to me. Balbi's son and daughter who also worked in the office were arrested. Each held a bond of 1.5 million dollars. The high amount was due to the fact each had dual citizenship and therefore considered a high flight risk. For the first few days the extent of our interaction was an occasional game of dominoes. Four days later Balbi was shipped to one of the other jails in Pompano Beach.

That same day, Zamor, who continued to torment me with police accusation, quickly got up from his seat and rushed to the kiosk as it was being vacated by an inmate. The inmate walked away without signing out. Zamor opened the inmate's message board and wrote a letter to the office, passing of as being that inmate. One hour later two guards came to the unit and took the inmate away. Xavier, a new trustee had witness Zamor write the message and so upon the removal of the inmate, he notified the deputies of what Zamors' action.

Zamor was despised, and hated by many; everyone wanted to beat him, but no one wanted the 30 days. Despite the guards knowing of Zamor's actions they were obligated to take the inmate away. Because this was not the first or second time Zamor had done this, several trusties knew where the inmate was headed to. Three days passed before the inmate returned to the cell. He said he was taken to the infirmary and placed in a turtle suit AKA straight jacket. Within 30 minutes of his return he became aware of what Zamor had done.

It was dinner time now and Zamor in an attempt to hide his actions, exclaimed, "Whoever wrote the message was wrong in doing so". I asked Zamor out loud, "why are you pretending? We all know who did it." Zamor looked around as if the perpetrator was amongst the crowd, and asked, "Who was it?" I stood up, as all eyes were fixed on me, and pointed straight at him, "It was you mother fucker." He denied it. Other inmates including Xavier jumped in. "I saw you do it". Another inmate that had several months there also jumped in. "This is about the 3rd time you do that shit and you think it's funny." Zamor was lost for words. He quietly sat down, ate his food and returned to his room. In jail, pointing at an inmate, who I was now guilty of, is considered a no-no. It's an invitation to fight. Something I was ready to do.

As usual, several more days came and left. Zamor managed to get under the skin of John, a trustee who was facing pill traffic charges. A traffic charge refers to a high amount of drugs. The name is misleading as it has nothing to do with transporting or moving drugs. John had had enough of Zamor and also invited Zamor to the room for a fight. One thing I could not understand was that even though they hated each other, they would sit together at the table to play spades.

John's cell was at one end of our unit, on the second tier. One needed to stand directly in front of it to see inside. One day John and I formed a plan to lure Zamor into Johns' room. We, as well as other inmates, had agreed if ever anyone had a fight with Zamor, we would all say, "we saw nothing". Zamor knew better than to enter anyone's cell, or room as we called it. My room was adjacent to Johns. The only thing that would bring Zamor near us was the shower. It was eight feet across John's room.

For several days Zamor continued on a regular basis to make the police siren sound every time he was in my presence. I had warned him several more times to desist. He would just laugh after his outburst as if it were funny. Although John and I had set a plan to lure Zamor into the room, he managed to stand clear. He knew how to drive someone to the edge and then backed off.

Knowing my bond issue would soon get resolved I managed to restrain myself. Here, days turned into weeks. Many a times I was disappointed with delays and extensions forced upon me. One of the things about the delays that bothered me the most was telling Abby for the fourth time that I would be home in two weeks. Her birthday was now approaching and I was not sure if I would be there. I always downplayed the discomfort I withstood in jail, when speaking to her. Last thing I wanted was to have her feel sad for me. I would always be upbeat and ask her not to worry. I mentioned some plans I envisioned for a portable gym.

In jail there were no weights. I managed to put a routine together that would help conserve my muscles until I got out. In exchange for breakfast items, I managed to get a trustee to bring me a few plastic garbage bags. The bags were clear plastic and very strong. I would fill them with about 50 pounds of water. I would then rap my bed sheets around it and use it to exercise. It worked out quite well. I also told her of a pulley system made to straddle any door. Plastic bags would then be filled with water creating a desired weight. Abby knew I was a business man and listened carefully to my ideas. She even made a suggestion or two.

Again a few more days have gone by. It was mid-afternoon and Zamor had not let up. This day he would make a mistake. Upon exiting the shower he heard John talking with his roommate. Each sat on his bunk as Zamor enters the room and engaged in conversation. From my cell next door I could clearly hear Zamors' voice. I immediately jumped off my bunk and from within my cell looked towards John's room. At the present moment we were not in lock down mode and so my door was ajar. Zamors' torso was inside John's room but his left leg was still hanging outside as he held on to the door with his right hand. Quietly I made my way towards Zamor. A trustee, standing by the fixed table, looked up at me and took notice. I placed my finger on my lips signaling him to keep quiet.

The door to John's cell was only about six feet away from where I stood. Upon reaching Zamor I lifted my right leg thus shifting my weight onto my left. I thrust my leg forward, planting it squarely on his spine. His torso moved forward as inertia made his head and neck tilt upward and back. The length from the cell door to the end of the room was only about 10 feet. Zamor landed on his hands and knees. His head only inches away from the brick wall. It took him several seconds for him to stand fully erect and realize what had taking place. His face revealed his pain. He arched backwards a bit trying to comfort himself. He looked at me and I could see the fear in his eyes. No words were spoken, non-needed to be. John, who was sitting on the bottom bunk, drew his legs in and gave space.

The trustee that was downstairs by the table had made his way to the entrance of the room. However he did not enter. Zamor was now standing at the end of the room with his back against the wall. There was only one way out, and that was through me. He made a move towards me. I again shifted my weight to my left leg. Instinctively I raised my arms upwards although I had no intention of using them. (In most fights your opponent keeps his eyes fixed on your hands.) I used them as a decoy. Again I raised my right leg and thrust it forwards. With a force he had never felt before I planted my foot across his chest and pushed with all I had. That reversed his forward movement. Momentum carried him backwards causing his legs to lift in the air. Finally his back reached the wall and his buttock the ground. His head hit the wall with a loud thump and with that he was unconscious.

For a few seconds I watched to see him recover, but I knew he hit the wall hard and was out. In my past I have experienced knocking out a man for more than five minutes. I knew Zamor was in the same place. I exited the room with my back facing out. By now, other trustees made their way to the cell. How they moved so fast was beyond me. Again I put my finger to my lips signaling for all to hush. John and his cell mate, along with the trustees looking in, were in disbelief. I could hear John repeating, "Got Fucken knocked out", I entered my room, closed the door and stood by waiting for Zamor to pass by.

More inmates came running over to see what the commotion was about and one of the trustees exclaimed, WOW! "You got knocked the fuck out"! After several minutes Zamor recovered and walked to his cell. He glanced over to me through the door with reinforced glass. I smiled at him as if to say, "That's all you got?" Quietly he continued five cells down and into his room. I rested on my bunk and replayed the event, after which I plotted my next move. Now I told myself I really had to be on guard. I knew if it had happened to me, there would be no way I would let anyone get away with such an event. From this point on I could not let my guard down, even though I knew he did not have the will to fight. Just like in chess, I played out different scenarios. I could not allow him near me. At dinner time I waited for him to take his usual seat, and then I sat two tables away. The tables are square and sit four people in all. He looked at me as I took my place. I told him, "if he for any reason, he came near me, I would consider that as an attack and would defend myself." I promised to break his jaw this time. Zamor had earned the respect of no one. Many at the feeding was commented, "I heard someone got knocked the fuck out". Even one deputy, repeated the comment as he smiled at Zamor. For the deputy knew Zamor was an instigator and a loud mouth.

Three days have since passed and Zamor had not spoken a world. Things were quiet, when two BSO police entered the unit! From my room I could see they were not your regular jail deputies; one of the two, made his way to the stairs and calls out Vargas? For a moment I knew this was not good. I exited my cell and acknowledge. He continued up the stairs and into my room. "Pack all of your belongings. Leave the blankets and towels behind." "What is going on?" I asked. "Just do as I say". With that he handcuffed me, walked me to the deputies' office, cut my bands and led me towards the elevator.

6 BRONX, NY

Did it begin in the Bronx? The place where I was born: or did it begin in Puerto Rico where my mother and father met, married and had their first born, Ismael Jr. My father passed on many of his genes to me. Ismael Jr. took many of my mother's genes. Often I made the argument that a lot of what we do in life is a result of our genetic composition. What we perceive as being a choice might just be a reaction or a consequence of those genes. We do not choose to be tall nor short, white nor black, smart or dumb. We don't choose to be straight or gay either. So again I wonder when did the decisions to do what I do, to do what I did, and to do what I will do, were made.

My earliest memories were of living in a beautiful two bedroom apartment in the South Bronx; corner of 156 street and 3rd Avenue. The 3rd Avenue train station or El, short for elevated, stopped there. Its entrance was on the corner opposite from mine. A candy store or newspaper store, depending on how you chose to see it, was on the corner. It was a frequent stop for us. The owners being so vigilant prevented pilferage to some degree. The building I lived in was a five story walk up with four apartments per floor. My aunt Sheila, as well as her mother lived on the second floor. We lived one story above. Sheila's house was Spanish speaking only. That was about forty seven years ago. To this date, Sheila and her husband are still living and together. The entire block I lived on consisted of mostly Hispanics and Jews. Across the street and around the corner lived the African Americans. Each group stayed within their boundaries without crossing into the others territory, unless of course only to pass through.

Some of my fondest memories were of being in my aunt's house. They were evening people and loved to play Bingo, Dominos and cards. Throughout my entire life, Sheila would make fresh coffee for my brothers and me, at any time of the day or night. All we needed to do was ask. Late nights were common, especially when school was out.

Due to an experimental medicine administered at a local hospital my father lost his hearing. He was 18 at the time. No one bothered to explain to me that Dad could read lips. For years I shouted to get his attention and so that he could hear me. It was strange that he would easily understand me if I did not yell, How ironic! Dad was always a loving, caring, soft spoken, wonderful human being. Every time he was present I could feel his love for me, no words needed to be spoken. Many nights I tried to understand what it was like being deaf and so I would often plug my ears at night and ask my brother questions. As much as I tried to understand what it must have been like, I never really knew. Years later dad said it was a blessing being hard of hearing as he did not have to hear his wife's nagging. Several blocks away from home, was to be found a stuffed toys factory which dad owned. Sheila worked with dad and many days after work, she would come home with candy bars for us; purchased of course from my favorite corner store. Dad would close shop about 4:00 pm and Sheila would be home about 4:15 pm.

My mother on the other hand was a complete nightmare. I think the only reason she had children was because of a lack of birth control! Now that I sit here and write, at 1:00 am, it makes sense to me why we spent so many nights at Sheila's house. I felt we were always a burden to mom. When I was about eight or nine, my parents divorced. Instead of being told the truth we were told dad was starting a factory in Puerto Rico. I missed my dad dearly. He meant everything to me.

My fondest memories of my mother were, none. It is actually a blank. I don't have any recollection of my mother hugging me or loving me. For that matter, I don't recall her ever saying the word's "I love you!" All I can remember were countless, horrifying beatings that would have landed her in jail, by today's standard. She had an arsenal of weapons to be used against us. There was a long extension cord, which she often used. She would fold the cord over several times before striking us numerous times. Welts and bruises were an almost every day occurrence. There was the belt off course. We were hit with either side depending on how she grabbed it. There were magical flying shoes that always found its target and also flying frying pans. Oh, let's not forget the cast iron one that landed flush on my forehead. Last but not least was the cheese grater. Where she came up with this one, I don't know.

That was a common item among Spanish households. The side that was perforated with outward sticking edges was used to make a dish known as Pastelles. Mom would place two graters on the floor with the outward perforated side facing up. As punishment we were forced to kneel on them for several hours, all the while wearing her see-through nighty. Blood was no reason to stop the punishment. She made sure to display us to any our friends that might have been in the house. Throughout this and in all my years of living with her and my step dad, I never once gave them the satisfaction of seeing me cry. Joey my younger brother was a different story. He would cry upon seeing any of her weapons. Ismael would sometimes cry. Up through the age of 18 I recall having cried only twice. Later on in life I often found myself crying twice in one hour.

Two blocks beyond dad's factory was our school St. Peter and Paul; a Roman Catholic grammar school. Often we would be escorted to school by a black man that lived across the street. Mom would give him coins for doing so. He was known throughout the neighbor as Mr. Two Pennies; for he walked with his hands stretched out and always asked for two pennies. Never more, never less! I would imagine him dead now.

Tuition at that time was $29.00 total a month for the three of us. One day when I was about 10 years old, I decided to take some of the tuition money mom had in an envelope within her pocketbook. After school I crossed the busy 3rd Avenue and went to the toy store. There of all things I purchased a chess set. Whatever drew me to such a game, I have no idea. My brother and I read the instructions and taught ourselves to play. We would do so at Sheila's house so that mom would not ask questions as to how we obtained it.

Sometimes when we were home I often found myself throwing thing at pedestrians below for entertainment. As I write about it I do so with a big smile. One day Joey, my younger brother of one year, and I were watching people walking by. I had a habit of throwing hot water in the winter time and cold water in the summer. One day we decided to throw raw eggs at people. I was pretty good at hitting my target. I learned to release it a second before the person was to be in position. There was a couple walking by one day. It was summer time and the lady had a bonnet, rather large I might add. I threw an egg at her and landed it right on her hat. I could clearly see it open and scatter about. Joey and I quickly hid out of sight.

After several minutes passed I told him to stick his head out to check. That he did. To his surprise the couple was looking up and pointed the finger at him. A few minutes later they came knocking on the door. Mom let them in and they pointed him out. After they left mom took out a plastic bat and started to beat Joey with it. On one swing she missed him and struck the wall. That caused her finger to bend backwards so much that she needed to go to the hospital. To this day she cannot fully stretch out that finger. As far as I can remember this did not curtain my antics. I enjoyed throwing things at people, especially the water. Also it did not prevent mom from inflicting further punishment.

Our next move was to Riverdale, in the Bronx. It also was a nice roomy place; a three bedrooms, two-family house. I shared a bedroom with Ismael and adjacent to ours was Joey's room. Because of the stained glass window in the dining room, I thought this was an expensive home. As usual, my brother and I continued playing jokes on each other. One of my favorites that always worked was the boot on the door. I would often leave my bedroom door ajar and on top of the door I would place a boot which would be leaned against the wall. When the door was opened the shoe would fall. One evening I set it up so as to catch my brother Ismael who went to the kitchen. While he was away, Raul my stepdad decided to enter the room. As planned the boot came crashing down. He was a little startled but I think he was also somewhat amused. No punishment this time. I explained it was an ambush for my brother, and with that he exited. This went on for several years until we moved again; this time to our own private home.

7 DID IT HAPPEN IN ROSEDALE AVE.?

It was summer when my parents bought their first house. I was about 14 then. The house was on Rosedale Avenue in the Parkchester Area of the Bronx. A two story building from the front view, but in reality had three levels, as the basement encompassed the entire length of the building. Our living area consisted of the entire first floor plus the basement. The basement had a huge recreation room in which my brothers and I spent much time playing in. There was a folding ping pong table as well as a small weight lifting set. It was comprised of a bench press and 110 pound weight set. The weights were made of cement encase in a blue plastic shell. In addition there were 4X10 pounds metal weights, which to this date I still own.

From the very first time I laid on it and pressed some weights I was hooked. I had no idea what I was doing, but I loved how I felt after using it. For the next year or so I would lie on the bench and do bench press on a daily basis. Every dollar I could save was used to purchase body building magazines. For the next 10 years I did so and saved them until I had a collection of about 300. It was upon my marriage in 1987 that they seemed to disappear. To this day I don't recall how.

The side of the house had a long deep sloping driveway leading to the backyard. The adjacent semi-attached house protruded about 15 feet beyond ours. A basketball rim was attached on its cement wall. My brother Ismael and I would spend hours playing ball with our neighbors Robert and his brother Junior who both lived in the house directly behind ours. The front of their house faced Nobel Avenue. A four foot high fence separated our homes, and enclosed my yard. We jump that fence back and forth every day as if it did not exist. Our German Sheppard's prevented others from doing the same. Jumping it took about one second (nothing to it at all). If trespassing was a crime then we committed it several times daily.

Often to get away from my mother we would go to the yard to shoot some hoops. From there we would jump the fence and make our way to Nobel Ave. Several houses away were the local corner grocery store, otherwise known as a Bodega. Across the Bodega was a park with several entrances: one on each corner of its long rectangular shape. One entrance was on Rosedale Ave. and one on the corner of Noble. Closest to our side the first thing you would encounter was a basketball court. Mom did not allow my brother or me to play there. However, that meant nothing to us. We would go to our backyard to play ball and after 10 minutes or so would jump the fence and sneak into the park trough the Noble side entrance.

My mother would sit in the front room on the first floor. It had four windows facing the street. She would spend hours there reading or watching the T.V. while at the same time observing any movement in the front of the house. We would therefore escape through the back yard so that she would not be aware. At the park we would lose track of time. About once a week for the next two years she would come looking for us at the park with the belt in her hand. By that time we were so accustomed to the belt that we were immune to the pain inflicted by it. Many of the kids in the neighborhood knew of the lady with the belt. To all of us, it was just a joke. She would enter the park through the Rosedale avenue corner. As she did so, you could hear the warning, "run your mother is coming". Before they could finish the sentence we would already be on our way with our basketball in hand.

The escape was always the same, run opposite her towards the Noble Avenue entrance, cross the street, run six houses down, turn into the driveway, jump the fence and enter through the basement door. There we would await our beating, after which we would drink water and laugh. As punishment she would sometimes take the basketball away from us. Little did she know we always had an extra basketball plus a volley ball for added measure.

Notwithstanding this we were good, respectable and well-mannered kids. Of the three, I got in trouble the most. Despite all the beatings, we were getting a good education, had a roof over our heads and a warm meal every day. Every so often I challenged mom when I was to get a beating. I would stand in front of her as I would get belted and would tell her, "That didn't hurt". This would infuriate her even more and she would strike harder. I would continue with, "that still didn't hurt." One would think this was a dumb thing to do, but with me it was a matter of pride. I could take all that she could dish out. I needed to show her and myself that she could hit me all she wanted, but she could never break me.

The following summer, something profound happened. As I sit here and think about it at 1:30 am, I still get the chills. No, I did not kill anyone, at least not yet. It must have been around 1:00 pm when Ismael came running in through the side entrance of the basement door. "Hurry up and come with me." "Where?" I asked. "Just hurry up, I want you to meet someone, new friends," he replied. Girls, I thought, great, before I knew it, I was at the top of the driveway ready to make our usual right turn towards the park, but instead he turned left. How odd, I thought, no good looking girls that way. We raced almost to the corner about 12 houses down.

There he called out towards the second floor, "Pamela, Pamela!!!' As he did so, my life forever changed. Leaning against a park car in front of that house was a tall, dark haired girl. She was accompanied by someone else. I froze in my tracks as I looked at the taller of the two. For a moment, time stood still. I could barely breathe. I had not noticed Ismael yelling at me: calling for my attention so that I could see his new friend, who was now looking out from the window. I turned to look at his friend Pamela, and quickly turned back to the girl. I do not remember saying one word the whole time.

Why would Ismael be calling out for Pamela at the window when there was this beautiful mesmerizing girl standing but only a few feet away? Had he lost his mind? Ismael called me several times, what could be so important? By the time I realized it, his friend that was previously at the window was now standing beside me. "Ozzie meet Pamela". Pamela said "hi" and introduced her two friends; the same two girls that were standing by the car. One of the two was also named Pamela. Her sister, the taller one, was the focus of my attention. I'll just call her "The Girl". "Oh, shit! Run" mom is coming. Mom had her best friend with her, the belt.

That same summer Joey Delgado, a chubby kid who lived on Gleason Avenue, (the corner right by my house and where the park is), and I were talking in front of the grocery store, which his parents owned. Joey asked if I was going to the party. Not knowing of it, I replied, "No", and with that he invited me. At the time I was dating a girl name Jeannette. Jan was tall with long dark hair. She would often sneak to my basement room where we spent much time kissing and enjoying each other. Joey told me of his girlfriend. It was "the girl". The girl that made me freeze in my track. The girl that made me feel something deep inside. A feeling I have never known.

Joey was lying. Numerous were the inquiries I made about the girl. She was respectable and did not have a boyfriend at the time. Although I knew he was lying, I struck up a deal with him on that day. We traded girlfriends. There was no way I was going to let him acquire her. He could have Jeannette and in turn I was to have her. But how? In what capacity? Oh Well! It did not matter much, in a way, I got what I wanted. She was now my girl, even if she did not know it. Joey thought he got the best deal ever. He thought he sucker me. However, I knew better.

Saturday was the big day; the party day. The girl and her other sister, Tanya, were there. It was early evening and the sun had not set. At the party they started to play the kissing game. This is how it went; one person would go in a room, then come out and pick from among the crowd someone of the opposite sex. He or she would then bring the chosen into the room. Once in the room the very first person would give the next person a kiss on the cheek, in turn that person would give the next in line a kiss and that would continue down the line till the last person in the room was kissed. "The Girl", who was also playing, was chosen and entered the room. Low and behold, when she came out she chose me. "Yes", I said to myself. She does like me.

Finally I was going to kiss her. I followed her into the room and watched kisses go from the first all the way down the line until it was her turn to kiss me. I leaned into her for my kiss. Bang! She quickly raised her hand and landed a hard punch across my cheek. What the fuck? I thought. What a cruel joke. As people laughed I wondered what had I ever done to deserve this? I lifted my left arm to rub my cheek. This girl struck me with a vengeance. Did she uncover my trade with Joey? I was about to turn around and exit. She grasped both of my hands and apologized. She then leaned into me and gave me a kiss. That kiss was well worth the blow and humiliation. I asked her why did she hit me and she replied its part of the game. Oh, OK! Hit me again I thought. From that point on I can't remember who the game finished with, maybe it was with me, for I don't recall kissing anyone after me. Nor did I want to. I don't even remember if Jeannette, who I had traded for was there. Several years would pass before the girl would hear of my trade with Joey.

8 PAUL REIN

“We have been instructed to move you. There has been a threat against your life.” "By whom?" I asked. “I don’t have that information.” My eyebrows lifted and I now looked at everything and everyone with suspicion. I was taken to a holding cell and isolated: from there onto a paddy wagon and then whisked away to Paul Rein Facility in Pompano Beach. The time must have been about 7:30 pm. The reception at the intake unit was all the same, strip down, lift up your balls, squat and cough. Thereafter you pass a metal detector and then sit on a chair that also detects metals, just in case you have an item buried within your anus. Next step was another holding cell; until they could figure out where to place me.

There I waited forty five minutes before being taken to the third floor, which was the top floor. The corridor looked more like a hospital than a jail. Wow, I said to myself. This place is nice. The unit is huge. The ceiling is about 20 feet high. This particular unit held nonviolent criminals and because of that the sleeping quarters had no doors. Each room holds three or four bunks. The design is an open floor plan. The eating area consist of about 16 squares removable folding tables. Thus four people per tables. The chairs are all plastic. That area leads into the main recreation room. Several comfortable lounging chairs can be found there. Forming a divider to the sleeping quarters is a row of eight upright telephones. Each spaced out about two feet apart and standing about 5 feet high. Plastic cylinders are used as seats while you place your call. To one corner is the television. Like the facility it too was modern. Its volume however left a lot to be desired. Just like the hallway the entire area was reminiscent of a hospital waiting area.

I was given a bunk and introduced myself to the two roommates. After I placed my belongings down I went to the T.V. area and for the first time in months sat on a non metal chair. The lounging seats had a big rectangular ottoman in which I rested my legs. Although I was in a comfortable seat I was not comfortable at all. For I now found myself looking backwards and sideways every time someone approached. Was I being paranoid or was I being cautious? Was it the Cuban cousins that made a threat or was it Zamor, with his games. Of the two, the threat from the Cubans would be taken more serious. How could I know who it came from? Who would be able to tell me? By now the phones were shut off, but it didn't matter for I had no one to call. That night, just like most other nights, I laid down to sleep but could not. My demons tonight were replaced by worries and concern. Then it came to me, (as answers often do, late into the night). Jerry! Jerry would know.

Chow time, as it was referred to, was the same throughout the Broward system. That morning, I eagerly waited for the phones to be available. They usually get turned on right after lunch; about 11:00 am. By the time they were activated I was already seated on the small plastic cylindrical seat, labeled "not a step". The connection was completed and Jerry answered, yes Ozzie! He knew it was me before I ever said a word.

Ø Hi Jerry, I was moved to Paul Rein on the basis of having a threat on my life.

Ø Yes, I know!

Ø Was it the cousins?

Ø Yes, we have informants that overheard one of them telling the story of how they were brought back to the main jail and in anger they said they would hurt you. Although they seem not able to go any further than just talk, they have been warned of the 20 years sentence for tampering with a witness. Also they do not appear to have the means to do anything. However, because the mail jail is more transient, we thought it would be better to keep you separate and somewhat isolated. It's just a precaution more than anything. While I have you on the phone, there is something I would like you to do for me. In your unit there is a man by the name of Balbi. He was in your unit at the main jail. Keep your ears open. If there is any info about him you become aware of give me a call.

Ø Ok Jerry. Will do and thanks for the info.

Five minutes later I was back on my bunk. What nerve of Jerry to ask of such a thing? I was no snitch. The info I gave on the two cousins was initiated by someone else, although there was a murder plot of which I did not want to be responsible for. Damn, is Jerry setting me up for something? Did he move me here intentionally to help him gather info on someone? What should I believe? It did not matter much anyhow. My bond was posted, bail paid; only a slight issue to resolve and I'll be out of here in a few days. It seems I was always about to be out in a few days.

It wasn't till dinner time that I noticed Balbi. I sat at his table and we talked for a minute. Although seats are not designated, friends usually sit together and are accustomed to sitting in same spot. I was politely made aware of that and so I removed myself to a different table. I caught up with Balbi later that evening in the TV area. It seems that all Hispanics hung around the back of the room. He introduced me to several Spanish inmates and we all had made small chit-chat.

Prince, whom I had met at the main jail, was also in the TV area. African Americans like to occupy the front seats. He stood up and turned around as he began walking away. He glanced at me and we exchanged Hi's. Happily he walked over and we exchanged handshakes. Prince always had a smile on him. He seemed to be a wonderful guy and in his own mind was a big celebrity with celebrity stardom. At 6'3" and 340 pounds, Prince one was a big one. He grew up in NYC and Long Island. He was well spoken and educated, for he obtained a degree from Hostra University, on a football scholarship. Prince was a computer geek and hacker. During college he worked at a Brokerage Firm as the main I.T. guy. His principle job was maintaining the hardware and software. He also helped implement new computer software security. The firm he worked for was a mid size brokerage firm. Although not a Goldman Sachs, it moved hundreds of millions of dollars daily.

One evening while on call, Prince was summoned to work, as one of the main computers went down. He determined that it was best to reinstall the system. All he needed was the backup disk which was in the hands of the owner and locked up in the firm's safe. Access to the firm's computer security system was reserved for less than a hand full. If ever there was a time to get complete access, this was it. Prince was given the backup disk as well as several others. The entire set of discs was numbered. Disc four was the firm's stocks and funds exchange. Without giving it much thought Prince popped the disc in a second computer using software he had on a USB stick and copied the complete disk onto it. As well he popped a blank disc in the machine and made an exact hard copy. The password for the software was written on the sleeve of disk 4. Now, he would have unsupervised access to the entire firms' daily transactions at his leisure. It is needless to say the very first thing he did when he got home was to load his new software on to his laptop. He remembered feeling like a kid in a candy shop. Up till this point I was not sure what to call him. I did not like referring to him as Big One. It's too close to Big O. That's what Jackie called me. O for Ozzie and O for orgasm, (our favorite pass time).

At the main jail we often sat together at dinner. He would tell that story to every new member. We also spoke of business in real estate, stocks and bonds. He seemed to have taken interest in my design for my portable gym.

Ø Hi, Ozzie! How have you been?

Ø Hi, I guess as well as anyone could be in jail.

Prince sat down next to me and made himself comfortable.

Ø By the way, what shall I call you?

Ø Just call me Prince.

Ø Ok, Prince it is, you the Prince of Pentium (This referred to a Pentium chip).

His book was about computer hacking and computer crimes. According to him, a movie deal was in the making. I was not sure if that was true or not. From what I could gather it seems he did have some celebrity status, as was evident in some photos he had. Over the next few days Prince and I talked often and spent many hours in the recreation yard. The rec yard is a large room just outside the dining area. A large heavy metal door stood in between both areas. The rec. yard was totally enclosed around the bottom perimeter. About 10 feet high were metal gates through which the sun came in. Because of the height it was impossible to see anything other than the sky's above.

In the yard one could feel the Florida weather. I say this because if one did not frequent the yard then one was not aware of it; for the housing units were kept so cold that that all the deputies wore jackets. Many inmates wore a gray sweater underneath their blue uniform top to keep warm; especially at night. At the yard the sun shinned through the gate while inmates took turns either sitting or standing while basking in it. We were allowed to exercise there, although there were no weights. Make shift and improvisation were certainly needed to do so. At one end of the yards was a basketball ring. Mainly the black guys would play ball and the Hispanic would bathe in the sun as they talked about. Myself… I was never much of a talker; I was more reserved and listened carefully. If I had interest in one's conversation, which more often than not I didn't then I would engage. Every so often the basketball would bounce towards the sun bathers. They would always kick the ball back as if kicking a soccer ball.

Because I often slept late into the morning or early afternoon, I would come to the rec yard about 3:30 pm. One day, while at the yard, Prince asked, "Why are you up all night"? I quickly replied, "It's just my sleeping pattern. I'm an evening person." Little did he know that I was unable to sleep at night. I was not in the mood to reveal the true cause. He knew I had trouble sleeping because on several occasions he would get up to visit the bathroom. This brought him right past my room and he would waive hi.

9 STEVE UPPER

It's been about two weeks since my move. The first week or so I had not had a chair during dinner that I could call my own. Steve Upper, an Irish American I had often seen exercising in the rec yard, noticed me looking around. He kicked back a chair at his table and invited me in. "Have a seat", he demanded. "It takes a few days to settle in. That seat is mostly empty. This is Joe my roommate." I was not sure I wanted to sit next to Joe. Rumor had it he killed his wife. Like myself, Joe was a quiet man. He would spend almost the entire evenings in his room reading, or doing crossword puzzles. I took my seat opposite to Steve and adjacent to Joe. Dinner was the usual tasteless junk; two hotdogs with beans and a piece of bread. Often times you were not sure what you were eating. To mentioned salts, flavor, condiments was to blaspheme. After dinner I watched a little TV and retired to my open room.

The following day I caught up with Steve in the rec. yard to thank him for the invite. We made small talk about exercising. Having been a trainer, I gave him some pointers on certain exercises and routines. Anyone who liked to exercise was a friend of mine, and so it seems Steve was to become one. He stood 6 feet tall, with light blue eyes and a full set of hair, which he wore short. Tattoos covered 80% of both arms. Steve kept to himself most of the time.

- Ø Steve, your roommate Joey, what's he in for?

- Ø Oh, someone said Joe killed his wife.

- Ø Oh, not so! I saw his charges.

I'm not sure if what Joe was rumored to have done made a difference in my life, as I also would associate with one; that is, an assassin with several hits under his belt.

- Ø Steve what are you in for?
- Ø Trafficking cocaine, over 400 grams.
- Ø OH, that is my same charge. What is your bond?
- Ø It's $325,000.
- Ø Why is it so high? I asked.
- Ø Well I also have conspiracy and prior arrest.
- Ø Well mine has been reduced to 75k. I posted bond already and should be out in a few days.
- Ø I wish I could get out. My bail is too high and don't have the collateral.
- Ø So Steve, who is your judge?
- Ø It's Lisa P.
- Ø Oh, same as mine. Word is that she is a fair judge.
- Ø Yes, I heard the same.
- Ø Well Steve, she is preventing me from getting out. I needed to prove where my bail money came from. I needed to prove that it wasn't from drug money. The problem with my bond according to her is that there was no actual property as collateral. The bondsman issued my bond on a signature. Next week I have a hearing on a motion for bond reduction. I'm sure it will all be resolved and I will go home. I've had to hire a private att. to file a motion as I have not been able to get in contact with the public phantom, Mr. Brian Greenwald.
- Ø Hey that's my lawyer.
- Ø I have not met, nor spoken to him yet as well. The system is a joke.

Over the next few days, I tried to settle in and relax while my court date arrived. Abby my 14 year old daughter was aware of my court date and awaited my arrival. I promised to take her jet skiing, as it was one of her favorite activities. Abby loved the water and the beach. For many years she was on a swimming team in Coconut Creek. She was tall and athletic for her age. Her schedule was busy as she also took dance classes twice a week.

Apparently she was an adrenaline junkie, for she consistently pestered me about taking boxing lessons. She often left torn yellow pages on the kitchen table. They were clippings of martial arts schools, and boxing gyms. I would always brush it off as I did not want to picture her pretty face all bruised up.

So far during my stay at Paul Rein I slept on a plastic portable bunk on the floor. It stood 11 inches high and that was with the mat included. I was the fourth man in a three bed room cell. Apart from the standing space between the bunks, my portable plastic make-shift bed occupied the only open floor space in the room. Anthony Hodge a white man in his mid-30's with long black hair, was in for an armed home invasion. That's a PBL, (punishable by life). All PBL cases have no bonds, meaning you can't get out until your trial or you plea out. Anthony would order every week from the law library, the same four items;

Florida model jail standards – 82 pages.

Jail house lawyer's handbook – 152 pages.

Patriot Act - 100 pages.

Florida state constitution

Ø Anthony, why do you have so many of the same items on the desk?

Ø I like to give them a hard time and waste their money,

I picked up the jail standard manual and laid down to read. As I did, Dwain another roommate or bunkee, as we called ourselves, prepared his cup of noodles. That was something most inmates with commissary would do prior to retiring for the evening. Dwain loved his cup of noodle and could show you about 100 different items to put in it. I myself came up with a few. It seems that the only way to satisfy your taste buds in jail was through commissary items. My favorite combination was shrimp picante soup. After the microwave, you let it sit for 10 minutes. This way it soaks up the water and grows. I would add hot blazing peanuts to it, and then dip BBQ pork grinds. Although it was while not nutritional, it was tasty and helped kill the hunger pains.

With the jail standard manual in hand I noticed on page 27, section (5.08) that "Multiple occupancy cells shall contain a minimum of 40 square feet of floor space per inmate in the sleeping area". I immediately counted the tiles on the floor. Each tile is 1 square feet. The room measures 9 X 15, thus a total of 135 square feet. Dividing that by four gives us 33.75 square feet per person. Broward was in clear violation of the state's law. Upon further reading of the manual I came across page 40, section (8.02). It states "Sheets, towels, and pillow cases will be laundered at least once a week". Funny thing is I've not seen one pillow case or any pillows.

On page 51, (12.06 c) states, "Sufficient space shall be provided in all living and sleeping quarters to satisfy sanitary needs of all individuals incarcerated. Every bed, cot or bunk shall have a clear space of at least twelve inches from the floor. There shall be a clear....single beds, cots or bunks shall be spaced not less than thirty six inches literally and end to end. Sleeping arrangements shall insure that a minimum distance of six feet is provided between inmates' heads, if a solid barrier is not used...." Unless math has changed since I was in school, Broward County is in numerous violations; for the cot is only 11 inches off the ground at its highest point. Also the portable cot was placed at the end of the metal one, both running the length of the wall 15 feet in length. So how do two 6.5 feet beds align to a 15 feet wall when you need 36 inches in between? Did I need a refresher course? But then this was Broward, land of opportunity, home of stupidity, where one is guilty until proven innocent.

Over the next few days as I waited for my court day, I took to playing chess. Two games tables had a chess boards printed on its surface. A cabinet which was opposite to the TV housed a sink and microwave. Underneath the microwave were game boards, including dominos, checkers as well as the chess sets. Of all the chess players', only one man was a challenge for me. He was a brother with dreadlocks three feet long. When he played against me, a strange thing would occur. The palm of his hand would start dripping sweat. Sometimes it would drip into the game board as he moved a piece. As much as I welcomed the challenge, I detested touching the pieces of the game.

- Ø What's that all about?
- Ø Oh, that happens when I get nervous.
- Ø What and you so nervous about?
- Ø I don't know; it's you. I hate losing.
- Ø Well you win sometimes and you're ahead now.
- Ø Yeah, but you have a habit of sneaking up in the end.
- Ø Well, that's all that matters. That you win.

The next few days I spent most of my time at the game table. By then the really good players had enough of me and would not play me anymore. I would play with anyone who sat down. If you were a novice I ended up giving lessons. Steve happened to have walked by and I asked him to sit and play.

- Ø I'm not that good. I know how to move the pieces, but no strategy.

- Ø Okay! The game is broken down into three states; 1. The opening, 2. The middle and 3. The end. In the beginning your strategy is to gain control of the middle of the board and place your pieces in a position where you can move them, or utilize them.

Steve was an eager to learn and picked things up quickly. For us it was just a way of killing time. As we talked, Steve revealed more about himself and his case. It was apparent that he was a loyal and trust worthy man. He told of his stories over the past 20 years. All that time he was selling drugs on a low level end, choosing not to deal with large amounts as those penalties were severe. He loved women and was twice married. He had a thing for black women and has two children from his second wife.

According to him, his black relatives treated him better than his white relatives did. I think his white daughter from the first marriage was not too fond of Steve's children from the second wife who was black. It was clear he loved all his children, especially his granddaughter. His son Steve Jr. was street smart and had numerous friends who were in the drug game. Jr. was living with Steve at a house in Lauderhill. Jr. had a live in girlfriend who was the mother of his two year old daughter. Throughout most of the twenty years, Steve Sr. had a fence business that allowed him to live comfortable. I think the low level drugs were because he used to entice the females with them. As time went on people felt comfortable buying from him and trusted him. He believed that if he needed a gun to do business, then the business was not worth it.

A few days later during a chess match or I should say lesson, Steve told his story of his arrest. His story sounded just like mine. Steve was set-up by a friend who was caught selling drugs and so decided to save himself by doing the substantial assistance program. The night Steve was arrested he was driving his truck with a friend that was just breaking into the drug business. Both Steve and his newbie friend were being followed and pulled over at a gas station. They were cuffed and Steve was taken to his house to execute a search warrant. There they found one half of a bird. Not a wing or feathered creature, but a kilo of coke.

Later, Steve's friend that was arrested with him that night confided to him that based on the lawyers recommendation he opted to do his civil duties. I think in reality Steve mentioned this to me because he wanted to test the waters. It's a subject you don't talk about in jail. The last thing an inmate wants to be labeled in jail is a snitch or a rapist. I was aware of the program also, but did not say much to Steve about it. My life was already in danger. I knew he was holding back on something. There was more than what he wanted to say. I did not press him for info. We left it at that and focused on the game.

Later that night as I watched Dwain put Fritos Chips to his cup of noodles, I asked him for some advice. Dwain had been arrested several times during the years and knew how things worked. He was familiar with my case by now. Dwain was the son of a preacher and he spoke several times about getting out of the game as he put it. As he put it, "The game has changed and there were many snitches." Every night he would kneel by his bunk and pray. I thought how ironic that all the worshipers were not in church but in jail. Here everyone and their mother prayed. Anyhow, Dwain was a genuine person. He thought about my options and said,

- Ø 15 years mandatory if you take it to trial, or perhaps lose five to seven years if you plead, or possible probation if you talked. If they have a very strong case, then you don't want to take it to trial. The Florida State statue demands a minimum of 15 years plus a fine of $250,000. Since there was an informant involved, a motion to disclose the identity of the informant could be made. Often times if the informant is involved in other ongoing investigations, the police might refuse to reveal his identity. As a result a motion to dismiss might be granted and the case dismissed.

By talk he meant doing the substantial assistance program. I saw this as a long shot, however, one I would contemplate. I was caught red handed; taking the case to trail did not seem the way to go. Dwain also mentioned that, that at the moment you start asking the state for discovery, they start taking offers off the table. He said, "If you are doing the substantial assistance program, you need to decide quickly."

A second option was to draw the case out as long as possible. Dwain asked about my lawyer. I said,

- Ø Who? Casper.
- Ø Casper is that your lawyers name?
- Ø No, my lawyer's real name is Green.
- Ø Oh Brian Green?
- Ø Yes,

- Ø Wow, are you lucky, that guy is great.
- Ø Great! Are you kidding? The guy is a ghost. That's why I call him, Casper the friendly ghost. I've not met him once. He does not exist.
- Ø Oh, no Ozzie you are wrong, that man knows his stuff. I tried to hire him once. He got my cousin off, and my cousin was guilty as can be. You better keep him. Here is a plan.
- Ø Dwain does it make more sense to get out on bail and use a public defender or stay in and hire a private lawyer?
- Ø Here is your plan Ozzie, you want to fight your case from outside, and not while you are in jail.

Anthony who was listening jumped in.

- Ø I rather put in some time; you might get a better deal that way. The state will have to pay you for imprisonment if they lose. They will give you a deal if you already have some time in.
- Ø Look, said Dwain; bail out, use Green to do the motions, all the discoveries and the depositions. He can tie up about two years that way. In the meantime gather money for a private lawyer. Since much of the work would have been done by Green, a private lawyer would then charge less than normal. That lawyer can drag out one more year or more. By then, anything can happen along the way. The informant can disappear, and so you can then order new depositions. There could be discrepancies in people's depositions as memories of the event get jarred with time. The officer might not be around by then.

To me this sounded like the plan. Dwain went on to discuss the last option,

- Ø You could do civil duties.
- Ø What's that? (He lowered his voice), do what they did to you.
- Ø What do you mean?
- Ø If you setup people, you might get probation or house arrest, because this was your first offence. If you don't have any one you could turn in then you can't go that route.

For me, the substantial assistance program was not an option. I knew of no one in the drug business. Till now, most of my acquaintances were doctors, business owners, and professionals.

That night, I thought about that which Dwain spoke of and started to formulate a plan of attack for my defense. I also thought about my childhood, about my lost friend (the girl), about Jackie; perhaps if she were not in the picture I might not have ended up in jail. I thought about Jenelle my first born and Ozzie Jr. I thought about the life I was responsible for, the life for which I was paid blood money, the life of an exuberant, happy, joyful, and playful person.

This night it hit me hard again. I had the blanket drawn completely over me. I laid on my side, in the fetal position. Tears started pouring out once again. Despite this I managed to reframe from making audible sounds. Usually I know hours in advance when my demon is coming to visit. Any number of memories can trigger it, such as, when I think of my own childhood past; when I think about the good times I shared with my brothers and all the games we played together, as well as all the jokes we played on each other and of course all the beatings we shared. When I think about high school, and when I hear the disco classics. That evening after thinking of Dwain and my new plan, I remembered being in my bedroom in Coconut Creek. It was a big, beautiful two story house. During that time I owned a furniture consignment shop in Miezner Park, Boca Raton. My wife Nancy would instruct the workers to load onto the truck any item she thought would look well in the house.

Nancy was a sexy, beautiful Puerto Rican woman. Not only did I love her, I was also deeply attracted to her. She had a knack for decoration, and our home always looked like a model home from a magazine. This night I had a vivid recollection of being there. I stood looking down out of the second story window onto the back yard. Time slowed down as it often does for me. I looked at the ground and then up at the telephone pole in the adjacent yard. I again looked down to the ground and back up to the top of the pole. As if that wasn't enough, I again looked down to the ground, and up to the top. This I did numerous times. The top of the pole was about 49 feet high. By now I knew how high 49 feet was, for I often measured it. Not the pole itself but rather the length itself. I have a long measuring tape at home. Several times I stretched it out and measured 49 feet. This I did for about two years.

I closed my eyes as I stood there and I could still see the ground and the top of the pole. With my eyes still closed I looked back down and then to the top again. Then back to the ground, and back up the top. Nancy and Abby were on the bed. I had given up on taking Abby to her room, for somehow almost every morning she was curled up between us. I opened my eyes and turned the night light off, which was to my side. I then placed myself under the covers. I was in anguish, and in deep pain. From under the covers I could see the ground and the pole within it. I looked at the ground and then up to the top of the pole. I had become accustomed to look at poles everywhere I went. I would look at the ground and then at the top and try to figure its measurement. Is it longer or shorter than 49 feet?

For the first year I did that, often masking the accompanying pain and tears. From under the covers tears started flowing; my breathing was hard as I gasped for air. Abby and Nancy knew what was going on. They knew I was in pain. A pain they could not comfort. A pain I could not control. No words needed to be spoken. No words could console or comfort my pain. There was nothing they could do nor say. There was no escaping. I sat back on the bed, with my tears rolling down my cheeks. I looked at the table next to me to reach for a sleeping pill, but the pills were not there. The table was not there, the lamp was not there. All I saw was a pole 49 feet high and an empty ground. I was ready to jump out the window, not because I wanted to kill myself, not because I wanted to die, but rather to escape; to escape from my vision; to escape from the 49 foot pole. To escape my demon that visited me. I wanted the pole to go away, but it would not.

Abby sat up next to me. How can I take another life away? How can I do that to her? She kneeled behind me on the bed. She rested her chest on my back, and she hugged me. Her face leaned to my side as she looked at me. She lifted her right arm and brushed away my tears. She brought her hand to her side and whipped her hand. She then brought it up and hugged me again as she gave me a kiss on my right cheek. Nancy had made her way around the bed and now stood in front of me. She leaned over and hugged Abby and I. I grabbed her by her waist and held on. I did not want to die. I did not want to jump. By now the table came back to the side of the bed. I could see the things in front of me. I could see the aspirins. I grasped Abby and brought her upon my lap. I hugged her for an eternity and told her I loved her. I then stood up and walked downstairs to the kitchen where of all things I made a cup of coffee and immersed myself in my laptop. It would be 3:00 am before I passed out.

10 AUGUST 31ST

It was now Friday, August 31st and three weeks into Paul Rein Facility. Friday evening is visitation time for my unit between 8:00 pm and 10:00 pm. The time was 1:30 in the afternoon. Steve Upper and Ozzie Vargas get ready for visit. How strange I thought. Who would visit me at this time? We were instructed to take off our sweaters stand by the door. Beyond that door is a short corridor that leads to the next unit. Within the corridor you will find a tiny counselor's office as well as another door that leads to a stairs going down. To reach the bottom requires about 30 steps.

Corridors are designed so that only one door at either end could be open at a time. Beyond that door at the bottom is a security booth. It is the guard's duty to supervise visitation. There are two forms of visitation. One requires family and friends, to sit outside of the room you are in. Cement walls and a reinforced window create a barrier. To communicate each party needs to pick up a phone placed at each end. All calls are recorded, and guards walk around to make sure no other form of communication is established; in other words, no sign language or writing. Also, if they determine one party is exposing themselves then that visitation is over and noted. The other visitation is reserved for lawyers and police. They get to sit in the same room with the prisoner, the size being about 6 X 5ft. It's a semi private room, with windows through which the guards can see. Your visitor sits opposite you with a table placed between the two. Conversation here is not recorded and thus private.

Once downstairs I was instructed to wait for the man in Booth 3 to exit. As I looked towards booth number three I noticed through the glass that it was Steve Upper. Sitting opposite him was a man I had seen in court for about one minute. Steve had made his way down before me by about two minutes. So he could not have been talking for more than that. To my surprise he stood up and exited. Although the room was tiny it had two entrances, one on each end. I was instructed to enter through the same side Steve exited from. I nodded to Steve as he exited. I entered the room and said hi. The man behind the desk did not stand. There were no handshakes. He responded with a nod as if to say, how's it going? "Have a seat", were the first words from the man.

- Ø I am Brian Green you attorney.
- Ø Wow, you really do exist?
- Ø What do you mean?
- Ø Well up till this point you have been a phantom. I heard good things about you, but I'm not sure what good that does, if you are unreachable. I've left numerous messages on your phone. I've called the main number and made a complaint about not being able to reach you. I've had my brother call you several times, unsuccessfully. I've been in court three times and saw you once. You would not even come over to introduce yourself. In court I noticed several lawyers speaking with the inmates.
- Ø Yes I know you were in court. You had an attorney present to help you with the motion for bond reduction, because of that I was not needed.
- Ø Yes, I needed to do so because I could not get a hold of you.

Mr. Green just sat there the whole time. He wore a shirt and pants that did not match. There was no tie. He had no fashion sense and to say the least did not look professional. He slumped backwards on his chair with his left arm pointing straight down to his side. His legs stretched out in front. He looked at me with no expression at all, almost as if his mind was somewhere else.

- Ø Can you tell me how to proceed on my case, I asked.
- Ø No, I cannot.
- Ø Any reason why?
- Ø Today is August 31st, the last day of the month. There are many people I need to see. I am here to meet my quota.
- Ø You got to be kidding me. I don't know if I should keep you or hire a private lawyer.

- Ø Under the law you have an obligation to hire a private lawyer if you have the means to. So, can you hire a private lawyer?

- Ø No, not at this time. Can I ask the court for a different lawyer?

- Ø Sure, you can put a motion in for that.

- Ø Wow, I think we have gotten off on the wrong foot and now I'm scared.

- Ø Well how would you feel if the first thing out of my mouth was, you're a ghost?

This whole time I thought to myself, what a fucking idiot? Green showed no emotions the entire time. He had not bothered to view my case; to me he was just that, a ghost. To him I was just a number.

- Ø Ok, I know you are a busy man. I've been hearing about the substantial assistance program. Can you tell me anything about that?

- Ø Do you have a number of people in the game, people who you could turn in?

- Ø No, I don't.

- Ø Well, the program is not for you. It requires one to plead guilty, then go out and work for the police. I've heard stories of police holding a gun to the head of the C.I. (confidential informant) and pressuring him to produce. Is this what you want?

- Ø No. Is it possible to?

- Ø Anything is possible.

- Ø You are not letting me finish,

- Ø Does not matter. You started with "is it possible", in court anything is possible.

- Ø Ok, I said I have a hearing tomorrow.

- Ø Yes, the lawyer you hire for the motion will be there is that correct?

- Ø Yes.

- Ø Ok, thank you

Green was an arrogant man. However, by the way he answered I knew he was intelligent. I exited without a handshake. He stood slumped on the chair as I turned my back. I proceeded to the door concealing the stairs going up and opened it. Once I reached the top I buzzed the office to let me through to my unit. The entire trip back and forth was less than 10 minutes. By now it was 15 minutes to 2:00 pm. In five minutes, at 10 minutes to 2pm locked down begins and continues until till the next shift change, which starts at 3:00 pm. During lock down you have to stay in your assigned room. The front of the room has a 36 inch walkthrough at the center; perhaps the term opening is more appropriate. It's flanked by two walls each about four and a half feet high and three feet long, so that the width totals nine feet across. The wall that separates the adjacent cell runs 15 feet long with a portion of it also being four and a half feet. The second half of the wall runs from floor to ceiling. Double bunk beds run parallel along the second half or should I say towards the back part of the room. Lock down is sort of a misnomer, for in jail you already are locked up. What is actually meant is room confinement. Because our unit has communal bathrooms, we are allowed to exit the room for bathroom visit. Oftentimes inmates converge there during lock down to chat or get a message across. Inmates also stand by the wall chatting with the neighbor from the cell next door.

Before lockdown began I spoke to Steve who was sitting by the eating table.

- Ø You have the same attorney as I do?
- Ø Yes, I guess so, if Green in yours.
- Ø Yes, he is so? I call him Casper the ghost.
- Ø Oh, I thought it was only me. This is the second time I see him.
- Ø So, Steve we have the same charges, the same judge, the same state prosecutor and the same lawyer. That guy, Mr. Green is arrogant but straight to the point and no nonsense.
- Ø Yes, that is how I see him.
- Ø OK. We'll talk later.

Shift change takes place at 3:00 pm. The first call of duty is to do a head count. Every few hours there is an official inmate count. After shift change lockdown gets lifted. The phones as well as the TV get turned on and we are free to move about the unit. At about 15min. to 5:00 pm we go to our units again in preparation for dinner. Dinner is at 5:00 pm. We get called to dinner by sections 1 – 5, 6 – 10, 11 – 15 and 16 – 20. Every day the sections are called differently. As soon as we are done eating, we must pass by the deputy and lift our shirts slightly. We must also lift up our pants to expose our ankles. The purpose of which is to make sure we don't take contraband back to the unit. What could that contraband be? Well food. We are not allowed to bring back food to the room. Deputies that have been around for many years don't seem to mind. Mrs. Humphrey a newbie makes it a habit to check. She gives you extra lockdown time for taking food to the room. Little does she know that her method is ineffective.

After watching her for a few days, one realizes that while she checks as you approach her, she never checks behind you. So instead of hiding food under our shirt in the front we simply hide it in our backs. One morning while on breakfast duty, I asked a different deputy, "why is it that some don't check at all and some are hung up about it?" He replied, "I've doing this a long time. I know all the tricks in the book. People hide food under their armpits, on their back, in their socks. They lower the pants and raise their underwear up high. That forms a pouch. Our duty is to stop it if we catch it, but we know some gets through. "Many inmates will save bread or cookies for a snack". Here was a deputy that knows what goes on.

Broward jail is a business. You can have all the food you want in your locker as long as you pay for it. That's where commissary comes in. A cup of noodles which you can buy at the store for .69₵ sells for $1.19. The amount of food served for dinner is not an adequate amount for a grown man. It's barely enough for a child. Those who don't have commissary, usually go hungry. You can tell the ones that have been in jail longer, as they are thinner. After we head back to the room we stayed there for about half an hour, while the dinner crew cleans up. We are then free till 10:00 pm. Those trustees that help out during dinner get extra food, which some of them then sell or exchange for commissary items.

I caught up with Steve after dinner, at the game table. Chess with him is not challenging, however, I do manage to kill time. We made small talk about Mr. Green. Steve was concerned about not being able to bond out. His house was confiscated upon his arrest and could not be pledge as collateral. His mother and brother were not willing to help him. It seems he was to be incarcerated for a long time. At 50, he said he did not have the fight in him anymore. His two charges could land him 30 – 40 years. Steve was nervous, but contained himself.

At about 9:20 I retired for the evening. At about this time inmates start preparing their evening snacks. A line for the microwave forms as people heat up water for their noodles. People walk back and forth to the restroom, showers or final chit-chat before the evening ends. Dwain was already in his room as usual. He was eating his noodles with what bag of chips he could find. For the moment we were alone in the room.

Hey Dwain thanks for helping me out with my problem.

Don't mention it.

- Ø I'm afraid I will have to do many years. I'm concerned I might not be there for my daughter's High School years.
- Ø Don't worry too much Ozzie. It's your first offence. You might get an offer for maybe 5 – 7 years.
- Ø What about you Dwain? What is your plan?
- Ø I'm weighting my options also.

Dwain had violated probation with a new traffic charge, on a VOP, (violation of probation), with that you don't have a bond. You must go before the magistrate or judge within 10 days. Sometimes, if it's a minor violation or technical violation, such as you moved and did not informed them, or you missed a probation date, you will get reinstated. Meaning you get released, otherwise you get a no-bond hold. That is, your shit out of luck. Your issue needs to be resolved which can take months.

- Ø Pssss, come here. Why don't you talk?
- Ø What do you mean?
- Ø Talk; turn in a few people for your freedom.
- Ø I don't know of anyone.
- Ø Buy them.
- Ø Buy them. How? That's easy.
- Ø I'll explain later.
- Ø Is that your plan?
- Ø I can't say much. You have to be very careful around here. I have someone working for me.
- Ø Working for you, where, how?

- Ø My wife is working for me out there while I am in here.

<Anthony Hodges walks in.>

- Ø You have to let the noodles sit for 10 – 15 minutes. This way it cooks and soaks up water. It's more filling that way.

- Ø Ok, Dwain thanks for the cooking lesson.

With that we all made small talk and settled in. Like myself, Anthony would stay up till past 1:00 am. He either read or played solitaire. Sometimes he would do a little of both.

That weekend came and went. For now I was just killing time, knowing I would soon be in front of the judge and then be allowed to go home. I called Abby again and inform her that I had the wrong date. It would be the following week that I would be home. I played an upbeat tempo when I spoke to her. Like me, she is not much of a talker. I usually find myself dragging things out of her. She said ok dad. After a few minutes we exchanged I love you's and hanged up.

Two nights have passed since I spoke with Dwain. Once again in the evening I found myself watching him prepare his noodles. He would make a project out of that. Anthony would play cards till as late as he could. So this was always a good time. Buy now our other bunkee was released and I had taken to sleep on the top bunk over Anthony.

- Ø Dwain, I'm curious can you tell me more about what we spoke off, two nights ago. I'm curious.

- Ø Look Ozzie, I'm already 40. I've been in and out of jail several times. I've never hurt anyone, although I've sold drugs, I have a nice home in Coral Springs, a nice wife and a beautiful daughter. I want out of the drug game. My wife prepares taxes for people and does it part time for a firm during tax season. There are other ways to make money where the penalty is not as severe. It's also harder to get roped, (roped is the street term for caught by the police).

- Ø So how do you have someone working for you?

- Ø My wife.

- Ø Your wife?

- Ø Yes, my wife.

Ø How so?

Dwain knew I was a quiet man. He also knew I was concerned about helping Nancy and being around for Abby. Other than that I don't know what made him confide in me.

Ø My wife was in the game with me. We both want to get out of Broward and move to Georgia to raise our two children. She is talking?

Ø Talking?

Ø Yes, it was her idea. It's not the way I wanted to go. It's what the Lord has in mind for us. She contacted my arresting officer, prosecutor and our lawyer. She is talking to them.

Ø What is she talking about?

I was not naïve. I wanted to hear it from him.

Ø Talking, dropping peoples' names and setting people up.

Ø Shouldn't you be doing that?

Ø Yes, but I can't get out because of my no bond hold. That will be resolved within a few weeks. Everyone she turns in, I get credit for. Maybe I will get less than a year or just house arrest.

Ø Wow, one can do that?

Ø It's working for us.

Ø How many people in a case such as yours do you need to turn in?

Ø Well it depends, cops like to go after pills now a day, and just a few blues will get you a trafficking charge. Many people are out of the dope (cocaine) business, because of the severe fines and sentencing (blues are pain killers).

Ø How do you get the pills? Don't you need a prescription?

Ø Yes, that's why you have several friends go to the pill mill.

Ø Pill mill, what's that?

Ø That's a doctor's office. They will give you a prescription of about 180 pills for a fee.

- Ø So, I can walk into a clinic and say I have pain and leave with a script.

- Ø Yes, back pain is undetectable, so you go in and complain. You will be charge a visit fee and then a fee for the prescription. The second time around you will pay just a higher upfront fee. There are several places you can go to in one day. You can pick up a few hundred pills. The only thing is that you need to have them filled at different pharmacies. Since the prescription is for a certain amount of time you can't get more until that time has passed. The way around that is to go with two or three different people who will give you or sell the pills after they have them.

- Ø Hey Dwain, there is a guy here that made the newspaper for running a pain clinic or rather a pill mill.

- Ø Yes, I know my wife has a prescription from him, that she did not fill because she heard the news. She was in the area when it happened and saw all the police. She got scared and put the prescription away.

By now my mind is thinking fast. Am I on to something here? Can this be my ticket out? Can I really help break this case? Or is this guy Dwain telling me a story? For a moment, Jerry came to mind.

- Ø So Dwain, are you saying that this guy Balbi wrote you a prescription himself.

- Ø No, but we have seen him there several times. I think there were several doctors there that would write the prescriptions. I'm not sure who wrote my wife's, as she said that she had a prescription from that guy as well as her friend.

- Ø So, your wife and her friend each have a prescription written by Balbi himself?

- Ø I don't know that. I know for sure it's from his office.

Dwain sat on his bunk with his cup of noodles. He sat down and changed the topic. I wanted to hear more but I did not press on. Moments later Anthony Hodges came to settle in. Dwain must have been aware of the time. Anthony settled in as so did everyone in the unit. I jumped onto my bunk and stared into the ceiling. I could hear the cards being shuffled underneath me. Nighttime was hard for me as I had no distractions to get me away from my demons that came regularly.

At about 12:00 am I could felt it, but I did not want to feel the pain. I jumped of the bunk directly to the floor. Anthony looked at me. He was playing solitaire. The green stool, disguised as a seat, was really a foot step to jump onto the top bunk. I sat on it and watched Anthony. It has been over 30 years, since I played solitaire and did not remember it well. For an hour or so I watched until I started to feel a little sleepy. With that I laid myself on my bunk. The next two days were uneventful. I killed time with Steve on the game table. I would correct him when he made a bad move and allowed him a better move. We made small talk mostly about girls.

11 SEPTEMPER 6, CALENDAR CALL

The 11:00 pm. shift change, is labeled alpha shift. It's the first shift of the following day. First call of duty is head count. Guards walk by and take a count to make sure no prisoners have escaped, I don't see how prisoners could escape from there, but nonetheless it's done several times throughout the day. Razors are brought in about 11:30pm and distributed to those who subscribed on the list. Everyone who is to shave tries to be fist in line. There are only a limited number of sinks to shave in. Those who are not fast need to wait in line for a sink to become available. That wait could last a half hour. Because of this shaving time becomes a race to the front desk to acquire a razor. To those that are shaving, it's a fun event; not the shaving part but the race itself. When Deputy Hosan turns the lights on, it's the signal to get ready for the razors.

We now stand in the room at the foot of its entrance. No one is to be on the outside part of the room. It's quite comical to see a whole group of guys standing in the room ready for the word. It's similar to a horse race where the buzzard rings and the stalls open. Hosan's first words are "Okay, gentlemen if you are going to shave you may do so now." By the time he finishes the sentence, the race is over. I have it down to a science. When I hear his voice I take off. I'm only about 20 feet away. Needless to say I am always in the top three. I knew I had court in the morning, so I made it a point to shave that night. My usual shaving days are Sunday, Tuesday and Thursday nights.

After he has finished writing our names on our Razors and passes them out, his next call of duty is to announce the names of those who have court in the morning. There were only two names that caught my attention Adams and Vargas. For Adams is the government name of Price. Going to the court house was not something anyone liked. On the contrary, it seems everyone despised it. It goes like this.

Breakfast is always served at about 3:00 am. By 3:30 it's over with and we are usually back in bed by 4:00 am. 4am is also the time for those going to court to get ready and come forward. We are not allowed any sweaters. Only one pair of underwear and/or a t-shirt under our uniform is permissible. Before we depart our unit we get searched, handcuffed and walked to the elevator to be taken to the first floor intake unite. Once there, we are released of our handcuffs and place in a holding cell that fits about 30 – 40. Most of which is stand up only. At 5:00 am we are handcuffed to another inmate and board the bus in pairs. The inside of the bus is dark as there are no windows to see out of. The bus ride to the courthouse and main jail takes about 20 minutes. We are first taken to the main jail. The main jail has a pathway directly to the courthouse, as both are in different buildings. Upon arrival at the main jail, the bus enters an enclosed area. There we exit and enter a large elevator to the second floor. Once we exit the elevator, we come to a finger scanning device. Our finger prints are checked and a screen reveals our mug shot if you will. Yea, mug shot is an appropriate term for usually the picture is taken right after our arrest. By then we would have been mugged and maybe shot by the police. I myself looked rather beat-up. Other info such as the judge's name, dictates which holding cell to place us.

The holding cells are kept very cold, mainly to kill germs and bacteria that might be floating around. There is nothing in the cell to entertain the mind. A long metal bench that runs for about 20 feet lines both sides of the yellow walls. At the end of a cell is a toilet with no walls, curtain, covers or partition. During the next two hours inmates from the other jails, including the main jail, march in. There is nothing to do but listen to stupid inmates revealing their ignorance and low I.Q. Every so often a fight will break out. By the time most inmates have been admitted, the noise level becomes unbearable. People are yelling over each other telling their pathetic stories, while others in fear discuss their case.

Although I was full of anticipation about resolving my issue and being released it was there that once again I worried about my future. This day as my cell door opened, I recognized a face. It was Dominguez. A trustee I had known from the main jail. He came over and I moved a little to the side so as to make space. After the usual formalities he lowered his voice.

Ø Ozzie would is the Cuban guy has put a hit on you.

Ø You're kidding.

Ø I don't know how true it is, put it was all over the jail when they moved you. Word is he belongs to a gang. You need to be very careful.

Ø Well, I'm not that worried about it.

Ø Anyhow, I'm not trying to scare you but they say his gang is big in Florida.

Damn! What a mess. Was all this worth love? As much as I tried I could not see the bright side to this. I sat quietly for a while. Dominguez took conversation with someone else. By now I had my arms across my chest. I had pulled them in from the sleeve so that the sleeves to the uniform were bare. All uniforms with the exception of jump suits are short slaved.

At 8:15 am the doors opened, a metal chain is placed around our waist and our hands cuffed to it; looped over the front of the chain. If you need to scratch your head you are out of luck. Once in the courtroom we sit to the side away from the civilians. My attorney, Mr. Wolf was late. That did not seem to matter much, as they call according to whichever party is present; as expected Casper Green was not there. However, Anthony, my bails bonds man was. It was 9:30 am when Mr. Wolf arrived. He made his way over to me and within three minutes it was over.

- Ø "Is there a house with collateral?" asked the Judge.
- Ø "No", you honor.
- Ø "Motion denied", asserted the judge.
- Ø Wolf tried to make an argument and suddenly Anthony spoke up.
- Ø"Your honor I am the bail-bonds man. In today's world many of the houses are under water."
- ØIf there is no house to key keep him tied, I am not releasing him!" exclaimed the judge.

I tried to speak up and called for Wolf's attention. He looked over at me and said no. There is something that I want to say. The judge looked at me for a second and then proceeded, "next on the docket". Shit, all that for nothing, I'm fucked, I thought. Now I also have to worry about getting shanked in jail, on command of the Cubans. It was clearly not a good morning for me. Wolf, walked over and said,

- Ø "I'll get you out. Don't worry."
- Ø Sure, I don't see how.
- Ø "Let me talk to the prosecutor."

I knew he was just saving face. Several minutes later I was whisked away. As the door to the holding cell opened, I could see Prince setting down; the look of despair was upon his face. There was no need to say anything. I sat next to him and neither of us spoke one word. Once on the bus we compared not notes and disappointments. As we exited the bus we were handed our lunch (A small package with four slices of bread, a small package of peanut butter, two small jellies and an apple). From there we entered a tiny room, undressed, lifted our balls, turn around, squatted down and coughed. We then dress up again and past the metal detector, and then back into a holding cell.

Once back in the unit, as my handcuffs were being released, Dwain looked over at me. I shook my head from side to side and made my way to my bunk where I ate my lunch. For the next few hours I took to sleep. It was 5:00 pm dinner time, when Dwain woke me up. "We'll talk later" he said. After dinner I would not come out to the game table, instead I got on the phone with my brother and Abby to inform them I would not be out this weekend. I took solace in talking with Dwain. We spoke about the unspeakable topic when Anthony was not present. Dwain knew I wasn't going home yet, and gave me my space and time. He waited for me to start the conversation.

Ø Dwain, the fucking judge did not even give me a chance. It took her all about three minutes to deny my motion.

Dwain was the son of a preacher and it showed. He was soft spoken and very positive.

- Ø Don't worry Ozzie, this will pass. Just believe. The Lord will find you the way.

Being an atheist I simply humored him.

- Ø You need to talk that the way. Come clean.
- Ø That's easy for you to say Dwain. You have a number of people you know that you can turn in. I don't know of anyone.
- Ø It will come. Get a girlfriend or friend that is familiar with the streets and the game. You will find it easy to buy all the pills you want.
- Ø I'm not sure I want people coming after me. I don't want to be a target.
- Ø Look, almost every one getting rope is talking. As far as I see it, it's the only way out for now. Of course you can always do your time.
- Ø How can I get out if I can't get a house with enough equity?
- Ø That's simple. Once you enter an agreement your bond gets reduced drastically.
- Ø How sure are you about that?

- Ø I'm very sure Ozzie. I am working something out, but I can't talk about it. You need to talk to your lawyer Casper.
- Ø I would if only I could see him. Thank you Dwain!
- Ø Don't worry about your secret. It is safe with me.

By now the time to settle in was approaching. I met up with Steve at the table. As he played I sat by his side for a moment.

- Ø I take it; it did not go so well.
- Ø What gave you that idea?
- Ø I saw you as you came in. Both you and Prince were quiet. Besides he already informed me. I am sorry to hear. It looked like you were on your way out.
- Ø All right, I'll let you play.

Prince was by the microwave when he decided to walk over to me. It seems he was preparing to eat. In his hand was a cup of noodles.

- Ø What's up Prince?
- Ø Man Ozzie, This shit is fucked up. I have book signings coming up and I am losing a lot of money being here. I can't even get a bond on my VOP. They're throwing the book at me. Broward County sucks, if you only knew how much money I am going to lose you would flip.
- Ø Tell me.
- Ø No, I can't say other than it's a lot.
- Ø Damn! I said. We're going to have to figure it out.

During the next few nights I thought about my future, like in a game of chess; I calculated all my options. Dwain opened an avenue that I have not seen. Look for a way Ozzie. Look for a way. There is always an answer. As off yet I could not see it. Again like in chess you don't make that move until you can see five or six moves ahead, so I wait.

12 THE AVENUE; HIGH SCHOOL

Fuck, holy shit, holy cow! For those outside on New York, it's not to be taken as to fornicate. It's just a part of speech, so forget-a-bout-it. That would be holy shit for the rest of the country and holy cow in India or should I say sacred cow. Yes, yes, I got it. I got it. "I think I can, I think I can, I think I can, so come on ride this train and ride it, come on ride this train and ride it." I'm doing my happy dance. I got a hunch; it's been four days now since my last talk with Dwain. If only he were here to hear my idea. I see it, I see my chess move. I see the avenue Dwain spoke off, if I can put it together. I think I can, I think I can. I think I can, yeah baby!

Its 1:30 am. It's only one, of a handful of happy times that I've experienced while in jail. I don't want it to end. The positive thought that is. Only happy thoughts tonight; for tonight I figured it out. This plan just came to me. I will see where it will get me, how far it will go, and who will come on board? Tonight, there will be no demon to visit me. I don't want to think about that. I'm going to sleep now. Thank you Dwain, thank you! For you showed me the way. It's because of you that I have formulated this plan.

Last night was a good one, after a few days of looking for an avenue, for a new way to go, for a way out, its come. I can see it. It's a hunch and might take some swage to implement, but for now it's a good turn. Being in joyful spirits these past few nights has allowed me to fall asleep quickly, All the while keeping my demon away. It's as if once again I was with Jackie. With her I kept my demons at bay, for with her he rarely showed up. With her being out the picture I wonder if there is a way to make it go away permanently; a way other than going mad, and a way other than hurting myself. Can I find that inner peace and love I once knew? There are new worries at bay. I am now a target, a marked man with a price on my head, but for the moment I need to stay positive and focused. Not only was I being positive, but for the first time in about four months I was happy. Thoughts about growing up with my brothers came, and for about 20 minutes, I was transposed. I remembered a time when both my brothers and I slept in the basement in Rosedale Ave. Sleeping together every night, was an adventure. We never knew how the evening would end. The hour before bedtime was always filled with expectations.

The house we lived in consisted of three apartments. Two were on the second floor. One apartment was a two bedroom and the other a single. To conserve money, my frugal mother, would have us turn the second story hallway lights off at night. (I sometimes wondered what law suit might have arise if someone fell at night.) The circuit breaker for that area was located in the same panel of the first floor apt. Two sliding doors in the first floor living room revealed a library that housed the electrical panel. It was our responsibility to make sure the lights were turned off every night. The last man to bed was in charge of that task. However this created a problem in that the basement bedroom light we slept in was also tied into the same circuit. So when the second floor lights went off, so did the basement light.

The events of the last man to bed went as such. After preparing the bed to lie down, he would have to walk up the stairs, open the basement door quietly, walk to the living room, open the sliding door, open the breaker box, turn the breaker off and then do everything else in reverse. If we rushed the entire process could take 20 seconds, but as we needed to do it quietly 40 – 45 seconds was average. That was enough time for the rest of us to load his bed with countless item and objects. It's amazing to see the amount of things two people can throw on a bed in 30 seconds or so, especially with preparation. We would throw anything within reach; the only thing off limits was a 30 gallon fish tank. And that's only because it was too heavy to carry.

For about six months straight we did the same; it never got old. One day my younger brother Jose and I managed to put the entire five drawer chest on Ismael's bed. Another time we put two bikes on the bed. But most of the time it would be the drawers, clothing from the dresser or closets, shoes. Sometimes there were so many items that the lights needed to be turned on. So on the way up we would remove all the items from the bed, but that now left a problem, the lights needed to be turned off again, so that the cycle would be repeated. My mother would sometimes sneak up by the top of the stairs and introduce the visitor, the belt. It wasn't always fun and games. Sometimes we would have fist fights, I can't even remember about what. Despite all that I loved my two brothers, as well as my father whom I dearly missed.

During the first year at Rosedale Ave. we made numerous friends. Many of the neighborhood kids would come over to look for us. They all got accustomed to seeing my mother with the belt in her hand. Sometimes they would beg her to let us come out. I think my mother got off on that. She needed to feel and exercise power. The following year I attended Cardinal Hayes High School; a private Catholic School. My dad flipped the tuition bill. By that time, Ismael and I were good friends with Tayna, Pamela and the girl. The girls' parents had a three family house. In the basement was a pool table which we often used, as we listened to disco music. Ismael and Jose would dance the Hustle with the girls. I mostly watched. Often we would go shopping together. Despite spending so much time with them; I never really made a move on the girl. Perhaps I respected her too much. I was a horny kid growing up. I would get an erection if the wind blew. The girls had strict parents and they were not allowed out in the evenings. Although I had several girlfriends, I did not push for more than a simple kiss with the girl. I valued, cherished and loved being in her company, and that's the reason I call her the girl. She was the only one that has ever captured me. Other than sex with other girls, there was nothing more that I enjoyed more than being in her presence.

Two summers after moving to Rosedale Ave, I turned 16. My mother and step dad for years constantly argue. By now I had enough of that as well as their beatings. Most of the arguments I believed were because of us. I don't think we were bad kids. We just seem to be in their way. At least that's how I felt. I was a burden to my parents. That same year I came across a lady that had a large efficiency apartment for rent, and so I decided to strike a deal with her. As long as we put all the garbage by the curb three times a week, I could rent the place for $50.00 per week. That was a no-brainer. I knew I was not going to drop out of school and knew I could not move out alone, so I managed to convince Ismael to move with me. We would be free of the tyrants and maybe help save their marriage; as of today they still are together.

I remember the afternoon I told my mother, that Ismael and I were moving. She demanded for us to stay and threatened to call the police on us if we did not obey. I thought that was a dumb idea, but she pressed on. I was never really into talking too much and did not say much. For that matter there was really nothing to say. My decision had been made. With a look of a mad man, I told her to move out of the way. She did for a brief moment and then returned. I knew what she was up to. I knew she would be back. I just stood there and looked at her. Once again, the belt was in her hand. She proceeded to swing the belt at me. I raised my hand and caught the belt halfway through its middle. I step forwards into her space while clutching the belt. "Look, you have managed to hit me all these years simply because I have allowed you to do so, but I do not allow you to ever hit me again. I am moving out today and I am not asking for your permission. Let this be the last time you raise your hand to me." With that I went into my room, gathered my clothing, and left. All the while I never bothered to look back at her. She must have had been frozen with surprise as I could tell by the lack of noise on the wooden floor that she had not moved.

The following day, there was a knock at my door. My first visit, but who could it be? I asked "who is it?", but there was no answer, it's as if the person behind the door was either deaf or playing games. I decided to open. Immediately I threw my hands up in the air; I step forwards and brought them down around the back of this man. We smiled for a moment and with that I gave my dad a hug and kiss. He was alone and had no bags. We both entered and he surveyed my living area. With dad, there was always some form of non verbal communication. He spoke both English and Spanish but it was the quiet moments that spoke loudest. There was always a deep unspoken love. It was different than the love for my brother. With dad, I knew there was at least one person in the world who loved me and there was no denying it. Dad asked me if I was okay, and I said yes. Ismael had not arrived yet and I think he was about the neighborhood getting a pizza. Dad was not aware of all the beatings and abuse we had received over the years. My mom had always painted a different picture. Dad apologized for what we had suffered.

Ismael soon managed to find his way to what was now home and also gave dad a big kiss and hug. We then walked three blocks to a mall and enjoyed dinner together. After dinner he called for a cab back to the airport. Before he did so he took out several large bills and handed them to us. It was enough to buy food and many items we needed, including furniture. (Dad, for that and all the wonderful things you have done for me. I thank you and I love you.)

By the following month we had settled in. September was here and I started my sophomore years of high school being emancipated. At 16 I was my own guardian. That became a joke in school and made Ismael and I popular. We were known as the only two kids that could write our own absent letters. However I enjoyed school so much I did not abuse it. By the end of my first year I ranked 16 among 400 freshmen students. By the end of my second year I ranked number 12. By my junior year I completed all the state requirements needed to graduate. My senior year at Hayes I enrolled in three advanced placement classes. One of which I took because the minimum grade you could possibly get was a 90. For that, all you needed to do was write your name on a paper. It was American History. There were less than a handful of exams in that class. I spent most of the time cracking jokes with my friend Eddie. Eddie and I were pranksters. Many a times I raised my hand for minutes on end, only to let the priest know that my friend Eddie who was being ignored had a question. "Good morning! Every day at Hayes is a holiday." Those were the first words of each the day over the P.A.

Throughout all this, Ismael and I had managed to keep our pact. Prior to moving out from our mother's house, we promised each other that we would never do drugs and that we would finish Hayes and move on to college. The only crime we committed was repeated almost every day. At school we were required to wear a sports jacket and tie. I always made it a point to purchase jackets that had deep inside pockets. At the lunch line I would slip a long hero wrapped in plastic onto my inner part of the jacket. I would buy a hotdog and soft drink. But it was the big hero that filled me, and the reason for being on line.

With the money my dad gave us I purchased a yellow 10 speed bike. By then I obtained a part time job selling shoes, and on the evenings that I was not required to work, I would hop on my bike and ride by my mother house. She was about 15 miles away from me. Taking short cuts would allow me to reach her in about 15 to 20 minutes; if I took the train from my place to hers it would take over 30 minutes. I enjoyed riding my bike as fast as I could. Why, you might ask would I want to visit my mother. Well, there were two reasons. If it's one thing she did was always provide me dinner or something to eat. But in reality I was not there to see her. Sure I could always use a meal. The real reason for the trip was to see my friend, the girl. I was around her often. She and her sister were not aware until a year later that we no longer lived with mom. Although I was somewhat reserved, I was confident and popular with the girls. For sexual gratification, I had more than my fair share, but for companionship, there was only one.

13 THE PLAN

Dwain, pack it up. The order came from the central unit. It gets re-laid to the deputy, where the inmate is housed. Pack it up means, you are going home, or at the very least, you are leaving the unit. Possibilities include you were written up for misconduct in which case you are taken to the main jail for 22 hours of confinement, or if you have been sentenced to prison. Dwain new it was coming, but did not reveal it to anyone. He had been in contact with the state and has managed to work something out. When the announcement was made, Anthony, Dwain and I were in our room. Dwain and I looked at each other and he smiled. He seemed to play it off well. Anthony was surprised and got up from the bunk, flipping over some of the cards he was playing with. With that he said,

- Ø Man, are you going home?

- Ø Yes! My wife posted my bail.

- Ø I though you did not have one.

A smirk came on Dwain's face.

- Ø "Oh, okay!" said Anthony.

Anthony knew what was going on, for he knew that Dwain had a VOP with a no bond hold. He also knew Dwain had not had a court date as of late. They only knew of each other for about two months. It did not matter to Dwain, as chances were, they would never cross path. Beside he owed no explanation to anyone.

Anthony looked at me and I shrugged my shoulders as if to say "Oh, well!" Dwain proceeded to pack his items. Several minutes later the deputy walked in the room and handed him two brown paper bags. The sheets and towers with lumped together inside of the blanket. When you are told pack it up-you are gone within ten minutes. Today was no different. There is no time to waste. As Dwain finished Anthony stood up again and gave him a hug and a good bye. "Take care of yourself." Dwain replied; "you do the same." With that he turned to me. I gave him a hug. As I let go I shook his hand and said in a low voice, Thank you! He nodded; we both knew what I was thanking him for.

No sooner, a deputy entered the unit, for him. A few inmates came over to Dwain to say their farewells. Everyone else was just as surprised. With that he placed his arms in front of him while holding the two paper bags and was handcuffed. Like most inmates do upon their departure he walked forward without looking back. From the entrance of the room I watched him exit the unit. As I turned to walk the few feet to my bunk Anthony said;

Ø Of all people I would never had expected Dwain to talk.

I played as if I didn't know what was going on. He continued,

Ø There's only one way to get released in situations like that, and that's to be a snitch. That's why I don't discuss my case with anyone, because one never knows who the snitch is.

Ø Are you sure that's what he did?

Ø Of course I'm sure. If it's one thing I would never do is to be a snitch, to rat out my friends.

Ø Would you do it if you could gain your freedom without ranting out your true friends; if it consisted of acquaintances or people that you have bought or sold to?

Ø No, although my best friends did.

Ø Well, how did you feel about that?

Ø That's a little different; I grew up with him and have known him for 26 years.

Ø So it's ok, for your friends to be a snitch but no one else?

Ø That's not what I'm saying.

Ø Sure it is. You're just not admitting it.

Ø My friends would not turn in his close friends and I know that for a fact.

Ø I get it! One can be a snitch, but not towards their friends? Anthony, if you could buy your freedom, would you?

Ø Buy it, how?

Ø Well, let's take my case. Let's say you are caught red handed. You know you have a case you can't beat. You're facing a minimum of 15 years mandatory with the possibility of 30 years, if you take it to trial and loose. Your second option is 5 – 7 years prison if you settle. In this case you have a 14 year old daughter who needs you, but you know you won't be around for her. And your third option is you might not get anytime or maybe just a year or just house arrest. And all you have to do for this option is turn over people who are not your friends. Maybe people you don't know. Your acquaintances gave you their info because you gave them money for that info. Let's say that instead of having a $20,000 lawyer, you can accomplish this with a public defender and dish out $5,000 for the info you need to set you free, saving you $15,000 along the way. Would you snitch?

Ø Man, I never looked at it that way. But being a businessman I can see this as a business transaction. I would not do it myself Ozzie, but having a friend that had done so I can understand.

Ø Well, it's something to think about.

I knew Anthony was facing life, and so he had no-bond hold. He's been already in two years waiting for a trial and was not expecting to leave any time soon. He needed to protect himself. He needed to say no. I could read through all of this. I knew he would talk in a heartbeat, if it could set him free. The substantial assistance program was not available to everyone. And so it seemed he did not have that option, nor decision to make.

Ø "On your bunks for head count."

It's already 11:00 pm. It's time for shift change. Deputy Hosan was on this evening. I reached for a deck of cards I acquired through a trade. After watching Anthony play solitaire I figured it was a great way to pass time. But more importantly it kept my daemon at bay. I was fortunate to have Ismael put money into my account, so that I could purchase commissary. Playing cards are listed at $3.25. I traded two items for a deck. A honey bun which contains 500 calories, mostly sugar, at a cost of $1.69 plus a cup of noodle at $1.19. Total cost $2.88, at least by my math. Let's not forget, I am in Florida.

By the time Anthony awoke me it was 10:15 am, otherwise known as lunch time. Sebastian Monslave was already occupying Dwain's bed. He must have arrived with the 9:00 am influx. They are shipped out from the Broward's main jail early in the morning, and sent to one of the three Pompano jails. This day I managed to sleep till lunch time.

Sebastian was a 21 year old, Columbian young man. He spoke English and Spanish equally well. I stood up and walked past him without saying a word. As I reached the bathroom, I thought about this young Spanish man. In the brief seconds it took me to walk past him, I sized him up. The vibe was not good. His right forearm, right knee and leg were bandaged heavily. He had signs of scrapes and scratches as well. I surmised he must have fallen off his motorcycle and landed on his right side. I was not concerned about that. My concern went deeper; I was concern for myself instead. Something was instantly triggered. I asked myself, who is this kid? Where did he come from? Does he belong to a gang? Was he sent by the Cuban cousins? While I washed my face I prepared myself mentally for what was to come. Any little sudden movement from him was going to prompt punches from me, with intent to knock him out. Because I managed to keep myself active all my life, I still had the reflex of a youngster. Mentally I played out different scenarios. Could he possibly have a shank? Although highly unlikely, I was not going to rule it out. If he does, and we are in the room, how would I escape? A kick to his chest or face was one answer. I prepared myself for possible strikes from him; One from overhead, one from his side, a jab, a round-a-bout. For each one there is a slightly different defense as well as offence. Worst yet I thought, what would happen if he came at night, while I slept. He could strike me and or shank me several times before I could react. By then, damage would have been done, with him being the victor. I was not about to let this happen. There was no way I was going to sleep.

For a few seconds I lost track of time. I looked at the man in the mirror and I thought about who he was. My name is Ozzie, Abigail's dad. For her sake I was not ready to die. Of all the rooms in the unit, mine was the closest to the bathroom, the distance being eight feet. I slowly walked my way back so that I could further read and study him. He watched me walk into our room. I looked him in the eye. I could tell he was up to no good.

Something was in the air and I could not put my hands on it yet. I lifted my head slightly upwards and back down. It's really a nod, a gesture; it says, "Hi, what's up?" He understood and reciprocated. I walked by him as he steps to the side to make room for my passage. Although I knew a welcome was due, no words were spoken. To me this was normal; it's part of who I am; a reserved individual. People sometimes tend to find me arrogant because of this, for I can easily ignore anyone. But I think I just grew up this way. Was this a lack of etiquette? A lack of education? Or could it be I simple did not care? Was it a defense mechanism? As I grew up, I preferred to warm up to people. Then I would decide if I would allow them into my world. With Sebastian, I needed to feel him out, and I knew I would have to get some answers before my bedtime, 4:00 am, else I would not sleep.

The signal for lunch came. I placed my towel on my bed and walked out the room.

At the lunch table I said my usual "Good morning gentleman", both Steve and Joe replied good morning. Not being a morning person, I did not talk much.

- Ø I see you have a new roommate already. (Said Steve)
- Ø Yes, some young kid. It looks like he fell of his bike.

Normally after lunch I would go back to sleep till about one. Lock-down is brief and gets lifted at about 11:20 am; it's enough time to clean the dining area. The laud TV volume is the signal for all to move about freely. Today, there would be no shut eyes for me. I needed answers and I needed them quickly.

As I walked in my cell room I discovered Sebastian had not arrived. I placed my foot on the green cylindrical stool, (the one with the labeled not a step) and climbed onto my bunk. There I stretched out and turned slightly over as I reached for some items from the head of the mat. First, was my playing cards, followed by my weapon, a five inch #2 yellow pencils. This one was not to be used for writing. Its point was kept extremely sharp; its purpose to jab someone in the eye or the cheek. It's something I witnessed in the streets of N.Y.

I sat up with my legs crossed and placed both items between them. Moments later Sebastian followed Anthony into the room. Anthony started conversation.

- Ø Hi, rolled your bike over?
- Ø Yeah, I was fleeing from the cops in Hollywood. The patrol car bumped me from behind as I went to turn. I fucked up my right side.

He lifted his arm. A bandage covered his elbow to his hand. He then pointed to his leg. I looked him over as best as I could, screening his tattoos, checking for any gang affiliation.

- Ø Is that where you're from, Hollywood? (asked Anthony)
- Ø Yes!
- Ø Are you Puerto Rican?
- Ø No, I was born in Colombia. I was about seven when I came to Florida.
- Ø Ah, so maybe you can teach me Spanish. Ozzie has thought me some.
- Ø Hola, Como estas?

- Ø Muy bien. Me llamo Sebastian.
- Ø Y yo me llamo Anthony y el se llama Ozzie.
- Ø Hi, I said. So, you have been in Hollywood for a long time?
- Ø Yeah, I know a lot of people there.

I was not going to ask him about the Cubans. I had other ways of getting the info I wanted.

- Ø Any relatives here? My mom and step dad, a brother and cousin.
- Ø What's that you have tattooed on your finger?

He raised both hands out away from his body and made a fist in each. The back of his hand facing up and his finger nails facing the ground. Both fists were side by side. His thumbs were not showing. "Thug life" was written.

- Ø Oh, thug life. I thought the writing represented your gang.
- Ø Nah, I don't belong to a gang. That's the first thing the police asked me when I was fingered printed. I mostly hang out with a few friends and my brother.

If he was in a gang, he wasn't going to let me know. Letting my guard down was the worst thing I could do. At dinner I sat with Steve to play a game of chess. I was waiting for the right moment to check out his things. So I kept eye on him all afternoon. As soon as he entered the shower, I excused myself from Steve and went to my cell. I waited a minute or two to make sure Sebastian was bathing. As quickly as I could, I lifted his mattress and checked it carefully as well as his clothing and locker. Anthony asked me,

- Ø What are you doing?
- Ø I'm checking to make sure this guy is not hiding anything.
- Ø Man, you are wrong. I hope you don't go through my shit when I'm not around.
- Ø Anthony, I never looked through your things. This is different. I'll explain later. I'm being cautious.

Steve who was on his way to the bathroom was standing by the entrance looking in. He knew I was up to something, but did not know what. He proceeded to the bathroom and I made my way back to the game table.

- Ø Ozzie, are you okay? You seem to be a little on edge today.
- Ø Is it that obvious?
- Ø Well, you have not been your usual self today.
- Ø Steve. I don't know if I should be telling you anything. It's a delicate situation, and being in jail one can never be sure, if one is speaking to friend or foe.
- Ø I understand. We have similar charges and similar circumstances. One reason I had so much business is because I never fucked anyone. I managed to stay under the radar for a long time. If there is anything I can do for you just ask.
- Ø Steve, no one else here knows what I am about to say. So if word gets out, I'll know it was you.

I explained to Steve the reasons why I was moved. I also told him about what Dominguez told me in the holding cell. All the while we acted as if we were playing as we moved some pieces.

- Ø Ozzie, this is a minimum security cell. Look around, most of the people here are lame.
- Ø Yeah, tell that to Mr. Stevenson, who killed his wife, or to Radio who has numerous burglaries.
- Ø Yeah, but no one here has a recent violent history.
- Ø That means nothing to me Steve.
- Ø So you think your new Bunkie is a hit-man?
- Ø Steve to me everyone is possibly a hit-man. Remember this is Broward, where one is guilty until proven innocent.
- Ø I wouldn't worry about it in here. If it were prison, then you should be concerned.
- Ø What's the difference?

- Ø In prison you have people doing long term sentencing or life. They have to fight to show they are not weak. That's where you find most of the gang members.

- Ø If it helps I'll start a conversation with him and get a feel.

- Ø No need to go out of your way but thanks for the offer.

I watched Sebastian exit the shower and go to the room. After speaking with Steve, I felt a little relaxed, but I wasn't about to let my guard down. That night there were no demons. I was now cautious and preoccupied with the thought of staying alive. I knew there was nothing I could do but be prepared. Either I would take a chance and get some sleep or I would have to stay up all night and through the next day. If there was someone that might know anything about this young man, it would be Jerry. For sure I was going to have to call him ASAP the next day.

- Ø Hi, Jerry, it's Ozzie.

- Ø Hey what's up?

- Ø Jerry I'm so sorry to bother you, but I have a concern. You mentioned there was a threat against my life and so I was moved. There is a young man in my room today. I saw a look in his eye that I did not like, because of that I've not slept much.

- Ø What's his name? Sebastian Monsalvo.

- Ø Call me later today. I'll look him up. By the way Ozzie, have obtained any information I can use.

- Ø Jerry there is something I came across, it's quite a coincidence. Man, I don't know if I should even say.

- Ø Look Ozzie I know you are a nice guy, I know what you did was your first time. The smartest thing you can do is help yourself by helping me. I am friends with your prosecutor. I can't make you any promises, but my recommendation goes a long way. Off all people I would hate to see do time, it would be you. Especially when you could of helped yourself to a short time.

- Ø Jerry, I have been considering the program, can you tell me more.

- Ø Ozzie, I'm a little busy now, but later today when you call me I'll tell you more. So what about the info you have?

- Ø You asked me to keep an eye and ear out for Balbi, the pill mill guy. It turns out that my roommate that just left has a wife with two unfilled prescriptions from his office.

- Ø Ok, that's good. What is the guy's name?

- Ø Jerry, I'll get that info in a little bit as I am not sure of the last name. I did write it down, but there are people by the phone next to me and I have to be careful.

- Ø What is his first name?

- Ø The name is Dwain. Ok, thanks!

After speaking with Jerry I headed back to my room. There was plenty of noise in the unit as the TV was on. For some reason it seemed lauder than normal. Perhaps I was irritated due to lacked of sleep. The entire night seemed like a week. Although I had managed to close my eyes a little, I was still vigilant. Any noise in the room would force my eyes to open. By now, I was sleepy. I know I had to get at least an hour in. Reluctantly I jumped on my bunk, covered myself under the sheets and closed my eyes. By the time I woke up it was dinner time. Anthony had knocked against the metal bunk bed to wake me. "Dinner time!" Wow, I was out. I let my guard down. I could have easily been hurt as I slept. Sebastian had already taken a seat in the dining area. I took my usual seat with Steve and Joe. Dinner was nothing special. It's always crappy food with way little flavor, and small portions. The first thing you feel after dinner is hungry. That night Mrs. Humpfree was on; the guard that doesn't allow food back to the cell, as if there was excess food to begin with. At about 6pm she let us move about.

The first thing I did was call Jerry.

- Ø Hi, Jerry, it's Ozzie again.

- Ø Hey, Ozzie that guys Sebastian was arrested for grand theft auto. As far as we know he does not belong to a gang. I'm certain he is not there on a mission to hurt you. I think you are worrying too much.

- Ø That easy to say when you're outside. I'm in here with nowhere to hide.

- Ø Again you are over thinking it, but if you want to come out just say so, I can get you out.

- Ø The judge and prosecutor hate me. They won't let me out even though I have had my bond posted for over six weeks.

- Ø I'm a man of my word. If I say I can get you out, I can get you out. I can get anyone out. All you have to do is say so. The substantial assistance program is designed to make bail possible. Bond could be as low or as high as $20,000.

- Ø Jerry, I have a bond. The problem is collateral.

- Ø Look again, think about it. If you want out, I will get you out. By the way as far as Dwain Jenkins, my partner is working with him.

- Ø How did you get the last name?

- Ø It's my job. That was very easy. Keep your ears open, call me if you have anything.

- Ø Jerry, thank you. Maybe I'll be able to sleep tonight.

Ok, Finally I can relax, at least a little. Steve was sitting down in the TV area.

- Ø Hey are you ready for a beat down.

- Ø Sure let's go.

After dinner Mrs. Humpfree sets aside four tables for games. The two table with the painted chess set is included. The rest are moved against the wall to make space for recreation. Anthony started playing cards with Sebastian, Vinnie and someone else. Vinnie was Italian. I called him Barbarino, after the sitcom. Vinnie was the only person who had a doctor's pass to carry a weapon. That weapon was a wooden, sturdy cane. I joked once or twice about grabbing it if ever I needed to defend myself. That is provided it was within reach.

- Ø Man you look better. You were looking as pale as a ghost.

- Ø No, Steve, I do not look like my lawyer.

- Ø Oh, you got jokes. So you got some good news.

- Ø Yeah, kind off, for starters Sebastian was arrested for grand theft; I think I was worrying too much.

- Ø I told you so.

- Ø I hope it's just worries and nothing more.

- Ø What's the second?

- Ø Well I have an idea, but I really can't talk about it. All I can say is that it might allow me to get out. Before I do, I need to be sure of a few things.

- Ø White or black?

- Ø You know the drill by now. One of each in your hand and I'll pitch white, I'm first.

- Ø Well, I happen to like black better.

- Ø Yes, I know Steve.

As I started playing I could feel myself relaxing. Being on high alert consumed a lot of energy. For the moment I did not pay too much attention to the conversation with Jerry. It's at night that I clear my mind and think things through. That's when I would give my plan from a few days ago, more thought. For now I was going to put a hurting on Steve. I know he is not a match for me, but I was going to have a little fun beating him quickly. No coaching today.

Over the next few days I tried to reach Casper Green. Just as his name implies he was not reachable. Three phone calls per day and numerous messages yielded nothing. There were answers I needed before I could commit to my idea. As for now I had to keep with the plan. By now, Sebastian and I had numerous conversations. He told me about his background and his charges. Because of prior charges, he was afraid he would get about seven years. Having a step son his age, I tried to console him.

- Ø Ozzie, my girlfriend is pregnant. I'm going to be a dad. I don't want to spend seven years in jail.

- Ø Look, the first few days are nerve racking, as we are not sure of what is to come. In a few days it will come together.

- Ø No, there is no way out.

- Ø Sure, there always is.

- Ø Besides I don't have money for a paid lawyer. I'll need to use a public defender. Now my girlfriend is pregnant and out of work, there won't be any money for commissary. I'm starving. Shit, I already lost a few pounds.

- Ø Hey Sebastian, how worried are you about the public defender?

- Ø I need a paid lawyer.

- Ø I have an idea. I'll help you if you help me. I've got to be very careful of what I tell you. My charges are very serious, 15 – 30 years. I could get off real lite if I want to. That's the part I need help with. In turn I can get you the money for a lawyer and commissary.

Sebastian's eye opened as wide as they could. He stood up from his bunk.

- Ø What cha mean? What do I have to do?

(His body was just a foot away.)

- Ø Look this is new to me. I have to be careful. Don't get the wrong idea, I want to get out, and you want to get out. A good lawyer will get you out and also do it quickly. The police that arrested me wants' me to help him with something. If I do, I can get a very short sentence. Problem is I don't have enough info so far to so.

- Ø Man, I'm not a snitch, if that's what you're asking.

- Ø No, listen to me. I'm not either. I could have been out of here if I were. Actually they might have let me walk at the time. I chose not to. I would never do that to anyone I know, but a few nights ago I got an idea. I decided to look at this as a business transaction. You have been on the streets for years and as you mentioned yesterday, you do all kinds of drugs. Surely, you must know a few people in the business. I don't want you to tell me of anyone you know well or care for. Just three or four people that you know will end up getting caught sooner or later. What difference will it make, if one is the game, eventually he will get caught? No one will even know the info came from you. I'll be the one getting credit. If in court then is discovery, it will be my name that appears. Nowadays, most people are talking. I rather pay your lawyer a few thousand dollars, than to hire one for myself and pay $20,000. It's a win-win situation for the both of us.

- Ø So, if I do this when and how do you pay me.

- Ø As good faith I will order some commissary for you. You give me one lead and if an arrest is made, I will pay you whatever amount we agreed upon. From there we move on to the next. I will buy as many as you can give me. With a few of them, you will have enough money for your lawyer. You can bond out, go to work and prepare a good life for your baby.

- Ø Ok, let me think about this.

- Ø Yes, I think it's a good idea. To think about it. If you do agree than I need for you to be sure and that will go through with it. My decision is tied in with yours. If I say yes and you don't come through I'm going to look for you with a Colombian machete.

With that we both smiled. My last statement was taken as a joke, but in a way convinced the seriousness of the agreement.

- Ø Ok, man, I'll let you know tomorrow.

- Ø Sebastian you can't discuss that with anyone.

- Ø Don't worry, I got you and I need to get out!

- Ø Ok.

That evening was a good evening. It was Saturday. Saturday was Ozzie and Jackie dancing night. Several days ago I purchased a radio and headphones from some guy in the unit for $1.00 or I should say one item. There is no actual dollar exchange in jail. Things are purchased and paid for in two ways. The first is to have someone outside of jail exchange money. The second way is through the exchange of food or commissary items. The radio I purchased has an initial cost $23.00 and the headphones $4.00. As people leave jail to go home they pass their items on to other inmates. The radio I purchase was given to someone who already had one. I managed to get it for a cup of noodles. Prior to my arrest, Jackie and I would frequent a club in Coral Gables, Miami on Saturday nights. Latin and Disco music was the norm. The station aired live on 93.9 FM. Although she was not physically present the music would take me back to those happy times. At 1:00 am the live broadcast ends. Sleep would soon follow. This allowed me to get in two hours before breakfast.

Ø Morning gentleman!

Ø Morning.

It was now Sunday (lunch time). Lunch is the same every day except for Monday and Thursday. Then its peanut butter and jelly time. Today was four slices of bread, two slices of bologna, one slice of cheese (that you cannot get to melt in the microwave, but we are told is cheese), one small mayonnaise pack and two mustard packs. The only thing that changes depending on the season is an apple or an orange.

Ø What time is the Dolphin game?

Ø Not sure, (said Steve).

Ø No matter it's not like we have anywhere to go. Sunday mornings I usually woke up with some chick next to me. After my morning fuck, I would get breakfast and com back home for the 1:00 o'clock game.

Ø Tell me about it. I loved my Sunday mornings also. Sometimes I would get up make a cup of coffee, do Jackie and then take off for breakfast. We would take a 20 minute ride to the Green Street Café in Coconut Grove. She loved that morning ride, especially with the top to the Benz down. Sometimes with Koby in the back seat.

Ø What for was she going to clean up after you ate?

Ø Steve, that's her dog a midsize mutt that would get a groomed like a lion. Not the vacuum.

Ø Yeah, I thought that was a dog.

Joe had managed to get up first. As Steve and I followed him to the garbage can I whispered.

Ø Steve I need to talk to you later.

Ø Do you want to meet in the recreation yard?

Ø Yes, about 1:00 pm. That gives me some time to sleep some more.

Ø Ok.

1 pm.

- Ø Steve what's up?
- Ø Hey Ozzie, what's up? I had a good workout.
- Ø Let's walk around.

The rec yard was always noisy. The basketball banging against the rim would cause the metal post that hung from the roof to vibrate loudly within the enclosed area. Players yelling also contributed greatly to the loud noise. The yard was so loud that in walking around the perimeter, one could barely hear the person next to him. Talking there was good if you did not want others to know your business, however one often needed to repeat things.

- Ø Steve what do you know about the substantial assistance program.
- Ø It's a way to get out of jail by turning in dealers you know.
- Ø Yeah, the part I know. What I am really asking you is what do you think about it?
- Ø There's a lot to think about. I knew of this chick that got caught with two kilos. She ratted out a lot of people she knew. Her sentence was probation. The problem is everywhere she turns she needed to look over her shoulders. I don't think that's something I would want to live with. I think I rather bond out and drag out the case. This way I could be home soon.
- Ø Steve like me, you were caught red-handed. Do you think you have any chance in hell of winning your case?
- Ø No, I can't take it to trial. I'll get minimum 30 years because of my priors, and I'm already 50.
- Ø So you will likely die in jail.
- Ø Man I never looked at it that way.
- Ø What do you accomplish by dragging your case for two years? All you are doing is postponing the inevitable.
- Ø So you're saying I should go CI route?
- Ø I was really asking you for me and not so much for you.

- Ø Ozzie be careful what you say around here.

- Ø Yes, I know. For some reason I feel comfortable talking to you. It seems there are a lot of people doing that these days. Steve I never snitched on anyone. For that matter I don't even know of anyone I could turn in. Many people I know are well to do. The police are not interested in those. They want trafficking convictions. I am only asking you because I don't know who else to talk to. If it wasn't for my daughter Abby I would not consider it.

- Ø I understand Ozz; I too have a two year old granddaughter. It hurts to think I might not see her again.

- Ø Ok, Steve thanks. I'm going in now.

Yes, "I got him", I said to myself as I walked to my cell. The smile on my face made Anthony take notice. I shook my head from side to side, as if to say, don't ask. He picked up on it. My smile was in part due to my success. I had a plan. That talk with Steve was calculated. I did to Steve the same I would to customers when selling a car. It's called planting the seed. You might ask your customer questions that will make them talk or think about an issue that you want them to think about. So that the customers ask the questions you want them to ask, as if it were their idea. You plant the seed; you get them thinking in a certain directions. Once you plant the seed you leave it alone. You let it simmer for a moment. Sooner or later the customer will open the door with a question and will invite you in. However it is I that pulls them in. Gently they are wheeled in. Don't pull to hard or they will feel it. You just guide them towards you. They will follow without realizing, that they are on your line. Steve has something I want. He has something I need. All I needed to do now is sit and want. This plan I saw several days ago. It's my chess move.

At 6:00 pm Mrs. Humpfree distributed the mail and the floor was open. One thing we liked about her was that she was quick to lift lock-down. I made my way to the game table and started to set up. Steve was still up in his room talking with Joe. Prince who had just finished reading his mail walked over to me.

- Ø Ozz look at my Hayabusa bike.

- Ø Nice, is that the one that was confiscated?

- Ø Yeah,

- Ø So how did you get it back?

- Ø I had my younger brother take delivery of it claiming he had a note against it. He took that note to the sheriff's office, paid the tow and the storage fee and picked it up.

- Ø Good thinking. What's the top speed?

Prince liked to tell stories about himself and now had an audience as he sat across from me.

- Ø It's legally rated for 170 mph. I modified it. One time I was running from the police and for a minute or two took it just past the 200 mph mark.

- Ø Damn, at that speed I would shit in my pants. How in the world can you hold on with all that wind pressure?

- Ø I had my helmet on and gear. You scout down into the bike as low as you can, cutting the resistance. At that speed you hope nothing is or gets in your way else you're dead.

I found his story a little suspicious, but I didn't show any signs of doubt.

- Ø Ok, let's play?

- Ø Nah,

- Ø I see you are avoiding me. You spoke of playing well in college. It's like getting on a bike, once you learn you won't forget.

- Ø Nah, it's not that, I need to call my lawyer. Maybe latter on. I'll halla at you.

- Ø Ok Prince.

By now Steve found his way to the table.

- Ø Hey Steve, take a look at my bike.

- Ø Wow, that's a Hayabusa.

- Ø You know bikes?

- Ø Sure, I had a Harley for many years.

- Ø Steve, Prince won't play me. I think his is afraid.

- Ø Of course, you are the chess king here. He is only a Prince.

- Ø Oh, that's low (said Prince as he pointed at us.) I'm coming for you later.

We all smiled and Steve sat down to play.

- Ø Ozzie, I've been thinking all day about what you said.
- Ø Tell me,

(I was surprised Steven would bring it up so soon; At least a few days I thought would pass.) I start with the black girl today. I am the king, while the Prince over they're plays with his bike.

- Ø I'll play with the black Queen.
- Ø So, Steve, what have you thought?

Ø Well, something you said really struck me. You said the only thing I was doing was postponing the inevitable. The sentence will be long. All I'm doing is pushing it of a little longer, but it doesn't change anything. I'll die in jail.

- Ø So, what is your solution?
- Ø The program you spoke of now looks good. It's scary Ozzie; in all my life I minded my business. I never told on anyone.
- Ø Steve, there is a time and place for everything. If you don't do it, someone else will. It's only a matter of time. So you might as well benefit.
- Ø Ozzie, do you know how many people I know? I think I have about 70 – 80 people I could turn in.

Bam, I knew it. Some time ago in the rec. yard Steve told me he knew a great number of people. That's what I was after. I hooked him. All I needed to do is bring him in slowly. So far, so good.

- Ø I need to talk to Casper.
- Ø Good luck with that Steve!
- Ø I'll have my girlfriend call him. She can reach him easier than I can.

I was cautious as to what I said to Steve. It was too soon to let him know that he had something I needed. I could not reveal my motive. He continued

- Ø There is only one problem. I can't get enough collateral to bond out.
- Ø What would you say if I told you I might be able to help you out with that?
- Ø You have a home for me?
- Ø No, Steve. There's a different angle. I know someone that can make this work. You just have to be sure that you will go through with it.
- Ø Ok, I'm not 100%.

Ha! The fish is swimming; I am not going to pull in anymore. I'll let him circle around and swim to me.

- Ø Your move Steve.

We made small talk as we played. All Steve could do was think about all the people that he knew. How easy it would be to get them. I listened carefully. He went on and on, as if he were a child in a candy store. Today his chess game was way off. He could not focus on it. That did not matter to me. My plan was taking shape. That's all I cared about.

Fifteen minutes to lockdown! Fifteen minutes to lockdown! Mrs. Humpfree always repeated herself. The time was now 9:45 pm. I made my way to my room and Sebastian was there. Anthony stayed behind played cards to the last minute.

- Ø Sebastian!
- Ø Hi Ozzie, what's up?
- Ø Have you decided on anything?
- Ø Yeah, I did. I told you I got you.
- Ø Oh, I thought we decided you would take a day to think about it.
- Ø Well, I did. I'm in. Question is how we are going to work this.
- Ø I should be out soon. I'll get with your brother and take it from there.
- Ø What about commissary money.
- Ø Will I need a name and number and description as good faith? I'll have it checked and then give you your commissary. Here is a soup for tonight. I know you are starving.

- Ø Thanks let me get hot water or else I won't be able to eat it tonight.

- Ø Ok, but don't talk in front of Anthony.

- Ø Got it!

Sebastian handed me a paper with two names. They were not government names but aliases. The real names I would have to get from his brother, as well as their phone numbers. That paper I placed in a yellow legal size envelope within my locker. With that I took out my cards and settled in. I was on to something, but still had a way to go. Would I get there?

Two days past before Steve and I spoke again about the program. He made a list of people he knew; people that either bought or sold drugs. The total was 63. He prioritized them by the bigger player to the smaller; also by those to which he had phone number to. He had instructed his daughter-in-law to obtain the numbers from his old cell phone. Included on his list, after the phone numbers was the words; buys, sells or guns.

- Ø Ozzie, come to the rec yard.

- Ø Ok, (I stood up from the TV area and followed Prince.)

- Ø What's up?

- Ø Yo-yo man, I am fucked. I just got 18 new added charges.

- Ø Eighteen, how the fuck? What the hell did you do?

- Ø I called my brother and asked him to contact several of the people to which I had their personal information and identity. Those names were on a list I carried when I was arrested. I told my brother to contact them, and inform them that although I had their info, they were in no danger. One of those people contacted the police. The police in turn retrieved a copy of the phone call to my brother. So I just picked up 18 new 3rd degree felonies, one for each person I had my brother call. There is no way I am going to be out soon. Each charge is punishable up to five years. Also I won't be able to get a bond on my VOP.

- Ø Damn nigger, what the fuck?

- Ø Yo – how stupid was that? Fuck man, fuck.

- Ø When did you find out?

- Ø I just got off the phone with my lawyer. He was looking at my case and saw new charges. I have magistrate court in two days. Ozzie, I'm about to lose a shit load of money.

- Ø Well, I know how that goes. This whole mess has cost me seventeen thousand.

- Ø Ozzie, I'm talking millions.

- Ø Millions, (he paused for a second), well a lot of money. Something I can't talk about. But I have book signing soon. My mortgage is due in a few days and my lawyers' fees will total about $30,000, but that's peanuts. Man I was working on something, but that's going to go down the drain. It can't be done without me.

What a dummy, I thought, for speaking like that on the phones. He was fully aware that all the calls are recorded. There was something Prince was not saying, but then, in jail people tend to hold back info. What could it be? Was he losing millions of dollars? Is that what he was so worried about? Or was it just simply the charges? Prince had been a con man. Con men are able to get you to think just about anything. I listened to him, but for the most part had no interest in him. He was not part of my plan and so his problem meant nothing. He was only minutes, a tick of the clock, and passage of time. Like everyone here he was insignificant. Because of this I would not even bother to ask people their names. Maybe I was cold hearted with a heart of stone as my brother often said. Truth is I never cared much for anyone.

- Ø Well Prince, I don't know what to say.

- Ø Ozzie, believe me when I say, I fucked up at the wrong time. This was my shot.

- Ø Prince, this too shall pass.

- Ø Fuck man, Fuck!

- Ø Prince how serious can it be?

He looked at me square in the eye. We were in a corner of the rec yard. There I was pinned between the wall and his big body.

- Ø Ozzie, I'm losing millions.
- Ø Millions!
- Ø Yes, Millions!
- Ø How the fuck?
- Ø Can't talk about it.
- Ø Wow, that's a lot. Where do you have that? Are they freezing your money?
- Ø No, I don't have it yet. Look I can't talk anymore. I'm so fucken pissed off.
- Ø Wow, this is some fucked up shit.

I knew Prince was a story teller. Not for a second did I believe him. We walked back in together. He walked back slowly with a look of despair. I made my way back to my favorite place, the game table. Steve was there in a match. Sitting to the side, I got a different perspective of his game.

- Ø What was that about?
- Ø Tell you later. Ok!

As I watched Steve play, I thought about what I just heard. There was a sense of despair in Prince's voice. I read people well and although I knew he liked to tell stories, there was something to be said about his body language. I could not figure it out, but he left me thinking. Shit, did he just plant a seed on me? Now, I myself am curious? Did he just hook me? Was he really losing millions or was he just concerned about the new charges? Yeah, that mother fucker. He hooked me? Although I know he was a con man, I was going to bite and play. Let's see if he was smarter than me?

14 FELLOW INMATES

Once again a few more days went by. That's the common theme. Everyone seems to be waiting for a few more days. A few more days, turns into a few more weeks, and a few more weeks, into months. Harold Escalante, a tall, copper-toned gentleman was admitted to my unit. He was accompanied by two other inmates. His short white hair revealed his age. His face told a story. It said, "I was in a fight and I lost." Not only did he lose, but was sent to the hospital. Harold's left eye was blood shot as well as deeply black and blue. His left cheek was swollen. Stitches on the upper left side of his lip were visible. He walked slowly with the help of a cane. I watched him walk into the unit. His face caught my attention. But just the same, he also was insignificant. I took my eyes away from him without a concern in the world about him or anyone else. I wouldn't talk to new people until a few days have passed. I'm sure he had a story to tell, but that was his and not mine. I was on a mission. Either you can help me, or get the fuck out of my way. First thing Harold did was sit on the lounge chair within the TV area. New arrivals are told to do so until a bunk gets assigned to them. Two or three of the Hispanics took up conversation with Harold. They tend to quickly greet all Hispanics.

- Ø Hey Ozzie they are pointing at you, said Steve.
- Ø I put the newspaper down to turn around on my seat. They waived at me and I waived back. Immediately I knew he was Puerto Rican and probably from the Bronx. Steve also picked up on it.
- Ø I guess his Puerto Rican. Maybe he's your father.
- Ø Fuck you, Steve.

Steve spoke to me some more. Every time we met he spoke about how many people he could turn in.

- Ø I'm waiting to talk to Green, I need to get out of here and get laid. With the number of people I have, I hope for a very short sentence.

By now I had explained I could help get him out. However, I had not yet mentioned I needed his help. That was to come the following day. I let the thought of getting, simmer. All he wanted to do was get some action from his female friends. He even talked about several booty-calls that knew of sellers. Surely they would be able to help him out. Although I did not say much, I was watching my plan working. Time was now 1:45 pm and thus lock down time; Time to retrieve to our rooms for head count, which would then be followed by shift change. As I made my way to my room, I passed by Prince and said,

Ø Hey Prince, I need to talk.

Ø Ok, holler at me later,

Ø Will do!

At dinner time, Harold sat to the table behind me, with our back almost touching.

Ø ¿Boriqua?, (Harold asked.)

Ø Si, y tu?,

Ø De pura sepa, pero me crie en el Bronx.

Boriquen was the Taíno name for the island of Puerto Rico. Boricuas were the natives who lived there. Boricua means "Brave and noble lord". Borinquen means "Land of the brave and noble lords". Pura sepa, meaning from a pure vine, or in this case 100% P.R.

Ø Me llamo Ozzie.

Ø Harold!

Ø Bueno hablamos despues.

Ø Bien!

Ø What's that about? Asked Steve.

Ø Oh, he is 100% pure P.R. raised in the Bronx.

Ø That's what I thought,

For the most part Joe would not talk. He was Portuguese. His Brazilian jail mates would often bring him food. Balbi and Calderon often gave Joe their apples or extra bread.

Ø Hey Prince, rec. yard.

Ø Fuck yeah! What's up?

- Ø Look Prince, I don't know you well enough to come at you like this, but I am willing to go on a limb here. I have a hunch. At any point if I overstep my boundaries just let me know. I'm not trying to get up in your business, but I need to know something and with your permission I think I can help you out.

With that I was going to turn the table and plant a seed on him. But was I really? Was he to be on my line or was it his hook that was reeling me in? Either way I would humor myself with the conversation. Prince was all ears. His eyes were wide opened and focused on me. He had two favorite lines, one, "Eat a dick" and two, "Are you fucking kidding me?"

- Ø Help me out. Are you fucking kidding me? I don't see any way out?
- Ø You're saying you could help me out?
- Ø That's what I'm saying Prince.
- Ø So, why are you still here?
- Ø I'm getting out soon.
- Ø Are you fucking kidding me?
- Ø Nope.
- Ø Are you fucking kidding me?
- Ø No I said. I'm not kidding you.

His eyes opened wide and his round pudgy face looked comical.

- Ø You're fucking getting out?
- Ø Soon working on it.
- Ø Wow!

I'm not sure if he believed me at this point, but he was listening.

- Ø How are you doing that?
- Ø I can't tell you yet Prince. If I'm going to confide in you, you need to do the same. So how bad do you need to get out?

- Ø Fuck, let's go sit over there. Yo Ozz, I've got to be careful with what I say.
- Ø Look Prince I'm not sure how much I should tell you.
- Ø Yo, Ozzie, I know it's hard. I promise you, anything you tell me will stay within these walls. I also have to be careful. If you can get me out, I could make you a millionaire.
- Ø You fucking kidding me now, right?
- Ø Nope!

I did not buy one word, but I had nowhere to go, and so I entertained myself.

- Ø How so? I asked.
- Ø Look Ozz, I need to get the fuck out. I was working on something in which time is of the essence. I can lose a few million dollars.
- Ø How much?
- Ø A few million. I guess as low as $6,000,000. up to maybe eight or nine mill.
- Ø No fucking way, that's a lot of money!
- Ø Yo, I'm not messing around. I know things but I can't go into details about it, but I promise you, I could use some help, especially you being Hispanics. I can make you rich,
- Ø The flip side is I could die trying, right?
- Ø No you can't.
- Ø I don't know Prince. I don't want to die.
- Ø Ozz, just get me out of, if you can. I'll pay you big dollars.
- Ø How big?
- Ø I'm not sure. For starters I'll get my lawyer to represent you. What will it take? Let's get together and talk tomorrow.
- Ø Ok,

Ø I'm coming at you first thing tomorrow. Ok, but you better not wake me up,

Ø Got it!

Prince knew I was up most of the night and therefore I slept late into the morning. We shook hands as we departed the rec. room. I made my way back to the TV area. The lounge chairs were always comfortable. I rested my leg up on the ottoman. I had not noticed Harold next to me. I was too busy wondering what the hell just transpired. Was I being played? Did he bate me, entice me with money? Was he looking for a way out, so that he could skip town, thus making a fool cut of me? Ah, fuck it! What did I have to loose. Tonight I'll let it come to me.

Ø Hola Boricua, y que. No pienses mucho que te pones Viejo, said Harold.

Ø Harold, I'm sorry. Yes, I was thinking of something and did not notice you. For that matter I do not even remember sitting down. Sorry, I wasn't trying to be rude.

Ø I figured that Ozzie. So you were from the Boogie Down Bronx?

Ø Yes Harold. And you?

Same, but mostly my teenage years, I then moved to Chicago.

Ø Where about in the Bronx? I lived on 3rd Ave., right by the El.

Ø Yeah, I know the area. I took that train many times. Where about 3rd Ave?

Ø 156 St.

Ø Harold, Your' kidding me, that's the corner I lived by.

Ø No way! (Exclaimed Harold).

Ø Sure, there was a candy store right on the corner.

Ø Yeah, it was owned by two fat Puerto Rican brothers.

Ø I was young then and I don't know who owned it, but I ate a lot of candies from there. That's the building I lived in.

Ø I lived right around the corner on the same block. There was a good pizzeria there.

- Ø Yes Harold, that right. They also sold hotdogs. A pizza at the time was 35 cents.

- Ø I remember then when they were 25 cents and sodas were 10 cents. I lived in the building on top of the pizzeria. Do you remember the toy store across the street?

- Ø Of course.

- Ø It was owned by some Jewish people. It was right next to the meat market.

- Ø Yeah, that's right, I remember one day in winter I was by the toy store and I kept passing by the meat market. I would opening the door and then run; letting all the cold air in. About the fourth time I opened the door I got showered with a pot of water. I ran home trying to hide from my mother, but she saw me. After I told her the bad man wet me for no reason, she spanked me. So, what's up with you Howard, looks like you were in a serious fight?

- Ø I got beat up by the Hollywood police department.

- Ø Where you restricting arrest?

- Ø No, I was being watched as I rode my pickup with my wife. I got rear ended by the police. They searched my car and threw something in it. Then turned to me and asked me, "Where did that come from?" I told him, "I pulled it out of your mother's pussy." That's when they started throwing punches at me. As I fell on my hands and knees, one of the cops kicked me in the face. My wife tried to intervene and yelled, "Leave him alone. He just had open heart surgery." So, they arrested her also. They charged her with conspiracy. I spent nine days in the hospital cuffed to a bed. My left eye has a few fractures and I'm having a hard time seeing out of it. Also, I can't stop bleeding from my nose. You should have seen my face the first few days; I could not open my eye.

It was obvious Harold was reliving the moment. His breathing deepened and he seemed rather upset.

- Ø Ok, Howard calm down. Just relax. Where is your wife?

- Ø She is here on the first floor.

- Ø Have you spoken to her?
- Ø No, there is no way to.
- Ø Sure there is. (He was bewildered). Harold, do you want to talk to her?
- Ø Are you serious?
- Ø Sure, I am
- Ø How?
- Ø Hey, Prince!

Prince turned around. He was standing under the TV, looking up at it. I signaled him over.

- Ø Yo, what's up? (asked Prince)
- Ø I need a favor. This is Howard, an old time buddy from the Bronx.
- Ø Hi, Howard. I know the area well. I traveled many times to the Bronx to play with the girls. I spent most of my time in Long Island.

Prince did not make any mention of Howards face.

- Ø Prince, Howard got beat up by Hollywood police.
- Ø Mother fuckers! (Exclaimed Prince).
- Ø His wife is here on the first floor. He needs to talk to her.
- Ø I got it. What's her name?
- Ø Jackie!
- Ø Ozz, that's your girlfriends name right.
- Ø Yea, ex girlfriend.
- Ø I need her last name. When do you want to talk to her?
- Ø As soon as I can, replied Howard.
- Ø Ok, I'll need to send her a kite. Write me a small message for her. I'll send it down tonight with one of the trustees.

- Ø Oh, I thought I would be able to speak to her.

- Ø You will I'll arrange it and let you know when. Just have a message for her in about 20 minutes and bring it to me. I'll call my secretary to let her know your wife will be calling;

- Ø Prince, is there anything you need? I asked.

Prince got on the phone. His big butt hanging over the over the plastic stool. Ozzie what's this going to cost me?

- Ø Nothing Howard.

- Ø Come on, there is always a cost.

- Ø No cost. Don't worry, were here to help each other. Just relax. The important thing is for you to get well.

- Ø Ok, thank you Ozzie.

- Ø You got it!

Howard's words were sincere. I knew when he said Thank you, he meant it. Prince was the go to guy for things like that. He was getting many commissary items for helping people out. It seemed money was not too much of an issue. For him, the attention was more important than the food. He asked me for nothing and I offered him nothing. We were beyond that. Besides he owed me two Honey Buns.

One more day was coming to an end. That night I was full of anticipation. As I settled in I read Jenelle's letter again. It saddened me for a moment. I knew I would soon address the issue. For now I choose not to look at the pictures of my granddaughter. For I have a plan. Something is developing. I needed to focus on bringing the plan together. There is a new player now. I put the letter under the mat and kicked back and thought. How do I proceed? I'll wait until I can see the next move. That's when I'll move; when I see it. That night I managed to get some sleep. The past few nights my demons had eluded me. If only I could find a way to make it go away, I would be a truly happy man.

That next day I seemed to be popular. Everyone in the unit wanted talk to me, even Joe.

- Ø Gentleman, good morning!

- Ø What's up with your compadre? Asked Steve.

- Ø He got beat up by Hollywood police. Spent nine days in the hospital; his wife was charged with conspiracy and is here on the first floor.

- Ø What he charged with?

- Ø Trafficking I would imagine. He seemed distracted yesterday as he told the story so I tried not to ask too many questions.

- Ø Ozz, we got to play a game later. (I knew what Steven meant.) Ok, you want a lesson or a beat down.

- Ø I think I need a lesson.

- Ø Ok, lesson it is.

Steve needed to tell me something, I guessed.

- Ø Well off to bed I go, Steve, I'll talk to you later.

It's was now Friday about 4:00 pm. As soon as lockdown was lifted the first thing I did was grab the chess pieces. That gave us about 45 minutes to get a game in before dinner. Steve whispered as he sat,

- Ø Ozzie, are you sure you can get me out?

- Ø Yeap!

- Ø I made up my mind. I spoke to my son and he said it was a good move. At first I was embarrassed to tell him. I did not want him to think of me as a snitch. He told me he would help me set people up. He had thought about it but was also afraid to mention it.

- Ø You see Steve, that's what family is about. You know he loves you.

- Ø Yeah, I know that. My son knows a shit load of people also. He said he would do whatever it takes to see me free.

- Ø So you in?

- Ø Yes!

- Ø Are you sure?

- Yes, but I do have my doubt about getting out. So what is the plan?
- Look, Steve, I can get out, but I'm not sure I want to get out. I need help with some things.
- What's that?
- I don't have enough people to turn in. What happens if I plead guilty and can't produce? I'll be fucked with a long sentence. So Steve, I can help you, but I need your help along the way.
- Ozzie, if you can help me get a low bond and help with the collateral, so I can get a much reduced sentence. I'll help you in any way I can.
- Steve, before I get this going this is what I need from you.

As Steve and I talked Howard made eye contact with me as walked over.

- Hi, Ozzie can I talk a minute.
- Sure Howard, have a seat. Steve have you met Howard?
- Yes, how are you? Ask Steve.
- Well, I'm hanging in here. Ozzie, I will be talking with my wife at 7:00 pm. I already got a message from her that she is ok.
- That's good Howard. I'm happy for you.
- How did Prince work that out? (Asked Steve).
- I don't know how he got the message to her, but he did. My wife called his secretary today. The secretary told her to call back at 7:00 pm. She will be doing a conference call. Prince will be calling her also at the time and will pass me the phone.
- That was easier than I thought.
- Thank you Ozzie, well talk later.
- Foods on post, foods on post!
- Ok, Steve time for Diner. We'll finish off then. Talk to you!

Back in my room I leaned against the wall as I look out. Which section will they call first for dinner? Sebastian, who was standing near me, had a habit of sitting on a small writing metal table in our room which was attached to the wall.

- Ø What's up Horsee,
- Ø Nothing much, same shit different day.
- Ø What's up with the commissary?
- Ø You should be good for next week. I need to have something checked out.
- Ø Ok, Horsee.

For some strange reason he would call me Horsee, but would not tell me why.

- Ø Yo, us let's go eat.
- Ø Ok, Horsee.

Steve and Joe were already at the table. Sebastian sat with the Spanish speaking people. Prince looked up and nodded. That was his way of saying hi. He was probably looking for recognition for helping Howard. Steve also picked up on that. I leaned into him and whispered, "Steve, after dinner, I need to make a call. I'll need your full name." Joe looked over at me, but did not say much. He never does. I was not sure if he heard what I said to Steve. Steve nodded his head and understood why.

- Ø Hi, Jerry!
- Ø Hi, Ozzie!
- Ø Jerry, I have someone that wants to do the program. I think you'll want to work with him. He has a shit load of people. Also I've made up my mind 100%. I also want to do the program. That kid Sebastian I had you look up is giving me some leads.
- Ø Good for you Ozzie. I'll be able to throw something your way. What's your friend's name?
- Ø Steve Upper.
- Ø Ok, call me Monday.

- Ø Will do Jerry!

- Ø Steve I spoke with my guy. The one that will make this happen.

- Ø I'm not sure you can do this. My bond is $325,000 and no collateral.

- Ø Steve, I told you, it gets reduced considerably. Don't worry about that so much.

- Ø Man Ozzie, I'll be amazed if this happens. I still think I'll need a property.

- Ø Let's wait till Monday. I'll know more by then. In the time being, let's get a game in.

During the next half hour Steve must have said, "Man Ozzie" about 50 times. All he could think about was getting out and setting people up, and getting laid. He was confident he could produce numerous arrests which would get him probation.

At night, I thought about the plan I had set in place. Can I see it thought? Will I be able to pull it off? Things were now in motion, like a downhill ball of snow, I don't think there is any stopping it. After about 20 minutes, headcount was completed, and the lights were turned off. Tonight there would be much noise. The floors were about to be stripped and polished. The tables from the dining area needed to be moved, onto the blue-gray carpeted TV area. Jay a trustee, made plenty of noise as he stripped the floor. He was tall and thin and did not look menacing at all. The machine required muscles to be handled properly and although Jay had experience with it, he seemed to tire easily. Jay needed help. Knowing I did not sleep at night, Husain made his way to my room.

- Ø Ozzie, do you want to work?

- Ø Sure,

I jumped off my bunk without giving it any thought. To work means extra food. Extra food means weight gain as well as less hunger pains. Also I could now barter with the other trustee.

- Ø Great, Jay will show you what to do.

- Ø Ok,

- Ø What's up Vargas?

I pointed at the ceiling. He was lost. It was a joke between my brother and I. Jay instructed what to do. For the most part it was to assist him. I did not mind at all. By now I had lost so much muscles mass that I would have done just about anything. All that mattered was that at breakfast I was getting a few extra trays to eat. Saturday morning breakfast consist of two hard boiled eggs. I must had eaten six eggs and still managed to save four for the following day.

The following morning on alpha shift, Husain called me to his desk.

Ø Ozzie, would you like to work permanently?

Ø Well, what exactly does that entail?

For, I knew that his regular clean up guy, Mario, washed the showers and bathrooms every night, four showers on each floor, as well as the bathroom on each level. Despite being eager and hungry I really did not want to clean up after grown men.

Ø I don't mind serving breakfast, but I don't really want to do Mario's job.

Husain agreed. With that I helped Jay wax the dining area for the second night in a row. At about 3:45 after breakfast was served I sat with Mario and Jay to share the left over trays. Over the next few days Hosan asked me twice again to help him with his problem. He was fed up with Mario, as Mario constantly question Husain, and often made stupid suggestions.

Ø Ozzie, please help me out here. I can't take Mario any more. You can get someone to work with you and split the work load or do whatever you can work out. But for the next few days I need you to help.

Not wanting to lose my portion, I agreed to help. The next evening Mario was fired. Fired from a job that did not pay? Mario told everyone he trained me because he was going to quit. However, everyone knew else. I offered Steve the job of my assistant. "There's no way I could stay up at night. I can't do it." Steve replied. Claudio, a Brazilian doing time for credit card fraud approached me and asked if he could work.

Ø Ok, (I said), but you have to clean every night. When I leave in a few weeks, you can move up and have someone assist you.

Claudio was fine with that agreement. Since then, I would always bring back extra food trays which I then passed out among a few of cell mates. Steve was first, then Harold and others. All of this I did for free. My generosity was well known. During breakfast itself Husain did not like the extra cups of hot oatmeal or grits to be given out. He preferred to throw them in the garbage so as to avoid fights. As soon as breakfast was served he would leave the area and do a check. As he did, I would grab the left over cups and pass them to the inmates. Every night I would pick different people. The exception was Steve and Howard. They got an extra cup from me every night.

15 BACK TO THE BRONX

Its 1am again. The only noise you can hear is that of a few snoring and a few breathing hard. For several days I managed to get away from my demon, as I focused on the task I needed to accomplish. Tonight, however things would be different. I allowed myself to escape into my past, and so tonight my demon would strike; there would be no escaping him. At this moment as I write, I am sitting by the entrance of my room. There is enough hallway light coming in for my aging eyes to clearly see. The stool I sit on is the same green cylindrical one found thought out the jail. My eyes are bloodshot and I am trying hard to contain myself. When I cry it is not for me, but instead for the life that I have taken.

Just like my actions that have brought me here, it's something I can't reverse. If only I knew back then what was in the future, I never would have left. Several tear drops now sit on the paper I write on. I can't help it. I can't stop it. It's my entire fault. How much pain do I need to take? How much suffering do I need to endure? They say time heals all wounds but as of yet it has not happened. Only Jackie was able to make my pain go away. I hear a noise beyond, but I'm afraid to look up. I don't want anyone to see my crying. Although I hate living with this pain, I don't want to die. If I could bring back time, I would.

Tonight it started with my friend, "the girl". I remembered going to my high school, arch rival football game with her. It was Thanksgiving Day. After the game, about 2 pm, we boarded the elevated train and headed back home. We stood near each other as the train approached. When the doors opened she quickly walked to the opposite door and pressed her back against it. I however, did not go any further than one foot into the train. The door shut behind me and I pressed my back against it. A vertical pole stood between us and so I leaned ever so slightly to my right to get an un-obstructive view of her face. You would think I should be standing close to her, but I knew better. I was observing her, capturing her, and admiring her. For a minute or two she stared towards her left and I continued to watch her. I was mesmerized. Her eyes disengaged from that she had focused on and she turned towards me. As she caught my eyes, she smiled.

Tonight, I clearly see that beautiful smile. It was a caring and loving smile. As our eyes locked on each other, I made my way to her. Time slowed down. Our faces were only inches apart. She looked at me as if expecting a kiss, but it did not come. Was she perplexed?-Perhaps. With two of my senses I took her in. Her aroma was to die for. It was different, one I have never known. It captivated me. Instead of giving her a kiss, I just smiled. I needed no kiss from her. Her presence alone was more than I could ever ask for. She was special to me and I wanted to keep it that way. I adored her, and felt something for her that I had never experienced in my life.

I missed my friend when she was not around, but for some reason I was afraid of asking for more. I did not want to mess-up that strange wonderful feeling I already had. Till then the only love and affection I received was from my aunt Sheila. The woman I think I should have received love and attention from, I despised. That was my mother. It was only from my dad that I felt loved. So I found it strange for me to feel what I did for my friend, "the girl".

I must have been about 20 years old, when for only the second time in my life, the same strange thing happened to me. By then I had my own two bedroom apartment. The second bedroom was my gym. It contained about 400 pounds of weights which I used almost every day. To the corner was a stack of muscle magazines. A big calendar on the wall allowed me to note the body parts I did that day. To the opposite wall was a huge mirror. Next to the mirror was a message to myself. It read "Remember your goals". For I always believed in being strong, both mentally and physically.

One evening after a workout I sat on the bed to relax for a moment, as music played in the living room. That's when it happened. It was about 11:00 pm. and although the light was off, I was not ready for sleep. Without moving the blanket I rested my feet on the bed with my shoes still on; both feet hanging over the side. I leaned back onto the bed, placed both hands behind my head and intertwined my fingers. As I stared at the ceiling it started to come. It was a feeling; a strange one, one I never knew before. As the song played I realized what it was. I knew what I was experiencing. I sadden, as I now knew, what I had been missing my entire life. I thought about my friend the girl. By now she was gone. She was far away studying in Ecuador. I never told her what I felt as I never knew what I was feeling. Tears came out as I sang to the music on the radio by Foreigner.

I wanna know what love is
I want you to show me
I wanna feel what love is
I know you can show me
I'm gonna take a little time

A little time to look around me

I've got nowhere left to hide

It looks like love has finally found me
In my life there's been heartache and pain

I don't know if I can face it again

I can't stop now, I've traveled so far

To change this lonely life

My friend, I love you. Where are you? I want you to show me what love is. Although she was not there, I could see her smile. The same one she gave me on the train. For the first time in my life, I felt love. I felt love for a woman. I felt love for my friend. My tears continued down my cheek. I stood up and walked to the living room. As I stared into the box where the music was coming from I cried out her name. Where are you? I love you! I want to hold you me. I want to know what love is, and I want you to show me. By the time I realized what the strange feeling was, it was too late. My friend, my love, was gone. Never to be seen again.

Many minutes had passed before I came back to reality. The clock on the wall above the guards' desk, read 1:30am. Breakfast would be served in just a little oven an hour. With pen still in hand I thought about my other love, Nancy, my second wife. She was young when we met. I was 21 and a few years older than she. At that time I was working selling real estate. It allowed me a decent income for the time. By then I had already purchased and sold my third house. Her dad lived across the office I worked in as so many-a-days, she would pass by. The office perimeter would take about 15 minutes to walk. However, she must have had a car beyond the view of the office. For she would walk in front, look in through the window, disappear, and three minutes later would walk in front again still traveling in the same direction.

She was a beautiful young woman. The first thing any man would notice was her bosoms. We had hit it off for a little while. Because of the age difference, I felt I needed to let her go. It was then that I meet Maria. Maria was my sister in law, and then became my first wife. Her older sister was married to my older brother Ismael. She too was very beautiful. I believe she was runner up to Miss P.R. or similar. Despite her charm there was something I would later find rotten within her. It's ironic that two of the few people I love most in this world, came from one of the two people I have ever hated. Jenelle and Ozzie Jr. were the products of that marriage.

I remember the day Jenelle was born. I was working at the real estate office. A call came in, it was her sister Lourdes. Ozzie, you need to go to the hospital. Once there I witness the birth of a beautiful, healthy girl. That evening I held her for the first time. It was an incredible feeling. How can one person feel so much love for another? I was in awe; in another world. I loved my daughter and I was happy. Jenelle was a good quiet girl. I could not understand why people complained about the terrible twos. That was until Ozzie came around.

His birth was the second happiest day of my life. Compared to his sister, Ozzie was a terror. As soon as he could walk he was climbing everywhere possible. I was afraid he would hurt himself. If Ozzie was awake you needed to be on guard. His energy was endless. Like Jenelle, Ozzie was extremely bright. By High School he was six feet tall, handsome and popular. When he was three, his mother and I divorced. In retrospect, I think we were too young and did not know how to deal with each other. For the third time in my life, I found myself departed from the people I loved the most; First my dad, then my friend the girl, and now my children. I was devastated. Maria loved to find ways to deny me visitation. My two children would grow up thinking I did not care for them, but that was not so. My frustration with Maria was so great that I sometimes thought of ways to eliminate her.

By the time Abby was born, I was traumatized and afraid; afraid to love again, afraid to bring a new life into this world. What good was life when everything you love eventually departs from you? Thus I lacked the emotional support Nancy needed during her pregnancy. I felt guilty about that for many years.

Well I'm tiring. Finally I put my pen down and for about the next hour I hid underneath the bed covers. There was to be no sleep for the moment. My mind was in an emotional uproar. I started to think again about what I had done and, the life I took. I was tormenting myself; I was in pain and in anguish. Breakfast could not come soon enough. After it, I would be exhausted and would be able to sleep.

16 DEALS

It's been a few days now since I've been helping at breakfast. Claudio and I have befriended each other. After we cleanup we sit at a table in the corner of the dining area. Most of the inmates are asleep. Twelve extra trays are available for us to share. We relax and gouge ourselves. Claudio tells me about his friend Balbi.

- Ø Ozzie do you know Balbi?
- Ø I read about him in the paper.
- Ø You know he is innocent?
- Ø How would I know that?
- Ø Balbi is not a doctor. He met the chiropractor through his wife. Both Balbis' wife and the chiropractor are Brazilian. The doc is American.
- Ø By Doc. You mean the chiropractor.
- Ø Yes. He wanted to open an office and asked Balbi for startup money. Balbi took partnership and did the books. He brought in his son and daughter to work. Balbi kept very good records of the money coming in, because of that he will be able to show that he was not aware the doc was selling prescriptions.
- Ø So why was he charged?
- Ø The doctor tried to cut a deal with the state after he became aware of the investigation and blamed Balbi. This way the doc could get out easy.
- Ø Well Claudio, Balbi went to the magistrate and bond was set. There was probable cause found, right?
- Ø Balbi has dual citizenship one from the U.S. and the other from Brazil. They think he will leave the country. So they set his bond at 1.5 million dollars. His daughter and son each got a bond of $500,000. They know his daughter was innocent but they charged everyone in the office.

- Ø That's a very high bond.
- Ø His daughter is being released this week. He has 50k, which is 10% of the bond.
- Ø Did he have that money lying around?
- Ø No, he did not put up that money. His brothers did.
- Ø So his family is here?
- Ø Not his blood brother.
- Ø Oh, he has black friends.
- Ø What do you mean?
- Ø Never mind, it's a joke I said.
- Ø Balbi is a Free Mason.
- Ø Oh, so the Masons put up the money?
- Ø Yes! In Brazil Balbi's grandfather was a high degree Mason. Balbi's dad is a Mason. His brothers are Masons, all with status and positions in Brazil. The Freemasons had a meeting to decide if they were going to help him. They decided they would.
- Ø That's a lot of money to give one person.
- Ø There are millions of Masons in the world. They have a system, when someone needs help; they ask how much money is needed? Then through the internet a message goes out. Many people give only a few dollars. With so many members a few dollars each adds to millions. They also hired a team of lawyers for him. That bill with be about $200,000.
- Ø Wow, I want to join.
- Ø You have to be invited by one, or you must request for them to allow you to join. They then interview you and check you out often they will visit your home. You pay a fee based on your money you have. They also set up commissary account for him and are helping his wife with the bills.

- Damn Claudio, talk about being connected. So, is he going to make bail?
- No, he preferred to use the money for trail instead of getting out. He knows he is innocent, so he is not afraid of trial. As long as his daughter is out, he is ok.
- What about you? You said you are leaving soon?
- I am being deported. I already have my flight info. I would like to get out for a week or two before I leave so that I can gather my stuff. But they will not allow me.
- Claudio I might know of a way.
- A way for me to get my things?
- Yes!
- How?
- Well, there is a program that allows for inmates to work something out with the state. It requires turning in a few drug dealers.
- Ozzie, I know a of a few Brazilian drug dealers. Also, I know a lot of people doing credit card fraud. That's the crime I committed.
- Claudio, you have to be guilty to go this route. I will make a phone call to someone I know. In the time being, I need you to prepare a list of people you might know. The police will work with you only if you have enough people you can set up.
- So, when will I know?
- Make your list first. Then I will call them.
- So you want me to put addresses down. I need to call my brother.
- Do what you have to do. Don't make up anything or you will get in trouble. They will file new charges if you lie.
- I know of a few clubs in Pompano Beach that cell cocaine.
- Write down as much info as you can.

Ø Tomorrow I will give it to you.

Claudio and I finished our breakfast. We cleaned our area and I made my way back to my room. Upon passing Howard's room I threw a package of food onto his bed. It startled him. He took notice, placed it under the sheet and gave me the thumps-up. Sleep came relatively quick.

Ø That afternoon, Prince grabbed my attention. It's been a few days since our talk in the rec yard.

Ø Yo Ozz, what's up?

Ø What's up? (I replied)

Ø I've been waiting for you. Let's talk.

Ø Sure, have a seat.

Ø Ozz you know I like my talking in the rec yard.

Ø Yeah, that the furthest you can get from the telephones.

He quickly picked up on the reference to the eighteen charges. He pointed at me and smiled. Steve made his way to my table and sat. I excused myself and proceeded to the rec. yard with Prince.

Ø Yo Ozz, I really need your help. I need to know if you can do what you say.

Ø I told you I could.

Ø So, what's the hold u?

Ø Well Prince, I wasn't sure you were 100% in. You sounded like you were, but for some reason I just wasn't sure.

Ø Are you freaking kidding me? I needed to do this yesterday.

Ø Look Prince, I have to contact someone who has a high position in the sheriff's office. He is usually very busy.

Ø Whatever it takes, just get it done.

Ø Prince, are you fully aware of what you need to do to get out?

- Ø Yes, I need to talk!

- Ø There is a program called Substantive Assistant Program.

- Ø Yo Ozz, if that's how you plan to get me out forget about it.

- Ø Why have you decided not to talk?

Prince leaned into my personal space. If there is one thing I hate is to have my space invaded by anyone, much less by a man. I turned my face to my right, my left ear inches away from his lips.

- Ø I tried to go that route. The officer, who arrested me, did not want to work with me.

- Ø Who is this officer?

- Ø Someone from the Hollywood Police Department.

- Ø Fuck that, you were dealing with the wrong person.

Prince knew I was on to something or in this case someone.

- Ø Prince I'm sure you have heard the saying, "it's not what you know, it's who you know". In your case it's what you know and who I know.

- Ø Ozzie, if what you are saying is true and you can get me out, I can pay you well.

- Ø Prince it's not a matter of money. I have other motives for getting out.

- Ø Look, I know about the program. I know of a few gangs that are dealing. I don't want to turn them in, but for 6,000,000. Fuck them! I need to get the fuck out of here. I can also use your help. Shit! I'll even throw you a few bones.

Bam! That's what I needed to hear. Before I plead guilty, I need to be sure I have enough material or people to turn over to the police.

- Ø Prince let me have you full name. I am also going to need a list of people you know that you will be able to turn in. Give it to me at lunch and I will make a phone call.

By now he was lite on his feet, almost jumping up and down, even though it was less than an inch off the ground. I told Prince I would help him. I was not sure I could for he was already rejected from the program. My confidence hid my doubt. We left the rec. yard together. He made his way to the TV area and I sat down at my table with Steve.

- Ø What's that about?
- Ø Can't talk about it.

I'm not one to make up stories, so instead I just said I can't talk. To some I come across as rude, but I'm only being genuine; true to myself. Steve was a street guy, he could tell something was brewing, but did not press on.

- Ø Ozzie, I managed to talk to Green.
- Ø You're kidding.
- Ø No, for once he answered his phone.
- Ø Shit I've been trying to reach him. I've had my brother leave messages for him to no avail.
- Ø Well, he was in his office today.
- Ø So what does Casper say?
- Ø I asked him about the program. He did confirm that it would be the lowest possible sentence provided I gave them enough information. He did say I was still going to need a house as collateral.
- Ø Are you sure Steve?
- Ø That's what he said. He should know.
- Ø I thought different. I thought a low bond was set, and it did not matter if you had the collateral or not. A thought a signature would be ok.
- Ø Ozzie, according to Green that info is wrong.
- Ø Let me talk to Jerry and find out. I have to call him anyway.
- Ø I'm scared; if I don't have the collateral then I can't get out.
- Ø Fuck Steve, I'm in the same boat.

Immediately I went to the phone and called Jerry.

- Ø Jerry, its Ozzie.
- Ø Hi Ozzie!
- Ø Jerry, I have a question for you. I also have two people that want to do the program.
- Ø What's the question?
- Ø Do we need a house as collateral?
- Ø That's up to the prosecutor. I know bond is set very low so one can get out. I'll have to check with the prosecutor to be sure.
- Ø Ok, get your pen and write these two names out.

I gave him two legal names to write and then continued,

- Ø Claudio has the Brazilian connection. However Prince is part of a gang I know you'll want. He has friends who sell guns from NJ through Florida. He also knows of a cocaine selling ring from California to NY and Florida. They Fed Ex kilos at a time in a microwave oven. Usually one per oven, this way the weight does not increase too much, but more important because the microwave oven has a barrier that does not allow its content to be scanned accurately. The scanners can't penetrate the inside of the oven, so it goes through as an empty oven.
- Ø Ozz, that's the first time I hear of this. What else?
- Ø That's it for now. I'm learning a little about Balbi, but I have a feeling he might be innocent.
- Ø Look, call me tomorrow.
- Ø Ok, Jerry.
- Ø Steve, I spoke to Jerry regarding the collateral issue. He wants me to call him back tomorrow. I'll keep you posted.

I made my way to Prince and told him I'll have some answers in a day or two. "Fuck Ozz, I need to get out." That's all Prince would keep saying. The following day at about 1:30 pm, I called Jerry again.

- Ø Ozzie, according to the state, it's up to each individual prosecutor. Most want to see a house even if it has no equity. As far as Claudio goes he is out, it is very difficult to get someone out of jail that has an immigration hold. Tell Steve and Prince I will come to visit them tomorrow. They have to have a list ready for me. I need to provide that list to the prosecutor. My partner arrested Steve, so it's not a problem working with him. As far as Prince goes if his arresting officer does not want to work with him, then I can step in. Either way, if he has good info we can use him.

- Ø Great Jerry; about what time tomorrow?

- Ø I'll visit them around 2:00 pm or so; that is provided I don't get called on a case.

- Ø Ok, Jerry and thanks.

Bam! I'm on to something here. What`I saw a few weeks ago is materializing. It looks like I might be able to help Prince get out. Steve had a concern about collateral. If indeed he was going to be required to post a house he would not be able to do so. As for, in order to plead guilty I needed to know Steve would get out as he had the contacts I needed. That's when it hit me. I was going to be able to get Prince out, but it was going to come at a price. I knew Prince had a house in Weston and I was going to make sure he would put it up to bail-out Steve. In turn Steve would have to agree to give both Prince and myself leads. Both guys knew I was up to something, but I was not saying much yet. With that I made my way to each, not revealing anything about Jerry's meeting tomorrow.

- Ø Steve, I spoke to Jerry and you are right. You are required a property.

- Ø Damn, Ozzie I knew it. It looks like I am never going to get out of here.

- Ø Steve, relax! I have a way out.

- Ø I don't see how I don't have anybody that will post their house. Just forget about it.

- Ø Steve, relax! Listen to me. I have an idea, a way to go, but I need your permission to discuss your case with someone else here.

- Ø Must be Prince?

- Ø Maybe yes, maybe no!
- Ø Well what's your idea? I can get you the house you need, but it's going to cost you. How much? I don't have much money.
- Ø Not in the form of money.
- Ø Then what?
- Ø You need to share some of your leads.
- Ø Share with whom?
- Ø I can make this happen. I need some of your leads which you said you would do if I could get you out, but to get you out you need a house. In exchange for the house you need, you will need to give some of your leads to this person.
- Ø Man, I know its Prince.
- Ø Maybe yes, or maybe no. I'll tell you who after we have an agreement.
- Ø Ozzie, I don't care who it is just as long as I can get out.
- Ø Steve, I need you to be 100% on this. Are you in agreement?
- Ø Sure! Ok, I'll get back to you later. In the mean time I need to talk to shall we say Prince?
- Ø I knew it!
- Ø Whatcha mean, I'm not saying it is him. I'm saying I need to talk to him.

We both smiled knowing it was Prince indeed. I was not fooling anyone.

- Ø Prince, need to talk.
- Ø Let's go.
- Ø Man, I hate talking in the rec yard. It's always so loud there.
- Ø That's why I like it.

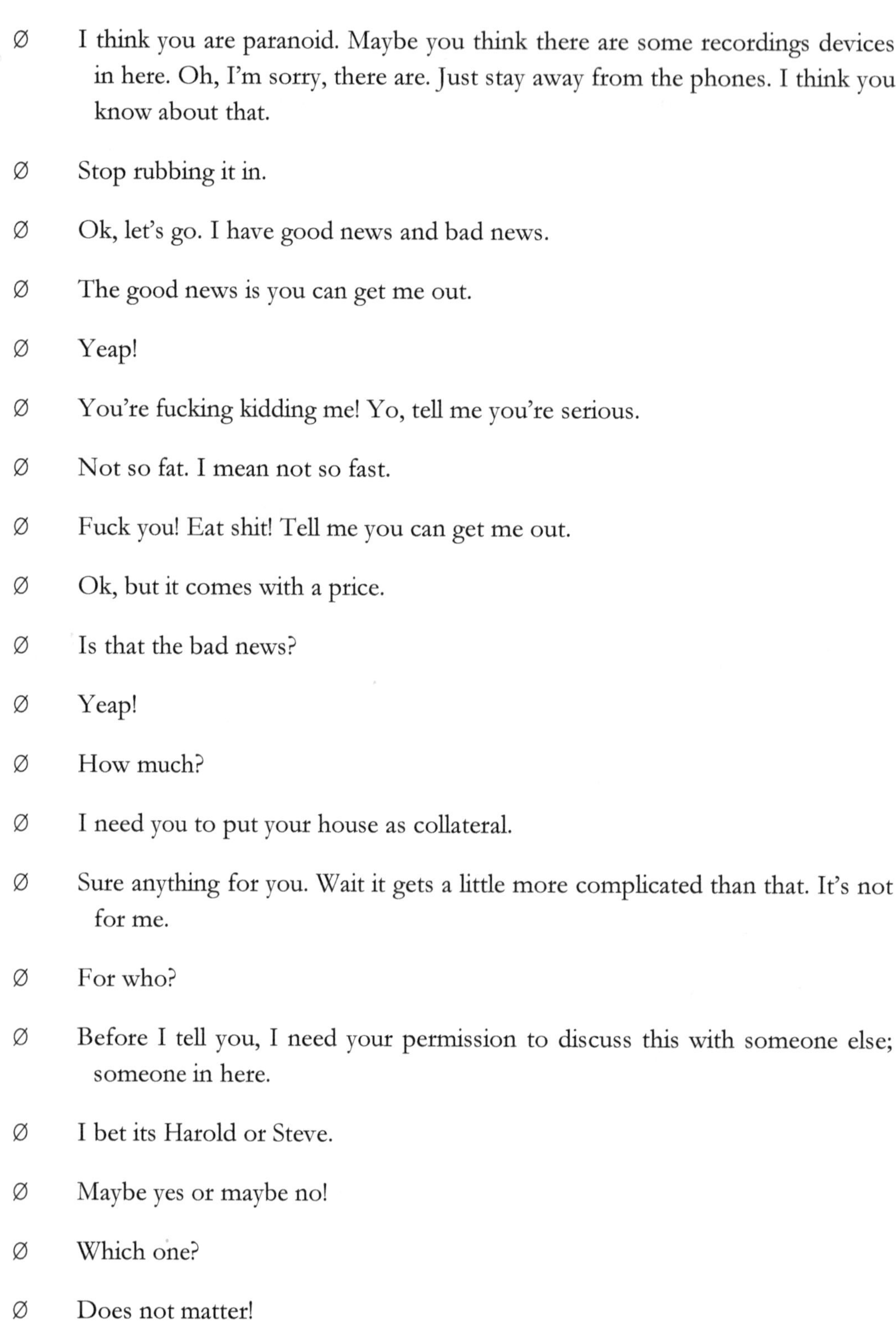

Ø I think you are paranoid. Maybe you think there are some recordings devices in here. Oh, I'm sorry, there are. Just stay away from the phones. I think you know about that.

Ø Stop rubbing it in.

Ø Ok, let's go. I have good news and bad news.

Ø The good news is you can get me out.

Ø Yeap!

Ø You're fucking kidding me! Yo, tell me you're serious.

Ø Not so fat. I mean not so fast.

Ø Fuck you! Eat shit! Tell me you can get me out.

Ø Ok, but it comes with a price.

Ø Is that the bad news?

Ø Yeap!

Ø How much?

Ø I need you to put your house as collateral.

Ø Sure anything for you. Wait it gets a little more complicated than that. It's not for me.

Ø For who?

Ø Before I tell you, I need your permission to discuss this with someone else; someone in here.

Ø I bet its Harold or Steve.

Ø Maybe yes or maybe no!

Ø Which one?

Ø Does not matter!

Ø I'm sure it's Steve.

- Maybe yes or maybe no!

- Yo, I'm not sure about this.

- Ok Prince let me know when you are sure.

- Wait, I'm not saying no. I just can't have anyone knowing my business.

- Prince you are going to have to trust me. I can make things happen. Look it is Steve. You have something he needs, and he has something you need. I also have something you need. Set the picture?

- So Steve needs a house as collateral to get out. Does he know about the program?

- Yes, and I am going to get him out if I get help from you. In return he is going to get me leads to make a few arrests. I need them so I can give them Jerry. That way I might get probation only. In return I will see that Jerry will get you out.

- How sure about that are you?

- I'm sure. All you have to do is agree.

- Yo, Ozz you think I can get a few leads from Steve and in return I'll turn over some guys I know to you? Reason is I don't want them to know I set them up. Besides I need help with the other money I told you about.

- I thought that was just a come on.

- Eat a dick!

- Yeah, I didn't believe you can get your hands on 6,000,000.

- Have you not been listening to me?

- Prince to me that is stuff you only see at the movies.

- Ozz, this is fucking real. Look, I'm in, let's get it straight. Steve will give me leads. Steve will give you leads. I will give you leads. I will give Steve my house as collateral. You will get me out, you will get Steve out. Right?

- Right!

Ø So, Steve is doing his civil duties?

Ø Yes!

Ø I fucking knew it. Ok, I'm in, but I don't want anyone to know about the hit.

Ø The 6,000,000. hit.

Ø Yeah, ok, not a problem. What shall we call it?

Ø Call it the $6.

Ø The $6., movie.

Ø Ok, you still don't think it's real? Why else do you think I would join the program? Besides I need your help.

Ø I don't know Prince; after all we are both joining a snitching program. Can we trust each other?

Ø Look Ozz, all this is real. I could really use some help.

Ø We can talk about that down the road but first let's get out of here. We are going to have to come up with some type of agreement.

Ø Ozz, word is bond; if I get out I'll owe you big time. Let's do this; we can discuss the details later today

Ø Ok, let me check with Steve. Then I have to talk to Jerry and give him the green light.

That evening I would have to visit Steve, Prince and Claudio. I needed to let them know of the news; the news about Jerry's visit. At around 9 pm I made my way to Steve and told him I had everything wrapped up. I let him know Jerry was going to meet with him tomorrow. After Steve it took me about 20 seconds to find my way from the game table to Princes' room.

Yo 2 pm tomorrow. Be ready with your list.

Ø You're fucking kidding me?

Ø Nope, 2 pm or so. They are going to call you for a visit.

Ø Yo, Ozz, you the Fucking man. I owe you big time.

Ø Yes, you do $6.00.

With that he pointed at me and smiled. It wasn't till 4 am that I sat down with Claudio and related the message.

Ø Claudio, I have some bad news.

Ø That's ok Ozzie. I did not think it was going to happen.

Ø I did and it's why I asked you for a list.

Ø Immigration works a little different. Sorry if I got your hopes up. Here is the list you gave me (little did he know I had made a copy of it).

Ø You keep it Ozzie. I have a few more to give you, especially the person who turned me in.

Ø What do you mean?

Ø A friend of mine had gotten arrested and set me up. He is still selling drugs and I want you to get him for me. I will give you all the info as soon as I get out and have access to a computer. It will be in a few weeks. I will be in Brazil by then. I'll leave you my email address so that you can contact me.

Ø What about Balbi? What is he going to do?

Ø Balbi is innocent and the police know it. He is just the fall guy. The other guy lied and decided to talk against Balbi. So they gave him a deal, but in trial everything will come out. The state will have to pay Balbi for false imprisonment and also for lawyer's fees. He will be ok.

Ø Ok, Claudio I can't thank you enough.

Ø Ozzie, just do me the favor and get the guy who turned me in. Also make sure Balbi gets extra food.

Fuck! Holy shit! Holy cow! My plan was coming together. For the moment it seemed I had things under control. My plan was a simple one. However it was a plan that contained many perils. I wondered if for the second time in my life there would be more blood money.

17 JERRY VISITS

Vargas, get ready for a visit. The time was 2pm. Although I was not expecting a visit for myself, I knew who it was; it could only be one person, Jerry. He was coming to see Steve and Prince. During any visitation we are not allowed our sweaters. For that matter we are allowed only one shirt and one underwear. Why such a rule? I wondered. What could we use the other underwear for; surely not as a weapon? Would be easier to sneak in contraband? Oh well. It did not matter much. After removing my sweater I made my way to the door that exposed the corridor with the stairs leading down into the visitation area. As I walked in I could see Jerry standing in one of the booths. It was the second time I have ever seen him.

- Ø Hi Jerry!
- Ø Gosh, you lost a lot of weight.
- Ø Yes, I know.
- Ø So how are you Ozzie?
- Ø I'm okay, Jerry. Apart from not eating too much, other than 10 slices of bread, some rice and other junk, I'm as good as can be.
- Ø Before I talk with the other guys I wanted to talk to you first and get your take on the matter.
- Ø OK!
- Ø I know about Steve already; my partner arrested him.
- Ø Apart from selling drugs, he seems to be a nice and sincere guy. He wants to get out of jail and out of the game. One thing is for sure. With the number of people he has to turn in, there is no way he can stay in the game. He prepared a long list of names.
- Ø What about Prince?

- Ø Prince claims to know some heavy hitters. He also has a list. He mentioned his lawyer tried to see if he could enter the SAP but was rejected. His arresting officer did not want to work with him. That's when I thought about you.

- Ø Ozzie, I'll make sure I throw a few things your way. What else do you have?

- Ø Oh, Balbi. If I had to bet, I would say he is innocent. I don't know the details but talk is he was set up. Seems he's got a good support team behind him. Rumor is that the chiropractor was the guilty one and tried to shift the blame elsewhere.

- Ø OK, keep your ears open and your mouth shut.

I thought to myself; it's because I opened my mouth that I am finding a solution, however, "I just said OK, will do." As soon as I was back in the dorm Steve was called. I wished him well. Several minutes after Steve was call, Prince was summoned to the waiting area. "Prince, get ready for a visit". He was standing by the deputy's booth, showing off the picture of his bike.

- Ø It's Jerry.

- Ø I figured that much.

- Ø So do you have your list?

- Ø Yea.

- Ø I'll talk to you when you're done.

2pm to 3:30pm was lock-down time. Talking to Steve and Prince would have to wait till then. A few days ago my room was changed. I was now on the upper level. Steve was on the same and so I waved at him and pointed to the bathroom.

- Ø How did it go?

- Ø Good, Jerry is eager to work with me. He also said my bond would be reduced.

- Ø Good, what did you think of him?

- Ø You know, he really seems like a nice guy.

- Ø I told you so. I know they are trained to play the nice cop role, but with him, there really is something different and genuine. That guy has the lightest blue eyes I had ever seen.

- Ø You know Steve, that's the first thing I noticed also. Prince is down there now.

- Ø Yes I know we will talk to him later.

Make sure your bunks are made. Floor is open.

- Ø Prince, how did it go?

- Ø Rec. yard!

- Ø Yo, I'm tired of this rec yard. I can't hear shit out there.

He just started walking and I followed.

- Ø How did it go?

- Ø Good! Good!

- Ø So tell.

- Ø We spoke for a few Minutes, and then I took out my list. As I pointed to the people on it, I told him what each sold. Some people did tax fraud. I have the names of people who are big in the game, but I am a little worried. I left out some guys I know really well. I just don't feel right pointing them out. You think Steve will give me some people?

- Ø Sure Prince, we are in this together.

For a moment I asked myself, why would Prince need help? Should he not have enough people of his own? The more I questioned him the less attention I paid. Was I starting to doubt? Was something wrong? How can I go and join him in a $6,000,000. heist if I can't trust what he says. I was going to need more convincing about his big money claim.

- Ø Ozzie! What cha thinking about?

- Ø I'm listening to you Prince.

- Ø Are you worried? Are you uncomfortable turning your best friends in? What would you rather have in your pocket? A few friends or $6,000,000?

- Ø Yo, you are right. Fuck it, it's a dog eats dog world. How sure are you about that anyway?

- Ø Look Ozz, as soon as we get out, I'll start planning. First I need to do some phone calls that I can't do from in here. I might need some help. If I'm turning people in I don't want anyone of them to know about this. That's why I really need you. Besides you speak Spanish. It might come in handy.

- Ø Wait, I did not say I was in.

- Ø Don't worry, you will.

- Ø What makes you so sure?

- Ø I know once I start revealing details about the money you're going to want in.

- Ø OK, we'll see. Let's get the fuck out of here first.

- Ø You think we will be out by Thanksgiving?

- Ø I hope so, this just 1 ½ weeks away.

- Ø How fast can this go?

- Ø Well Jerry has to set up a meeting with you, your lawyer, and the prosecutor. After that it should only be a day or two. Good, good, hope to be out by then.

- Ø OK, talk to you later.

Prince mad his way to the front row seat of the TV area. I sat to the back on the comfy lounging chair; Harold was also there.

- Ø Oye que tal.

- Ø What's up Harold?

- Ø Ozzie, those mother fuckers stole my jewelry.

- Ø Yeah, you mentioned that.

- Ø But now it's official.

- Ø How so,

- Ø I got a list of items that were placed in my property bag. There was no mention of any of the jury. Those fuckers, mother fuckers!

- Ø Who?

- Ø Hollywood P.D.

- Ø Are you sure?

- Ø Ozzie, my arrest was probably a planned hit. My jewelry totaled over $35,000. I had all that costumed made. Those mother fuckers planted that shit in my car, arrested me and my wife, who was innocent of everything, and then stole my jewelry. To top it off, they beat the shit out of me, knowing I had heart surgery. But that's ok. They fucked with the wrong guy. These mother fuckers don't know who I am.

- Ø Harold, first off all, calm down. You get too excited every time you talk about them. Take a deep breath. Now I'm afraid to ask you, but who are you.

Harold was sitting next to me. He turned sideways and slightly forward. He grabbed the collar of his V-neck shirt and pulled it down as far as he could.

- Ø Ozzie, very few people know who I am. You see this tattoo?

- Ø That's from a gang. Right?

- Ø Yes, but a little different than all the others. This one is special; anyone caught carrying this tattoo that is not supposed to have it will be killed. There are only five people in the world with this same tattoo. You see these teardrops.

- Ø Yea!

- Ø There are four. Each one represents a murder.

- Ø Fuck, Howard you're scaring me.

- Ø Ozzie, You and I are cool. Don't you worry about anything! I appreciate you, I am going to give you a gift.

Ø No, no! Howard you don't owe me anything.

Ø That's why it's a gift. I see you play chess all the time. At home I have a chess set that I purchased in Japan for $2,500. The pieces are carved out of Jade. It's yours. I never used it at all.

Ø OK, Howard. I replied.

I wasn't expecting to actually get it, but I'll still accepted, that's if, if I ever get out.

Ø Howard, what were you doing in Japan?

Ø Ozzie, I was a real gang banger growing up. I'm talking real hard core. I was sent there to help bring back some members we sent there on a mission. It turns out some of my guys were owed money by a small group of Japanese dealers. They decided to fee to Japan without paying the drugs. So our leader sent a few of our guys to Japan to collect. They were then held captive and so our leader sent me as well as a few others. Once there, an insider showed us around. On the second day there we came in contact with the group. We were instructed to collect and then kill all. You see this scar.

Ø It doesn't look like a scar.

Ø It's an old gunshot wound. I took a bullet. It went right through my arm, but I took out the mother fucker that shot me, plus his cousin and I collected the money.

Ø Are you serious?

Ø Ozzie, I'm a grown man. If you knew about gangs then you would know of my tattoo. Lower ranking members come up to me, kneel down and kiss my ring.

Ø Fuck that is power!

Ø I don't like it anymore. It reveals who I am, and I don't like the attention. My ring was specially made for me. It has a diamond cut in five corners.

Ø You mean it has five pointed sides?

Ø Yes!

Ø So, then that would make it a pentagon?

- Ø Yes, just like the building. By the way we have members in there and in Washington D.C. All of our members know the signs. They all know that there are five leaders throughout the world. Whatever command we say, goes. No questions asked. Anyone found wearing the ring other than the five leaders will be killed. Once you are a leader, you are so for life. That ring cost over $7,000.

- Ø How do you become a leader?

- Ø I started in the gang 35 years ago. It was a small group first. It formed to protect ourselves from other gang members, especially in jail. The Hispanics were always picked on. That's why the gang was formed, to help and protect each other. Now there are over 1,000,000 members throughout the world. I am the leader from Canada to Florida all the way to the Mississippi River.

- Ø That's a big area.

- Ø Yes, I have the largest area. Believe me, when I say those mother fuckers from Hollywood have something coming.

"Foods on post, food on post"!

- Ø Dinner, we'll talk later.

- Ø Don't talk about what I said.

- Ø Don't worry I won't.

- Ø I know Ozzie. I know who you are.

- Ø What do you mean?

- Ø Don't worry, you're my people, we'll talk later.

Fuck, fuck! Why did Howard have to tell me so much? I did not need to know all of that. Besides what the fuck did he mean? "I know who you are." He struck fear in me. Do I need to kill him, before he kills me? Did the Cuban cousins send him to kill me? Now, I am fucking worried. He did not even tell me the name of the gang. As I looked out from within my room, the first thing that came to mind was to grab my little sharp pencil. Waite, I said, If I was going to kill him, it would not be with that. My heartbeat started racing, as I now planned a way to kill Howard. I'd rather be tried by 12 people than to be carried by six. I thought about grabbing the cane from Vinnie. I could knock him with one blow to the head, and then make the cane break and splinter. Then I could ram it through his heart. If someone was going die it was not going to be me. The best place to kill him would be in the rec yard.

After plotting for about five minutes I told myself to relax. I reasoned, "If he was going to kill me, he would not have told me anything." So was he trying to scare me? ; If so, he did; but for what reason? He has been here for a week now. The bruises on his face were real; it's obvious he was beat up.

- Hey Ozzie, that's not your usual chair.
- Duh! I know Steve. I figured I always have my back to the crowed. Today I thought I would see the crowd.
- Seems like you've seen a ghost. Did your lawyer come by?
- That's funny. I think I would really be scared if I saw my lawyer. Joe, are you part of the mafia?
- Why?
- Because you always get extra food thrown your way. Every day you get extra bread, apples, cookies and sometimes half of people's dish. I know you are not getting commissary, so what's the deal?
- Ozzie, he does postcard drawings for people.

Ø Hum! I know you belong to the mafia. I'm watching you Joe. You know in this place you could never be too sure of whom one is sitting next to. That old man killed his wife; we have drug dealers, rapists, gang leaders, and innocent people like Balbi, as well as free Masons and mafia Joe.

- So tell me Ozzie, are you in the drug dealer category or the innocent?
- Neither Joe, but I'm guilty as hell. I was in the "in-love" category.
- What does that mean? Steve asked.
- Never mind Steve, that's a long story, one I don't talk about, besides it usually take me 30 minutes to explain.
- So, Joe, which organize crime family are you from?

- Ø He's from the Freemason.
- Ø No, you kidding, no wonder. I knew you had to be connected. That's why Balbi always passes you food.
- Ø You know about Balbi.
- Ø Yea Joe, a little bird in the rec yard told me about him.
- Ø Hope they told you the truth.
- Ø What that he is guilty.
- Ø No, he is not.
- Ø Relax Joe; I'm just fucking with you. I was told he is innocent.
- Ø Yea, we Masons know he is. The police know he is also. In the end it will all come out.
- Ø What's that Joe, all the corruption?
- Ø Yes.
- Ø Do you think there are good cops out there?
- Ø Sure, there are good and bad cops. Just like there are good and bad people.
- Ø Are there other Brazilian Freemasons here?
- Ø No, just Balbi and I. But I am Portuguese and not Brazilian. Our language is the same, so it's like being in the same family.
- Ø That makes sense, Joe. I want to join the Masons.
- Ø You have to be invited in, or you must ask to be invited.
- Ø That's what I'm doing Joe. So invite me in. Actually now that I think about it, my in law-James is a Mason.
- Ø There you go. He can get you in.

- Ø First, thing first, I need to get the fuck out of here. Weeks have turned into months, my bond has been posted since Sept 23 and I'm still here with you guys. Thanksgiving is right around the corner.
- Ø Ozzie, we'll be out by then.
- Ø Sure hope so Steve. I'm so tired of this place, especially the same crappy food.
- Ø I'll eat to that.
- Ø Joe do you consider yourself as being in a gang? I asked.
- Ø Oh, no! It's a club. Most members are doctors, lawyers, politicians and working class citizens.
- Ø Yea, I know that Joe.
- Ø Hay, do you guys know anything about gangs? (I asked).
- Ø Ask Prince, he's in one.
- Ø Really I did not know.
- Ø Which one is he in? It's a motorcycle gang called Broward's finest.
- Ø Shit that is why Broward is so corrupt. The police are gang members.
- Ø No, it's not Broward's finest. That's the name of the gang.
- Ø Yes, I know. I just fucking around. But you know the saying, "If the shoe fits, wear it."
- Ø OK Ozzie, it's 'Broward's Most Wanted'.
- Ø Fuck Steve, that's for from Broward's finest. So, you know for sure that he is in a gang.
- Ø Yea, everyone knows that. Don't you remember he showed pictures of his bike?
- Ø That doesn't mean he's in it.
- Ø He rides with them.

- Ø So, he really is a gangster?
- Ø Looks that way.
- Ø Oh, Steve. We have to play a game later.
- Ø Sure!

That's our code for, we should talk. For the first time in a while Joe spoke much more than normal.

- Ø So, what other gangs are there?
- Ø Ask your father sitting over there.
- Ø Howard! Is Howard in a gang?
- Ø Sure, I noticed his tattoos. Man Ozzie, you need to get out move often.
- Ø No, thanks Steve, one night I did and I'm still locked up.
- Ø What did the ground taste like Ozzie?
- Ø Fuck you Steve. So what gang is my father with?
- Ø Latin Kings!
- Ø Fuck! Are you sure?
- Ø Yeah, you see the tattoos! Your father must be the real deal
- Ø From what he has told me, I would have to say so.
- Ø I saw you guys talking earlier today. Btw, is that what was on your mind at dinner?
- Ø Maybe yes, maybe no!
- Ø Ozz, I think you're a little panic.
- Ø Steve, have you ever lost someone who was closed to you?
- Ø No.

- Ø I have. It hurts. I'm trying to stay alive for my Abby. After all that's who I am, Abby's dad.
- Ø I can understand that. I think you should talk to Howard about gangs. There is a Cuban gang in Miami. I don't know of the name, but I've heard they are ruthless. Real mother fuckers you don't want to play with.
- Ø Shit Steve, to me this is no joke. I need to get to the bottom of this, but how? I don't know anyone.
- Ø Talk to Prince and Howard, they might know.
- Ø I'll have to find a way to approach Howard about it. Talking about Prince, guys are wondering what is up between the two of you. You and I always talk while we play, so people don't suspect anything, but they notice you and him in the rec. yard.
- Ø I've invited him to talk inside, but he likes it out there and honestly I don't give a shit about what those mother fuckers in here think.
- Ø Try not to let it be known about the program.
- Ø Steve, half of these mother fuckers in here are on it. They just don't have the balls to say it.
- Ø Because, it's not a smart.
- Ø Ok, Steve. So, I could sleep tonight, without having to worry about Howard?
- Ø I think so. Besides they just changed your room to upstairs. How do you like it?
- Ø Oh, much Better. They can't see me doing exercises in my room. Also it's a little further away from the flushing noise of the bathroom.
- Ø Yeah, I told you would like it there.
- Ø Ok, let's play, I'll think about talking to Howard later on.

For the next hours Steve and I relaxed as we entertained ourselves. It was just pass 8pm, time for the guys in the rec yard to come in. And time for the adjacent unit to enter the rec. yard. About 5 minutes after 8, there was a loud bang on the glass. Someone from the other side was trying to communicate; since its common, I didn't bother to look away from the chess game. Steve took notice of a man pointing at me. "Hey, Ozz, this guy calling at you" said Steve. I looked up to see three fingers pointing at me. It was Zoe a brother from Pompano. "Steve it's your move, let me go say hi to this guy."

- Ø Yo Ozz, what up? I thought you would be out by now?
- Ø I should be out by next week.
- Ø Yo, let me give you my number.
- Ø I still have it.
- Ø I have a new one write it down. It's the number to my baby's momma. I will be out in a month and would like to do business.
- Ø OK Zoe sounds good.
- Ø By the way I heard some guys in the mail jail have a hit on you.
- Ø Do you know who?
- Ø Not sure. After they pulled you out of our unit, the talk was that some guy on the 8th floor with a big scar on his head wanted to kill you, so that you would not testify at court against him. The trustee you beat up started the whole shit.
- Ø How serious do you think the threat was?
- Ø Yo, they say he has a cousin in a Cuban gang.
- Ø What's the take?
- Ø Don't know, this jail is lame, but the main jail is full of crazy niggers. Just lay low for a while. Yo, and don't forget to call me. We gonna make some serious money.
- Ø Ok, thanks Zoe. I'll talk to you later.

Fuck Steve! This Cuban guy seems to be following me. That's the 3rd fucking guy to tell me about a hit on me.

- Ø Shit, where do you know this guy from?

- Ø He was in my unit in the main jail. He runs a drug distribution in Pompano. After he became aware of my charges, he wanted to do business with me. I played along as if I was connected.

- Ø Look it's been going on two months since you have been here since the time it happened. I'm sure there were lots of rumors, but I bet it's all forgotten now.

- Ø Steve you always have a way to down play it. I'm not taking this lightly.

- Ø Ozz, if you keep on like that it's going to drive you crazy. You know most people just talk garbage to try to look strong and powerful, but the truth is most can't back up what they say, especially these young thugs. It's the quiet ones that you need to worry about.

- Ø Like Howard, Steve?

- Ø Yeah, like Howard. But like I said before, if he was going to do you in, he would properly get a younger gang member to do it.

- Ø Well, even though this unit is full of older and lame guys, they are still a number of Chico's and Jits. So I'm not letting my guard down.

- Ø Stop worrying and play.

That night I tried to stay confident and focused on the plan. There were brighter days ahead. I told myself to relax and try to get a nap before breakfast.

It was Tuesday morning, two days away from Thanksgiving. "Vargas, you have a visitor", said the guard. At least that's what it sounded like. I was not sure I heard correctly. At 8am I am usually in a deep sleep. By now I have become accustomed to tuning the morning noise out. I don't even notice when the nurse calls, as I've become accustomed to tuning everything out. If it was me that was being called they were going to have to call again. I wasn't about to get up because it sounded like my name. "Ozzie, room L8, get ready for pm court." Fuck, I heard it clearly. But why was I being called to pm court without any prior notice?

Walking half asleep to the front desk I asked Mrs. Chapman, "I have pm court?" Yes, get ready. They are coming in five minutes for you. As I made my way back up the stairs I thought about Jerry had his promise to get me out by Thanksgiving. Before I could finish washing up, the deputy came for me. I'll be right there. "Only one shirt and underwear on" he said. Got it! I stated.

I was handcuffed, walked to the elevator and taken to the intake unit. To my surprise pm court lacked all the commotion of numerous inmates yelling, or could it be I was starting to adjust to such experience. I do have to say this time I enjoyed it. The weather had changed since I was incarcerated. It was a cool morning with almost no humidity. For the minute it took me to board the bus, I took several deep breaths of the fresh air. On the ride I did not know what to expect for I had no warning, no notice that I was to appear in court.

At the court house I was placed in a different holding cell then the one for Judge Porter. The wait was just as long as PM court starts after lunch. At 12:30pm I was called up. This time they placed shackles on my feet as well as the usual handcuffs bounded to my chains around my waist. Walking in shackles becomes difficult if you happen to have a long stride such as myself. The shackles are only about 16 inches long, whereas my normal stride is about 36 inches. If you take too long of a step they tug away at the ankle and into the skin causing pain and discomfort.

Judge Porter does not require her inmates to wear the ankle shackles, so I know I was not going to her court room. Where could I be going to? Was I to testify against the Cubans? If so, I was not going to say a word. Did they manage to scare me? Yes, they did. I did not want to worry forever, about any repercussions. As the elevator closed the deputy pressed the 5th floor button. "5th floor, that's civil court, right?" The deputy responded you're going to meet with the prosecutor and your lawyer for an agreement. Ah, yes, what a relief, finally I will get to go home.

The walk to the office was a long one. The hallways were full of people walking to and fro. A young boy, about 7 or 8, stared at me, as he walked with his mother towards my direction. As I glanced up and meet his mother's eyes, I felt humiliated. How could I have put myself in such a position? I could not walk fast enough. My steps at that point were very short and it seems like it took forever and a day to pass through the hallway.

As I walked to the office, the first person I noticed was Jerry. He was standing up 15 feet away from the entrance; sitting to my side was Casper. "Hi, Mr. Green!" Hi, Ozz! Casper did not stand up nor shake hands. Next to Jerry was the state prosecutor Mrs. Salomon. She immediately said hi, and invited me in. One deputy accompanied us into the room. Jerry also followed.

For the first time since my arrest I was surrounded by civilians, instead of inmates. When I was among the inmates, I felt totally different than I did in this room. Inmates were not a normal part of my life. I did not care one bit about any of them or about what they thought about me. However, today I felt strange. Although I never committed a crime prior to this, I felt like a monster. The civilized world was now upon me. There were in my presence and I in theirs. I was sure that in their eyes I was a man to fear; a big time drug dealer who was guilty and should be put away for life. For a brief moment I felt I was beneath them. I was an outcast that no one cared about.

- Ø Hi Ozzie, have a seat. Are you sure you want to go through the program?

- Ø Yes!

- Ø OK, did you bring your list?

- Ø Yes, it's in my shirt pocket.

- Ø Let's review it. The chief state prosecutor has to review it and give the green light on it.

- Ø OK.

- Ø Ozzie did you get a house as collateral?

- Ø No, I thought that was not going to be necessary? Green had mentioned in a phone call that everything was taken care of.

- Ø Ozzie, it was, but my boss likes to have a house as collateral even if it's worth very little. We called you here thinking everything was resolved. Besides your lawyer is very hard to reach and he does not returns my calls. Mrs. Salomon, I am not fleeing anywhere, I have a 14 year old daughter and I was hoping to spend Thanksgiving Day with her.

Mrs. Salomon looked at me straight in the eye.

- Ø Ozzie, I'm trying to help you. Jerry told me all about you; believe me when I say I feel for you, but it's out of my hands, I have to answer to my boss. He says he wants a property. Some people have gone this rout, only to flee, so it's not a personal thing.

I looked at Mrs. Salomon and felt her to be sincere. Deep down inside I longed for her to understand that I was not a monster. I wanted to feel like a trustworthy human. I wanted to be believed.

Ø Is there anyone you can think of that will put up their house? We can set bail at $25,000. So the collateral won't kill you. If you want to use the phone to call someone you can.

Ø Mrs. Salome I thank you for trying, but as of now I don't have anyone. Maybe my brother in PR, but that's a long shot.

Ø Well, unfortunately we are going to have to reschedule.

Ø OK, I understand.

Once again I was let down. It was easy for me to put the blame on Casper. On the ride back, I thought again; you're never going to get out of here. By the time I got back to my unit, it was feeding time. I made it back in time to sit with Steve and Mafia Joe.

Ø How did it go?

Ø At the very last minute they said I needed a house as collateral. I was not sure I could get one so I did not go through with the meeting.

Ø Wow, it looked like everything was set up to go.

Ø Yes Steve, That's what Casper lead me to believe. In this case he is not to blame. After speaking with the prosecutor, it was green lights, but once there, her boss insisted on some type of collateral; no matter how small. So I'm here. Now I have to try to get one, and I don't believe I will be able to.

Ø Damn Ozzie, that sucks.

Again, I promised my daughter I would be home. Looks like I'm having Thanksgiving here.

That evening I ate rather quickly and for the most part quietly. Joe and Steve sensed I was not in a pleasant mood. After dinner I went to my room and sat there for a while. The evening medication rounds came and left. During that time I made a list of people that might be able to help. My brother, my mother and Jackie had already said no; so I knew not to ask. I thought about a female friend, Rene; she had a paid condo. A few years ago I lent her $5000, for a crisis that came up. Turns out her ex-husband got arrested for real estate embezzlement, and she needed the funds for a lawyer. I thought surely she would help; all I needed to do was get in contact with her. Asking my brother to help was like pulling teeth. He always procrastinated and seemed too busy. By 8:30pm I decided to call Abby and tell her the bad news.

Ø Hi Nancy!

Ø Hi Ozzie.

Ø I won't be leaving today. For that matter I don't know if I will ever get out.

Ø What happened?

Ø At the last minute, the prosecutor said I needed some type of property or business. Because I don't think I will find the collateral, I did not continue with the meeting.

Ø Sorry to hear. Abby was looking forward to being with you. She has mentioned several times that she really misses you.

For a moment, I had to contain myself. I remember telling myself that unlike my cold mother, I would always be around for my children.

Ø How is she?

Ø She is fine, don't worry about her too much just take care of yourself. BTW you father emailed me. Wanting to know what was going on.

Ø Please email him back, tell him of my problem. If my brother Tony will put up the business, I'll be able to leave.

Ø Alright, I'll let him know. I'll get Abby for you.

Abby was polite as always and said that it was Okay as she understood my predicament. How ironic is life? Nancy was a person I shared 18 years with and then abandoned. She was the one I hurt the most! She did not see the breakup coming! I broke her heart. Despite all this she was now the only person that was truly concerned about me. She was also the most understanding. To her, it did not matter what I did, for she knew me well. She knew I was a good provider, and acknowledged she was grateful for loving her and for raising of her two children from a previous marriage; Axisa, her oldest daughter and Justin both now 27 and 25.

She also knew I was the best father any little girl could have. She had seen me suffer many times when I was told I could not see Jenelle and Ozzie. Nancy knew I had loved her and she loved me. She knew I dealt with her depression for the last 8 years and kept the family together. I left her thinking the grass was greener on the other side. Was it fate, destiny? I don't know. Should I go back? Can I go back? I think the damage has been done and healing has taken. It's been four years now. It's better to let nature take its course. Time tells all and heals all wounds. On the other hand, the people I thought would help me turned their back to me. Even those who claimed to have loved me. When in jail you realize who your friends really are.

It's now Friday. Three days since I spoke with Nancy and Abby. Yesterday at Thanksgiving dinner I sat with Steve and Joe as usual. There was nothing different about that day in jail. I laughed at all the idiots who thought there would be turkey, for the Thanksgiving Day menu read; turkey gravy, mashed potatoes and two other items. For a week I told many that nowhere on the menu does it say turkey. Sure it does, right there turkey. That's turkey gravy. Gravy is the subject, its gravy you fools. Anyway, although there are some very intelligent people in jail the average IQ is probably less than 100. After all, this is Florida, the state that can't even count votes. Even the recount has to be recounted.

Howard came over to me a little while ago and thanked me.

Ø Ozzie, yesterday, I spoke to my wife again for Thanksgiving. Prince set it up for me. Why are you still here? I thought you were leaving Tuesday or Wednesday?

Ø Well, I'm having some trouble with my collateral.

Ø How much is your bond?

Ø I have a bond posted already, but they are asking for a house with collateral. It's just my luck the judge seems unsatisfied with it. In any event it's going to be $25,000.

Ø How much?

Ø 25k

Before I realize it, I had put my foot in my mouth. Howard knew what my charges were. Surely he would ask himself, "Why would it be reduced so low?" Did I just reveal to him what I was doing? After all, he knew how the system works. He reached over to me, put his hand on my right shoulder as he taped it twice and said;

Ø Don't worry; maybe I can help you out. (I looked at him, what the fuck thought, I thought.)

Ø What do you mean?

Ø Don't worry; we will talk in a day or two.

Ø OK, Howard thanks.

As he walked away I watched him, making sure he was not going to strike me from behind. What is this talk of; "Maybe I can help" Is this, an attempt to get me out so that they can kill me? Was he part of the Cuban connection? Are the Cuban cousins' parts of the Latin Kings? Something did not add up. Although, Howard's' "thank you", seemed sincere, I wasn't going to let my guard down. Right after my brief chat with Howard, I made my way to the phone. The furthest away from the TV is about 20 ft. It's my favorite, as it's a little quieter.

Ø Hi, Nancy!

Ø Hi, Ozz.

Ø Any luck with any of the three people I wanted to reach.

Ø Axisa, was able to reach two. Both said no; Renee and John. The other number has changed. Your dad emailed me. He wants you to call your sister. They have a few questions and concerns. Hold on Ozz, let me call her.

Ø Hello!

Ø Hello!,

Ø Hola Sarita, como estas?.

Ø Muy bien, y tu?

Ø Well, if you were to see how skinny I've become you would feel bad, but apart from that I am as well as expected for being in jail. (With that she started balling on the phone.)

Ø My God, I'm so sorry for you. I want you to know that I love you. I love you. I love you so much. Even though we only spent summers together I love you just like I love Tony and Mom and Dad.

With that a tear rolled out of my eye. I could not speak. Without looking up or around I wiped the tear. This was new to me. How can someone love me so much? Never in my life has anyone told me three times in a row that they loved me. It was good to hear someone else, apart from the few I knew of, say, I love you.

Ø When dad was given the news he had to sit down as he felt ill. We had to calm him down. Mom, dad and Tony are truly concerned for you. Dad received Nancy's email and asked for her to call me as there seems to be a problem with your brother.

Ø Sarita, I don't know what is going on with him. He told me I had embarrassed the family and that I am getting what I deserved. He also told me that he instructed the family not to help me. Not having access to anyone's numbers I was left with very limited options.

Ø He told us to send some money for you which we did. He also said not to worry about anything that he would be in charge of helping you out. So we thought everything would work out fine. You know at one point he did say not to help you, but I think that's because he was upset.

Ø That decision of his has cost me dearly. I would never have thought he would have acted in such a way.

Ø Why did he do that?

Ø In part I believe he has my mother's genes; smart like dad, but temperamental like mom.

Ø What about your mother.

Ø Oh, no, the first thing she said was she would not help, but that's typical of her.

Ø You know I remember all those stories you and Ismael would tell about your mother. I thought you were just being kids and exaggerated. How can a mother be that way?

Ø I don't know that's what I grew up with. That was what I thought was normal. I've told you many times, growing up that she did not love us. Can you see it now?

Ø Yes, but how can it be?

Ø I would watch dad and your mother pick you up so much and I thought that was strange. It was not till my children were born that I realized the love one is capable of having for their children. I do have to tell you that I knew dad loved me and I always loved him.

Ø Yes, we all know how much you always cared for him. To me that was normal.

Ø Look Ozz, after dad and Nancy emailed each other, he asked for me to see how we could help, as Tony is very busy with the three pharmacies. Nancy and I spoke and I we were shocked to hear of the way your brother behaved. He told us not to put up our house as collateral.

Ø Sari, I don't know why. There is no danger in doing so. If I can get out I can do a program with the police and possibly just get probation. If I don't get out, I am looking at many years. So it's in my best interest to get out and help myself.

Ø OK, that's what we wanted to know. We are here to help you in anything you need. We want you to know that we all love you.

Once again the tears rolled down my eye. To be told they will help was one thing, but for me to be told they love me, well that's was just too powerful.

Ø Sari, thank you! Tell everyone that I am doing fine. I don't want dad to worry too much. As far as what I need, I just need anyone to put a house as collateral.

Ø OK, let me speak to mom and Tony. More than likely, I will be the one to do it. Remember my husband is an engineer. We designed this house.

Ø Yes, I remember passing by as it was being built. Sari, again I want you to know that there is no harm to you in doing so. Skipping out is something I could never do, especially to you.

Ø I know you won't,

Ø Let's talk tomorrow.

Ø OK, Love you!

Ø Love you also.

Ø Nancy?

Ø Yes! Thank you!

Ø You're welcome. I'll call you tomorrow and will speak to Abby.

Ø OK, Ozz, take care of yourself. By! By!

After my call with Nancy I sat on the lounge chair. My mood had now changed. For the moment I was relieved knowing that I found an answer to one of my problems. There would be more, but for now it was a victory towards getting out. The smile on my face revealed I was Ok. Prince who was making his way to the microwave veered off course and sat next to me.

Ø What's up Ozzie?

Ø Yo, I just got some good news. I believe my sister is putting up her house as collateral. Now I can do what I need to do, my civil duties.

Ø Good! Good! Maybe in a week or so, we can get out of here.

Ø I sure hope so. Every few weeks it's the same thing. Just when I think I am leaving something happens. It's almost as if I'm supposed to be here for a reason. I've given up on fighting my fate. I'm not saying I'm giving up on getting out and doing what I need to do. I've had to adjust my thinking so that I don't become bitter at life. I always say when given lemons, make lemonade.

Ø Well how is the juice so far?

Ø You know Prince, for some strange reason I've taken to writing. I don't know why, I don't know if it simply to kill time. Surely I'm not expecting anything to come out of this. I do believe it has something to do with my daemons.

Ø What's your demon? Are you seeing things?

Ø No, I'm not mad. Something happened in my life that has changed the person I've become. However, I don't talk about it. It's a tragedy, I won't say much more than that. It keeps me up at night. Now that I'm in jail I don't have too many distractions so it comes to me more often. When I was with Jackie, it all went away. For now it's just him and I. The fucker comes knocking on the door whenever he wants. One day I will put him to rest. It's like a splinter in your thumb. If you can't get it out you eventually get used to the slight pain. Even when you don't feel it, you know it's there. You know sooner or later you have to take it out or else it can get worse. But anyway Prince, for the moment I am OK. Actually, I was feeling quite well.

Ø Yes, you look relaxed. Yo Ozzie Is there is anything I can do to help you out?

Ø What do you mean?

Ø Well with your demon problem. Do you need to kick someone's ass?

Ø Oh, no, no, it's nothing like that.

Ø OK, if you need anything let me know.

Ø Well, now that you mentioned it, what about if I do need to kick someone's ass?

Ø Just give me the word, I have many friends out there; might cost you a few dollars.

Ø What do you mean?

Ø If your problem is you need to hurt someone or get back at someone, then I know people. I have friends.

Ø You mean your gang buddies?

Ø Browards' Most Wanted Baby.

Ø So it's true? I heard rumors you were in a gang.

Ø Oh, it's not rumors. It's not a secret. I ride with some bad dudes.

Ø So it's a motorcycle club?

Ø For the most part; but there are people in it that don't ride. It's more a matter of being connected.

(I started laughing, as an image came to mind.)

Ø So it's like old moms and pops riding with their "Depends" diapers on Harleys?

Ø Fuck you nigger. Do I look old?

Ø No, but you look like you haven't eaten for a long, long time.

Ø Such a dick nigger, stated Prince.

The mood was joyful. We were beyond that. Prince and I laughed.

Ø Prince, on a serious note, I have a concern and might need some help or at least some advice.

Ø What's up?

Ø I was moved from the main jail because of a threat against my life. I'm glad for the move, although there is now a looming concern. That concern I now have is that, there is a price on my head. His gang members are looking to kill me.

Ø Are you sure they are in a gang?

Ø I don't know that for sure I. Jerry told me not to worry about it too much. He said he did not believe they will do anything.

Ø Well, I know of a few gangs around here. I can look into it for you.

Ø How?

Ø How? Remember my specialty, hacking; I have access to all 50 states Department of Motor Vehicles, just the same, I can get into some government agencies files. I'll have to wait till I'm out. In the meantime I'll ask my boys to check with some other gangs about your Cuban guys. I'll need their names. Also Ozzie, you should talk to Howard.

Ø Howard! What do you know about him?

Ø He is in one of the biggest gangs. The Latin Kings.

Ø Did he tell you?

Ø Didn't have to, his tattoos tells the tale. In his gang, once in, you're a member for life. He is old, so he might have some rank and pull.

Ø What happens if he is part of the same gang as the Cubans?

Ø Then you would have been gone by now. But I don't think that is the case. Besides it's mostly the young guys that are used for stuff like that. They make a name for themselves and move up the ranks. At his age, he is beyond that.

Ø So he is not here to do me in?

Ø Na, relax.

Ø Good, so where is your gangs tattoo?

Ø Right here on my arm BMW – Browards Most Wanted.

Ø Shit Prince. All the while I thought you were just happy of owning a beamer.

For a moment we both laughed out loud. Prince gave me a little shove as he leaned into my space. He could not contain himself.

Ø Damn Prince, I got to get with the program.

Ø You're not kidding.

Ø So, Howard saw your tattoo and you saw his and both knew what was up. Right,

Ø Now you talking.

Ø What happens if your gangs are rivals?

Ø Well this is jail; it's a little different than prison. In prison there are rival gangs. You just stick with your own. Here in jail you are trying to get out, so you respect each other for the time being. Last thing you want is to pick up an assault or battery charge. That can complicate things a lot. Howard and my gang are not rivals. We respect each other. There is nothing wrong with being in a gang. Howard is not concerned about gangs, he asked me who had connections here; connections to the prosecutor, not connections to gangs. I told him to talk to you.

Ø Could that be why he told me I know who you are?

Ø Might be. I told him a little about you and me. Nothing to do with the program.

Ø OK, that makes sense to me. IF there is anyone to talk to about gangs it's him. All right Prince thanks.

Talking with Prince about Howard put me at ease a great deal. I had been a little concerned and anxious about Him. So if Howard has nothing to do with the Cuban cousins, then what could he possibly want to talk to me about? Questions came to mind as they often do. Was he going to make a demand or a threat against me? If so, how do I handle it? Prince might have offered a clue but I could not be sure about anything. Fuck it!!!

Fuck it!!! Fuck it!!! ; That's a euphemism, meaning, (don't worry about it, There is nothing you can do.) Do not take ownership of someone else's problems. Fuck it Ozz!!! Let it go, for tomorrow is another day.

Ø Howard, let's sit by the game table. It's apart from the other tables, making it good a good place to talk.

As we set the pieces, Steve came by.

Ø "Hi, Steve, we'll play later."

He knew what I meant as I did not offer him to sit and watch.

Ø Ok! Replied Steve.

Ø So what's up Howard?

Ø Just wanted to talk a little. It's been a few days and I want to see how my NY brother from another mother was doing.

Ø Well my dad did get around at 74; he could be your father. (Howard cut right through the chase.)

Ø Ozzie at 58 I can't do this anymore. I was set up. Those charges make me a habited offender. If they stick, I will spend the rest of my life in jail. I was thinking of taking on my wife's charges. She is innocent of all this. All she did was yell at the police about my recent heart surgery. She should not be suffering in jail like this. ON the phone she tells me she is OK, but I know she is not. She just doesn't want me to worry. If I have to die in jail I will, but I am going to get that mother fucker cop from Hollywood. I already put some guys on notice. If I can bond out I would, but I now have a no bond hold.

For the moment I just listened, it's what I do best. Howard's frustration was clear and I was his vent, but there was something to his story. Maybe the Hollywood police did plant that cocaine, but did Howard deserve it? Was it just his time and his destiny? What about all those sales he did and never got caught? If the drugs were planted, was it his payback for all the sales he got away with? After he carried on for 10 minutes I asked him;

Ø You're from the Latin Kings?

Ø Yes, I didn't tell you the name before right?

Ø Right

Ø I forgot.

Ø Howard, I have a few questions about gangs. I am concerned about two Cuban guys in the main jail. Talk is; they have a price on my head.

Ø What gang are they from?

Ø I don't know. I don't even know if they belong to a gang.

I explained to Howard everything that happened. He took a deep interest in what I was saying.

Ø Ozzie, if they are in a gang it's not the Latin Kings. If it's true that they have a hit on you, you have to take into consideration the gang and their rank. If it's one of our friendly gangs then I can put a truce and end it.

Ø You could do that?

Ø Ozzie I am a very powerful guy.

Ø So how will I know Howard?

Ø I need their names; from there I can get their arrest info and give it to one of our members in Washington.

Ø Are you serious?

Ø Ozzie, it's a secret, do not mention this to anyone.

Ø What are the gangs around here?

Ø Well the brothers have the CRIPS, the Bloods, and GD – Gangster Disciples. The whites in the south have the White Supremacy. Those are real racists, KKK type. The Cubans have the Zulus, real gang bangers; they will take you out in a heartbeat. If the two guys are part of that gang then you need to be really careful. There is also a motorcycle gang BMW and then you have gangs that are our friends. Those are the Netas from PR and up-north, mostly New York and New Jersey. There are also the Stones, divided in two parts, the PR Stones and the black Stones.

Ø Howard, you know your gangs.

Ø It's my life, over 35 years in it, but I'm old now, too old for this shit now. I can't spend my life in here. I promised you, there is going to be a blood bath in the Hollywood PD.

Ø Howard if I told you I could get you out, would you believe me?

Ø Why are you still here?

Ø I'm getting out any day now.

Ø You know Ozzie there is talk about your friend Prince getting out even though he had no bond hold.

Ø Damn, Howard, it's hard to keep a secret around here.

Ø I see you guys talking in the rec yard. That's why I don't talk to you too much. They say you are helping him.

Ø Maybe yes, maybe no!

Ø I don't care about that, I'm worried about myself.

Ø Howard, I can get you out, but it might require you doing something you might not want to do. Besides, I don't want you to get the wrong impression about me. Last thing I need is for the Kings to come looking for me.

Ø Ozzie, I give you my word, you won't have to worry about us. I am the one that gives the commands, especially in Broward and Miami.

Ø Howard, I don't know what I am getting into. Maybe I should just leave this alone. I have a beautiful little girl that I need to be around for.

Ø Ozzie the Kings were formed in Chicago to help and protect each other. We don't go out and kill people for the hell of it. When we do, it's because it was deserved. Many of our members sell drugs, but there is an order of command that keeps everything in place. The FBI knows that we do not go after the innocent.

Ø Are you saying no?

Ø How is it you always say Ozzie, maybe yes, maybe no. As for myself, I don't bring attention to me anymore. I stopped calling-in favors years ago. As for the Cubans, don't worry, I will protect you. So what can you tell me about getting me out?

Ø OK, Howard, I'm only telling you because you are asking. You are coming to me.

Ø Don't worry I have an idea I know more around here that you might think. There are ears all over.

Ø Ok, the program is called substantial assistance program. You cooperate with the police and help them arrest dealers and in return they give you a much shorter sentence.

Ø Yes, I know about it. I can't deal with the Hollywood police. Part of the reason I want to get out is because I am personally going after that mother fucker.

Ø Howard, you know when you fuck with the police they all come looking for you.

Ø Fuck those mother fuckers. I rather go out with them then to rot in jail. It's too late. That cop sealed his fate. This can't be stopped.

Ø Howard, you're telling me too much.

Ø Ozzie, I know, I'm telling you for a reason.

Ø Howard, I don't want to die.

Ø Ozzie, you and I are family. I promise you I got your back and will protect you and your family. I already told you I know a lot about you. There is one thing I need from you. I know I won't have to worry about you. You are a good man, concerned about your daughter, which is why I am telling you all this.

Ø Howard I need to get this straight, please don't take this the wrong way, but are you threatening me? If there is one thing about me, it is that shit does not work.

Ø Ozzie, I respect you. Don't take what I said as a threat. It's more about trusting each other.

Ø Ok, since you put it that way I guess I can understand.

Ø It's like going to war with your neighbor, or better yet when you play chess, you know all about your opponent and he about you. There comes a time when it is better not to move. So, I know about you and you about me. We know not to ever move against the other. I promise you one more time, you are completely safe with me. You have my word on that.

Ø OK, Howard. I understand. So what do you need from me?

Ø I need your contact to get me out.

Ø Howard, are you sure you want to do this?

Ø I wouldn't be here talking to you if I wasn't.

Ø How do you know I can get you out?

Ø I did a little investigation and I know you are cool. I know this was your first transaction; I knew about the two cousins. Like I said earlier don't worry about them. I'll handle that for you.

Ø What I don't know is your contact guy.

Ø Howard, you're not going to do him in right? If you are, please wait till I get out.

Ø Don't worry; as long as he had nothing to do with the guys at the Hollywood police, he is fine.

Ø OK, before I call my guy. There is something I need.

Ø What?

Ø You need to prepare a list of the guys you could turn in.

Howard, look all around. He leaned in and said

Ø Ozzie, I could give them the whole cartel.

Ø Yea, ok Howard, for real? I have to tell my guys what you could bring to the table.

Ø Ozzie, I'm not saying this again. I could bring down the entire cartel, both Mexican and Colombian.

It took me 15 seconds to respond. Time slowed down, all of the sudden I was taken to another world. Howard had in a few minutes taken me to a new land, with a new game. One I never asked to play. One I did not even want to know about. Why me? I don't want to play Howards game, but is it too late? I either play or get beaten; one thing I hated was losing. It seems I am now a player. That's why he told me so much. Once I knew what he had to say there would be no way out. Fuck it! Fuck it? Fuck it

- Ø Howard! Let's play.
- Ø I can't play chess.
- Ø Howard, fuck it, let's play.

With that a big smile came upon him. He caught on. Howard stood up and extended his hand. I also stood up and we shook hands.

- Ø I'll come to you in a day or two, as soon as I contact my guys.
- Ø All right Ozz, thank you.

Shit Ozz! Shit! What have you done? You have just entered a dangerous game. Although I knew it was a new dangerous game, I was not about to stop. I was now more intrigued as to how this would all play out.

18 TRANFORMATION

In the course of a few months, I have undergone a transformation; going from a naïve puppy in love, to a felon drug dealer, involved with gang members, thugs, and murderous. Soon, I'm to become a thief. That is, if Prince's $6,000,000 scheme materializes. I now know of a powerful man who can take down an entire drug cartel and who also has a plot to riot against an entire police department. Adding to all this, I have a contract on my life. What more can a man ask for within the course of a few months? I never did. My entire life was spent walking a straight path. In an instant it changed. There is no going back. First, thing I need to do when I get out is to get a life insurance policy. If I get taken out, my children will be taken care of. For now, I fell powerful knowing what I know. The question now becomes; how do I play the game? What are the rules? Who are all the players? Am I a pawn in the game, being moved by someone's hand? Or am I the hand moving the pawns. It's not clear to me yet. Until it comes, the best move is, not to move. I'll move when I can see it.

Without realizing I had been walking I found myself sitting on the green stool at the base of the phone. Subconsciously I was there to get in contact with my sister. I did not remember sitting down or picking up the phone. I'm not even sure for how long I've been sitting. All I know was the phone was now ringing, but who was I calling.

Ø Hello!

Ø Hello! Ozzie,

Ø Yes! Who is this?

Ø You called me.

Ø Jerry!

Ø Yes! Oh so sorry. I was day dreaming, I meant to call someone else, but now that I have you on the phone I might as well give it to you.

Ø Go ahead!

Ø Jerry, I have a guy here that wants to do the program. This guy is a big fish, the real deal. He says he can deliver drug cartel with ties to Mexico and Colombia.

Ø What's his name?

Ø Howard Escalante.

Ø I have to check with his arresting officer.

Ø Jerry, he is not going to deal with them. He said they beat him up, sent him to the hospital for nine days and also made some charges against his wife because she was yelling at them during his arrest. On top of that he claims they stole all his jewelry during the arrest and now it does not show up anywhere. I can tell you he is not going to deal with them at all.

Ø Okay, call me Monday.

Ø Well do, I said.

Ø Bye!

Ø So, long.

Without giving it much thought I called Nancy.

Ø Hello Nancy!

Ø Hi Ozz!

Ø I am well. How are you and Abby?

Ø We are fine. Hold on Ozz; let me dial your sister.

Ø Hello! Hello Ozzie, go ahead.

Ø Sari, Hola, como estas?

Ø Muy bien.

Ø Where you able to talk with the family?

Ø Yes, dad is relieved that you are ok. He is still a little heartbroken for you and wants to see you out. Don't you worry about anything; I am putting up my house as collateral for you. Dad also has some money aside for you if you need it.

- Ø Sari, thank you! I am ok with money. I just needed a property. Now, I can get out and help myself. Maybe this would be as bad as it first looked. Thank you again. I will let the lawyer know and will give the bonds man your number.

- Ø That's fine.

- Ø When do you think you can get out?

- Ø I now have to get another meeting set up between the police, the prosecutor and the lawyer. My lawyer is very hard to reach. He does not return any phone calls. All we need to do is set up a date and then I can get out. Hopefully within a week or two at most, but then being in Broward you never know.

- Ø Ok, do you need anything else?

- Ø No, nothing I can think off. Thank you again and I love you!

- Ø Love you too! Bye!

- Ø Bye.

- Ø Thank you Nancy!

- Ø Your welcome! Call me if you need anything.

- Ø Ok, I'll keep you posted. Bye!

That night I fell asleep early; perhaps 10. The confirmation about my collateral was surely good news. I now had the tools that I needed to help myself. For several minutes I thought about how my brother seems to have purposely extended my time in jail. If I left it up to him, I might have had to settle for many years. I've lost all my love for him and will make it a point never to see him again. Why did I get this treatment from him? I don't know. For the moment I had positive things to look at.

Howard was now the new player in my destiny. He told me things I did not want to know. But also I relax knowing he can possibly put an end to the Cuban cousins coming after me. Howard has forced me to ask new questions. If Jerry is able to get him out, and Howard commits a blood bath, will I be to blame? Did the Hollywood police department fuck too many people over? Do I tell Jerry of Howards motive and so run the risk of being killed by Howard? All the while, I found a sense of adventure in all this danger and I was going to see it play out. After all, it seems to be my destiny.

With that I looked around. It was now late into the evening and my bunkees were asleep. I slid my underwear down and started stroking myself. Maggie and Jackie came to mind. We were at the beach basking in the blazing sun. Their buttocks, barely covered by a skimpy bikini, faced the sun. Sweat ran down their backs. After some time they decided to cool off and so we made our way to the water, walking hand in hand. I was between them and each was holding me as I too held them by the waist. Once neck deep in the water, Maggie wrapped her legs around my right leg and Jackie wrapped hers around my other leg. The salt water made their buoyancy effortless.

As I held both around their waist, Jackie reached in front of me and grabbed Maggie by the waist. I took Jackie's left hand and placed it on Maggie's ass. One of Maggie's breasts came out of her top and her nipples stood erect. Jackie looked at her and gave her a kiss. As they kissed Jackie placed Maggie's breast back inside the bikini top. She then stood in front of me and lowered my shorts exposing my manhood. As she stroked me, Maggie made her way behind me. Jackie now standing in front of me straddled her legs around me. She pulled her bikini to the side and took me in. I placed my hands around her waist and ass. After a few minutes of thrusting she climaxed. She then stood up and turned me around towards Maggie. As Maggie placed her feet around me, she fixed her arms around my neck. With that, Jackie stood to my side. She grabbed my penis and guided it into Maggie. It took Maggie a few minutes also to reach orgasm. As I was about ready, she got off and stroked me several times as Jackie held on to my balls.

Just as I was about to cum, I heard a cough. It was not coming from the beach or the girls. It was from one of my roommates. I awoke from my wonderful dream. Fuck, I guess I'll just have to settle for the shower.

It's Monday afternoon. Thanksgiving came and left. The routine here has been the same. It seems in jail, you are looking forward to the next day. You take each as it comes, as you await your departure. It's been a few days since I've spoken to Jerry.

- Ø Hello Jerry!

- Ø Hi Ozzie! Some good news, I managed to speak with the prosecutor this morning. She has both you and Steve schedule for Dec. 12. Your lawyer, however, has to confirm. He stated that was the soonest available day for him. Where did they get this guy?

- Ø I don't know. Damn Jerry, that's another two weeks away.

- Ø Sorry Ozzie, I tried for next week, but it was not possible.

Ø Ok, I understand. What about the guy I talked to you about?

Ø Tell him I will be there Wednesday to talk to him. I know about him.

Ø Ok, Jerry thanks! I'll see you in two weeks.

Ø Viejo!

Ø What's up Ozzie?

Ø Come over here.

Ø What's up? "Jerry", my guy, is coming on Wednesday to see you.

Ø Ok, that's good I guess.

Ø Yes, it is. If he were not interested he would have said no.

Ø Ok, good. Did he say anything else?

Ø No, just to give you the message that he will be here. He did say he looked you up and knows about you.

Ø So, he knows they stole my jewelry.

Ø I have not discussed that beyond the first call.

Ø Ok, mi hermano. Thanks,

Ø Your welcome Howard.

Ø Steve, I have some good news and some bad news.

Ø What's the bad news?

Ø Looks like we both have a day set up for the meeting with the prosecutor.

Ø Finally, so we are both going on the same date.

Ø Yeap!

Ø So what's the bad news?

Ø It's on Wed. Dec 12.

Ø Well that's not bad news for me. We been here so long what's another two weeks?

Ø That's the problem Steve; it's always another two weeks, then another and another.

Ø Relax Ozzie; at least there is some light at the end of the tunnel.

Ø Yea, two weeks away. We can always see the light coming as the two weeks near but as we go up the road so does the light. It's a tease. Here I am and there it moves.

Ø Man, you should listen to yourself.

Ø Ok, Ok! I'll go back to bed. In a few days I'll make some phone calls so that my new bond can be ready.

Am I becoming institutionalized? In a few weeks I will be out. While being here I have become discontent with the outside world. Watching the news on TV and reading the paper is not what I am referring to. Two more weeks, three more weeks, it was now all too familiar. I stop thinking about the outside world. Not about my loved ones, just the world in general; about work, about buying a new place to live in, about getting a new vehicle. In here none of that mattered. I don't know if it's my writing that has calmed me down during my time spent here; allowing me to relax and accept anything and everything that comes my way, or if it's something else. For some strange reason I have embraced the time of my incarceration. For the first time in my life, I actually have some me-time. Yes, it's been forced upon me; However its time that has allowed me to evaluate and assess myself. I need not worry about paying any bills. No need to worry about working, no need to worry about food on the table. Sure, it comes at the expense of something else; nonetheless it's a new experience in my life.

Is it my destiny to write a book, or am I writing a book about my destiny? Truth is it doesn't fucking matter. "In dying he taught me more about living than I could have ever taught him while alive." For life is a journey through time. It's not the destination that's important, for the destination is death, it's about the ride; yea, yea, some will argue the destination is life after death. When you can prove it to me, I will change my mind. By prove it, I mean really prove it. Please people, don't belief all the stuff we have been propagandized with, as we grew up. Life is about living. It's about enjoying life itself. It's about dealing with the bumps on the road; new turns in the road. It's about the joy of being on a bus ride with the one you love. For we go through life overlooking every day. We strive for what tomorrow might bring, all the while ignoring the one thing we can never bring back. That is, time itself, and life. Before we realize it both will passed us by. I've learned to take life everyday as it comes. It's that life I helped take away, that has taught me so. Enjoy it; love it, no matter how bad it might seem to be. We are here today and we are gone tomorrow. For some, tomorrow has come today.

So, what is my destiny? For I have now sealed a deal with criminals, drug dealers, scammers, thieves and murderers. What have I become? Who have I become? For that matter who am I? My handshake with them was my word; my promise of my involvement; a commitment to help three individuals as well as myself, get out of jail. No written document was made, for no written document could hold up this agreement. It was sealed with something more important than any pen and paper. It was sealed with a simple handshake and backed by a commitment, for the handshake sealed the agreement; an agreement that death would befall anyone of us that would cross the other. It was our pledge to ourselves and to the others that we would stand behind each other, and more important behind our word. For we agreed not to turn against anyone other, no matter what the situation might be. From now on, anything that would happen, anything we would uncover, anything we would say or do, would remain a secret amongst us. Failure to do so would get us killed. This I promised to myself, I promised to the others, and they to me.

So again who am I? I came in to jail one way, but I leave with something more, and something new, and all for what? Each man had his own motive; as for myself I too have a selfish one. All I wanted was to get out. Get out so that I could get my girl back, for she was the only cure for my pain and suffering. Jackie was my escape from my demons. As of today I know of no other way to do so. So, is it her I really need by my side, or is it the demon by my side I need to loose. I have a date set for Dec. 12. I shall be out then. The plan is set. All I need now is to get out and execute the next phase. Playing chess during the evening will occupy my time, as well as writing will distract me from him.

It's now Dec. 10, which brings me to my current time in my writing. Not much has happened the past few days. Prince, Steve and I are filled with anticipation. In a few days we will all be out. First thing on the agenda for me is to get laid and put some muscles back on. Off course, executing the plan and seeing it through is off the upmost importance. Staying out of jail is the ultimate goal. There are off course other things to consider. Staying alive is one of them, as I am too aware of the price on my head. Then there is the matter of the $6,000,000. That one is on the back burner. I'm not banking on it. For me I view it as a slight possibility and nothing more. Tomorrow, Prince is due to leave first. His appointment is for early am courts. That means he will be processed and freed by the evening. Steve and I have pm court the following day. So it might be Thursday morning for us when we get released. By now, what's one extra day?

Thursday morning, 8am, "Steve Upper, Ozzie Vargas, get ready for pm court." Yes, finally we are getting out of here. The drill is all too familiar for us. However, this one we will savor. We were cuffed to each other and taken to the intake unit to wait for the bus ride to the courthouse. The bus that came was not the usual big one. It was the small paddy wagon van with three compartments in all; the front for the driver followed by a small section that holds two people, and then the rear which holds eight. The driver was not the typical Broward deputy female. This one was a slim blond, blue eyed woman. It's not being blond or blue eyes that was so different, it was that she did not look like the regular females deputies. Of all things, this female deputy looked feminine. She did not look masculine. She did not have mustache hair; she did not weight over 175 lbs. For the most part she was just a regular girl.

Steve and I sat in the middle compartment, our backs facing forward. To see out through the front we had to twist our bodies sideways. Looking straight back towards the rear, through a dark tinted partition, we could make out four inmates. They were wearing green uniforms. Those were the inmates from the next jail, which was only one block away from us. The first 15 minutes of the ride was mostly quiet. By now we had the rout figured out. Steve kept turning sideways to see out the front, all the while handcuffed to me.

- Hey Ozzie!
- Yeah!
- I think we are turning around.
- What makes you think that?
- It just seems to me, we are going back.
- Na, I doubt it.

From the rear you could hear someone say, "We heading back. Maybe they left someone behind." Several minutes later we were at the main gate of the adjacent jail. Much talk is coming from the rear. "Steve, we probably have to pick someone up." As the pretty deputy opened the rear compartment she announces "there will be no court today. There is an evacuation of the entire courthouse due to a natural gas leak on the adjacent construction site. All buses have been dispatched to pick up all the inmates."

Ø Just our fucking luck Steve! What are the odds of something like this happening? Off all people we know, it happens on the day that we are scheduled to leave.

Ø Ah, shit Ozzie, looks like we won't be out this week.

Ø Steve, I can't believe this. It will take at least one more week to set up a new meeting.

For some reason I was not surprised; after all it's always one more week for me. The most disappointing thing was, having to call Abby to tell her of the news. Will I ever get out? Will Abby be convinced that I will ever get out?

As we made our way to the intake unit, we undressed for inspection, got dressed again, and then were given four slices of bread with peanut butter; which we were to take to our cells. As we entered our unit people were not surprised to see us so soon. The news of the courthouse evacuation had just finished playing on TV. I shook my head to Howard, and I made my way to the table. He came over and I explained the drama. Howard said,

Ø Ozzie, you were not supposed to leave today. It's not in your cards. You'll be out soon.

Does Howard know something I don't know? Did he plan this? Is he a god? If there are gods, what do they say? If there are gods, is there one assigned to me? I think not. It's just plain destiny. It's my fate.

First thing I did after lunch was call Jerry.

Ø Jerry.

Ø Hi Ozzie! There's been an evacuation at the courthouse.

Ø Yes Jerry, I know. I was en route and the bus was turned back.

Ø Ozzie, I'll try to set it up next week. I know you want to be released. Just, be patient.

Ø That's easy for you to say.

Ø I'll call the prosecutor and will let you know.

Ø Ok, Jerry. Thanks! I'm sorry to bother you so much. I could never reach my lawyer. So far, all the info I get is from you.

Ø Ok, don't worry.

Ø Thank you!

The next call was to Nancy. She was on standby to pick me up. I explained the bad news and asked her to make Abby aware. As usual she told me "Not to worry about anything. Just take care of yourself and let me know when there is new info." For some eerie reason, I was not so disappointed. Was Howard right? I was not supposed to leave that day. Why? Because I still have not met Edwin Tejada. You see, he is part of my destiny. He had something I needed and something I needed to know. Would there be a price to pay for what Edwin would tell me? Only time would tell. For the time being I just needed to continue to be patient. There would be enough time to be out by Christmas. The important thing was to be there for Abby, so that she did not have to suffer or worry about me, during the holidays.

Ø Boricua?

Ø Si!

Ø Yo Lo sabia. Bienvenido,

Ø Hablara contigo?

Ø Bien!

He was assigned to room 3.

Ø I take it his PR?

Ø Yeap! How would you know that?

Ø Steve, I told you that I spent many summers in PR. Puerto Ricans come in all sizes and shapes, from blue eyed blonds to black hair, black skin people. The natives of PR were Taino Indians. They called the island "Boriken". So we refer to ourselves as Boriqua. The term differentiates us from the rest of the islands in the Caribbean. There are no more native Indians in PR. The last 500 years has brought Europeans, mostly the Spanish as well as slaves from Africa. His size, color and especially his hair tells me he has Indian descent. Dominicans and Cubans, as well as Mexicans have slightly different features.

Ø Ozzie, that's the guy the Cuban cousins sent to kill you.

Ø Fuck off! If there is something I know is that this guy is not a threat.

- Ø How can you be so sure?

- Ø Instinct, just a feeling.

- Ø So you know for sure he isn't going to kill you?

- Ø Just as sure as I am about you.

- Ø Man, I can easily pull the trigger on you.

- Ø Steve you couldn't hurt me if you tried. It's not your nature. I'm not saying you wouldn't do so if you needed to protect yourself, it's just not your nature.

- Ø Yea, you got that right.

- Ø That guy that just came in, because on his age and the way he carries himself as well as the tattooed teardrops, tells me has killed, but to me he is not a concern. Yo Steve, after this game I need to make a phone call or two.

- Ø I also need to call.

- Ø Hello!

- Ø Hi Ozzie!

- Ø Hi, Jerry!

- Ø Ozzie, I got a hold of the prosecutor. The earliest day available is Jan 2nd at 1:30pm.

- Ø Fuck man. I won't see Abby for Christmas.

Ø I'm sorry Ozzie. I tried to get you out by Christmas, but your lawyer and prosecutor could not work it out. Jan 2nd is the soonest. The judge will also be away from the 21st through Jan. 1st.

- Ø Ok, Jerry. There's nothing I can do. Thanks for your help. If I relied on my lawyer I would not know what was going on.

- Ø Your welcome!

Once again, one more time, another few weeks, it's a never ending story; it's a broken record. There was nothing I could do. Worrying and getting upset would do me no good. I made my way over to Steve and told him of the news. Steve asked me if he was set for the same day.

Ø I'm not sure Steve.

Ø I'll have to check with Jerry again. I assumed it would be the same day.

Steve expressed a little disappointment. He also had plans to spend Christmas with his son in law and granddaughter. That evening I got back on the phone and called Prince.

Ø Yo Prince!

Ø Ozzie!

Ø Yea!

Ø Yo what's up?

Ø More of the same fucked up news.

Ø Yea, I heard about it.

Ø How,

Ø I've been spending some time with Jerry.

Ø That soon?

Ø Yea, same day out; this guy does not play. So I heard it's going to be right after New Year's?

Ø Yup, a few more weeks again.

Ø Well, I'm waiting for you to come out. There are some things we need to discuss. That $6 deal is looking good, but I need you.

Ø Ok, Prince. I'll see you soon.

Ø You got it!

Knowing I had two more weeks to go, I decided to relax again and make the most of it. My writing had taken me this far and I knew there was something missing, a small piece that would tie up everything and everyone. Like Steven Hawkins, the astrophysics who tried to unify Einstein's theory of relativity with time, space and quantum's mechanics I too needed something to tie up Prince, Steve, Howard and myself. The answer would be

Edwin.

Edwin Tejada, the man called in the states by his nickname, Indio Canovana. Indio meaning Indian and Canovana, being the town in PR he grew up in. The plan I had set in place was a good one. Getting out was going to happen with or without Howard, but Howard had something on me; He had the upper hand. He promised me help and protection from the Cuban cousins and for that I was to help him get freed through Jerry. But Howard had put the scare on me. He knew I had learned too much about him. That put me in an uncomfortable position. Knowing too much might end up costing me my life in the future. I reasoned, after everything was set and done, I might be eliminated. Why, because dead man tell no tales. Edwin was the answer. What I would uncover over the next few days would put me in a winning position. He would be the extra pawn that would make the difference in this new

game I've been forced to play. This pawn was to become a queen.

Again, Howard was right. Dec. 12th was not my day to leave. My day to leave was destined to be in the future, Jan. 3rd. I recognized this when Jerry told me the new date. Subconsciously, I knew there was a missing link. Within the next few days I would learn why Edwin was that link.

Two more sleepless nights passed. Calderon had been picked up by immigration. Husain, the alpha shift guard approved of my recommendation for help with Breakfast. Keating a long haired, midsize Italian American had expressed interest in taking Calderon's place. He seemed eager to work, where others saw it as a chore. It's been several days now that he and I served breakfast together. Keating, did not like the bologna fed to us during breakfast, thus he would not save any of the extra trays. Therefore, I had almost every night over 20 slices. I would pack 5 or 6 bags of sandwich. Each bag consisting of four slices of bread, four slices of meat and one apple sauce. Steve was always on the list, so was Howard, and Rico Acosta, a 49 year old, Christian Cuban, as well as some others. My change to them for the food was nothing.

- Ø Ozzie!

- Ø Yes, Howard! Come and talk.

- Ø Boriqua, what's up?

- Ø Hello Ozzie!

Ø Ozzie, Edwin is from my town in Hollywood. We know some of the same people. Ozzie, Edwin is waiting for his commissary on Friday. If you can help him out, I'll give you a few items.

Ø Oh, don't worry Howard. Edwin, are you hungry now?

Ø A little.

Ø I have a sandwich. Would you like it now?

Ø A little later, (Edwin replied).

Ø Edwin, Ozzie is writing a book.

Ø Well Howard I was just writing to kill time and because I don't sleep at night. I don't expect to make a book out of it.

Ø What is it about? (asked Edwin).

Ø It's about my life. I am trying to find answer as to what were the events and encounters that have brought me here. During my stay here I encountered people that became entangled in my life.

Ø So why don't you sleep at night?

Ø I don't talk about that.

Ø I understand.

Ø So, Howard is Edwin part of your group.

Ø I know him for a few years now from the neighborhood.

Ø But does he run with you?

Ø Edwin is from the Netas, straight from PR. He is an old timer.

Ø Shit! You, kidding me?

Ø I was first locked up in PR at the age of 17. That's when I had to join the association.

Ø What do you mean association? Is that your term for a gang.

Ø Oh, it's not a gang as you think. It's a long story. The group is recognized by the government of PR as an association.

Ø So the Kings and the Netas get along well?

Ø Yes, the Kings are more like a gang. Howard was a real gang banger. Ozzie, do you know who Howard is?

I looked at Howard for a clue as to whether I should reveal what I know. Howard just nodded without saying a word.

Ø Yes, Howard told me who he is.

Ø Howard is one of the leaders. The decision maker, the Latin Kings is a worldwide group. The Kings and the Netas are brothers. Many PR are either from one or the other. My brothers in NY are Kings. I was raised in PR so I became a Neta. But when there is a rival group we join each other.

For the next half an hour Howard and Edwin told stories about being in jail. One in particular stood out. It gave me a real insight as to Howard's character. Howard went on to say,

Ø I remember one time in prison. I found myself being surrounded by over 20 Crips. A Mexican, who was also surrounded, had a machete cut out from a metal plank. I'm sure he must it paid a lot to whoever made it for him. He threw me a shank and we started fighting. Luckily we were the only ones with weapons. One thing you learn in jail is that you do not let go of your shank until you are finished with it. We were charged and I managed to stab 6 or 7 guys. In a group fight, the minute one or two guys sees blood, they back up and run away. The Mexican also inflicted much damage. Before I knew it, there was a big guard that grabbed me by the neck and shoulders. As I turned to stab him I noticed the uniform. I poked that mother fucker two times in his side. All the guards came running over to help him. The guards beat me and the Mexican. I was sent to 30 days in solitary confinement. At the trial the judge ruled that we were not guilty, as were acting in self-defense.

Edwin had already known the story and kept nodding in acknowledgement of what Howard was saying.

Ø Most of the Kings I know, have heard about Howard's story.

Ø Ozzie, I was a real badass. I used to knock people out with one punch.

Ø I know the feeling Howard. Big adrenaline rush.

Ø That's right!

Ø Edwin, I'm fascinated with the story of the Neta. Within the next few days I would like to learn more.

Ø Sure Ozzie, anytime you want to.

Ø Ok, fellows well talk later.

Christmas was fast approaching. The mood seems to be a little happier. That was evident by the new festivities at Alpha head count. If there was a memo sent out, I was not privy to it. At about 11:15 each night Hosan would go into each room for head count. He had to check that the person assigned to the room was there and alive. If one was sleeping he would kick the post of the bed, and wake you up; turns out there was now a competition. Each room would have one guy that would pose as sleeping. As Hosan would call his name, that person would release a thunderous fart. As disgusting as it might seem, it was hilarious; the louder the sound the louder the laughter. For the next three nights, as punishment, Hosan would leave the lights on till 7am. I don't know if he broke us or we just did not find it funny anymore, but on the 4th night we stopped.

It's 5:30am. Rich Acosta, who is sleeping in the adjacent room, has been snoring for the last one and a half hours. It was shortly after breakfast that I laid myself to sleep, but as of yet have not been able to. It's not Rich that has kept me up. My demon is coming and going. I'm trying to shift my thoughts. Tonight I keep thinking about my children. Ozzie keep coming to mind as well as Christian. Christian is away in college at Albany. I say he's away but to him, he is home. For he and his mother left the city in search for a more peaceful place. Like Ozzie Jr. and myself, Christian has a great physic and loves to work out. His Facebook page has clips of him and I, lifting in the gym together; he also has a few clips dunking the basketball at school. Ozzie is also away. I try not to think too much about him. It's almost six years now.

Tonight, as I sit on the stool, the plastic one, that which I call my seat, I write. Writing is my escape. My left shoulder is leaned against the wall of the entrance to the room. It's at that spot where enough light comes in for me to see what I am writing. My left leg sticks out of the entrance as my right lies within. Yes, the writing keeps me distracted. Like my body, my mind is also halfway in and halfway out. There is a saying; I think therefore I am. Having said that, am I dreaming, or am I going crazy? I realize I need professional help. I want to cry. I am hurting deep inside and I can't escape it. The clock hanging on the wall across from me reads 6am. From where I sit, it's just below my eye level. Right under it sits the deputy. A support beam about 16 in diameter obscures him. It's a good thing, for the post covers my face; tears once again flow on to this pad I write on. When it happens, I don't make any noise. I also do not look up or out. My face stays looking downwards. Why is that? Am I ashamed? Maybe I am, for the first few years after it happened I would not look into my eyes while in front of a mirror. I hated the man looking back at me. I hated what he did. It's all, my fault. Yes, the reason for my writing is not to tell a story, it's an escape, and a self-analysis. If I want to continue living, I will need to seek help. I don't want to resort to any drugs. Also, I don't think I will seek a woman's companionship as an escape. For that matter, I don't think I will ever open up my heart again to anyone. Spending money foolishly is also not the answer. Now that the blood money is gone, so is the woman. However, my demon is loyal. He has not abandoned me. He sits in the background patiently and when all is calm and quiet he appears. I wish I had a better friend. I want to get rid of this loyal guy. Is he driving me crazy? I think, therefore I am.

19 EDWIN TEJEDA

Edwin Tejeda, Yes! Yes, it was, Edwin, the least unassuming character of them all. The insignificant short little Indian; the one no one would bother to take a second look at. The one no one cared about; yet it was Edwin that would change the course of my life and the one that would have the most profound effect? He made me open my eyes and made me see. As the saying goes, good things come in small packages; to which some might reply, and so does poison. So Edwin, unbeknownst to me, was my destiny. Harold was right. December 12 was not the day I was supposed to go home. September 12 was my destiny. So, now that I have met him, was he my destiny or was I his? Was he to be the great thing in a small package or was he to be a poison? Will we uncover more blood money or would he create it? Yes! Yes! Yes, it was Edwin my new destiny and so maybe, I his?

Following is a copy and paste from a local newspaper.

Broward Courthouse gas-leak evacuation disrupts busy morning

December 12, 2012|By Tonya Alanez and Rafael Olmeda, Sun Sentinel

FORT LAUDERDALE — It wasn't court as usual Wednesday morning.

A gas line rupture at a construction site next to the main Broward County Courthouse caused a 90-minute evacuation of the building, disrupting hearings, trials and weddings of couples eager to mark their nuptials with a 12-12-12 anniversary date.

Three people went to the hospital with complaints of nausea and vomiting.

"It was a little crazy," Iris Siple, chief administrator for the Clerk of Courts, said. "It's just a hub of activity all the time here, and any kind of break in service causes a lot of chaos and uncertainty."

Once the courthouse doors were reopened at about 10:40 a.m., business and weddings — about 16 by 2 p.m. — quickly resumed, Siple said. "The weddings went off without a hitch and they're happily married couples now."

When a backhoe ruptured a high-pressure underground natural gas line at about 7:30 a.m. at the construction site of a new courthouse, hissing could be heard and the pressure sent a small cloud of dust into the air.

A now-demolished parking garage used to sit on the site, about 25 feet south of the Main Jail and adjacent to the existing courthouse at 201 SE Sixth St.

The evacuation began at about 9 a.m., sending hundreds of lawyers, litigants, jurors and judges to mill about outdoors until the doors reopened.

First-appearance court was halted, a Sawgrass Middle School field trip to the Sheriff's Office crime lab was cut short and a sequestered jury that was to begin its deliberations early Wednesday in the Seth Penalver murder case was seen leaving the courthouse in vans. The jury resumed its work at about 11:30 a.m.

Traffic was diverted and dozens of construction workers were evacuated while Fort Lauderdale Fire Rescue's hazmat team secured the leak. Firefighters checked each floor of the jail with a monitor to ensure there was no danger, said Matt Little, spokesman for Fort Lauderdale Fire Rescue.

Gas supplies to the jail and courthouse were turned off, and the repair to the broken line — approximately six to eight feet below the surface — was expected to be a "daylong project," Little said.

Despite the disruptions, Broward Chief Judge Peter Weinstein said he would rather be "safe than sorry."

"We made a very fast decision, better to evacuate people and be safe," Weinstein said. "I just didn't want to take any chances."

Back in September, two men suffered minor injuries at the same site when a four-story parking garage collapsed during the structure's demolition. A thunderous sound could be heard and tremors could be felt inside the courthouse.

20 THE DAY HAS COME

The time has come and I was now ready. I saw the plan, I arranged it, and structured it. This time, I knew it was to be. I knew I was leaving. I knew I was going home; but where was home? Having lived on my own since 16, has thought me how to survive. But has it really? Could my survival be attributed to the genes handed to me by my father? Oh, well! It doesn't really matter. At the very least, it gave me the confidence of knowing I could survive anywhere on earth. Because of this, I was now relaxed; knowing I was getting out today. For some reason I am leaving with more than I came in with. For I came in with a pair of sandals, a pair of jeans with a whole on one knee, a black Hugo Boss t-shirt, a driver's license, one credit card and one gold ring. Oh, and my loyal friend the demon. He has not escaped. He came in with me and now leaves with me. Today I also leave with my plan, my writing and most importantly my new destiny.

Arrangements have been made within the past two weeks. I sat with Jerry, Casper, Mrs. Salomos and her boss Galliger. His office was full of Baseball memorabilia. It was there I plead guilty and signed my substantial assistance papers. It was there that, for the second time, I sealed my fate. The bondsman had prepared the paperwork for collateral and had already presented it to the court; all that was needed was for the honorable Liz Porter to sign off. From Galliger's office we proceeded to the judge's chamber, where she signed it and so now everything was complete. I was allowed to leave or should I say be processed, because in Broward County jail it is easy to get in, but slow to get out. I knew 10 – 12 hours was the time needed for the internal processing of papers and I also knew there would be a 90% chance of having to wait for the next morning. And so the next morning it was. It was about 11 am and Sheila one of my favorite person in the world, my loving cousin, was to pick me up.

After being released, my first order was to go to Casper's office and sign a paper. And so I left the entrance to the jail. As I walked across the street, I had an eerie feeling; for I was free. There were no chains, no handcuffs, and no uniform to reveal that I was a criminal. People did not seem to notice me. People did not seem to care. My altered eagle was ahead of me. He knew who I was. He knew where I was going. He called me a criminal, but no one heard him. I caught up to him and put him away. I was free, yes, free at last, but at what price?

At Casper's office I made a call. Sheila, I am out. She was ready: ready to pick me up. Where are you? At the corner of 2nd ave and 6th St. it took her 30 minutes to arrive. By now, I have grown to become patient. For all I did in jail was wait. It was January, the air was cool and I was free. The sunlight was everywhere I went and everywhere I looked. It was warming me, as I stood on the corner looking down the street towards the oncoming traffic. One would think I would be filled with anticipation, but that was not the case; for as I stood waiting I was grateful for being able to bask in the sun. I was grateful to be out, happy to smell the fresh air; happy to be able to walk around at will; with no chains on and with no one watching me. More importantly, I was happy to be alive. Despite my loss of muscle; I was still a healthy person. I was taking it all in. It did not matter to me if I needed to wait a minute, an hour or a day. I was free for the moment, and I relished every minute of it.

Finally I saw it; the gray mom mobile. Sheila was a mom of two beautiful girls, and wife to a loving husband. The van was across the street and fast approaching. I noticed she was alone and as she neared the corner I waived at her; just as someone would flag down a taxi. She pulled right up to me and I entered the front passenger seat. With that she leaned over and gave me a kiss and a hug. It was the first time in six months I had been hugged and kissed. It was a warm feeling, one of love and concern. How are you she asked; hungry I replied. With Sheila, there was no need for formalities. She asked,

- Ø "What would I like to eat?"

Holy shit! I thought. I have a choice? I can decide where and when I want to eat. It really made no difference to me.

- Ø Fast and cheap was my reply. At the moment I am broke, not a single penny.
- Ø Don't worry; I have some money for you. Mom and dad game me $100. And I also have $100.

These people were truly a loving family, and so I swallowed my pride and said *thank you*. Just as it was with my dad, it was with Sheila. Not too many words needed to be spoken. Love was always there and it was felt.

A few blocks down the road I saw an all too familiar place. Nope, not the jail, but a hamburger place. *There I said.*

- Ø Order me the biggest burger with large fries and a soda.

As I ate, I did feel like a king. It took me about three minutes to devour that food.

A yummy greasy burger!

As I ate in the van, Sheila proceeded to drive to Coconut Creek. That's where my mother lives. To this day I still find it odd to say mom. Nonetheless, I was headed there; for it was there I had some of my clothing. The ride took no more than 20 minutes. Along the way, Sheila brought me up to speed on people and events. At the gated entrance Sheila announced herself. My mother buzzed her in. Two quick left turns is all it took. As we approached her house, she waited by the curb in anticipation, almost as if she loved me.

As I exited the van she took a good look at me and hugged me. Tears rolled down her eyes. How odd, I hugged her and said hi, it was my second hug and kiss within 30 minutes and it was strange. What was wrong with me, I thought for a second, for I felt nothing. Not only did I not feel anything I did not want anyone's pity. Raul, my stepdad, came out and hugged me also. Ok, now this is really getting weird. I said hi and with that we all entered the house. Raul had opened the garage door as he knew there were thing there I needed to get.

As usual my mother offered me food and invited me to the kitchen. She took out two plastic bags which she filled with can goods and things she knew I liked to eat. I told her I needed to get some items I had left in the upstairs bathroom. For the first time in six months I looked at my complete self in the mirror, a full glass mirror where I could see my head through toes. Not a plastic distorted 8 X 12 inch mirror, but a clean full floor one. Immediately I lost myself. I lost track of time, who is that? I thought. There was a frail looking creature staring at me. I could see his collar bone. I could see his pronounced jaw. I could see his thin arms. I realized why my mother cried. I was someone else and not the strong muscular Ozzie she once knew. I was now a frail unkempt aged man. I too felt sorry for the person now before me. For it was not the man I once knew. It was someone else, both on the inside and outside. It was a person I did not want anyone to see. It was someone I needed to burry. That person looking at me consisted of two different people. It was not since my high school years that I looked like the man in the mirror, but more importantly, that man, the creature that was staring back at me, was not me. That man was dead and I knew it. That man who occupied my body was gone, no longer allowed to exist.

The man looking at his reflection was now a different person; a person with the knowledge that I would have to kill again. He was a sinister, person. If I saw what my mother just saw I guess I would also cry, but crying was never my nature. Only one thing ever brought tears to my eyes, but I was not going there now. I had lost track of time. How long did I engage the man in the mirror? Was it a minute, or 10 or perhaps an hour? Surely if it was an hour I would have noticed. So maybe 10 minutes, but then again I wasn't too sure. Before I realized it, I was standing in the garage with a few things I had gathered while in the bathroom. My mother offered me a bag to put things in. With that she also handed me $150. I just took it and said thank you. I am not sure if I said love you, for that was all too strange. Sheila and Raul helped me carry a few bags to the mom mobile and with that I was off to my next destination, Coral Springs. It was only a short ride.

21 JUSTIN'S HOUSE

It's all vague, the ride to Justin's house, only five minutes from my mothers. Justin my loving stepson, whom I raised since he was three, who was a wonderful kid growing up. He was a child with no malice. He was an artist by the age of three and was already doing cartoon characters. A few years later he was drawing portraits. If there was one thing he loved to do apart from drawing, it was dancing. I often wondered why the bottom ends of his long sleeve sweaters were always cut opened. It wasn't until one day at a restaurant with Jackie that I figured it out. Ok, I did not figure it out, he disclosed it to me. While break-dancing he would put his thumb through the rip so that the bottom material would allow him to spin on his hand while reducing friction.

Anyway I now find myself in front of a mirror again. This time I don't know how I got here, for I don't recall going up to the third floor where he resides. I don't know how I got in or how my items I brought in. I do recall a shopping cart with some of my personal belongings by the kitchen. Justin was at work, as well as his beautiful girlfriend Asia. I did not have keys, all I knew was I was in his home. For a second time today, I found myself in front of a mirror. This time I stood naked as the shower was ran. The mirror was starting to fog, which I thought was a good thing. I did not want to see that man anymore.

What had happened to me? What had made me change? Was it September 9th, 2006, or was it my plan? Was it Jackie or was it Edwin Tajada? I was glad the man in the mirror was fading with the fog. I stood there and for a moment thought about Abby. I could not allow her to see that man in the mirror. That man was a dead man. I knew I needed a day or two to feel comfortable with my new self and with my new person.

For the first time in six months, I had a shower all to myself. I stood under the hot water for a while. Was I thinking? Was I daydreaming? None of the above. I was relaxing, enjoying and savoring the moment. I was out of jail and it felt good. I did not realize it but I think I was there for a long time. I think I tried to scrub myself of all the cells in my body that have been in direct contact with jail. Maybe I was daydreaming. No matter. It felt good to be free. It felt good to be alive. I excited the shower and blow-dried my hair, followed by a shave. I tried to make the least possible eye contact with the man in the mirror. But, I do have to say, he now looked clean.

Within minutes of exiting the shower I found my way to the kitchen. Everything in the refrigerator looked good. Some items were not so healthy. What's the difference I thought? I might be killed soon anyway, might as well depart happy. I sampled different items and quickly settled down on the table with my laptop. The short term priority was to gain some weight and get laid. If there was something I loved, and at this point missed a great deal, it was females. Several minutes on my laptop, I discovered old unread e-mails. From there it was on to 'Plenty of Fish', a dating website. After reactivating the account I manage to send out about 50 Hi's; for I kept it short and simple, after all I had some nice pictures of myself. It's what people look for anyway. If they like what they see they may or may not read through the profile. I just threw it out there about 50 Hi's, to see what would stick, who would respond. Before I knew it Justin and his girl arrived from work.

It was now 7 pm. It was a nice long welcome hug. Once again I felt loved. We chatted for an hour or two and then we retired for the evening. Well for me that meant, I was in my room; actually my nearly acquired occupied room. As the bed there was a small 2X4 mattress, not my size at all. I laid on a rubber mattress on the floor with my laptop within reach. By now I had a few replies from, the fish in the sea. So, as usual it was in the early morning I feel asleep. This time however, I chose to sleep when I wanted, in a room all by myself with no one looking over me.

Next morning was my favorite; my scrambled eggs with ham and cheese, as much as I wanted and accompanied by all the coffee I wanted. I was alone in the house as the occupants were off to work. As per our arrangement, Sheila picked me up at 12. First order was to go to the flea market. There I would have my cell phone flash to Metro. Within a few minutes I had a number, not one that identified me, but one that would give me access to others. A cell phone number! Quickly I started to integrate myself into the system, or should I say the main stream; for I had different opinion than most people do about the system. What system you might ask? Well that's for another topic. Suffice to say, that for the moment I was becoming normal. I was glad to have a cell phone again. Being in jail has thought me how significant small things can be. Simple things we take for granted.

Next stop of the day was? Anyone? Anyone? Well the gym; one of my favorite things in the world. I don't know which I like better; getting laid or working out. Anyways, once there I found myself at the leg section. It was the same gym I went to before my incarceration. There were a few familiar faces. Two of which asked me what had happened to me, without giving it much thought I replied; I was locked up. One was in disbelief, but it was obvious I was away; away from the weights and away from food.

I never really cared about anyone and for that mattered never cared about what people thought about me. I found no reason to lie. With me it is what it is. No sense in hiding from the truth. Actually, the truth does set you free. Being back at the gym felt good. I felt free and I was grateful; grateful for life and grateful to be alive. I knew in a few months I would bring my body back to speed or at least would add 10 pounds of muscle. After the gym I walked back to the house about a mile away. The Florida weather was cool and I relished the moment. I now had a phone and a gym membership.

Next on the agenda was to see Abby. I would give myself another day to do so; for I started to feel comfortable in my new own skin or I should say in someone else's body. Mentally I had changed; I was not the same person I used to be when I entered jail. I was now someone else. I just did not know who.

Third day out - Abby Day. Finally, the time has come, for the first time in six months I was to see the most important thing in the world. Abby was the joy of my heart, the greatest love of my life. Sure I loved all my other children as well, but Abby and I were attached to each other. For years on end she would get up in the middle of the night and make her way between her mother and me. The person I should have the least fear off was now the one I was now most afraid off. But afraid of what? Afraid why? To her I was just dad and to me she was still the greatest love of my life. But I was now a changed man. Someone else in the body she once knew. Would I be found out? Would I be able to keep my composure? Justin had picked her up. As she made her way into the house I got a good look at her. She was grown up; a young girl in a woman's body. I made my way to her and hugged her. All of a sudden all my fears went away. Nothing seemed to matter. A tear rolled down my eye. I could not say one word. Justin walked over and hugged us both. For a brief moment, the old me was back. Love had prevailed. Nothing needed to be said, no words needed to be spoken. I was once again Abby's dad. Just as I had an unspoken love for my dad, I had an unspoken love for my daughter, far beyond words. As we separated we could see each other's watery eyes. It was a wonderful moment, with that we sat in the living room and just started talking. I explained to her what had happened. Something I never did, was lie to any of my children. Today would be no different. We shared dinner and talked some more. She seemed rather fascinated by how things worked in jail. Without going into to detail I told her about it. After several hours Justin and I took her home and then we retired for the evening.

My new friends were now waiting for me. That is the girls from POF. Two things were on the agenda. First was getting laid, followed by hooking up with Prince. It would be a few days before I would catch up with him. Through my laptop, and phone, I now had contact with old and new friends. Vickie was first on my list. I e-mailed her that evening and she responded. Vickie was a sexy, beautiful, voluptuous Colombian woman. She was all tits and ass, with a beautiful face to go along. I had met her right before I got locked up.

Jackpot! That was my first impression.

She was surprised to hear from me. She thought I had dismissed her. After explaining the situation we agreed to meet. Vickie was well to do and owned several condos in the heart of Miami, a perfect catch for any man. Little did she know how often I caressed her and myself while in jail. Two days later we met at her place. She was wonderful and I quickly took a liking to her. Life was getting good. By now I had a few dates lined up. You know the girls or should I say the fish in the sea. I was eating well, working out and well on my way to normalcy.

22 PRINCE

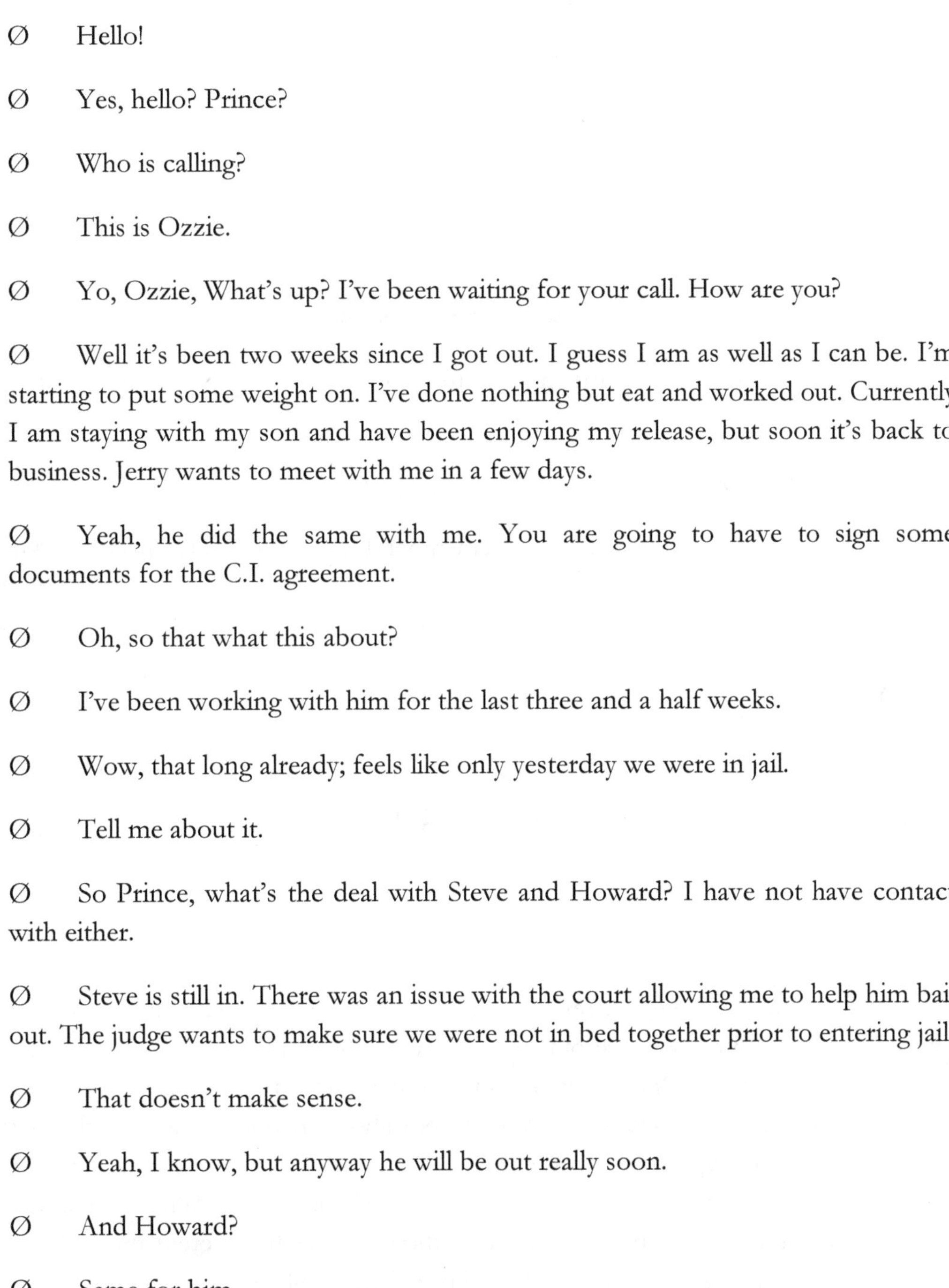

Ø Hello!

Ø Yes, hello? Prince?

Ø Who is calling?

Ø This is Ozzie.

Ø Yo, Ozzie, What's up? I've been waiting for your call. How are you?

Ø Well it's been two weeks since I got out. I guess I am as well as I can be. I'm starting to put some weight on. I've done nothing but eat and worked out. Currently I am staying with my son and have been enjoying my release, but soon it's back to business. Jerry wants to meet with me in a few days.

Ø Yeah, he did the same with me. You are going to have to sign some documents for the C.I. agreement.

Ø Oh, so that what this about?

Ø I've been working with him for the last three and a half weeks.

Ø Wow, that long already; feels like only yesterday we were in jail.

Ø Tell me about it.

Ø So Prince, what's the deal with Steve and Howard? I have not have contact with either.

Ø Steve is still in. There was an issue with the court allowing me to help him bail out. The judge wants to make sure we were not in bed together prior to entering jail.

Ø That doesn't make sense.

Ø Yeah, I know, but anyway he will be out really soon.

Ø And Howard?

Ø Same for him.

Ø How do you know?

Ø Well I don't, but I believe he is still in.

Ø Ok, I'll ask Jerry. He will know.

Ø Be careful with Jerry Ozzie.

Ø What do you mean?

Ø Remember he is still the police.

Ø Yes, I know.

Ø So Prince, when can we get started on the plan?

Ø Hush; don't say anything on the phone about anything. The government has ears.

Ø Are you paranoid?

Ø No, I just know things. Remember I was a computer hacker. I know how things work.

Ø Ok!

Ø So Ozzie, let's have a beer in a day or two and catch up; Just like we used to do in the yard.

Ø Ok, I got you! Tell me a time and place.

Ø Ok, be ready Sunday.

Ø Got it!

It's Sunday morning. A few days have passed since my talk with Prince. Seems like every day I feel a little better about myself. My energy has greatly increased as well as my muscles and sex drive. Once again I find myself waking up every morning with my stiff wood. Maybe there was some truth to the rumor about chemicals added to the water in jail in order to reduce aggression and sex drive. As I await a call from Prince, Vickie prepares some breakfast; as usual the very first order of the day is playing. What's a man to do with the presence of a woman such as her? Well, there are plenty different things I could think about, but for the most part they would all just a form of play.

Vickie served breakfast in the balcony overlooking Brickell Ave. The view from the 28th floor was fantastic. It took me several days to get used to that balcony. My first time froze me in my tracks. Not from fear of heights. It took me back to September 9th, 2006. However, we were far above 49 feet. For some reason I calculated we were probably five times the distance. Luckily, I had step out by myself as she changed her garments. Anyway, I try not to think too much about September 9th anymore.

Vickie ate across from me. It was a small table and rather romantic. The air was cool just breaking 70 degrees. Her attire was my shirt I wore the previous day. I could not help notice her erect nipples under the soft cotton. They were calling at me and I responded. I stood at attention in reply. She asked

- Ø Is that for me?
- Ø But of course.

Breakfast was delicious, but I don't remember if I ate it all. I do remember savoring her for the next hour. After all, that's what Sundays are for.

It was almost twelve when my phone rang.

- Ø Hey, what's up?
- Ø Shooters restaurant in Ft. Lauderdale at 2
- Ø Ok!

Vickie followed me into the shower. You would think I had had enough sex by now, but you would be mistaken, for I was an optimist, and there was twenty minutes available before I would head out to meet Prince. That meant 20 minutes to play some more and so, it would be written and so it was done. Once in there she lathered my back with a soft sponge. She pressed me against the wall and continued to wash my back. Soon after she turned me around and hugged me. Hey, this is strange. A hug. Why. What is going on here? I'm not used to this. She looked me in the eye for a second as if to say something. No words were spoken. She knelt down in front of me and went to work; Water pouring all over her. What a beautiful site. What a beautiful woman. What more can a man ask for. This girl had it all. I lifted her to her feet, turned the water off and continued in bed until she once again reached orgasm.

Shooters' was a nice place. It was adjacent to a bar called Boot Leggers. A long swimming pool separated the two. A wooden plank ran the length through the middle of the pool. Early Sunday was wet T-shirt time. The place was packed with guys and girls drinking and having a good time. Girl from the audience were allowed and encouraged to participate in both the wet T-shirt contest, as well as the skimpiest bikini contest. The place was situated on the mainland part of the intercostal highway. Having picked this place I figured Price wanted to see tits and ass. As I waited the waitress asked if I cared for a drink.

- Ø Galliano, I replied.
- Ø What that?
- Ø Yellow liquor, comes in a tall slim bottle on the rocks please.

Galliano was one of my first drinks. I was 16 when I first tried it and got hooked on it; was once a popular drink. Some places won't carry it because it's rare. After working out and sex, it's my next favorite thing. However, it was always with moderation for I never allowed myself to get drunk.

As I stood to relieve my pocket of some change, I noticed Prince walking in. My raised hand eluded him to my presence. I asked the waitress not to leave as my buddy would need a drink. Although we were now free we greeted each other with the jail hug. We extended our right hand, clasped them, and leaned in pressing out right shoulder into each other. The left hand comes around and pats the back with that we sat and he ordered a drink.

Prince was a big guy and it seems he also liked living large. His clothing's were of fine quality and his watch worth several thousands. He pulled out a cigar and sampled its odor, then lit it. The aroma of the cigar, the salt in the air accompanied by the view of sexy girls while strutting their stuff fulfilled the senses. Adding to the senses was my drink; I was zipping it and had the fresh memory of Vickie's erected nipples in mind. Ah yes, once again life was good.

- Ø Ozzie, you cleaned up well. You look different.
- Ø Yes, I put on a few pounds. I am clean, shaved, cut my hair and blew it out, as you have never witnessed before.
- Ø You know, in jail you looked like a criminal, but here.

How ironic I though as Prince continued to speak, for I was not the same person leaving jail that I was going in. Prince has only known the person that was transforming into who I now am. Will he uncover that I am not the person he thinks I am or will I uncover that I am indeed the person he thinks I am. With that I smiled. He must have said something amazing as he also smiled along. I said yea too. No matter. I've been known to shut people off while in my presence. It's easy to tune them out, especially if they are stupid. And remember we are in Florida; don't think I am trying to bad mouth the state, truth be told, it's a beautiful place to live in, but we can't get a vote count right.

Ø So Prince, you look good as well.

Ø Well, I have someone who has been catering to me, a good longtime friend that's been with me over the years.

Ø Your wife?

Ø Oh, no! My wife was out of convenience. It's only to raise my son that I am with her. My friend, she really knows me and cares for me. The only thing my wife cares about is our big house.

Ø So why this place? Haven't you seen enough tits and asses yet?

Ø True that!

The waitress brought over his drink. He asked for a menu, handed her his credit card and asked for a tab. I knew he was about to start talking as he started looking around to see if he was being watched.

Ø Hey Ozzie he whispered. Do you remember Lindsey? He was on the second floor with you at Paul Ryan?

Ø Was that the Navy seal team 6? The demolition expert?

Ø Yea, yea, him!

Ø Ok, isn't he awaiting a trial?

Ø Yes, but he is going to get out soon. His family owns this place.

Ø Tell me you not here for free drinks.

Ø Come on Oz I don't roll that way.

Ø So, you do roll?

Ø Eat a dick.

Ø I am listening.

Once again Prince started looking around.

Ø Ozzie, the $6 is real. Lindsey is a bomb expert and I need him.

Ø So he knows of your $6 plan?

Ø Not entirely. I told him I needed his help with something and that I would pay him 50k for it. He said he would, but also wanted me to give a message to his brother.

Ø So his brother is here?

Ø I'm not sure. I'm waiting for a call from him at any minute.

Ø Prince, how many more people do you need for your plan? The more people involved the greater the chances of being discovered.

Ø Ozzie, the $6 is real, it's in a vault. He can easily get in and out, but I can't say anymore until I talk with his brother.

Ø Why is that?

Ø Part of the money he will get will go to pay off someone in Broward court. It's in the works already. His brother will put up the funds needed for that. He needs a guarantee from me that if he does get out and follows through I will pay him and in turn he will pay his brother.

I did not like what I was hearing. It seems like a plan for disaster to me, but as I often do; I played along. I was good at that. I always preferred for people to underestimate me. I seemed to thrive on it.

Ø So what's the plan?

Ø In a few days we will meet again.

Ø Ok, I said and left it alone.

The clapping towards my left forced me to turn to the side. Holy, shit! Fuck! What a girl? She must be Puerto Rican or Colombian. This girl was nothing but tits and ass. That's not a bikini that's a fucking shoe lace she is wearing. If there is one thing south Florida has, that is beautiful people and it seems this afternoon they all come to Shooters. As I sat, the waitress once again found herself at the table. The plates that she carried have two delicious steak burgers accompanied by sweet potatoes fries.

Ø Hey Prince, what's the deal with Steve?

Ø Yea, yea, he replied.

How odd I thought. I have spent many months in jail with Prince that yea, yea sounds familiar.

Ø We are working on it. He will be out soon.

Ø You sure? I am depending on him to help me stay out.

Ø Yea, yea, I got it he replied.

Prince ordered another round of drinks. He pulled out a second cigar. I did not say much. I never do, but my mind was working and this time on overdrive. Prince took in the atmosphere. He was now focused on the girls. As for me I much rather be fucking them than looking at them. I quickly finished my drink and with that, parted ways.

The ride to Vickie's place was about 45 minutes. The visuals left me somewhat excited and so it seems I was speeding for some Vickie juices. She knew I would return, and so had left some meat to marinate. As she opened the door I reached for her and pulled her to me. I hadn't noticed my erection pressing against her. We headed straight to the bedroom and for the third time today we played. After about an hour I disengaged, not so much physically but mentally.

Ø What's wrong? How did it go?

It was the first words spoken since I early left the house. It dawned on me that since I arrived and kissed her we did not say one word. By now I was gone; to another world, for I did not answer. I did not tune her out for surely she was not dumb. Quite contrary I enjoyed her mind, as well as her body. My mind was focused on something I saw today. Not on or near the pool, not around Prince and I, but rather at the table; Namely Prince, if my instincts were to be right, something was wrong. I could not grasp it, but my instincts have never failed me. Then it came, "yea, yea", that was it! It was the "yea, yea"; his response to the question, what's the deal with Steve? Prince is lying. I know it. His "yea, yea", is his way of pushing the subject to the side. I've seen it twice before in the rec yard. What was he lying about? Was he able to help Steve? Was he willing or did he know Steve would not get out?

Ok, so now my guards are up again. At least I knew there might be a problem and can plan for a change of course. Ah, a sigh of relief. Vickie picked up on it. She knew I was now back. I could relax for the moment knowing that things might be different. This would encourage me to make new calculations. A plan B, in case A would not materialize.

Vickie leaned into me, put her arms around me and gave me a kiss. It was a warm loving welcome move. I embraced her; I excused my brief mental disengagement and proceeded to explain; though not in to many details as she was not privy to my plans. All she knew was I needed to get some arrests under my belt. I reached down for my underwear and put it on, then followed her into the kitchen. She poured some wine and I took in the aroma. She placed some meat on the stove, and so I stepped out to the balcony. The sun was low to the west, as I looked on, I thought about Jackie. Sunset was her favorite part of the day. I wondered how my friend was, my friend that wanted nothing to do with a criminal. What has become of her? Oh, well, I thought. Time goes on, time goes by. It's a new time for me; A new world.

Vickie had music playing in the background. It was bringing me back to my younger days. I looked down for a moment and got lost; 49 feet, 249 feet. I caught myself. I knew better. Change the scene, change the music, and remove yourself. Do not awake him, run! And that I did. I went inside and turned the TV on. It was to distract myself, to distract myself from myself. No, no, no more demons tonight. This time I won. I had control. Twenty minutes later Vickie summoned me to the table, as she set the dish down. The food was delicious, and the evening was beautiful. I thanked her for it with a kiss on her cheek. After dinner we retrieved early. She turned the TV on as we digested; I was out like a log.

23 A CALL FROM JERRY

During the next two or three days, as I awaited a call from Jerry I continued to eat and sleep well. It would seem that after 6 months in jail I would be eager to get back to work. I think I am starting to itch a little but maybe just a little. My priority was to put some weight on and manage to do things to help stay out of jail. As I was relying mostly on Steve, I knew there was nothing I could do, or at least not much I could do, until his release. So for now I was content with the motto "Eat, sleep and be merry". I often leave out the "for tomorrow we shall die" part as I am not looking forward to it. In my world if you call it, it will come. As it was in jail, two or three days turned into one week. Surely this time I did not mind at all. I was regaining my health, my strength and my sanity. Vickie was taking care of me and several times I had visited with Abby and Justin. Now, I was spending more time at her place than at my own.

- Ø Ring!
- Ø Hello?
- Ø Ozzie?
- Ø Hi Jerry.
- Ø Hey, what's up?
- Ø All is well.
- Ø Ozzie, I need to see you on Wed to sign some papers. I will call you Wed morning and give you a time and place. Also remember to keep your eyes and ears open.
- Ø Got it!

Wednesday was two days away. I would ask Jerry then, what is going on with Steve. Jerry knew I had set up the guys release with his help.

Wednesday was a beautiful day, but then, here in sunny south Florida almost every day is a nice day. Jerry and I met for the first time since my release. The Broward Mall parking was full for the most part. We met at the north east end. I jumped in his vehicle which I don't think I should disclose at this time.

Ø Ozzie you look well.

Ø Yes, I feel well. My strength is up and I put on some weight.

Ø Yes, I can see. There are some papers here I need you to fill out. They are mostly confidentiality agreement papers. As of now you work for us. You are not to buy any drugs or do anything that might get you into any trouble with the law. One little fuck up, one little mistake and you will be taken back to jail. Then you will really be finished. Ozzie, I want to see you succeed.

There was something authentic about Jerry. I knew people. I could easily read through anyone. I knew Jerry was a good man, one with integrity. I could feel it. His words, actions, demeanor were all genuine.

Ø Jerry, what is happening with Steve and Howard?

Ø Looks like Steve will not be able to get out. Turns out that your buddy Prince does not own the house he said he owned. He is renter. I don't know what his plan was, but he can't help Steve.

Ø Fuck Jerry! I based my decision on Steve being able to get out and help me with some leads.

Ø Well looks like you are on your own. You have three months before your sentence. If they are going ok, I can ask for an extension. The prosecutor will give us more time if we are doing what we are supposed to do. You need to start making your own contacts and you need to start right away.

Ø So, Prince knew he could not get Steve out?

Ø I would say that.

Ø What about Harold?

Ø Harold will be out soon. Any day now, it's just a matter of all being able to meet with the judge.

Ø Will I get credit if Howard turns in some big fish?

Ø Yes, but you still need to provide a few trafficking charges. Ozzie, you must check with me every other day. Stay busy looking for people.

Ø Ok!

Next stop, of all things was the gym. Yes, I was upset at myself, and upset at Prince for deceiving me. Most men would be furious with such news. One's first reaction would be to confront the situation; in this case, Prince; and express anger and frustration and possibly even revenge. I was different. I would dissipate my anger and frustration through a good workout. I would convert these emotions and energy into a logical and calculated plan. It's how I worked. How I did things. It's what I did that infamous Sunday, September 10th, 2006. I remembered it clearly. Some thought I was crazy for working out. How could you do after such a tragedy? But I knew better. The gym would bring me the peace and calmness I needed. It's who I am. It's what I do.

Anyhow, today's workout was a good one; chest and triceps. It was a push day. A term understood by gym guys and girls; between exercises I told myself to stay focused on the task at hand. Relax the mind, concentrate on the muscle. While at the gym, nothing else matters. I've trained myself over the years to focus on my next lift. I trained myself to visualize my next move; to mentally go through the motions of my next exercise from start to finish, tuning everything else out. Working out was a gift; a gift from me to me. A gift I would let no one take away from me or interfere with. In my life I was first, though I was not a narcissist I did love myself. As Abby's dad I needed to take care of myself so that I could in turn take care of her, and thus continue to love and protect her, as well as all my children.

After working out I was relaxed and hungry. I called Abby and had dinner with her. This time it would be at Chipotle, her favorite. I decided to spend the evening in Coral Springs at Justin's house. For the moment, I managed to keep the problem I newly encountered, at bay. The workout did its magic; for I knew that sometime during the evening I would think things through with a clear head. That evening I found myself thinking of my friend Vickie. I gave her a brief ring before I laid myself down to think things through. After thinking things through, I found myself with three different motives. To get things done; or rather, to start working on things. For starters, I needed to get to work. Although Dad and family have helped me and might continue to do so, there was no way I would continue to burden them with my financial situation.

Next, it came the matter of Prince. What shall be my next move? Surely, I would have to create a backup plan. Howard was still in jail and so was Edwin. Steve was not going to get out and Price could not be trusted. My mother of all people came to mind. Her tough love, to put a generously, has taught me, to fend for myself and rely on no one. Her motto was "you were born alone". Indeed I was. Not only was I born alone, but I chose then to leave early. That is to leave her womb at seven months and to leave her house at 16. I once again, found myself alone by myself and if I was going to stay out of jail, I would have to depend on no one but myself. Looks like plan B which has not been formatted yet, would have to bump plan A. Once again I find myself going with the flow, seeing how things would develop and making adaptations along the way. Plan B would entail formulating a plan that would not involve any of the thugs from jail. I would give myself a day or two to devise a plan, a day or to confront Prince.

Being curiosity, on the following day, I decided to do a little investigation work into Lindsey. It was a fact that he was a former member of the Navy Seal, whether he pertained to Seal Team 6 was up for debated. His family by now had lost their property in foreclosure to First Bank of Puerto Rico. The family had filed for bankruptcy in March of 2012 and changed hands by year's end. This was not an important fact. I do wonder however, if Prince was aware of this? Was he doing his homework, was he trying to impress me with his plot? Was he trying to set me up in some way? My plan was to act dumb. For somewhere in my high school English class I heard a phrase that stuck "Let any man utter but seven words, and I shall so hang him with them". It became a philosophy of mine. So when I say I like to play dumb what I am really saying is that I just shut up and listen. Let people speak, give them enough rope and soon they will hang themselves. Prince has already been found out by me. He doesn't know that I have caught on to him. Does it matter? As of now I'm not in any rush to go anywhere with him, I will sit and write for the next day or two. I'll wait to see how the cards play out. What does matter is the formulation of plan B. Also I need to find a job.

Finally I had the full itch; the itch to go to work. After my favorite meal of the day, breakfast, I decided to send a text messages out to people I knew in the car business. This morning I sent eight messages to friends and acquaintances. I knew I would have a job by the end of the day. One thing about the car business is that, a good sales person or closer will always be accepted to work just about anywhere. I was fortunate to have had a good reputation. Within the first hour I had two offers to manage. Sergio was the first to call.

- Ø Hey Ozzie, I need help. I'm running a store in Washington.

- Ø Washington? What the hell are you doing there?

Sergio once owned three different new car stores. He was well known in the business and made me an offer I couldn't refuse. However the court was not to allow it.

- Ø Ozzie, come up. I will give you a guarantee of $8,000 plus a percentage.

Ø Sergio, I did a stupidity and can't leave the state till I settle it. I was with a friend and picked up a trafficking charge. You know the guy Dustin from the tent sales.

Ø Yes. I worked a few events with him. Sorry to hear about your problem but if you are ever available do look me up.

Sequoia was next on the list. Just like the tree he was a tall man; at 6'6", I often found myself literally looking up at him. Sequoia was a ladies' man; tall and handsome. During our encounter at the Toyota dealership we frequently hit the bars together. He was now running a dealership somewhere in Georgia. Just as I expressed to Sergio I did to Sequoia. I could not accept his offer to manage because I was not allowed to leave the state.

Next call was Ralph. After leaving the Toyota store Ralph went to West Palm Buick as the used car finance director. He then moved on to a high volume used car store as the finance director. It was with him that I learned F & I. That's Finance and Insurance. Ralph's income was well over $25,000 a month. He promised me about $10,000 a month, but I would have to start in sales for a few months before moving on to finance. I made an appointment to meet him in three days.

It must have been about two when Helen returned my call.

Ø Ozzie, how are you

Helena, Sergio, Sequoia, Ralph and I had all once worked together at the Toyota store.

Ø Helena,

Ø I've been away; got into a little trouble. What are you up to?

Ø Ozzie, I am working for a small lot on 441 in Lauderhill. We need to get rid of the finance manager. Ed the owner could use some help.

Like Helena, Ed also was Brazilian.

Ø Well Helena I will come in two days.

Ø Two days? Come now.

Ø Helena, I can't now. Let's talk tomorrow ok.

Fifteen minutes had not passed by when Helena called again.

Ø Ozzie, I spoke to Ed, he wants to see you now.

Ø Helena, I can't. I'm driving an old car my mother had in her garage and it's not turning on, besides I have not showered yet. I made an appointment to see Ralph in three days.

Ø Ozzie, you don't understand the time is right. I will send Miguel, the lot man to pick you up.

Ø Ok, here is my address. Give me one hour.

Like clockwork, one hour later, my cell rung, it was Miguel.

Ø Hey I'm downstairs.

Ø Ok!

After several minutes, Miguel realized that he knows my brother Ismael. Miguel was the head lot attendant at the dealership where Ismael once worked. A few minutes more into the conversation I realize I knew his wife; for she had also worked at the same dealership for a brief time. Miguel made me feel comfortable and at home.

Helena greeted me with a warm hug. She was a short tan woman and true to her heritage, she had a big ass. She walked me into Ed's office and introduced me to him. We did the formalities and Helena told a story or two about us working together. After which she gracefully excused herself and left us to talk. Ed needed a finance person to replace the one he had. The guy was a Brazilian friend of Ed, who was inexperienced in the business. After 10 minutes it was clear to me, the department was not being run correctly. Ed had done several fundamental mistakes; for starters, the finance guy was paid a fix $1,000 per week. There was no incentive to sell Gap, or extended warranties and/or other forms of insurance. There was no back end money, and so no incentive to make money on the spread. That is, the difference between the percentage the bank buys the loan for and what you actually sell it for. Ed knew I knew what I was talking about. He wanted to bring me on board right away. However, he was not willing to pay me. I said

Ø Look Ed, you need help. You have no penetration. In paying $1,000 a week you are making a mistake. Per square foot the finance department is the most profitable part of the dealership. You can't afford not to hire me. For it would not be you that pays me, but rather I pay myself. I know what I am worth, besides I have an appointment with someone in three days. I have already been given a guarantee. If you want to talk again you can call.

By telling him this, I created some pressure. Truth be told I wanted the position; at a minimum of $50,000, working 10 – 7 with Sundays off, was fine with me for the moment. However I did not disclosed my price.

The following days, Helena called me. I was in the middle of breakfast.

Ø Ozzie, Ed wants to talk.

Ø Helena, I will call you in 20 minutes.

I knew it was an offer, and I knew that at least for the moment it would be good for me. Two hours later, Miguel called for me to come down. During the ride he tells me Ed really wants me, but that he also feels sorry for his buddy.

Ø Well, its business.

Ed's offer was $1,000 a week plus a percentage of the gross profit. My counter was 8,000 month, plus a percentage, as well as a demo. After an hour we finally agreed on $6,000 base pay, plus a percentage, plus a car, per month. It was not a lot of money. But it was good enough for the moment, especially for my circumstances.

Ø Works for me!

Ø Works for me as well, replied Ed.

And so just like that I was working again, plus I now had the pick of the litter as my ride. For the moment, life was good. I had disclosed to Ed my situation and he knew that from time to time I would have to leave to do my civil duties.

Out of curiosity I gave Ralph a call, it turns out I did not have to excuse myself from our engagement for I asked him if they would forgo a background check, to which I was quickly dismissed, besides I did not really want to travel to WPB every day.

That Saturday Prince calls.

Ø Hey Ozzie, can you meet me at 2 today.

Ø Sorry Prince I just started work yesterday and can't leave till 6:00 pm. I am free on Sundays.

Ø Ok, tomorrow then.

Ø Ok!

Sunday morning was almost a mirror of previous Sundays, sex, coffee, sex, breakfast and more sex. I departed about two and drove to the Hallandale Race Track. It was a beautiful place. The master plan called for a horse race track, a casino and an outside mall. As usual the sun was shining; a slight ocean breeze filled the air. The outside seats were all occupied with people having some type of edibles; some had Juice, others wine. Prince and I found our way to a table. I did not mention to him what I knew. The woman's big straw hats gave notice of an impending race and anticipation was a mist. I don't know which race was bigger, the horse race or the ladies race for the biggest hat prize. Aventura, which holds one of the highest per capital earnings, was only two blocks away. Maybe that's where all the big hats came from. Anyway, I thought today I would order a sandwich, a French one, made with American dough. I was not too concerned with what Prince had to say; for all I knew he was just a liar, a big one at that. Talk about pun. The ambiance was wonderful and I wanted to enjoy it.

Ø So, Prince how's it going?

Ø Good. Wow you look even better than before. You have some color to you.

Ø Yes, I feel great. I just worked out a deal at a small car lot, and for the most part I'm doing well. And yourself?

Ø Well I am a little stuck, but will find a way.

Ø What are you stuck with?

Ø Well it's the $6.

Ø So it's a no go?

Ø No I did not say that. It's just that Lindsey's brother never called me.

Ø Do you know that his family doesn't own the place anymore?

Ø Yea, but I just found out after his brother never called. I found it a little strange that no one there knew of his brother. In any event it seems that I will need a way into the Vault. Lindsey was a sure way in.

Ø Don't be so sure of that. Did you not have a plan B?

Ø I thought his brother would get him out, but it looks like it's not going to happen. So I did not give it much thought yet. There are a lot of preliminary plans to be made before plan B.

Ø So Prince you hack your way through people's computers. You take their info, wipe out their bank accounts, hack into the government agency and you can't find your way into a storage place?

Ø Oz, you don't understand. This is no regular storage place. I'll explain later, but be on notice this is going to happen. I am still finding things out, information. The money belongs to a really bad man. You and I are saints by comparison.

Ø So you are saying it could get us killed?

Ø No, that won't happen. But I can't mention anything yet.

Ø Prince, I know things also.

Ø What?

Ø I know that you can't get Steve out.

Ø Look Ozzie, it was always my intention to get him out.

Ø With a get out of jail free card? You said you would put your house as collateral. You knew you could not. So you deceived us.

Ø Not so, my landlord owes me a favor. I thought I would collect and ask him for help, but he disagreed on that. Besides Ozzie I needed to get out and I needed you.

Ø Needed me, are you kidding me! You used me, used me to get out and so now that you are out why are you really chasing me?

Ø Ozzie I trust you!

Ø Trust me? You don't even know me. You only know of a man that was in jail sharing my same name. Tell me, why should I trust you? You lied to me. How can I trust you? I don't trust my own mother.

Ø And that's a good thing. You are smart and calculating. Look there are two things to consider. One I am out, and it was you who helped me do so. If I did not need you I would not be meeting with you. I would not care. I'm sorry about Steve. I am sorry if you feel I lied to you. It was not my intention. I did believe I would be able to use the house as collateral.

Ø Prince if you already lied, what's to prevent me from thinking you would not do it again? Maybe you are setting me up?

Ø Ozzie the second thing to consider is that we made a pact, you Howard, myself, Steve and Edwin, a pact that would keep each other in check, one that would prevent the others from talking. There is a bigger picture here than you can see.

Ø Prince unless you give me something to dig into I will not meet up with you again. I have started to formulate a plan to generate my own arrest.

Ø Ozzie this agreement is bigger than you know. Howard has a lot to do with it. Howard had some people check you out. He knows everything about you. He is an influential man. The two Cuban cousins have a price of 10,000 on your head. That is real. Howard needs you. I need you. Surely you could use some money. Howard has put word on the street to keep tabs on the Cubans. You are in deeper than you know Ozzie, much deeper. You can play with us or you can walk away, watching over your back every minute of every day. Jerry will not be around to help you. It's up to you. Steve Upper was small potatoes. This is big. Besides we will be able to throw some arrest your way. Howard will be out in a day or two. I am sure of this. We will meet again sometime next week; sit tight for a little while. Howard will contact you.

Ø Prince what else should I know? If I become aware of anything else, that you should be telling me, there will be repercussions.

Ø Ozzie you have my word. We will tell you everything you need to know.

Ø Ok, I'll sit and wait.

As I munched on my sandwich Prince excused himself and departed. The empty space in front of me exposed three large hats sitting at the next table. I now found myself with three things to think about. 1. The beautiful creatures across from me. 2. The sandwich on my plate. 3. The words spoken by Prince. Politely I nibbled away at my food. It was delicious and I was going to finish it even if I had an audience. The middle big hat smiled at me; to which I reciprocated, but of the three things before me, pussy was the farthest from my mind, especially expensive pussy. Fright now came to me. I sat there looking towards the middle hat, but I was not looking at her. I was seeing Prince, his leaning over.

"Ozzie the Cuban cousins have a $10,000 price on your head", now alarmed me. I found myself lost. Holy shit! Fuck, Ozzie you did it again. You put yourself in a dangerous position. Will I be dead soon? Will Abby have a dad? How deep is this journey taking me? Why was Howard and Prince so interested in me? What key do I hold? There must be something; otherwise they probably wouldn't acknowledge my existence. The other possibility would be that I would be the fall guy, which is something that I will not allow. Surely it will backfire. So let the game begin. Ah, a challenge; an adventure. This thought brought a smile upon me. As I returned to earth I realized the three hats were gone. All the while I was looking in the direction and I had not noticed their escape. Talk about escape; I needed to formulate an escape route; an escape plan in case Howard and Prince were setting me up. With that I looked over my shoulders. I have to be very vigilant now. Everywhere I go I will have to look for an escape route. I knew the Cubans were in jail. Who would put the hit on me at $10,000? It could be anyone, can come from anywhere at any time. High alert was the name of the new game.

Twenty minutes later I found myself in my car courtesy of Ed. I don't know how I got there. Did I pay the tab? Did Prince pay it? My heart was racing. I was in fight or flight mode. Where am I going? I asked. Shall I go to Vickie, to Abby or home? Before I knew it, I found myself at Abby's door. Usually I will express my desire to spend time with her before I pick her up, for at times she is away with her mother visiting Luis in West Palm Beach. I phoned her from outside.

- Ø Abby?
- Ø Yeah!
- Ø I'm outside, want to do something.
- Ø Yea, the mall.
- Ø Ok, let's go.

How did I end up at Abby's house? What led me there? Was I still in panic mode? Why not Vickie's? Sex is always good. Why not home where I would be alone? Maybe it was the heart. I think I needed love. I needed a hug. I needed my baby. I needed comfort. After a short while Abby tried?

- Ø Let's eat dad.
- Ø Ok, what are you in the mood for?
- Ø Chipotle!

Ø Ok.

We ordered to go. After dropping her home I went home to relax. I decided to check in with Vickie. Six words were all it took. That is for me to go into my quiet mode, but more important those six words once again made me panic. She pressed a button; the wrong button. They were not threatening words, at least by many people's standards. They were not malicious words; maybe it was a single plain observation. "I think you're spoiling your daughter". That's all it took. How dare she? My daughter was my life, my blood. My daughter gave me something no one else did, true unconditional love. She was a part of me and I a part of her. She was my joy. I told Vickie I would call her back, but I was lying. Deep inside she took a jab at my heart and I was determined to protect it. With that I never called her again. Once again the word to follow was, "NEXT"!

Over the next few days, I decided to find a place to move to. A place I could return to without having to bother anyone. Justin needed his time and space with his girl. My sign on bonus at work was enough to cover the expense of deposits and rent; so that I did. One week was all it took to find a nice place. The house was huge. The two parking garage allowed me to set up some weights in a corner, as well as a pool table. I quickly moved in. Abby's house was only four minutes away. Elizabeth, the real estate agent had her house up for sale, I managed to get some good quality furniture from her. Among the items was a king size bed. It's the same I slept on before. Hum, fun!

Ø Ozzie?

Ø Yea, what's up Prince?

Ø Howard is out; he wants you to visit him. He says he has a gift for you.

I took the details and hung up. I was never much for talk on the phone. Small talk for me had no meaning. I was also more concerned about the facts.

24 HOWARD GETS OUT

Sunday with Howard. It's been two Sunday's since I saw Prince. It seems time was going by faster than expected. This Sunday was different than those previous Sundays, accompanied by Vickie. By now she was just a nice memory. I now found myself entertaining girls as well as being entertained by them. These were the girls from the vast ocean. And as the site implies, there were plenty. It was not a site for high maintenance girls, although there were some amidst. Not the site my friend Jackie would consider such as, "Select Choice"; little did she know I became aware she was a selected member, but I just kept it to myself. Anyway, for me, this was good enough. This Sunday I found myself in bed with a girl. Truth is I don't recall her name. She was just the NEXT. After a morning quickie I asked her to leave. I prepared myself a delicious breakfast, showered and left to meet Howard.

The address I was given showed on the map, a house by the ocean. The drive was a quiet one, no music, no NPR (which I would soon learn to despise as well as CNN), just quiet. As I approached the intercostal on Hollywood Blvd, the neighborhood started changing. The cars in the driveway were more expensive and the houses got larger. Once there expensive cars was the name of the game. The setback to Howard's front door must have been at least 75 feet. Two columns post flanked the double door entrance. No dogs came running up, for some reason I pictured Howard with some pit bulls running through his lawn. From where I stood the doorbell ring was a faint chime.

Ø Just a minute!

As the door opened a tall elegant woman with Coppertone skin color greeted me. Wrinkles revealed her age.

Ø You must be Ozzie.

Ø Yes and you?

Ø I am Jackie, Howard's wife.

Ø And true to his words very beautiful.

Ø Thank you! Howard told me you have a Jackie also.

Ø Well it's more like had a Jackie, as for now it's just me.

Ø Come please come in. Howard is out back. Shall I take those from you?

Ø Yes, thank you!

With that I handed over two bottles of wine, I had purchased for the occasion.

Ø It's a lovely home Jackie.

Ø Yes, we call it home. We have been here now over 10 years.

The kitchen view of the intercostal was spectacular. I could see Howard sitting in the patio. Jackie opened the glass sliding door and introduced me.

ø Viejo, hola que tal?

ø Bien, bien, mi niño.

ø Wow, Ozzie you look different.

Ø As well as you Howard. I remember your swollen eye when I first met you. You know Howard for some reason jail makes one look like a criminal. I met Prince and he looks well also.

Ø Yes, I too saw him a few days ago. Jail does make you look awful.

Ø Well Howard it's nice to see you again; this time under different circumstances.

Ø Yes, Ozzie it's nice to see you also.

Ø This is a lovely home, Howard.

Ø Thank you! Jackie and I have put much time and effort into it. It's our paradise.

Ø As well as it should be.

Ø Come Ozzie, let's sit.

To my surprise Howard pulled out two different bottles from within the bar. One was a bottle of cognac, the other bottle was unmistakable, a tall long bottle about 14 inches high and six straight sides; (an instant recognition of the obelisk) a phallic symbol, but that's for some other time. The bottle with the yellow liquid within was Galliano.

Ø Ah, my favorite Howard. How did you know?

Ø It's my job to know things Ozzie.

Ø Come on Howard, your scaring me.

Ø Ok, we once talked of a chess set I had. You mentioned you would often sit and play while holding a cup of your favorite drink Galliano.

Ø Ah yes, I remember that.

Ø BTW Ozzie, now that I am on that subject, I have something for you. Let me get it.

Howard walked away for a minute. During his absence two small boats passed by. They were only about 40 feet away. The intercostal was wide around this part. For a moment I wondered if I was being watched or was he, or both. Am I paranoid I thought or am I just at a heighten alert. Clearly the object Howard was caring had some weight to it. The open item exposed a rich marble surface. In it sat 16 green jade pieces. It was evident each piece was hand carved, for no two were exact another.

Ø Howard that's a beautiful set.

Ø Yes, and it's a gift for you.

Ø Thank you Howard, but I don't know that I am deserving of it.

Ø Ozzie, it's a gift. I have no use for it. In jail, I promised you this set.

Ø Yes Howard, I know you did, but I truly never expected to get it.

Ø Ozzie I am a man of my words. You connected me to my wife when I had no other means, and you asked for nothing in return, you are a good man and I know that. It gives me pleasure to give you this.

Ø In this case I will take it with honor. Surely, I will play in your name. The king is, the Latin King.

Ø Ok, Ozzie let's not get carried away. That set is over two hundred years old. I had it authenticated. I want you to have it.

Ø Thank you again Howard.

Ø Ok, Ozzie let's sit and talk.

Howard must have felt quite comfortable and relaxed in his home, especially in the patio we were sitting in. Without lowering his voice, without looking around, without leaning in he proceeded.

Ø Ozzie there are number of things on my table. One or two that I might need your help with. First of I want to thank you for helping me get out. Jerry is a good man and because of his ties to you I am here today. I was set up by a dirty mother fucker, a Hollywood police cop. There was no way I was going to get out, had it not been for you. Those mother fuckers wanted me in. Jerry being a BSO was looking to catch some big fish. That's why I am here. I know the big players, the cartels. I know how things run and who runs them.

Ø Howard, before you go on let me tell you that I do not want to die. Nor do I want to be responsible for the life of any man. For I already deal with the pain. It's a pain I will take with me to my grave.

Ø Ozzie I can assure you, your life is not as steak. On the contrary you can put an end to the price on your head.

Ø So it's true about the Cuban cousins?

Ø Ozzie that is true. They had put a price on your head. There are two things to consider; 1. They don't have $10,000. They don't even have one thousand, but word did go out. How they will be able to pay I don't know. 2. I am well connected. I can help save your life for now; I have put the word that anyone who touches you will have to answer to me. In the streets that means a lot. You don't have to worry about it for now. I am not telling you to stop looking over your back, but you need not lose sleep over it. As far as death goes, I have four under my belt. After a while you don't think about it anymore.

Ø Howard I am responsible for the death of a love one. It was September 9th, 2009 when it happened, and I am to blame. I live with it every day. There was blood money given to me for it. Money I did not want, money I could not live with and so subconsciously I blew away. I thought it could help erase the painful memory, but that was not the case. As for now I do not want to die. I do not want to kill and I do not want anyone else's blood money.

Ø Ozzie you are a strong man, a wise man. You are someone I can trust. And it's because of that, that I come to you. I need your help. The mother fucker from the Hollywood police is going down. I need to give Jerry some info. Things that might get me killed. I need to make a break from the Latin Kings. That part I might be able to negotiate. Prince had a real deal of a $6,000,000 heist. That's where I really need you. I need someone I could trust. Ozzie I don't trust Prince, but the money is real. If you and I, as well as Prince can get our hands on the $6,000,000.00 then I will be able to buy my way out. I can still be protected by the kings or at least I can quietly fade away. There will be enough hush money that will allow for this. Also I have some properties in Dominican Republic. It's a quiet place. No one knows about it here. There no one knows who I am. I don't trust bringing in anyone else. No one knows of my agreement with the state to work as a CI. Only you do, as well as my wife, my son and Prince. If anyone found out I also will have a price on my heard. This is why I need you to help me. No one knows who you are. You have no ties or connection to the people I know. That helps to put me in a better position.

Ø What about Edwin?

Ø I know Edwin a long time. He is from the Neta. They take a pledge with their life that they would not snitch. Edwin knows people I know. He has an idea of what I am up to, but I need him at a distance. We respect each other and will not interfere with each other's business. Because of his oath to the Neta it might be possible for him to turn his back on me, especially if people did know what I was doing. I know where he lives, I know his family and I know his people. It's best to keep our distance.

Ø I thought Edwin knew what was going on with you?

- Ø Edwin knew I was set up. He also lives in Hollywood and knows of the police that robbed me. He was in jail for a simple driving charge, nothing to do with drugs. We do not ask each other too many personal things. Edwin is also well connected. The Netas is a well-organized group. You should look more into it.
- Ø I will.
- Ø So for now Ozzie let's also keep our distance. I think the only contact should be for discussing the Prince deal. I don't want you getting involved with the cartels. Please don't talk about this with anyone. We will meet again to formalize a plan for the $6.
- Ø Ok, Harold. I'll sit and wait. Now give me one of those steaks your wife hides on the grill.

The next hour was spent enjoying the beautiful weather. Howards place was such that one could easily relax in; a large screened-in patio gave way to a vast lawn that bordered the river. As a gentle breeze blew, small and large boats quietly navigated by leaving ripples in the water. It's a shame for Howard to have to remove himself from such tranquility at this stage in life. I wonder if it was his own doing that might lead to his demine or is a crooked Hollywood police officer to blame. I guess I might never really know and truth is I really did not care, for I considered most people insignificant. He was no different; just another face in the passing of time. Howard set two plates on the small table for the both of us. The medium cooked steak was almost to perfection. His wife Jackie opened one of the Merlots' I brought, and joined us in a toast; soon after she quickly excused herself and departed, leaving Howard and I to talk further. Although I enjoy the wine I was eager to get back to my Galliano. Also, I think I was done talking. I did not have much to say, in part I believe because of a lack of interest, and so politely I engaged in small talk as I savored the steak and enjoyed the river view.

Today as I sit and write I thought about the last meeting with Howard. Why is that I never really cared to talk much with people? Why is it that I do not engage people? Jackie always told me I needed to talk more and engage more with people. I think there are a few reasons for not wanting to do so. Wait, that a poor choice of word, "not wanting". It's not a matter of not wanting to talk, but instead just did not care to do so. For starters, I find myself among a stupid, ignorant population; not that I am a genius, but by my first year in high school I was able to calculate how many atoms where within a balloon; taking into account the weight, volume, the air temperature, and the elevation or rather the air pressure. I could figure out how many jolts were stored in kinetic energy. I was well versed in history, science, math and many subjects. I was easily bored with people and as I saw it, they were just not worth my time and effort. On a much deeper and emotional level, I did not need to speak in order to feel the love and warmth of someone.

My love for my dad, as well as my children, was an overwhelming love. Because my loving dad could not hear, I needed not say much, for love was something I felt. If you stood quiet and listen you could hear it; you could feel it. You could hear its chime, its vibration, its existence. Love was something I never really knew, except that love between a father and a son. My mother's love was nonexistent. Thus I grew up not knowing what I was missing. I did once feel love for a girl, but I let her slip by my hands. Love for my children, that's what I knew. It's a deep feeling that needs no spoken worlds for it to be felt.

I do not think of myself better than any of my fellow human neighbors, nor am I stuck up or on a high horse. On the contrary, I am a humble, gentle, tranquil person. So the answer simple is I just don't care: not interested. Fuck love! It can hurt you. It can kill you. It can haunt you. That's if you let it. Ok, I know find myself going off in a tangent. I'm starting to think too much. I can see him coming. He is going to haunt me tonight. I must get away. No crying tonight. I must keep him at bay. I need to be strong. Fuck you! Fuck you! I think there for I am.

It was a bad night for me. There was no girl, no Jackie, no Vickie, no Abby, no Christian, no Jenelle, no Ozzie. It was just me. It was a bad evening; one I lost. That is, to my demon. I don't know how to confront him. While the girls are a distraction, the time will come, where he will either kill me, or I him. I don't know how to coexist with him. I don't want to coexist with him. I want him gone forever, but I guess it's my punishment. I must get back to the sea, to find some more fish to distract myself. This way he can stay away. It's a vast ocean with plenty of fish; some are easy to catch. Those are my favorites. For I'm not looking for romance, not looking for love, just looking for the catch of the day, a quick bite. A quick meal, bones to be discarded. The next wave will bring more. Am I running? Am I afraid? I think so and therefore I am.

It has been a week since I saw Howard. During that time, I've also not heard from Prince or Edwin. Work has now occupied my day, followed with a seven o'clock workout and then either Abby or some new fish. As of late, one fish has caught my attention. Browsing through the site I came across a picture of a sexy tanned woman. I told myself, "hum this one looks like she is wild"; but then many are, otherwise they would not bother to search. For me, that was the name of the game; no love, no strings attached, just enjoyment. I sent her a message. Because I was already backed up two weeks with dates, it would be two weeks before I met her.

In the mean time, at work, Ed had introduced me to a friend of his; his personal trainer. Anton was a huge well-built Brazilian man. It was clear he was juiced up. That's street talk for the use of steroids. Two years ago my physician, upon checking my hormone levels, prescribed testosterone. It was then that I became hooked on it. I did the research and spoke with friends I knew as to proper administration. There are things the doctor either does not know or will not tell you. Example, as well as the testosterone, one also needs to take an anti estrogen pill to prevent the conversion of testosterone to estrogen. Anton now provided me with what I needed, and because money was no object, I loaded up; however, I was on edge, as I was very scared of the law. There was always something fascinating to me about pushing the envelope, about walking on the edge. Why? I don't know. It was just inherent. Maybe it's why I got in trouble.

Two weeks have passed by since my meeting with Anton. I was feeling energetic and revitalized. Neither Prince nor Howard nor Edwin has contacted me. I was not going to press the issue. If I was going to have any involvement with them, it would be on my terms. I knew the rout they wanted to take was a very dangerous one. It could also be very lucrative, but at what expense. The burden of one demon visiting me was more than I could handle. I did not need another demon or blood on my hands. Now that I found myself with a decent job, a nice home, a nice car and more importantly, out of jail, I was in no rush to get with them. If I was to remain out, I would have to figure out a way to get things done on my own. With that I asked a few people I knew for help, namely for tips on drug dealers, and people I could turn in.

25 G

G was a fish among of many from the sea. She lived in Hollywood. It was Saturday when I met her. The Oakwood Plaza movie we were to watch was soon to begin. Being a typical Hispanic I figured she was Cuban or PR, since she was a little late; for we have our own time. It's called Cuban time. I was standing in front of the lobby looking around as I waited. As she neared, I noticed her. I turned away and exclaimed, "Yeah baby, that's a good fish." for she was tall, slim and delicious. Something exotic about her I could not place. We greeted with a polite hug.

- Ø It's late for the movie, how about a drink?
- Ø Sure.

With that we walked to a nearby restaurant. The name escape me, but it was has the name of one of the weekdays, not Sunday nor Saturday, nor Monday, nor Tuesday nor Wednesday nor Thursday.

- Ø Would you care for a drink?
- Ø Sure.
- Ø What would you like?
- Ø Chocolate milk.

For a moment I stared at her. Was she for real or was it a joke? She burst into laughter; a laughter that broke the ice, a laughter that would become common place. Two hours later I walked her to her car. Leaning against it, I encroach her space and planted a kiss. My right arm found its way to her back and I pressed her into me. After a minute I became erect and so I pressed into her.

- Ø Hum! Very nice!
- Ø What is?
- Ø Never mind. Thank you for the evening. Call me.
- Ø I will. Thank you.

It was a fun evening I thought, as I drove home. All I needed now was to relive myself.

Breakfast, breakfast, my favorite! Sunday morning I made myself my favorite once again; scramble eggs with ham and cheese and green peppers and tomatoes, bread and coffee. Yum, yum! As Jackie would say. I enjoyed my breakfast as usual. This day I was alone. That worked well for me. I enjoyed being alone. Girls were only good for playing; outside of that, for the most part, I was a loner.

- Ø Ring.
- Ø Hi Justin.
- Ø What up Oz? I have some info for you. Here is a number, I'm not sure of his name. He sells a lot of crack cocaine. You are going to have to make something up to get him to meet you.
- Ø OK, I'll figure it out.

I now had a lead, but not much to go by. However, I was not worried for I was quick on my feet. I worked great under pressure, and because I knew that, I felt no pressure. Maybe this is why I can always push the envelope.

Several days passed before I made the call. Some girl answered.

- Ø Hello
- Ø Hi, I'm looking for Will.
- Ø This is his girl I am handling thing while he is away.
- Ø OK, a friend of mine gave me this number to get some stuff.
- Ø What cha want?
- Ø Some dope.
- Ø Who gave you this number?
- Ø Some girl I know from the ave.
- Ø What does she drive?
- Ø Drive, she doesn't have a car. So has a bicycle.
- Ø OK!

She said she would call me back, but I did not buy it. "Well, that's that" I said. Need to look elsewhere. By the end of the week, G had already visited me two days and was with me when I a call came in. I told her of my predicament; of my unfortunate situation. She did not seem to mind. I think I was to her what she was to me, just a lay or perhaps maybe companionship. Whatever I was to her didn't really matter. G was good in bed and that's all I cared about; actually she was great. Wow, I thought, "I read her correctly". However, there was also something more to her. Usually after sex, I often found myself turning my back to my partner and would hug my pillow. Of all the girls I slept with, I could count with one hand the number of them that I would hold on to after sex. If so after sex I would lay on my right side with my left arm around my partner. This was something I never really thought about, until now. All my life I did it subconsciously. Two nights in a row I held on to G after playing. Why? I don't know. I never really thought about it. Anyway G was fun, a lot of fun. She always said a word or two that would make us both laugh.

It was Sunday morning when I got a call.

- Ø Hello!
- Ø Hey, what's up? You called my number this week.
- Ø Oh, hi! I was trying to get some dope. My regular guy is not around.
- Ø How much you looking for?
- Ø Well, I always get an ounce or two a week, but since I don't know you just a little to sample.
- Ø Ok, I'll call you back.

Here was my opportunity, however, it was Sunday. G and I had been out Saturday night and we spent a good deal of Sunday morning playing. I was not sure of what to do or how to proceed. I've never purchased drugs in my life. Do I call Jerry? "Ah, let it go", I thought, some other day. I felt comfortable with G. Why? I don't know, but I did. So I told her my dilemma. To my surprise she encouraged me to go forward and so that promoted me. It was already 1 pm. I made the call.

- Ø Hey!
- Ø Yea what up?
- Ø Can I get $100 worth? It's for a sample. If I like it I'll get an ounce.
- Ø OK, drive up to Delray Beach and exit on Atlantic. When you're close by call me.
- Ø Ok.
- Ø G, I need to go to Delray to meet this guy.
- Ø Would you like me to go with you?

For a second I thought to myself, "Is this girl for real?" Does she get off on this kind of stuff? Who am I sleeping with? After a second I responded.

- Ø Sure, if you don't mind.

Fifteen minutes later we took off. Having a girl with me might actually be beneficial. It could help him lower his guard. As I neared the exit I called.

- Ø Hey!

- Ø Where are you at?
- Ø Atlantic
- Ø OK, go to Military Trail, make a right and into the parking lot. Stay in the middle of the lot. I'll come to you.
- Ø OK, but just so that you know my girlfriend is with me.
- Ø OK.

Once in the parking lot I proceeded to the middle; away from traffic as instructed. After about five minutes a car pulled alongside my left. Will was in the passenger side. I got out and said hi, without any thought or hesitation he handed me a tiny plastic zip lock bag.

- Ø This is $100

As I put the item in my right pocket I took out a $100 bill and gave it to him, with that he drove away.

- Ø Call me if you need more
- Ø OK!

To say I was nervous would be an understatement. Here I was in a car that was not mine; sitting in the middle of a parking lot in Palm Beach County. If I got arrested I would not be able to finish my civil duties and would therefore be sentenced in Broward for many years. I quickly drove back to I95 and decided to exit where I saw the first gas station, once there I headed to the bathroom, locked the door behind me, and took out what was in my pocket. The items were crack cocaine, 10 small flakes. I dumped it all in the toilet and flushed. What a relief, no evidence on me. Once back in the car I told G what I did. She was glad I got rid of it. I wondered if she was testing me out. With that I decided to get a bite to eat.

- Ø Hey have you been to this movie theater?
- Ø No!
- Ø OK, let's go. We can eat there and take food and drinks into the theater itself.

It was a push place and well known. The food was moderately priced. There were many well to do people lounging around and eating. Some by the bar watching a game. G and I ordered, ate and proceeded to watch a movie. The seats in the theater were for two people. Sought of like a small couch with tray holders on the end. She seemed impressed. We bought our drinks we purchased at the bar, as well as a big soft drink and off course popcorn. For a trip to the movies is nothing more than a chore unless there is popcorn to be had.

Later that night Prince calls.

- Ø Hey Ozzie.
- Ø Hi
- Ø We need to meet tomorrow.
- Ø Prince have you forgotten I work. It will have to be in the evening, but it will be Monday and Monday is squat day. Can you meet me at the gym or somewhere in Coral Springs?
- Ø No, we have to visit a place in Ft Lauderdale.
- Ø Prince let's do it for Wed.
- Ø No, this can't wait.
- Ø Look, I've been working out for over 30 years.

Everyone and their mother, knows I don't skip my workout unless I am sick, and I'm not, so it will wait, perhaps Tuesday. Tomorrow in out for sure. If it were that important we could have done it today.

- Ø Ok, call me tomorrow.
- Ø Will do. BTW, have you heard from Edwin?
- Ø I heard he is out.
- Ø Can you get me his number?
- Ø Sure

G was resting next to me. She asked no questions and I gave no indication as to what was going on. However, she nudged her rear into me. That was enough for me to forget everything for the moment and get some more play time.

26 FIRST ARREST

Monday morning I was due at work at 9 am. The only thing enjoyable about the mornings was breakfast and sex; not work, for I was an evening person. My entire life was filled with late nights, especially after Sept 9th, 2006. Sometimes thereafter I would not even sleep. Time has passed by since then and I now find myself needed my beauty sleep. More importantly I did like my job and needed to be well rested for it. I was good at what I did and things came easily to me. It was about 11 am when I called Jerry. I exited the office through the back door and sat in the back patio area.

- Ø Hey Jerry
- Ø Hi Ozzie, what's up?
- Ø I meet someone that will sell me drugs.
- Ø What's his name?
- Ø Goes by Will; Male, black, 25ish a friend of mine introduced me to him and I met him yesterday. He sold $100 worth of crack to my friend. Will said, he could get me whatever I wanted.
- Ø Do you think he will sell you an ounce or two? You have to always try to get more than one ounce for a trafficking charge.
- Ø I think so.
- Ø Let's place a call, put me on hold and call him, then joins the calls. I will be recording. When you are finished make sure he hands up first before you talk to me.
- Ø OK.
- Ø See if you can get something for tomorrow.
- Ø OK, Jerry.
- Ø Also make sure he comes down to Broward. We can't go into Palm Beach County. So you must find a way for him to deliver.
- Ø OK. I got it. Should I call now?
- Ø Yes!
- Ø OK, hold on.
- Ø Hello!
- Ø Hi Will. This is Ozzie I met you yesterday.
- Ø What up cuz?

- Ø Yo, can you hit me up with an ounce or two for tomorrow. If so the price has to be right.
- Ø What time?
- Ø Around three, but I'll call you as I will be in Miami. Maybe you can meet me in Broward.
- Ø I don't know about that. I have to check with my ride.
- Ø Yo tell him I'll give him $50
- Ø OK, I'll talk to you tomorrow and I'll tell you how much
- Ø But can you get it for sure?
- Ø I got you Cuz.
- Ø OK!

With that I hung the phone. I was not sure Jerry recorded the conversation, as I was not used to doing three way calling.

- Ø Hey, did you get that?
- Ø Yea, good job! Let's shoot for about 3 to meet up. I'll give you all the details tomorrow. Expect me to call you around 12 pm
- Ø OK.

So far, everything looked simple. I was neither nervous, nor anxious, for I knew Jerry was a professional. Besides, it was not in me, to react in such a nervous manner. I entered through the rear door and returned to my desk. My evening squat session was on my mind and I needed to provide my body nutrients for the workout to come. So off to lunch, or as was usually the case I ordered lunch. After lunch I told Ed that there was a high probability that tomorrow I would need to leave early. Actually I told him why. He just said Ok. I'll be here to take over. Great I said and thanks. Ed knew of the program, for some reason I asked him how was he so familiar.

- Ø Where you ever in trouble like that Ed?
- Ø No not myself but I do have a friend that have had the same problem. Remember I am Brazilian, if I ever did anything like that, I would be deported after my jail time.
- Ø I would think one would be able to negotiate that.
- Ø Well you know Oz, I do have a friend that got in trouble, but he was actually set up. Talk is he won't be deported.
- Ø Why, is he that special?
- Ø He belongs to a group. His group will keep him here in the USA.

- Ø Wow, so that's what you call being connected, but then if he was connected why was he in jail?
- Ø He and his son were set up by some doctor who was working for him.
- Ø Wait, does this have anything to do with the pill mill doctor's arrest in Pompano Beach?
- Ø Yes!
- Ø What's his name?
- Ø Balbi
- Ø You're shitting me?
- Ø Why?
- Ø Ed, I was in jail with him. They kept him separated from his son. His daughter was arrested also.
- Ø Yes, what a coincidence.
- Ø Ozzie, we Brazilians are a tight group. We have our own people that we do business with. Talk is he was set up by some cop in Hollywood.
- Ø Ed, I heard they were doing a sting operation for one year.
- Ø Yes, but it was on the doctors in the office not him. He was the man with the money.
- Ø Well, they say it's the man with the money that controls everything.
- Ø He was implicated at last minute because they wanted to make the sting look bigger than just two or three doctors. The Hollywood police knew that.
- Ø Yes, but wasn't BSO involved?
- Ø Yes, they also knew.
- Ø What the fuck? Ed, something is wrong with this picture. How sure are you about what you are saying?
- Ø 100%
- Ø How can you be?
- Ø I told you, we are a tight group. Balbi is well connected, once they arrested him they realized that they made a mistake, but they did not want to look bad and dropped the charges. His first call was to his lawyer who placed a call to his group.
- Ø The Brazilians?
- Ø Oh, no we don't have power.
- Ø What power?
- Ø Balbi is a free Mason.
- Ø I heard that while in jail.
- Ø They did a quick investigation and determined he was not guilty. So they put up about $300,000 for his defense.

- Ø So, it's true!
- Ø Yes, it's true.
- Ø I heard that from a Brazilian guy named Claudio.
- Ø Hey I know him. Does he have a place in Boca Raton?
- Ø Yeah, that's him. He was exported to Brazil.
- Ø Yeah, for sure that's him.

Fuck, what a small world. Talking with Ed has made me ask a few questions about the system. But because I did not know enough about the true inner workings of the system, that is the political and judicial system, I dismissed them. I ate my lunch and carried on through the day awaiting my workout. On my way home G gave me a call.

- Ø Hey Ozzie, what are you up to?
- Ø Nothing much, just relaxing after a good leg workout.
- Ø Would you like a good leg massage?
- Ø I would not mind at all. How quickly can you come?
- Ø Is one hour okay.
- Ø Sure, but you must make some coffee.
- Ø Okay G, I'll see you in a bit.

It's now Tuesday morning. Once again I found myself not wanting to get up from bed, especially having G by my side. I did not mind seeing G for a fourth straight day. Normally, I would see the same fish, every other third or fourth day. However, she was different. She was fun. While with her, I found myself laughing more than usual. It seems that we would often burst out for the silliest of remarks. To top it off, the sex was fantastic. And so this Tuesday morning I found myself naked in bed with G. What's a healthy man supposed to do? She prepared some breakfast as I showered. I ate with her and departed to work. I had not noticed if she would be able to get in and out of the house, but by then I was almost at work.

It was 9:30 AM when I arrived at the office; No one was there, not even the secretary. I settled in and waited for Jerry's call. However it was about 11:30, when my first call came in.

- Ø Hello
- Ø Yes, hello?
- Ø Boriqua
- Ø Si, quien es
- Ø Holla Ozzie, its Edwin.

Ø El Indio Boriqua

Ø Si. That's me.

Ø Yo, Edwin what a surprise. I've been waiting to hear from you.

Ø Your boy Prince gave me a call yesterday, along with your phone. I tried to look you up but did not have your number.

Ø Have you been in contact with Harold?

Ø Yes a few times, why?

Ø Harold has my number. I'm surprised he did not give it to you.

Ø Hum, I've seen him twice, and he has not mentioned it.

Ø No matter Edwin. It's nice to hear from you. What have you been up to?

Ø I've been lying low, just trying to stay out of trouble: and what about yourself?

Ø Well Edwin, There are a few things on my mind, but I can't talk about them this moment. Actually I am waiting for a phone call. How about I call you later, and we can meet during the week?

Ø That would be great Ozzie, by the way, what about your book?

Ø It's still in the making Edwin. I guess I will have to include you in.

Ø Yeah, Yeah. This way my kids can read about me. I'll be a star.

Ø Edwin is this your cell phone?

Ø Yes

Ø Okay I will call you later on today. I am glad you called.

Ø Okay Ozzie. Give me a ring

Ø I promise Edwin. I'm looking forward to meeting you.

What a pleasant surprise. Of all my new found thugs, Edwin was my favorite. For despite his size, he managed to fascinate me. I was intrigued. Edwin knew several things about Puerto Rico, and its jail system, that captivated me, and I wanted to know more. But for now, the important thing was to get this arrest under my belt.

It was almost 1 pm when Jerry called.

Ø Hi Ozzie. Let's place a call to Will, and see if we can meet up. Ask him for one and a half ounce of cocaine, and make sure he meets you in Broward. Under no circumstance are you to meet him in Palm Beach County.

Ø Okay Jerry. Hold on while I placed a call.

Ø Hello

Ø Yo, What Up Cuz?

Ø Hey it's Ozzie. Are you going to be ready for me?

Ø I got you.

Ø Okay but I am in Miami now. Can you meet me around Commercial Avenue?

Ø I am not sure. I have to check on my ride. Let me see what's up with him, and I'll call you in a few.

Ø Okay, remember to tell him that I will throw a few dollars his way for bringing you down.

Ø Hello Jerry?

Ø I got it Ozzie, nice job. When he calls you back, you must insist on him meeting you in Broward. Otherwise we can't do anything. When he calls you back, do not answer the phone, call me first and set up the three-way call. Everything needs to be recorded.

Ø Okay Jerry will do.

Ø Ozzie, after he calls, you will have to meet us, and spend a few hours with us. So do not make any plans.

Ø Jerry, this is my priority. I've already made arrangements at work, to do this. Just tell me when and where.

Ø Okay as soon as he calls you, don't answer, but make sure to make the three-way connection before you speak with him.

Ø Got it Jerry

I was hungry by now, and I knew that I had better get something to eat. If there is one thing that can upset me, it's my hunger pains. So lunch it is.

Not even five minutes went by when Will called again. As per Jerry's order, I did not answer.

Ø Hello Jerry. I just got a call from Will; I am going to shoot the three-way call.

Ø Okay Ozzie, do you know what to say?

Ø Yes Jerry, I can think on-the-fly. Actually I excel at it.

Ø Hello

Ø Will

Ø Yo, what up Cuz.

Ø Hey I am running late. I am still in Miami. Are you going to be able to meet me?

Ø Yes I can, but homey, wants $100.

Ø Yo, that's a lot. Tell him $75. I will be here for another 2 to 3 hours. I will call you when I am driving up. Does that work for you?

Ø Yes I guess

Ø What's the damage?

Ø $1600.

Ø Okay, but the shit better be good. Just to be sure; it is cocaine and not crack, right?

Ø You got it Cuz.

Ø Okay, I'll call you in a while. Later!

Ø Hey Jerry did you get that?

Ø Yeah I got it. Okay Ozzie, the next step is to sit tight and wait for me to call you. It will be about one hour or so. When I see you, my team will prep you.

Ø Okay Jerry, got it.

It was about 3 o'clock when I met up with Jerry. I was instructed to meet him behind a big department store, towards the rear. As I approach, there were several large sport-utility vehicles. I counted at least eight, as well as about 15 police officers. They seem relaxed, as if this were something they did every day. Oh, that was something they did most days. It was new to me, and I did not have a clue. Jerry came over and greeted me. For a moment I felt like a criminal. Here I was amongst all of these police officers, and they all knew of my offense. I must have been projecting, for I thought they knew I was a criminal. Actually, I was a criminal. I committed a criminal offense, which they were aware of. So what would they think of me? How did they see me? Fuck it I thought; so much for projecting. That only lasted 30 seconds. Then my true self came out. I did not give a fuck what they thought; for I was a criminal. No matter, Jerry knew who I was, and I think that's all that really mattered.

Ozzie this is detective Joe. He is going to brief you a little, and is going to wire you up. Listen to his instructions, and I'll catch up with you in a little, during which you will make another call.

Joe was a heavyset guy. He seemed to wear his donuts well. Although he had a belly on him there was something graceful about the way he moved. Not to mention that he treated me with honor and respect. Joe made me feel and treated me like a human and not a criminal. Maybe I had the wrong notion of what it was to be working as an informant. He instructed me to lift up one leg of my pants and expose my calf. DNA testing? I asked. He just smiled; I have to wire you up. This is a transponder. It will be sending a signal to a backpack we are placing on the backseat. In turn that signal will be amplified so that we can hear it a block or two away.

Joe taped the transponder to my leg. He proceeded to raise my shirt exposing my side, to which he also taped a microphone, and then dropped a wire down my side from the mic to the transponder. He had me speak several times to make sure it was working properly. He also instructed me on how to turn it off and on. With that he did a few tests runs. Okay Ozzie you are ready. Just hang tight and Jerry will be with you shortly.

As I sat in the car awaiting Jerry, I observed the police detectives enjoying themselves. The atmosphere was relaxed. I was neither nervous nor anxious, but perhaps a little apprehensive. Am I doing the right thing? Do I need to wary about retribution down the line? Will this guy come looking for me, just as the Cuban cousins are? Fuck it. There is no turning back. Jerry came over and asked how I was doing; to which I replied," I'm okay."

Ozzie I want you to make a phone call. Tell him you are on your way to Broward and to meet you on Commercial Boulevard, just east of I-95. Make sure to confirm the price and the amount. Ask him how long, does he need to get there?

After the call, Jerry gave the command for all to move: For we were not at the destination for the arrest. With that everyone headed north on Interstate 95 for about 5 miles into Deerfield Beach. We exited on Hillsboro Boulevard. Jerry took me to a gas station and gave me instructions to have Will meet me there.

Ø Ozzie under no circumstance are you to leave this station. Tell him you have the money, and that is where you will be meeting. Try to get him to sit in your car. If for any reason you see a knife or a gun, make a comment such as, Wow there is no reason for that gun. Or knife. If you see a gun or a knife but he has not pulled it out ask him what type of a gun is it? Once he hands over the drugs and has taken the money, say, "That looks like good stuff." At which point we will make the arrest. Make sure you turn away from any line of fire. If he is in your car, you can exit if you like, and proceed away from him. There will be one unit responsible for your safety. Do as they tell you. There will be a different unit responsible for the arrest. Remember to stay as far away as possible. Don't worry about your safety. Your safety is important to us Ozzie. We are responsible for you. Just make sure to stay clear. My unit will have you out of the way before you realize it. Try to stay calm and relax. If he sees that you are too nervous, he might not want to do business. Remember to leave your mic on; we can hear everything you say even though you cannot hear us. If I need to talk to you I will either call you or text you. If he calls you try to put the phone on speaker so that we can record the conversation.

- Ø Do you have any questions?
- Ø No Jerry I think I got it under control.
- Ø Okay let's place the call, and see how far away he is. Do not tell him where you are now. If he is nearby or a few minutes away, tell him that you need to gas up and that you are approaching Hillsboro Boulevard. You must remember to make sure for him to meet you here. Otherwise we cannot do the arrest.
- Ø Got it Jerry.
- Ø Hello Will, where are you around?

- Ø Yo Cuz, I will be in the area about 10 minutes.
- Ø Okay, listen I am going to drive a little further north. I can be around Deerfield Beach in about 10 minutes. Exit on Hillsboro Boulevard and give me a call.
- Ø Okay Cuz.
- Ø Jerry did you get that?

A minute later Jerry gives me a call.

- Ø Okay Ozzie we heard everything. When he calls you tell him the gas station you are in. Make sure you stay put. Make sure you see the money before you give him the drugs. When he gives you the drugs make sure to say "it looks good". That will be our queue to move in. Does not make sense?
- Ø Got it Jerry.

The gas station was full of people. I was parked next to a garbage container and the store clerk was running garbage to it. There were several people pumping gas. Of all the available places, I thought this would be a bad one if bullets were to start flying. Fuck it. It's too late. Jerry surely knows what he's doing.

Two minutes later Will calls

- Ø Yo, Cuz. Where you is?
- Ø At the Station one block east of I-95. On the right. Black car. I already gassed up. I'm pulled up by the garbage dump.
- Ø Okay I will be there in three minute.

Three minute turned into four, than four into five, and five into six. He must be staking out the place I thought, or perhaps became afraid because of all the people around.

- Ø Hello
- Ø Yo Cuz, too many people around there. Let's meet somewhere else.
- Ø I can't do that, I don't know you and you don't know me, and if anything is going to go wrong, I rather have people around.
- Ø Yo Cuz, I'm not doing business there. So if you don't go down a few blocks, I am leaving.

I had my speaker phone on. I knew Jerry was listening in on the conversation. So I took it upon myself to follow his instructions. I knew I would be safe, at least I thought I would.

- Ø Cuz, make a right at the corner and go down a few blocks. I will meet you there
- Ø What car are you driving in?

- Ø Don't worry I'll tell you in a few. Just exit the gas station. Make a right turn. And go down a few blocks. I will be out of the car. Do not drive up to me. When you see me wave to you, pulled to the side and walk up to me. We will finish business in my car.

Without thinking, and totally disregarding my instructions, I exited the gas station, made the right turn at the corner and preceded down the road. Two blocks down I could see the silhouette of a thin person waving at me. As instructed I pulled to the side, exited the vehicle and waved at him. I looked all around but saw no big sport-utility vehicle, no detectives, no police, no Jerry. As I proceeded down the road I turned my eyes away from the silhouette, there was a parked car with a person in it. I tried to get a good look at the person and wondered if I was to be ambushed. As I turned towards the silhouette, I noticed he was laying flat on the ground. Several police officers surrounded him with guns drawn. The person sitting in the car just a few feet away from me exited and called me by my name.

Ø Ozzie, come to the car. I am detective Juan. We need to drive over and identify Will. I know you are new to this but you put yourself in jeopardy as well as the police officers; for we are responsible for your safety. Once you left the gas station all bets were off. We no longer have control of the situation. Luckily nothing went wrong. You could have been robbed at gunpoint. This is very common. We are set up to handle that situation if it arises. Once you made us move we lost control of that. After you ID Will, I will bring you back to your car and you must sit and wait there for Jerry. Do not leave.

- Ø OK.

It only took seconds to reach Will. His faced was pressed against the ground. As I neared him, he was helped to his knees. There was a bag of cocaine several feet away with a number placed by its side. There was also a pistol, some type of semi-automatic on the hood of a car. The gun was emptied and the cartridges to its side. A detective stood watch over it. Upon seeing the gun on the hood, I realized of how bad things could have gone.

- Ø That's Will.
- Ø Are you sure
- Ø I'm positive.
- Ø Okay. I'll take you to your car. Just sit tight and wait for Jerry.

It took Jerry about 10 minutes to approach.

- Ø Ozzie that was terrible. It was a good arrest for you, but it went totally out of control for a minute. You put yourself in harm's way by disobeying orders. You were clearly told not to move.
- Ø Jerry, it was clear he was not going to do business at the station.

Ø Ozzie these guys are motivated by greed, money. Had you stand your ground he would of eventually met you at the station. The last thing they want to do is head back home with the drugs.

Ø Jerry I am sorry. I sincerely believe he was not going to do business there.

Ø Ozzie this guy had a gun on him. His intentions could have been to show you the drugs and then rob you once he saw the money. This is common practice. You could have easily been shot. That is why we did not allow you to make contact with him. It was just too dangerous. We do this every day for a living. Luckily for you, he did have the drugs and he further complicated matters for himself by bringing a gun. That makes his crime much worse. It now becomes an armed trafficking charge. This is good for you. But it could have been an ugly picture. If you fail to listen to us in the future, we will arrest you and your chances of redeeming yourself will be over. I would rather call the operation off, then to have to go through this situation. I've seen it before. Once or twice it's turned out bad. For now go home. I will call you later with details.

As I drove away I could not help but smile. It was my first arrest and despite Jerry being upset, the only thing that mattered was that I accomplished the task. I knew Jerry's team would protect me. This was a first for me, and as the saying goes, "All's well, that ends well". For me it ended well. For Will, it was not such a good day. I knew he would spend the next few days in jail, and the truth is I did not give a fuck. He was insignificant. He was to me an escape route. That's all that mattered. I managed to get one step closer to freedom, even if I had to step on someone to do so.

By now it was already past 6 PM. I had lost track of time. My stomach was growling a little, but I did not want to eat anything heavy. Gym time was fast approaching, and my concern now shifted to getting some energy. A slice of pizza, with a soft drink, and two ephedra pills, will surely do the trick.

After the gym, I decided to call Justin and Abby. I was already in Coral Springs, and longed to see them. Before I picked them up, I made Justin aware. Abby had not a clue; for the moment she did not need to know the situation her father had placed himself in.

27 PRINCE AT THE HARD ROCK

Prince, how could I forget? Three days passed since I spoke with Prince. How could I have forgotten him? For his call seemed important. Well, maybe not that important to me; at least as important as I thought it or should be. By now, loss of interest, loss of trust, and disenchantment, had settled in. I was not so much a believer in Prince anymore. However, the possibility of $6 million was still there. There was still the slim chance that something might materialize. Besides, I was still intrigued. So, to call Prince, it is.

- Ø Hello
- Ø Hello Prince, how are you?
- Ø Yo, Ozzie I been waiting for your call. Listen, we need to talk, but not over the phone.
- Ø Okay Prince how about Friday.
- Ø Friday night sounds good to me.
- Ø Hard Rock casino 10 PM. That gives me time to work out. I'll meet you at the inside bar. Oh by the way, I received a call from Edwin. Thanks for putting me in contact with. Speaking of which, do you think I should invite him?
- Ø Oh no Ozzie. Edwin is not part of the plan. Howard wants to try to keep distance.
- Ø Prince who is running the show.
- Ø Ozzie we will talk about that Friday.
- Ø Okay you got it.

After that call, I decided to call Edwin. Why? I don't know. It's not like me to want to call people, let alone men. For the most part, if it's not about money, or getting laid, I'm not interested. So why in the hell, do I feel compelled, to call this Edwin, whom I really don't know.

- Ø Boriqua
- Ø Ozzie
- Ø Si. Como estas?
- Ø Muy bien, Muy bien.
- Ø Edwin, what have you been up to?
- Ø Same old, same old. Just chilling. Like I said before, staying out of trouble. Ozzie, I told my daughter, my friend was writing a book and I was in it. She wants you to mention her name.

Ø Sure Edwin anything for you. I have daughters also. So I know what it's like. So Edwin, when can we meet up? I want you to tell me more stories about the Neta, and your experience in Puerto Rico.

Ø Ozzie any time you would like. Not too early during the morning, because I always wake up late. Maybe Saturday or Sunday.

Ø Okay Edwin I will call you Friday or Saturday if I don't forget. We will set something up. We will have a few drinks and get a bite to eat, and shoot the shit for a little while. By the way, how are you with Prince and Howard?

Ø Well I'm not really tight with Prince. Howard and I do our own thing, but it's not really like we are tight friends. More than anything, we just know each other but we really do not cross paths. Once in a while, he might call me or I might call him, if we need some dope.

Ø Okay Edwin, nice talking to you. I'll try to hook up with you this weekend.

That evening, I had a new hook up. Another beautiful fish; sexy as can be. I met her at my favorite bar in Coral Springs. I have this dating thing down to a science. Before my date, I always announce, that I might possibly need to pick up my daughter. That was my quick escape. Just in case the fish smelled fishy. If all the scents were perfect, then, I would proceed to the next drink. This fish turned out to be a slimy one. The kind I like. Not that she had a bad odor, but rather she was loose. For as some often do, she ended up in bed with me. No big deal, it was part of the equation. As usual after some good sex, I turned my back to her and hugged my pillow. I started to chuckle; maybe a little louder than I realized.

Ø Are you okay?

Ø Sure I was just thinking about something.

Ø Anything you want to share.

Ø Na, it's about my daughter.

Truth is, I was thinking about the chocolate milk. The chocolate milk G requested on the first date. What the fuck. Why am I thinking about G, when I am in bed with someone else? This fucken girl; I hope I don't get attached. It's not in the cards. Sure G is a lot of fun, but I can't allow this to happen.

28 HARD ROCK CASINO

It was now Friday afternoon. The workday was very productive, and business was good. While at work I mentally prepared for my workout that evening. The question of the day was: After my workout should I invite G to accompany me to the Hard Rock? As my friend Felix from New York, often said," you don't bring sand to the beach". Friday and Saturday evenings, the casino is jammed with people. Many of whom are, sexy beautiful woman. What's a man to do? The choice was easy. Don't bring sand to the beach. Besides, I was meeting Prince. This was more a business meeting than a social call.

As usual Prince dressed well. Too well I thought. I myself have a fair share of expensive clothes, and know quality when I see it. Prince wore an Armani suit minus the tie. Alligator skin shoes, and expensive bling. A little too dressed for the occasion I thought, but to each man his own. As for myself, I was lean, with well formed muscles. Just about anything I wore looked good. We picked the spot to the far end of the semicircular bar. The noise level there was not as pronounced. I ordered my Galliano, and Prince his cognac. He placed a cigar in his mouth but did not light up.

- Ø So tell me Prince. What's going on?
- Ø Ozzie, I want you to go with me on Sunday to the vault. It's where the six dollars are. We need to reserve our own storage space. This way we can go in and out and do the things we have to do without raising any suspicion.
- Ø Prince so far I have played your hand. I helped you get out of jail. But I must tell you, the situation with Steve has really left a bad taste in my mouth. I've been around the block a few times. Truth is Prince, I have my doubts. In this world you get nothing for free, unless you are the Federal Reserve Bank, of which you are not. Nor do you have a reserve, nor resource. So tell me; what's the plan?

Ø Ozzie, if you remember, I once told you of this man in Long Island I worked for. He was a partner in a large brokerage firm. Hundreds of millions of dollars were traded every day. Both he and his firm were very successful. Being an IT guy for his firm, I was called to his office to fix his downed computer. I managed to get my hands on some backup disk that he had. One of the discs included the software necessary to do the trades. With my laptop I made copies of each discs. I also gained access to his password which he was later to change. After reloading the software I managed to set a back-door into the software, as well as into his personal computer. That back-door lay dormant waiting for my command. To me this was all, child's play. It's like letting the Fox into the hen house. Later that evening I pulled out a brand-new laptop, one that has never seen the light of day, and loaded his trading software onto it. I set my own password, and I now had access to all his daily activities, as well as profits and loss. Once I had it up and running, I went back to my regular laptop and did my usual hacking. I was part of a large group of hackers, and I was well known. My connections were many, spanning the entire world. Over the next two weeks I logged on to the software several times, and decided to create an account for myself. As luck would have it, he changed the password. I remembered writing the back-door password on one of the other disc that I had not bothered to look at. It was then that I discovered something strange. On one disc was a folder labeled, "SMITCIV". The file was encrypted, so I decided to find out what was on it. This guy's encryption method was stronger than that of the federal government. It took me only two days to break into the government files. It took me to weeks to break into this file. Ozzie, when I saw what was on it, I almost shitted on myself.

- Ø Ok Prince. Tell me more.
- Ø Guess what the SMITCIV means.
- Ø I don't have a fucken clue. It's obviously an acronym.
- Ø No, guess again.
- Ø Just tell me.
- Ø Read it backwards.
- Ø SMITCIV, Victims, so the file is a list of the victims he robbed?
- Ø It's worse than that.
- Ø How worse. Waite Prince. Do I really want to get involved?
- Ø You already are. Ozzie. This was a sick man. A dark man. There were pictures of mutilated people. Mostly young girls. Cut off fingers with jewelry still attached; Hands cut off. All appeared to be dead.
- Ø So, your man is a serial killer.
- Ø I don't know that. There were only pictures. Nothing else to tie him. Maybe he just got off on things like that. I checked the other disc to see if there was more, but they were just business records. In the same Victims folders was included his own firm. He had been skimming money for eight years, through the use of a dummy corporation.
- Ø How do you know it was a dummy corporation?
- Ø Well for starters, the giveaway was that they were included in the folder. One of my friends looked into it. He crossed checked it with the records from the trader software and determined that said corporation was owned by him. His name, of course spelled backwards. Embedded into the software was an algorithm that would

skim a fraction of a penny from almost all the accounts. The amount so small, that it was not flagged by the legitimate holders.

Ø How the hell did you figure all that out?

Ø Ozzie, it's what I did. It's what I once went to jail for. Some time has passed since I obtained all this info. I was able to hack his system again. He is still in business, doing the same thing. He has a second house here in Florida, in Ft. Lauderdale, right on the intercostal. It must be valued at over a few millions.

Ø So that is where he keeps the money?

Ø I know for sure. He has been buying gold bars as well as bearer bonds. Do you know what those are?

Ø Off course. Unregistered securities notes. The person, who holds it, owns it.

Ø Yes, since 1982 new issuances of bearer bonds have been severely curtailed. In the US, all bearer bonds have matured. There is over 100 million dollars outstanding. A few million of which are sitting in the vault.

Ø Prince, what makes you so sure that the bearer bonds are there, or for that matter that there are bearer bonds in his possession?

Ø Included in the file of mutilated people were pictures of the bonds. There were eight $500,000 bonds. He photographed the serial numbers.

Ø Well Prince that adds up to $4,000,000. Dollars.

Ø The rest is in gold and silver.

Ø That's one fucken heavy load.

Ø Actually not so. There were about 30 bars that seem to be in the form of the Kilo. At $1335 an Ounce. There are 32.15 troy ounces. So 30 X 1335 X 32.15 =$1,287,607. Plus silver and who know what else.

Ø Prince, each Kilo is 2.25 lbs. That's over 60 lbs.

Ø 67.5 lbs. divided by three people is just over 20 lbs per person. I have looked into some backpacks that can hold 100 lbs. You're not afraid of 20 lbs on your back!

Ø So, assuming these items are there. What is your plan to retrieve them?

Ø That's why we need to check out the vault.

Ø How do you know those items are there?

Ø I hacked into his home computer. I have the receipts, of payments made to the vault.

Ø Maybe he is storing other things. Maybe the bonds are in a bank.

Ø No, the pictures are of a small contained place. Does not really look like a bank. The only logical places to store these items would be there.

Ø Why there?

Ø It's built like Fort Knocks. Made to withstand Florida hurricanes. Once there, you will see why I wanted Lindsey. We have to figure a way to get in. That's where I am stuck. I know it's there. I just can't get in.

Ø OK, Prince. Let me get my magic wand from my back pocket. I'll say a spell, and when you get over there his gate will automatically open for you. You can mail me my bonds.

Ø Eat shit!

Ø So Sunday, we will go and take a look. I'll open an account and we can stake out the place.

Ø Ozzie. This is no joke.

Ø What do you expect me to do at this moment? If I cried would you considered me serious? Just relax. Nothing can be done today, other than enjoy the moment. Once we get there we can think of the next step. For now, look around. Look at all these sexy ladies. I'm going to get me one.

Ø Well, I'll be leaving soon. My girl is waiting for me.

Ø I thought you were a player! Is that your baby's mom you are talking about?

Ø Na, I'm talking about my friend. The one that cares for me.

Ø Alright, I'll give you a call Sunday morning. We can meet there around 1.

Ø Sounds good.

Several minutes later Prince departed. I ordered another drink, and took in the atmosphere as I pondered our conversation, although it was more of a monologue. But with me, that was usual. There was something strange about the entire situation. I felt Prince was being truthful base on the flow of the conversation. But I think he himself had doubts about being able to get into the vault. Oh well. Fuck It! Sunday I'll know more.

Ø Hi. Is that seat taken?

Ø No. It's all your.

I thought she wanted to pull it away. Instead she sat. Her name escaped me. Those are some tits, I said to myself. She was tall an elegant.

Ø Are you here by yourself?

Ø Not anymore

Ø Oh. I'm sorry.

What a fucken Bimbo I thought.

Ø What I mean is, not anymore since you're here.

Ø Oh. I get it.

It took her all but two minutes to get right down to the point, which sits well with me.

- Ø Do you have a room here?
- Ø No, I don't.
- Ø Do you want to get a room?
- Ø What's your rate?
- Ø $150 per hour.
- Ø No Thanks. I get it for free. I'll tell you what. You pay me $150. And I will give you the best fuck you ever had.
- Ø I'm sure you would.
- Ø Sorry sweetheart. Not interested.

As much as I love pussy, I never paid for it. Although in the long run it's all just as costly. Sometimes it cost you more to get rid of it than to keep it. This reminds me of a Joke by Charlie Sheen. "I pay them to leave when were done". Jackie came to mind also. "If you can float it, fly it, or fuck it, it's cheaper to rent it. However, renting it was never my style.

Well enough excitement. Tomorrow was Saturday, and I needed to be rested for work.

29 THE VAULT

Yum, Yum, Yum, Yum! Sunday morning was my favorite day, as well as my favorite part of the day. G and I had spent the night out. We visited a club in Ft. Lauderdale where anything goes. All the visuals had me aroused throughout most of the morning. After some play time she made my favorite once again; that being, a delicious breakfast. I was beginning to think she had a plan; a plan to win me over. Of all the things in the world, that was scary to me. I was not about to give my heart to anyone. No more pain and suffering for me. Despite this one thing I wasn't afraid of was to hold her. For I found myself doing so all night long, and the truth is, it felt good.

G knew I was to meet with Prince. She did not ask any questions, which is another thing I liked.

By the time I arrived, I had already staked out the place. What a wonderful map. Google Maps, that is: Perfect for thieves to formulate an escape route. For more than half hour I studied the map, laying out the land, which included different ways to and fro. The place is located west of Federal Highway. I-595 was elevated and so its wall ran just on the outside of the south side of the building. To the other side of I-595 was the Ft. Lauderdale airport. Several blocks to the East is Port Everglades. There, a few cruise ships were docked. Four miles to the East was I-95. That made the Vault landlocked on two sides. I had instructed Prince to meet me across the street from the storage, where an industrial park began. I thought it best we drive up in one car so as not to raise suspicion. From Google maps I could see that the Vault had several cameras on its perimeter.

Prince was there by the time I arrived. We parked just outside the view of the cameras. I jump in his car and drove for about 30 seconds across the street. By my measurements the building was about 150 foot wide by 300 ft long. The height must have been about 60 feet. That makes for a pretty big building. The roof had four separate and equidistant air conditioning units. Each was encased by a cement wall with no cover. Based on the position of the shade I determined that the photo was taken about 9 am. Not that it matters, but its things like this I often notice. Why? I don't know. I just do.

There was really only one main entrance to the building. That would be on the West side of the building. However I did notice some tire marks on the South side leading to the East side of the building. I guess some found it to be a short cut to the back of the building, as the entrance was on the West. OK, for you ladies, enough with the East and West. Just note that the beach is to the East, where you will find the sun in the morning. First impression upon seeing the building is, wow, this place is holding or hiding something. The only windows were those found on the entrance; only about 15 feet wide. So the entire building was never sun lit. That meant that some sort of power always needed to be supplied for one to be able see, (Unless one could see in the dark) which leads to the next obvious conclusion. Night vision lenses. Oh not that obvious. Well then, do excuse me. We were buzzed in from the outside. I wondered if we would also be needed to be buzzed out; although it's usually not the case. But at this point there was no telling. The staff was a bare bones ones consisting of only two people at the front desk. We asked for a brochure and for prices on available sizes. The young lady was regurgitating,

Here's How It Work

The Vault offers robotic storage for valuable possessions such as fine art, exotic cars, antiques, fine furnishings, wine, business and forensic property or smaller items such as jewelry, precious metals, currency or important documents. The Vault ensures a level of protection and security that is unprecedented. With no human access to the storage areas and unparalleled security features, The Vault provides the best defense against theft, vandalism and natural disasters.

Storage Unit Logistics

From the comfort and safety of your vehicle, input your pin number into an outdoor kiosk. The security system identifies you and prompts the robotic system to transport your self storage module directly to you into a private and secure staging area. Simply drive into one of seven staging areas inside the building, swipe your card, scan your fingertip and enter a pin number to gain access. Unload or access your possessions as needed. When finished accessing your module, the robotic system safely and quickly transports your secure module to the climate controlled storage area of the building where no one has access. Security features include private drive in access, biometrics, motion sensors, photoelectric beams, door contacts, networked closed circuit televisions and card access. Module sizes include 5'x5', 5'x10', 10'x10', 10'x15' and 10'x20'.

Vehicles Storage Logistics

Private garages and traditional automobile storage simply can't offer the complete range of automobile storage and protection found at The Vault. Vehicles are protected from harmful elements in a quality climate controlled environment specifically designed to preserve the integrity of your investment. Our facility is perfect to for antique and vintage automobile storage.

The access process is simple. Once you gain access to the private and secure staging area, drive your vehicle onto your storage pallet. The robotic system safely and quickly transports your vehicle to the climate controlled storage area of the building where no one has access. When it is time to retrieve your vehicle, simply repeat the process and your vehicle is returned to you. We also offer "Concierge" services including periodic inspection of batteries, fluid levels and tire pressures.

The Vault has been endorsed as a preferred storage vendor by most of the major insurance carriers. Clients who store their valuables at our facility may be entitled to a reduction in their insurance premiums. The Vault's proven and sophisticated robotic retrieval system transports your valuables without human assistance. Drive your vehicle into the building through one of several overhead doors into a private staging area. Using biometric and keypad recognition, the security system identifies you and prompts the robotic system to transport your storage module to the drive-in staging area.

Once you have loaded your valuable items into the storage unit and locked it, simply press the "send" button on the touch screen near you, the door will close and the robotic system safely retrieves and stores your items in a matter of seconds. The entry door you drove in through will open and you can be on your way. Simply repeat the process anytime you need to access your storage module again. Should you ever need any assistance, a friendly and professional staff member is always available to help with your self storage facility needs.

Dam, I thought, this person knows the entire brochure. I was impressed. Here was someone with a brain. OK, so do I make a move on her or just lay low without bringing any attention to myself. My second reaction was, fuck, this place seems impenetrable. Penetrating her was surely being much easier. It became clear why Prince seemed to show some doubt or lack of fate in getting into this place. For this place was not cyberspace. It was a real place. At first glance it appeared impossible to break in. The more impossible it seemed, the more intrigued I was. For now, it became a game; A challenge. Not against someone else. But instead a game against myself. Will I out-do myself one more time. Or will I die trying? At this point there could have been only $6. instead of $6,000,000. It was all the same now. A challenge... A new Chess game perhaps, or the game of life. Anyone? Anyone?

- Ø What size unit would you like?

- Ø Very good. You just assumed the sale. Is that part of your training?

- Ø Well, we were given a few classes before employment. We also have to know the brochure, or a good part of it.

- Ø Give us a minute.

Prince and I discussed it. We thought it best to get a 5 x 10.

- Ø 5 x 10 please.

- Ø Sure, let me have your info.

- Ø I thought we did not have to discuss any privacy matters.

- Ø You don't if you don't want to. I do need a name to identify you by as well as how you will be making payments. You can prepay three months cash in advance if you like, or you can pay online.

With that we gave some fake name and number. Prince opted for the three months prepay cash. No records of leasing ownership were recorded. It felt comforting to know that we could not be traced to the unit. The sales lady called for someone to get us and we were taken to the car entrance to the back of the building. There we were showed how to access our unit. We gave it a test run; again there were only artificial lights. Once the vehicle enters and the correct sequence of identification was established, an LED light on a giant elevator door blinked. One minute later it opened. A container 5 x 10 was behind the door. The area are car was in, was closed off to everyone else. We could freely enter the unit beyond the large door. We walked in our unit and looked around. We were confined within our unit itself. The units inside floor, walls and ceiling were all that was visible. There was only one vent within. It measured about 12 x 12 inches. Not big enough to squeeze in and out of. There was no escape from within. From here I could not determine if it could be entered from the outside. That is outside the loading area where it now sat.

- Ø Yo Prince. I don't see this happening.

- Ø I don't either, but then there always is a way.
- Ø For now we can only determine how not to brake in. That is until we find how to break in. Dam Prince. I feel like I'm conspiring for a big heist.
- Ø Shush. You never know what ears are listening.
- Ø True that.

I could see no vantage point to formulate a break in. At least, not at the moment, and I was not sure there would be one. As we left the unit I looked at the sliding door that close our unit shut. It was electronic, with a mechanic lever to open and close both from within and without if necessary. Seems this place was well thought out. After stepping out the unit, I hit the elevator button to take the unit away. The door to the unit first closed. There was an option to put a padlock on it. Sensors on the elevator door knew if there was an obstacle or person in its path. For the moment we did not have a padlock, nor needed one. We watched the elevator door close and the noise behind the wall indicated movement. At least that was my assumption. Once that door closed we were still confined to the area where our car was parked. Prince turned around and pressed a button. Another door now opened and we were forced to exit in reverse. Sunlight was now shinning in, and it was bright. Several seconds were needed for my eyes to adjust again. This place was not for the claustrophobic. I felt like I was in jail.

- Ø Yo Prince. This is not going to be easy.
- Ø Nothing good comes easy. But the payoff is justified.
- Ø According to you! What would you do if there was no money there?
- Ø What would we do?
- Ø You know Price. More than anything, I want to see how this plays out.
- Ø Ozzie, I know you are curious. When I first pitched it to you from jail, your face lit up. I knew you were hooked.
- Ø So, what you are saying is you planted the seed on me.
- Ø If that's what you call it.
- Ø Fucker you! You know what's funny Prince? When you first mentioned it that was my exact thought. Did you plant a seed on me, or me on you? Seems we both think the same. However, I'm smarter.
- Ø Eat Shit.
- Ø I can see why you wanted Lindsey. But you know Prince. That could have been a little more destructive in the end.
- Ø How do you mean?
- Ø Asshole, its, What Cha Mean? Look, blowing up the unit is tricky. There should be some way to get in. The whole place is electronically controlled. Therefore, through some electronic means, instead of brute force, should a break-in be attempted! You're a fucken hacker. Let's get to work and find the way in.
- Ø Let's meet during the week and start formulating a plan.
- Ø Sure, like I said before, I'll just blink my eyes and have the unit open. Talking of which, we don't even know the unit size he has, where his unit is, or how to access it. I would imagine the storage containers are placed randomly within the warehouse. Or let say, they could easily be moved around as people come and go. It's not as if we would be assured a stationary target.
- Ø True. We have a lot of work to get this done right.
- Ø OK Prince. I'm getting the fuck out. Let's sleep on it. I'm going fishing.
- Ø I did not know you like fishing.
- Ø Stupid, I'm talking about pussy.
- Ø Oh my bad.
- Ø Later.

I left the area from a different way from which I came; just wanted to see the surrounding and possible escape routes. G was home when I arrived. She had ordered pizza. It arrived at the same time I did. How perceptive or intuitive was she? Can she be spying on me? I think not... Coincidence? I hope so. The day was still early. I thought I give Edwin a call.

- Ø Hola Edwin.
- Ø Hi Ozzie. Que Tal?
- Ø Nada, Todo bien.
- Ø Hey. You up for a bear.
- Ø Sure.
- Ø What time?
- Ø 6 at Hard Rock. Outside pavilion. By the circle where they play music.
- Ø OK. Bien.

My intention to call Edwin was simply that; to call him, not to meet him. So why did I so quickly invite him for a drink? Oh well. Something deep inside must be pushing me to do so. Should I bring G. Sand to the beach? I think not. Besides, it's best for her not to know the thugs.

I wanted to impress Edwin with my knowledge of the NETA. At the very least, not appear so ignorant. So, research I did.

30 NETA

This following is a copy and paste from Wikipedia.

The **Ñeta Association** (Spanish language, **Asociación Ñeta**, or simply **Ñeta**) is the name of the worst gang that began in the Puerto Rico prison system and spread to the United States. Although Puerto Rico has hundreds of small street gangs claiming its poorer neighborhoods, Ñetas is by far the largest and most dominant, controlling the illegal drug trade on the island. The gang claims about 15,000 members in Puerto Rico, 10,000 in the United States & nearly 10,000 in other parts of the world.

History

The *Ñeta Association* was founded by a man by the name of Carlos Torres Irriarte, also known to others as "La Sombra" ("The Shadow"). It began in the late 1970s when several pro-independence political prisoners were incarcerated in the Maximum Security Prison called Oso Blanco located in Rio Piedras, Puerto Rico. He professed to believe that the rights of inmates were being violated by prison officials and vicious gangs. They formed as a mutual protection group in the late 70's, ostensibly to improve living conditions that were being violated by guards and other inmates and defend themselves against another prison gang called "G'27" ("Group 27"), or the "Insects" ("Insectos"). The G27s called the ñetas "Worms" ("Gusanos").

In the early 1980s, the Ñetas became the most dominant gang in the Oso Blanco prison after fighting both opposing gangs and crooked correctional officers by intimidating both correctional officers and rival gangs. The majority of the inmates were fascinated by Irriarte's way of thinking and did all they could do for the Association.

In an act of revenge against the Ñetas & Irriarte, the leader of the G27's - along with the help of paid-off authorities - plotted Irriarte's murder. They were to set him up and assault him when he left the watchful eyes of his followers on a routine walk to and from the prison chapel that he would make occasionally.

On the afternoon of March 30, 1981, Irriarte, who was accompanied by an officer (who was in on it), was attacked on his return from the chapel which was located just west of the Recreational Yard. He was stabbed in the chest, stomach & back and then shot in the abdomen by a .38 caliber pistol. He was pronounced dead sometime after sunset.

During the investigation of the murder of Irriarte, the correctional authorities found out that he was probably betrayed by his Lieutenants. His Lieutenants wanted to get into the business of drug trafficking in the prisons which was opposed by Irriarte. After the burial of their leader on March 30, 1981, the Ñetas exploded into an all out rampage and took over several wings of the prison compound. Rumor has it that the majority of the ñetas were drug addicts and in the drug trafficking business so almost every riot would end with an assault on the prison's pharmacy where they apprehended all types of narcotic medications.

They first showed their power and brutal force to everyone when they retaliated against the G27's leader "Manota" in retaliation for the "Hit" he helped plan against Irriarte. After a few days of digging and chiseling their ways through the prison walls with spoons and their bare hands, they broke through the wall of "Manotas" prison cell where members of the Ñetas stabbed him over 150 times and cut his body into 84 pieces. There were rumors that certain parts of his body were sent via mail to selected people: a severed finger was mailed to his mother, his ankle and foot were sent to the warden of the institution, and his eyes were sent to G27's 2nd in Command. The rest of his body was never recovered.

The news soared and the media depicted the story as a hostile takeover. Used to their advantage, they used the media coverage as a means to send out messages to other members in different prisons across the island. Their message was clear: They wanted justice and they meant business. They warned the administration and let them know that if their needs weren't met about improving the living situations within the facilities, there would be bloodshed and an all out war. By the middle of 1984, their numbers multiplied excessively. They took over 7 major prison facilities across the island and ruled them with an iron fist.

Until today, they still completely run a good amount of the prisons and work as the Administrators when sentencing convicted felons. They denounce and repent any sexual offenders, pedophiles and abusers & exile them to solitary confinement where they do not allow them to co-exist with the rest of the prison population.

It became such a force that the P.R.C.D imposed that their prisons be segregated imposing that the Ñetas have their own Buildings across their facilities and the rivals share another.

Reportedly in the late-80s, the association was involved in the cult of the "Holy Death" and performed several ritualistic murders at the Oso Blanco State Prison. In 1988 they branched out & expanded into the east coast of the United States and the forefront of

Canada. There they based their roots from Puerto Rico and continued to branch out as far as South Florida. Forming into separate Factions or "Chapters", they were constructed into an almost mafia-like umbrella, where there was a President, Vice President and lower hierarchy instated.

In the late 1990s, there were confirmed reports that Joanna Pimentel, known as "La Madrina," had been appointed council and leader of the New York City chapters. In 2001, Pimentel was convicted in federal court in Brooklyn, New York of ordering a gang-related killing in 1995 and sentenced to life in prison. [She is currently being held at the Federal Correctional Institution, Danbury, a federal prison in Connecticut.

Their rivals vary throughout territories. Because of their structure and form of moral breakdown they are usually in alliance with People Nation. Crips & Folks are usually on top of the list, as well as D.P (Dominican Power), D.D.P (Dominicans Don't Play), MS13, Los Sólidos, Grupo 31, and their lifelong sworn enemy G27 (Grupo 27). History shows that in certain areas of NYC they were even at war with the Latin Kings where the rivalry spread as far as Ecuador & Spain. Recent reports say the Ñetas have ended their problems with the Latin Kings and Bloods becoming allies around the New York City area. Reports also show the same for Spain, where the war between the Ñetas & Latin Kings claimed many lives in Madrid. One way to identify members of the Ñetas is by the beads they wear around their neck. Their rosary styled necklace usually embodies a cross and are worn with the colors white, black, and red. Another way is their clothing: they wear mainly white or the colors of the Puerto Rican Flag (red, white and blue, where sometimes blue is replaced by black). A white bandanna is also a good way to identify members. It's usually represented as their "flag" They may also be identified by using the letters "ÑDC" ("Ñeta De Corazon" - Nyeta From The Heart).

Upon a little more research I discovered from, The Florida Department of Corrections that there are six major prison gangs that are recognized nationally for their participation in organized crime and violence. THEY HAVE NO KNOWN OFFICIAL AFFILIATION WITH OTHER ALLIANCES. Each group is represented in Florida's prison system population; however some are not readily recognizable.

The six major prison gangs currently are:

1. Neta
2. Aryan Brotherhood
3. Black Guerrilla Family
4. Mexican Mafia
5. La Nuestra Familia
6. Texas Syndicate

Although their numbers are small in Florida prisons, if left unmonitored they could easily develop into highly predatory groups as they have in states with comparable inmate populations. The largest prison gangs in the Florida Department of Corrections are Neta and Aryan Brotherhood.

And finally from another source, The NETA Like to lay low and not bring attention to themselves. I wondered if this is why Howard and Edwin were different. For both personified the description.

- Ø Ozzie
- Ø Edwin, Que tal?

It was nice to see Edwin again. I had forgotten his short stature. Maybe I had just gotten a little bigger. We gave each other a warm hug. It was different than that of the others.

- Ø Edwin. Tell me something. We are not related, right?
- Ø With your height, even if we were distant cousins, I would be taller. Why do you ask? Do you know my mother?
- Ø Hold up. I'm not going that far. It's just I feel comfortable with you. Different than Prince and Howard.
- Ø Yea, I know what you mean. I do have a large family. Real large.
- Ø Well, I have a few brothers and sisters myself.
- Ø I have 16 brothers and sisters, of which I am the eighth. A few brothers have died, serving the brotherhood.
- Ø What brotherhood?
- Ø Los NETA.
- Ø Waite Edwin. Let's get a seat and drink before we get into all that.
- Ø Si, OK.

The day, once again was beautiful; nothing outside the norm for Florida. We picked an outside table within the perimeter of a banister. I stretched out my legs and leaned them on it, but not too high as to be inappropriate. I then ordered a drink.

Ø Cuba Libre, on the rocks.

Ø Edwin, too many Cubans around here. Just call it a rum and coke. Besides I feel funny drinking to the Cubans when I have two on my tail.

Ø Oh don't worry about that. The Neta have your back.

Ø Sure?

Ø Well. We can.

Ø Galliano Please. On the rocks.

Ø Que es eso.

Ø Galliano is Liquor. Made from a few different natural ingredients, including vanilla, star anise, Mediterranean anise, ginger, citrus, juniper, musk yarrow, and lavender. Neutral alcohol is infused with the pressings from the herbs except vanilla. You know what's funny? I've been drinking this all my life and never really knew of the ingredients. All I know is, I fucken like it.

Ø Sounds like a cocktail.

Ø So Edwin, tell me, how are you? I see you look good, but how are you.

Ø It's a tough world. I have younger brothers and sisters, and nephews that struggle with drugs and it bothers me to see them like that. Knowing what I know, I try to teach them to stay straight.

Ø But Edwin, aren't you in the drug business.

Ø Yea, but I'm low key. Just a handful of people that I've been doing business with. I am more of a runner now. I keep a small stash. It's the only way to make a living. I promised my mom I would look out for the family, before she died. There are just too many. I have about forty cousins, and about as many nephews.

Ø Edwin, don't you think you have to do for yourself first?

Ø I do. I also take care of business as well as help many people. Especially in PR.

Ø How?

Ø Ozzie. I am almost 50. I was in jail in San Juan, right after the NETA formed in Rio Piedras, P.R. It was formed to help each other survive. Every so often I send a small donation for that cause. I was a top guy. I know the whole story firsthand.

Ø Yes it started with, Carlos Torres Irriarte, an inmate.

Ø Yes. He was a good man. I met his cousin in jail.

Ø So why was he in jail?

Ø Who?

Ø Carlos Torres Irriarte.

Ø He did drugs.

Ø What about his cousin?

Ø Same.

Ø Tell me Edwin. I'm fascinated.

Ø During that time, there was a gang called the G27s. They would pick on all the inmates that were weak. Many inmates would starve because the insects would take their food. (It's what the NETA called the G27s). Parasites. Insects. The prison guards would never do anything to help out those weak inmates. It got so bad in jail that several inmates died. Many were beat up and sexually abused. The guards were in with the insects. Maybe for fear of the G27s. Carlos, decided to put an end to all the injustice, and so he started a group. He called it the NETA. Part of the mission of the NETA was to raise commissary money for the weak people that were preyed upon by the G27s. He also wanted to put an end to the sexual abuse as well as torture. The movement grew quickly. It was not a gang at first put an association which became recognized by the government of PR. The NETA started to murder the insects. Those that were the worst of the G27.

Ø How did they get away with that?

Ø Simple. The murder would occur in the bathroom. The bodies were cut into small pieces and the flesh stripped from the bones. All the pieces were made small enough to fit down the toilet bowl. The head was placed in a plastic bag, and then sent out through the garbage. There would be a trustee in charge of making sure the bag got to the outside.

Ø Edwin, your fucken kidding.

Ø No Ozzie. I was there.

Ø You mean with Carlos.

Ø No, I was in San Juan. We did the same there to the G27s, in that jail. At first, no one could explain how some prisoners were unaccounted for. There would be no signs of escape. No explanation. The NETA soon grew and took over the jail in Rio Piedras. A big war with the G27s broke out and then both groups were separated. The NETA were always low key. We have our own secret hand sign and recognize each other easily. The movement spread to the San Juan jail, where I was. I don't want to talk too much about what I did there, but let me tell you, a lot of awful things happened.

Edwin paused. He did not say a word. I recognized the moment, for I was there many times. He was containing himself. Whatever it was, it must have been terrible. But I was not going to ask him. I, myself, do not like talking about Sept 9, 2006. I gave him his space as I turned in all directions watching the ladies go by. I sipped my drink and totally disregarded him.

Ø I became a leader. There were a few higher leaders over me. Once we were recognized by the government of P.R., we were given rights which we did not have before. Power changed from the prison guards to the inmates. At first it was a good thing. When one was sentenced to jail, they would be asked by the prison guards, if they were comfortable being placed in that jail. The prisoner had the option of choosing. If you were a NETA, you wanted to go to a jail were the NETA were in control. And if you were a G27 then you would be sent to the jail where they were at. Once an inmate was admitted, the NETAs would take him to a room within the jail and ask of his crime? Certain crimes were not tolerated by us. Such as being convicted of rape, child molestation or abuse of the elderly. If so, then you would be held in solitary confinement during the entire stay. You needed to pledge allegiance to the NETA If you wanted to stay in our jail. Of all the worst things one could do was to be a rat. A snitch.

Ø What do you mean?

Ø If you were suspected of ratting out someone, especially a former NETA member, than you would be severely beat up on the spot. Death was possible. If you lied to us and were later found out, then the punishment would also be bad. At first the NETA, was a good organization. But after many years, young street thugs started becoming members. In P.R., the NETA only existed in jail. Once out of jail, you would not bring attention to yourself. In the US, many Puerto Ricans, started joining the group, and they existed as a gang outside of the jails.

Ø Edwin, Carlos the founder was killed in jail by the G27s.

Ø Yes. It started a war and that's why the groups were separated. The guy that put the hit on Carlos was killed in jail by us. You know Ozzie. A few times I sat in to judge the new prisoners. This way we would know of their crime. There was this big guy that had a cast iron pan from the kitchen. If it was believed you were lying, he was told to hit you on the head with it, until there was blood, or until the truth was told. It was tough, but it kept the prison running smooth and truth is, prisoners were treated well and also ate well. One of my cousins was there with me. He came from the G27 jail. I helped save his life in a fight that broke out. I got shanked for it. His son lives here in Ft. Lauderdale.

Ø So your cousin was a G27. No but his friends were. When he got arrested, he had to choose to go to their jail, or pledge with us. Almost all my family is from the Neta. So he went where I was.

Ø Edwin, what's the deal with the Latin Kings?

Ø The NETAs are from, Puerto Rico. The Kings were from Chicago. Many of them were also Puerto Ricans. At one time they were our enemy, but being that blood is thicker than water, the Kings would not fight the NETA unless it was really necessary. One of my younger brothers in NY is from the Kings. In Puerto Rico, there are no Kings. You are a NETA or some other gang.

Ø So what is your deal with Howard?

Ø Well, we respect each other. But we are both leaders from once rival gangs. If the word ever went down to fight each other, than we would. But for now, we get along. We keep away from each other so that other NETA or Kings don't start any rumors.

Ø Is Harold as connected as I think he is?

Ø Yes. He has a lot of power over what happens in his gang. But only on the East coast. Big decisions are handled by him and a few others. He is getting older and tired. But there is no way out. You are a member for life. I think you can buy your way out, but I am not sure. There are a few soldiers that bring news to him. They don't talk much over the phone.

Ø Edwin, he said he would protect me from the two Cuban cousins. What do you think of that?

Ø Down here in Florida, the numbers of Kings are not as great as up north. The NETA actually have more members. But if he said so, I would believe him.

Ø Hey Edwin. Let's go to Puerto Rico and do a documentary. Who knows, maybe we can make a movie.

Ø Make a movie. You don't know anyone in the movie business. You know Ozzie. All of that is controlled.

Ø By Who?

Ø By people you or I will never know. Puerto Rico, just like the United States has a corrupt government. There are a lot of things that I do know, but I can't talk about. Some of the top leaders of the NETA group were once approached by a few men working for the US. Some received money, but I wasn't included. I was not approached. But my leader was. They wanted to help the group form to help keep the jail under control. I think they also wanted to get us to convince people to help Puerto Rico become a state. I don't know much more as I left jail after a few months after they came. I just minded my business and did not ask questions. Do you know, that it is rumored that the legend of the Chupacabra, was an attempt to genetically modify animals and humans? Our women were made sterile through Operation Bootstrap. The cancer rate in Vieques is 27% higher than the mainland. Long before I was born, a doctor had given some people cancer cells. Many of which shortly died of cancer. The list of corruption is long.

Ø Edwin, you're going off a little here.

Ø You see Ozzie; many people don't know the history of Puerto Rico. I know a lot. But I just can't say much.

Ø OK, Edwin. So let's go there and document things. Besides I want to see my family. First, I need to do what I need to do here.

Ø Ok.

Ø Hey, it's getting late, I'm going fishing.

Ø You like to fish?

Ø Love to fish Edwin. Love to eat fish also.

Ø Me to.

Ø Edwin, I'm fucking with you. I'm talking about pussy.

Ø Well I like them both.

Ø Edwin lets meet up next week some time so you can tell me more things.

Ø Ok.

We hugged each other and exited different ways. What seemed like 30 minutes had actually been an hour and a half. I must have really been entertained, for I did not even remember asking for the second drink. Nonetheless, I do remember enjoying it. Edwin spoke without any hesitation. He did not blink. He did not look down. He made no micro expressions. He was not uncomfortable. He did not touch his noise, or cover his lips. Edwin was right handed, and when he once paused to recall, his eyes looked up and to the left. He looked me in the eyes many times as he spoke. I knew everything he said to me was the truth. Or at the very least, he perceived it as being true. And so now, I am even more intrigued than before. This guy seems to have more knowledge than I expected him to. Maybe that's why I was drawn to him from the get go. One thing that did struck me was when he mentioned, "I can't say much." I'll meet with him again and figure out why. I'll give him the rope he needs. I wonder what he really has to say, or wants to say. Surely, it will come. Anyway, enough for now. Its G time. I'm going to play. Yea baby! I like it. I like it a lot.

31 SECOND ARREST

Several days have passed since Sunday. I've not heard from any of my thug acquaintances. For the most part I was resigned to fend for myself. I don't think I will be getting any help from them. Jerry had called and asked if I had anything else going on. He reminded me it's been almost three months now since I was out, and if I wanted to get an extension, I needed to come up with something. "Fuck it" I thought. I called Jerry back and asked if he was interest in a steroid drug deal. He said yes, "But try and make it for several hundred dollars." he exclaimed. Not a problem. If it's one thing I knew, it was steroids. Eddie my long time high school friend had coached me on it, after telling him of my prescription.

I became good at spotting users, and by now I knew of a few dealers. Through a fish I meet two years ago, I was informed that a certain man was selling big quantities; No, not the Brazilian. He was too close to home for me to do anything. Besides I did not want those Brazilians after me. My first arrest was a black man. Someone I did not know or care for. Being an equal opportunity guy, I thought nothing of turning in a white guy. Fuck it. It was all the same to me. I had no preference. Well maybe just a little. I don't think I would like to turn in a Puerto Rican. Monday afternoon I called Jerry and then made a controlled call to the target. I don't even recall his name. Oh, yes. It sounds like Jerry, but begins with a B. I'll just say B. Jerry sent me a picture of some man after running the phone number I gave him.

- Ø Do you know this guy?
- Ø Yes, that the guy. B.
- Ø He is actually out on bond, awaiting a drug trial.

Oh fuck. That's not good for him. He's going to have a long weekend; Too bad. That was the extent of my emotions for him. Let's do this, Brutus.

Tuesday afternoon was the arrest day. Just like before I meet a team of over 15 detectives. I exited my car and was greeted by Jerry. Two other guys were with him.

- Ø Hey. I remember you. I tried to knock you down during your first arrest but you just stood standing.

The other police started laughing at him. Yea you had to beg the bad guy to get down on his knees.

Ø Look at the size of him. This guy is a monster.

I commented

Ø So you're the one that punched me on the side of my face.

They all started laughing.

Ø Sorry man. Things like that just happen.

Ø Yes, I know.

The atmosphere was relax and I wasn't about to foul it up. I laughed along. Truth be told, I had neither bad nor ill feelings towards any of them. They had a job to do, and it seemed they did it well.

I got wired up, made a call to B. and told him to meet me in Tamarac. Once there, I was given $700, for the purchase of four bottles of testosterone, four vials of Sustenon, and four vials of Deca; As well as fifty needles. The price was rather cheap and so I figured something might be wrong with the quality. No matter, I had to do my civil duties.

B called and asked if I can meet him somewhere else. I learned my lesson from the first time and told him my girlfriend was in the store shopping as I awaited him. He told me to wait about 15 minutes. Not being Hispanic, 15 minutes meant 15 minutes. B showed up and pulled next to me. I exited my car and shook his hand. He put a small box on the trunk lid and opened it up. I was glad to see it. As I handing him the money I said the magic words. "Man, my buddy is going to be happy". Before I could look up there was a detective that had flung himself onto B. B fell forwards and scrapped his knees. I was grabbed by two detectives and pushed to the side of the car. They leaned me over and handcuffed me. What the fuck I said?

Ø Relax Ozzie. We are making it seem like we are arresting you. Good job!

B was handcuffed and sat on the curb facing away from his car and myself. A big gun was taken out of a briefcase on the back seat. It seemed to be a Desert Eagle. They stripped the bullets and placed it on the hood of his car. Oh that's not good! I said. But I really did not care, for it's a dog eats dog world.

As my handcuffs were being removed I said

Ø Man that brought flash back.

The detective smiled. Jerry told me to go home and that he would call me later. OK. Off I go. I would make my way to the gym, but first a pizza. Although it was only my second arrest, I felt comfortable. I did not have to think of looking over my shoulders. I did what I did, and I was glad. The workout was a good one as usual. The only question now was who is going to reply to my booty call? As I waited for replies from my text messages, Jerry called.

- Ø Ozzie. That was a good arrest. Not a trafficking charge, but better than nothing. All the vials were testosterone. Passed on as other steroids. He was labeling it himself at home.
- Ø Thanks for the call Jerry.
- Ø Ok, keep looking into things.
- Ø Will do.

32 TIME PASSES

It's been two weeks now since I spoke with the thugs. I thought I give Edwin a call and chat a bit. Was I looking for a friend? Nope, just curious. Maybe it will make me write more. Maybe it will be a future distraction from my demons. Maybe it's therapeutic. Whatever the reason, I was softly compelled to call him. An oxymoron perhaps! Anyone? Anyone? I'm bored, as Abby would say. I'm not going to call anyone. Fuck' em all. I was born alone. I'll die alone. Research, yea, that's the ticket. I'll look into what Edwin spoke about. Then I'll call him.

It was Friday, and my regular fish called. She wanted to see a movie; of all places at the movies. I said that would be great, but I was lying. I was in fear. I'll be brave. Sooner or later, I will have to conquer all my fears. Deep inside I hated going to the movies. It was after my first divorce when I started to fear the movies; for I loved my Jenelle, Ozzie and Christian. Jenelle's mother was a nasty bitch. A fox in sheep's cloth. She hid behind her religion. She was vengeful and would hardly let me visit them. One of the first movies I saw after my divorce was, "Mrs. Doubtfire", with Robin Williams. It was a movie about me. Mrs. Doubtfire was a man disguised as a nanny, the purpose of which was to see his children that his wife would not allow him to. Although I never disguised myself as such, everything else in the movie was relevant.

I could not stay to watch it at the time, nor did I ever. My next movie was with Ozzie and Jenelle. They were still young. The movie was Peter Pan. In it was a character that looked exactly like Ozzie. My tears rolled down and I struggled to contain them. Never again. No more movies for me. It wasn't till Abby was movie age, that I started going again. I never let anyone in my family know of my fear. It was not so much a fear, but rather a pain. A pain of being removed from loved ones.

My movie date with G was an internal disaster. In it was a man that was a US Marshall. He often drank to mask his pain. Although I did not drink for such a reason, I knew what was coming. I knew he too lost someone. Later in the movie it was revealed that his young daughter of five had passed. It was a good thing it was dark at the theater. For it concealed my emotions. I knew that man's pain and I was forced to relive mine. G did not have a clue of what I was going though. There was no fooling around for me that night. She asked if I was ok. I gave the typical answer, but I wasn't. I was torn and tormented. For tonight I was to be paid a visit; A visit from a loyal friend. Although he has eluding me for a little, he returned tonight. I turned away from G and hugged my pillow. I found myself in the fetal position grasping for air. I was being chocked. Not a sound I made. Not a whisper, nor a whimper. My tears were flowing, as I remembered my lost loved ones. One of which will never be back. One life I am to blame for. Why? Oh why? When will it ever stop?

Several days have passed. My demon has not revisited. I did manage to do some research into Edwin's revelations. To my surprise I started to uncover some disturbing news. For the moment, I won't point them out. For it had lead me to do more research. It seems one thing leads to another. In many aspects, many things are related if not interrelated. I'm starting to see something here, though my thoughts might be a little premature. It seems Edwin was right of that which he spoke of. I'm beginning to see a pattern. Something is amidst. Lead by evil forces. If you can call it that. In my world there is no god, but there sure seems to be a Devil. Something dark and evil is at work. Not an entity, but man himself. Anyway, back I must go. Back to the laptop. Research some more. I was right about him. Edwin that is. The big thing in a small package. Not poison, but one that would expose it.

Finally a call,

Ø Prince.

Ø Yo, Ozz! What's up?

Ø I gave up on you.

Ø Sorry. It's just that I've been very busy working with Jerry. Got to do my civil duties.

Ø How's that going?

Ø Good, good. I can't talk about it but we are about to make a big bust. Might hit the news.

Ø That's good. I've been stuck with two arrests, and I am a little worried.

Ø Ozzie, you know that Jerry likes you.

Ø Tell that to the judge. That gets me nowhere. I was just given a two month extension to come up with some more things. I don't have anything Prince. My plan seems to have failed.

Ø I'll see what I can help you with.

Ø I know Harold is working on something big. I think you will get some credit because you helped get him out. Ask Jerry about that.

Ø I wonder if Harold can throw anything my way.

Ø Harold knows some heavy hitters. Be careful.

Ø Yea, I know. I am already a wanted man.

Ø Look Ozz, Can you meet me at my house?

- Ø My wife is away for two weeks, so we can talk.
- Ø Sure. How about Wednesday, after I get out of work. Somewhere about 7
- Ø Sounds good.
- Ø Great, see you then.

As usually, I looked up the address Prince gave me Southwest Ranches; just a few miles from Hollywood. It would take about 15 minutes from my work to reach him. The houses there are large, with some well to do residents; including some actors as well as baseball, and football players. The front lawns as well as the yard are huge. Three vehicles were parked in the driveway. One was his BMW. One was a new Tesler. The other not so expensive. The closed circuit cameras must have revealed my presence; as he came out to greet me before I could exit my car.

- Ø Hey Price. How's it going?
- Ø What up, Ozz.
- Ø Nice ride. Is that the wife's?
- Ø No. No. That belongs to my girl. The wife is away. I leased the car for her.
- Ø So, your girl is here.
- Ø Yea.
- Ø That's wrong. Tell me your wife won't show up here with a gun in her hands while I'm here. After I'm gone I won't give a shit.
- Ø Eat shit.
- Ø So, what's on your mind?
- Ø Come on in.

The house was impressive. The ceiling in the foyer was about 20 feet high. A white marble stirs gave way to upstairs. I wasn't really interested in a tour. I could care less about the features. The family room we sat in had a few boxes of sneakers that weren't opened yet. I guess he must have been shopping.

- Ø Where's the maid?
- Ø Don't have one.
- Ø Oh. So where is your girl? She is in the back watching TV.

Prince was not formal, or rather, not polished. His expensive clothing help detract this fact. As I say. Each man is his own. It really doesn't matter what others think? Well, to many people, it doesn't matter. I had a female doctor friend that thought otherwise. The house had a few expensive decors, but was somewhat unkempt.

- Ø So Prince. Talk
- Ø We need to get back to the vault and study it a little.

Ø I thought about that. Bring a four foot ladder, screw drivers, flashlights, and masking tape.

Ø Dam, what do you have in mind? To abduct someone?

Ø We are going to take a ride in the container itself. From there we can see where the unit is placed. Also, I think it's a good idea to rent a smaller unit. A security box. This will take us to the other part of the building.

Ø So you have been thinking about it.

Ø Prince, I thought all that up while we were still over there. I saw it as I stood within the container. I didn't give it any further thought thereafter. Once we go there again, we can plan some more. So what you got Prince?

Ø Well, I did not want to talk about this anymore as I have a feeling my phones might be tapped.

Ø So we meet in your house. How about if your home is tapped?

Ø I don't think so.

Ø Bring those items I asked. Also see if you can find a device that will reveal the presence of laser beams.

Ø What's that for?

Ø It's just to check on their security, once we start walking in the off premise area. I need to know where the sensors are. Don't want to cross the path of a laser and trigger an alarm.

Ø Good looking out, Ozz.

Ø We have a long way to go.

Ø Ozzie be careful of what you say when we talk on the phone.

Ø I think we should just go over and ride in the unit. The following week we should open up a small safety box. For now, I'm out of here.

Ø Ok Ozz. Thanks for coming over.

Strange. Weird. Ominous. I wanted out of there. I can't place it, but the vibe from Prince was just not good. He leased a Tesler for his girl. Was it in his name or hers? What's it costing him? How much money does he really have? I remembered him telling me in jail that his lawyer had chewed a large part of his money, and that he owned thirty thousand in plastic. I'm willing to play a little further. But proceed with caution is the name of the game. His girl never came out to say hi. I'm getting a strange feeling he is up to no good. I need to prepare a speech for any questioning I may get from Jerry or any other cop regarding my involvement with Prince. Just in case. Just in case. My faith in all this keeps dwindling. I find myself more interest in following or exploring what Edwin has mention than getting involved with Prince. What is holding me back? Is it the challenge? I think so. It's eight and I'm hungry. I shall call my favorite girl and see if she wants to eat. Not the playful fish, but a girl that I know loves me, Abby.

33 TOM

Happy dance! Happy dance! JT, I'm doing my happy dance; and one happier dance. Prince and I were to meet this past Sunday. He called to put it off to the following week. By now I concluded that all bets were off with the thugs. I am left to my own devices. It's up to me to generate some arrest.

The evening was cool. The garage door was raised and music played in the background. A glass of Galliano in one hand and a cue stick in the other. I often played by myself to relax. That is, when no fish were around. Tom, A white male in his fifties came over. His house was right next door to mine. Several times we had spoken and shot a game or two. Tom wasn't very good or well-coordinated. Every evening he sat in his garage with his door opened as he smoked his weed. Friends would come and go to his place. He was a contractor that developed a serious back problem after a fall at work. I knew he also took pain killers. For the most part he kept to himself just as I.

- Ø What's up Tom? Ready for a beat down?
- Ø Sure.
- Ø Ok. Grab a stick.
- Ø Hey Ozz. You care for a hit? I got some good stuff.
- Ø Fuck it. Let's roll.

Here was an opportunity. I had a feeling Tom had connections and I was going to uncover them. There was only one thing on my mind. That being to stay out of jail. Tom pulled out some weed and rolled it. Everything he needed was in his pocket. It's been many years since I had a hit. The weed had a nice smell, and we both smoked. Into our second game I asked:

- Ø Hey Tom. I'm looking for a connection.
- Ø What do you need?
- Ø I am trying to break back into the business. I have a friend that moves a lot of dope. If I can get a good source, I can get a nice piece of the pie.
- Ø How much are you talking about? I have some people I know. They will bring it to me.
- Ø To start, I need to sample it. If it's good as well as the price then I will buy maybe up to a kilo a week.

Tom had been in the business a long time ago and was happy to talk about it.

- Ø Are you going to cook it or cut it?
- Ø Neither. I need it as pure as can be. Price is not an issue if the quality is good. If it's bounced on to much I can't use it. I think my guy will cook some. His name is Prince. He moves a lot of shit. We became buddies in jail.

Tom picked up his phone and made a call.

- Ø Hey. Bring me a twenty and also a gram of butter. I'm shooting pool at the house right next to mine. The garage door is open, just come in. I want you to meet a friend. Make sure the butter is not stepped on.
- Ø Tom, how much is that going to cost. Well, I will take half. So just give me $50. If it's good we will do business.

A half hour has passed since his call. Mike, a short Haitian pulls into his driveway. Tom signaled for him to come over.

- Ø Mike, this is a friend, Ozzie. Ozzie was in the business and trying to get in again. If he likes your shit there he will do a lot of business.

Mike and I shook hands. I brought out a beer and some chips. I don't think he was of the wine type. Tom spoke freely and confidently. He knew I lived alone and often remarked about different girls coming and going. Tom gave the cue stick to Mike and I re-racked. Mike played well, but our focus was getting to know each other a little so that we could do business. Tom asked for his order. Mike reached in his pocket and pulled out a bag of weed and a small bag of cocaine. It's what Tom referred to as butter. Why? I don't have a fucken clue. And I did not care. Arrest number three. That's what I was looking at. Mike finished his beer, took some money from Tom and left.

- Ø Hey Tom. Thanks for the hook-up. Hope it's good.
- Ø Give it a try.
- Ø Will do.

Tom went to his garage and retrieved a small electronic scale. He set it on the pool table and weighed half a gram. He placed the coke in a little piece of foil that he brought along. He was not concerned about the garage door being open.

- Ø Tom. Aren't you worried about someone seeing you?
- Ø Ozzie, I lived here 20 years. I know everyone on the block. People know I have workers that come and go. I've worked on most of the houses on the block. There are no cops here.

- Ø Ok. If you say so. I trust you Tom. While we are at it. Do you have another connection, just in case?
- Ø I have many connections. If you really need big quantities, I know of two Cuban brothers in Miami. You have to deal in Kilos for that, and the first few times they might not sell to you. It will have to be through me. I also have a Puerto Rican guy called Ramon. I was in jail with him. Problem is he buys from some other guy I know and then he cuts it. Oh. I got James. You might have seen his car here. I think he knows of Mike. But they each have different territories.

Jackpot. Happy dance. I'm in business. I had another drink and gave Tom another beer. I was going to get as much info as I possibly could, without raising any suspicion. Yea baby. Fuck those fake thug friends I know. Tom and I spoke for the next hour. He offered to introduce me to James in a few days.

- Ø Tom, when he comes, if my car is parked, just let me know. We can shoot a game and talk.

Tom did get pleasure out of the pool table. Why had he not own one? His garage was as big as mine and empty, except for the lounge chair he often uses.

Wow. I could lasso a few guys here. My mind was working fast. The only reservation was about the Cuban Brothers. I was afraid. Not of them personally, but because of a possible connection to the price on my head. I don't need to die. I'll see how the others go first. The thing here was to get at least two arrest, maybe three.

Tom departed and I retired. For the moment, I was happy. Without giving it much thought, I picked up the phone and called G.

- Ø Hi G.
- Ø Hi Ozzie. What's the miracle?
- Ø Just wanted to say hi.

It was too late. I could not retrieve the call. I found myself reaching out to G. We spoke for a few minutes. Why did I call her? Why? Was I just happy and wanted to share? I don't want to be attached. I don't want to fall in love again. I do not want to open up myself to anyone. Oh well. Fuck it.

For the next few evenings I made it a point to quickly shower after my gym workout, and then spend some time in the garage. Of course with the garage door open. Galliano was always the order followed by a game of pool. G was getting used to coming over. Like myself, she preferred to eat healthy. She much prefers to cook a meal than to eat out. How convenient for me. I wondered if this was part of her plan. For now I was content with it. Every so often I would peak towards Tom's house. True to his word, he came over on the fourth day.

- Ø Ozzie, James is coming over tonight. Do you want me to bring him over?
- Ø Yes Tom that would be good.
- Ø Should I tell him to bring you something?
- Ø Yes, same as with Mike the other day. Just a sample. I'm on a tight budget.
- Ø Okay I'll pay for it and you can hit me later.
- Ø Sounds good Tom.
- Ø He usually takes about 45 minutes after I call. I spoke earlier with him and he said he was coming by.
- Ø Okay I'll be here in the garage shooting pool.

G brought to the garage a plate of food. I told her to sit and eat with me. She went to the kitchen and retrieved her plate. And so we sat down to eat.

- Ø Dam G, as usual this is fucking good.
- Ø I'm glad you like.

She always included greens as well as vegetables. Sweet potatoes were among her favorite, but she kept it down to a minimum because of the carbs. G was Peruvian and had a flair for seafood. I never asked what she was making, I just always chowed it down. G was fully aware of my circumstance. She knew of the plan with Tom and did not ask any questions nor got in the way. I had mentioned that James would be coming over a little later. She sat to eat near me only because I asked but I think she would much have preferred to be inside. My class of Galliano had empty. I found myself drinking from her cup.

- Ø Nice aroma G.
- Ø It's a merlot.
- Ø Is there more?
- Ø Sure let me get some.
- Ø It's okay G I can get.
- Ø No you sit and relax.

With that she went to the kitchen and brought the bottle to the garage. I poured a glass, but did not let it sit. No matter. For the most part it was all the same. Delicious… G quickly ate and headed to the kitchen.

- Ø Don't worry about the dishes G. Ill clean them later.
- Ø No it's okay. Just relax and wait for your friend.

Can it get much better I thought. The answer is probably yes. But for now this was good enough. I had business to take care of. Business that would turn off most woman. And G allowed me to handle my business without any pressure.

As I started to rack, I noticed a vehicle drive up slowly and pull into Tom's driveway. It had to be James. I played as if not to notice. Tom's garage door was open and James walked in. Several minutes later, Tom and James walked over.

- Ø Ozzie this is James.
- Ø Hi James, what up? Are you up for a game?
- Ø No, I can't stay long; my wife is in the car. Tom told me you were interested in moving some stuff.
- Ø Yes I was in the game and trying to get back in.
- Ø What are you trying to do?
- Ø Well James I have a friend that moves a lot of dope. He cooks some of it, and cuts the rest. If I can get a good connection, he will buy from me. However the quality has to be good.
- Ø Tom is a good friend of mine. He said you were good people, so just hit me up when you need something.
- Ø Ok. I'll call you in a few days.
- Ø Later.

James was matter of fact; to my liking. Tom handed me an ounce of coke and said, "I'll get you later." I now found myself sitting with a gram and a half of coke. I had no way of disposing of it. Who could I possibly sell it to? That was not an option in my book. In my figurative book. Tom departed, and I closed the garage door. Before I knew it, I was standing in the bathroom with the toilet seat raised. I flushed the coke and then retrieved the other. That also went down the toilet. I had no use for it. Nor did I want to chance getting caught with it. I then went to the room and laid next to G and told her what transpired. She was glad to hear I had disposed of it. I then showered. As I lathered, I was planning my next move. My mind was somewhere else. I knew I was going to take these guys down. The sad part for me was that, I knew I also had to move. There was no way, I could rope them and hang around. That would be foolish; suicidal. Upon returning to the room, I found G naked. What a sight. Fuck it! Planning the next move, that could wait a little.

Well I'm on my way. I see the light at the end of the tunnel; which brought me back to my High School days. Every afternoon, lunch time was a race to the cafeteria. It had different entrances. Sometimes after a certain class my route would take me through a long semicircular tunnel with a length of over 150 ft. Because of the curvature one could not see beyond thirty feet. Many a days on my way through it I would loosen the light bulbs so that they would go off. My friend Eddie usually joined in. We could not help our self. We would leave the tunnel in total darkness. Fun days they were. Anyway, back to reality. I waited for Prince to call. If he didn't, it was no big deal. I now had a plan. I was able to do for myself.

I waited a few days before I called Jerry. I knew my days in my apartment were numbered. My mother's house was an option. I could stay there for a few weeks until I acquired another place. The room was on the second floor as was hers. I reasoned there was no way I would bring my fish over for a swim.

I decided to rent a storage unit. Perhaps the Vault? I think not. There is a saying, "you don't shit where you eat". I wanted as little ties to that place as possible. South Florida is loaded with storage facilities as there are many Northerners that visit for a while, and/or move. I decided to rent one that was easily accessible to me. Within the next few days I took some items over, in preparation for my move. I knew what was coming down the pike.

- Ø Jerry
- Ø Hi Ozzie. What's up?
- Ø Through my next door neighbor, I meet two different drug dealers. My neighbor Tom is a pothead. He sometimes comes over for a game of pool. He introduced me to two different guys that sell dope. I meet with them and told them I was trying to get back in the game and was looking to purchase. They both said they would get me whatever I needed. Any amount.
- Ø Did you meet them together?
- Ø No. Separately. They bring drugs to Tom. I don't know if they know of each other. Tom also spoke of two Cuban brothers in Miami that sell only in kilos. But I have not made that connection.
- Ø Did you buy from them?
- Ø No, you said I could not.
- Ø Whatever you do, you have to play by the book. You are not allowed to do any drugs or buy any.
- Ø I understand. They did bring Tom some drugs, and Tom offered to give me. I have both their numbers.
- Ø How soon can we get them?
- Ø Jerry, I have to plan for a place to move to. I'm not going to stay there after I turn them in. It's disruptive to me, but I understand it's what I must do.
- Ø Give me a few days, or let's shoot for next week. This will give me the time I need.

- Ø Ok. Text me there number and name and anything else you might have.
- Ø Will do Jerry. I'll call you in a few days.
- Ø Ok. Keep your eyes open. See what else you can find.
- Ø Ok.

After two arrests I knew what to expect. I figured it best to do both these two guys on the same day and then get the fuck out. The following day, I took to the garage again. Tom popped in for a minute.

- Ø So how was that?
- Ø It was ok Tom. James stuff was better than Mikes. My buddy wants to buy a few ounces. I'm wondering if you have another source as well.
- Ø Why. How much do you need to buy?
- Ø Yea. Your right.

I was not about to make Tom suspicious. So I left it alone. For a bird in the hand is worth two in the bush. Two birds were even better. I let Tom know I would be calling the guys within the next few days to order some coke.

- Ø Let me know if you need anything from me.
- Ø Ok. And Tom thanks.

Despite having to move I was in good spirits. Things were looking up. Several more arrest and I would remain free. I thought of Edwin and looked further into my research. It started to consume me. Alarm was an understatement. I was dumbfounded, bewildered, and confused at what I was uncovering. What hypocrisy; The United States of America. It can't be so? But I was realizing that it was. There something evil, something dark. Do I write about it? For it has gotten many killed. But how can I live with myself if I don't do anything about it? Do I continue? Does Edwin know of all I am uncovering? If so, how can he live with himself? Is that what he meant when he said he knew thing but could not talk about them? Or was it perhaps that it could get him killed? What a dilemma. Where is this taking me to? Is this part of my journey? Is it my destiny? Was ending up in jail, just the first part? Fuck! This is scary shit. I never asked for this.

34 PRINCE CALLS

- Ø Hi Ozzie.
- Ø Yo, what's up?
- Ø Meet me tomorrow at the Vault. !2.
- Ø Do you have the items?
- Ø Yes.
- Ø OK. Pick me up at the same place as last time.

It was Saturday evening. I was packing some items. G spent the night over. In a few hours, it would be my favorite day of the week. Upon taking notice I sent Prince a text. It read, Need to meet at 1pm.; For I was going to enjoy my Sunday morning. Waking up naked with a beautiful girl, followed by love and breakfast. Oh, did I say love, instead of play? Did I say girl instead of fish? So maybe she has graduated to girl, but I'll continue to call it play, with emotions, different than those primordial one instilled on us to preserve mankind. Anyway, she was growing on me a little. I know she has a fucken plan. So far, it seems to be working.

- Ø What's up Prince?
- Ø Hey Ozzie
- Ø Come on. Let's go.
- Ø I'm assuming you have the things in the trunk.
- Ø Yea
- Ø OK. Let's do this Brutus.
- Ø What's that?
- Ø Brutus.
- Ø Never mind.
- Ø Should I have said, let's do this fat head.
- Ø Eat a dick.
- Ø Talking about fat head, there is no way you can squeeze that face of your through the 12 x 12 inch vent.
- Ø Oh, you got jokes.
- Ø Cheer up. What's with you? The wife came back?
- Ø Yea. She is such a nag.
- Ø Then get the fuck out.
- Ø Cant right now.

Ø Oh well. Let's go.

Prince was not in good spirits, and I really did not care. Nor was I that interest in his escapade. But my curiosity has not waned.

The drive to The Vault from where we meet was only 30 seconds. We drove straight to the back into a loading dock. Prince pressed a few numbers on a key pad, then his thumb into a reader. He pressed to have our container brought to us. To me this was adventurous. Doing something we were not supposed to do. Pushing the envelope, if you will. BTW, where the hell did that expression come from? I'll look it up when I get home. It took about three minutes for our container to arrive. I was going for a ride. Can I trust Prince to bring me back? I think so. Prince popped the trunk. We made sure once again there were no cameras. I grabbed the ladder and placed it within the unit. Prince grabbed a bag with items in it. First on the list was the removal of the vent; Phillips screwdriver, very easy. I was in the mood to keep fucking with Price. It was just one of those days. Once I get on a roll it hard to stop.

Ø Hey Prince. Stand on the ladder and unscrew. Make sure you climb on very slowly. Is that ladder capable of an extra heavy load?

He did not answer, but smiled as to say. OK funny. I got up on the ladder as nimble as can be and removed six screws. Without making too much noise I pushed the vent outward making sure it would not fall.

Ø Yo. Pass me the tape.

I used it as a rope. Gently I let the aluminum out of my grasp, holding only the tape. I extended my head out through the opening. There was not much to see if front. Unfortunately the hole was facing the side of the building. There was about a four foot clearance between the building and the container. Looking to my right I could see down the long side of the building: properly 75 feet. It was hard to judge. It was also difficult to tell what was there. There seemed to be stacked containers. I guess we were on the last bay. Looking to the bottom left was a wall. I think part off the bay where our car was parked. The air space above that was open. There was enough light to see without the need of a flashlight.

I put the vent back to its original position without any screws, all the while using the tape as a cord. I cut off about a four feet piece and unmounted the ladder. Prince just watched. There was a sensor on the elevator door. It was to make sure there was nothing in the way of the door closing. The gap between the container and the elevator door was less than half inch. Not enough to make sense of anything. I say the elevator door but reality was the door was not part of the elevator. The door was affixed to the wall. What would move was the container itself. So it was the elevator that sat on some type of elevation system, and moved around. I was now full with excitement.

- Ø OK Prince. Flashlight. When I tell you, stand outside the container and send it away. Then retrieve it in about five minutes.

Prince mind was occupied. Not with the task at hand. He proceeded with my instructions. As the door was closing he replied.

- Ø OK Ozzie. See you next week.
- Ø Eat a dick, fucker.

I could hear him laughing. However I was not scared. Off went the container. It was a sturdy move. No tipping or rocking. Whatever was carrying it was secure and strong. The first traveled direction was up. There was no light in the container. I turned on the flashlight and pushed the vent out. Some light came in, but only a little. The end of the container was still dark. The move up was slow. About 15 seconds, then shifted to the right. That would be with my head facing out. We were traveling towards the south part of the building. The box traveled for about forty feet or so. It then went a little up again and came to rest. I deduced that some type of robotic forklift must be at work, for the container came to rest on top of another. I could see that the adjacent stack was higher. So, the container was neither plucked from the top nor lifted from the bottom. That means there has to be a large enough space towards the other end of the container, opposite the vent, through which it is moved. Where it now rested, the temperature started to increase; Not unbearable, but noticeable. It was clear there was a strong a/c unit towards the bottom where the elevator door was. All of a sudden, the unit lifted. It jerked a little, but not enough to throw me off the ladder. Due to lack of noise, it was discernible the lift had not disengaged. It now traveled in reverse order. The time was about the same. The container door opened first and came to a complete stop. The elevator door immediately followed.

- Ø Hey. Nice to see you.
- Ø So what could you tell?
- Ø We are fucked. Too many uncertainties. The containers could be placed in any number of different spots. It rested on top of other units, with rows of containers to each side. I think you might be better keeping tabs on the man, finding out his pattern and everyday movements. And then approaching him as he pulls in. I can't think of anything at the moment. You're going to have to hack into the system and find out where his unit is.
- Ø Ozzie. I already did that.
- Ø Why didn't you say so? It must look daunting; else you properly would not use me.

Ø You helped me get out. I promised you a piece. Anyway, I do need some help. Going to have to look elsewhere.

Ø What does that mean?

Ø Not sure. But need to get creative here. Meaning thinking outside the box.

Ø Hey Prince. How did that phrase originate?

Ø With circles.

Ø Eat shit? Look next week I'll come and open a safety deposit box. It's to the other side of the building. We will learn a little more then. Something will give sooner or later. There is always a way. Just have to rule out the wrong ways. Let's get out of here.

Ø OK.

Ø Hey Prince. What's the deal with your girl?

Ø What do you mean?

Ø I don't know. Just curious. She must know you are married.

Ø Ozzie, I married for convenience. Not for love. I've been seeing this girl for many years. She knows my family and my friends. She knows more about me than my wife. Come to think of it, my wife doesn't know much of what I do. She just spends the money. And lots of it.

Ø So you have lots of money?

Ø As soon as I got out I was able to do a book signing and made a shit load of money. My book is doing really well.

Prince looked away and raised his hand to his mouth, as if to cover up. I knew he wasn't truthful. I know something was wrong. I do believe there is something in The Vault he wants to get his hands on. His confidence in talking about it convinces me. But outside of that I know there is something wrong. I'll continue to play along. I wonder if he thinks I'm stupid. Well come to think of it, he did plant the seed for the $6. as he calls it. "I think, therefore I am." Nope! Not this time. If it's one thing I know, I am far from stupid. But as I recently came to find out. I'm ignorant. Just like 99% of Americans. I've been bamboozled. My fellow American and Hispanic friends we have been sleeping. Basking in mundane, day to day activities of no importance. Sleeping, while the dark forces work. Again, I'm not talking of spirits or entities; I am talking about a handful of people; evil people with an evil plan. OK. I'm going off on a tangent. But trust me. I will get back to this. You are in for a rude awakening. OK, OK. I must contain myself. Hey, what the fuck? Where did I go?

Ø Yo. Let's go. You've been standing there for a minute. What happened to you?

Ø Oh Sorry Prince. Few things on my mind. Did you get everything in the trunk?

Ø Over a minute. Hello.

Ø So, you were saying you made a lot of money with your book.

Ø Sure did, and it just keeps coming in.

Ø That's great.

Ø Maybe, I'll write a book. Something along the lines of Don Quixote and Sancho Panza, and it will be about you and me. I would be Don Quixote and with your belly you would be Sancho Panza. But more appropriate would be Edwin and I fit the bill better. Or maybe I'll call it. Fat Prince eats dick.

Ø Fuck you!

Ø Let bounce. Oh BTW you said you hacked in the system.

Ø That was easy. I can get into any system, usually without a trace. Some systems will know when they have been compromised. I was able to get in without being noticed.

Ø So, what did you learn?

Ø The biggest problem we have here is that the units can be leased anonymously. I know he produces a bill that pertains to a box. But that box or container cannot be traced to him. The system is designed so that boxes show as paid without any connection to its owner. To retrieve your box you have to know the code that person created and also have to have your thumb print verified by the reader. You can set it up so that the thumb print is not needed but then you lose a level of security. Drug dealers forgo the thumb print and put drugs in a container and then have someone else retrieve them. Money is paid through wire transfer into some foreign bank, or sometimes money is placed in the security box. There are a number of ways of going about that.

Ø Is that what you used to do?

Ø No my crimes were identity theft.

Ø That's lucrative!

Ø Big time. I'm working with Jerry on that. Can't say much more.

Ø So. You know this guy has things in storage. But you don't have a clue as to which unit it is.

Ø That's the problem. There is no way of knowing which unit is his. Even we knew which unit it was, we would have to know where the unit was parked. Things get complicated further if it's placed high up. Breaking into it would be an issue.

Ø You hacked this man's computer. You hacked the storage place. Is there not a way to cross check both computers for links or connection as to the unit?

Ø I did that. Very complicated to formulate an algorithm that will give me that answer. I think he has it hidden well. On top of that he probably also uses his thumb.

Ø Cut his finger.

Ø I thought about that for a minute. But that's more stuff for TV. I spoke to a friend in Israel, a famous hacker, that might be able to produce a replica or mode of his thumb print if I can get lift a good finger print.

Ø Are you serious? A hacker friend in Israel.

Ø Ozzie. Several times I told you I was a big time, notorious underground hacker.

Ø Well, I would think underground would be appropriate. Hacking does imply that. At least it does have that kind of connotation. So you went so deep you came out on the other side of the world and when you poked your fat head out the ground, the police saw you.

Ø Eat shit. You've been funny today. I got to have some of what you've been eating.

Ø Try some pussy instead of that dick you are always talking about.

Ø Eat dick.

Ø OK. On the serious tip Prince; Is, what you saying, true?

Ø Everything I say is true.

Ø Well then. It's true.

Ø So, how many people are really in on your $6 deal.

Ø Ozzie. Hackers hack for the love of the game. It's a sport. We help each other out, without asking what the hack is. Everything that goes out through the Internet and all the phone calls in the US are recorded. There are computers that filter out key words. When they find those key words you get flagged. That's why hackers don't ask too much. Otherwise they self-destruct.

Ø Yea, I know this. Ever since the government blew up the Twin Towers, they implemented and enacted laws to watch us? Look up The Hegelian Dialectic and learn.

Ø What the fuck are you talking about? Everyone knows Osama bin Laden did that.

Ø Yea Price. We know. I'm just delusional. Last week I had sex with the tooth fairy. Her teeth were really white. I made sure to stain them.

Ø Yo nigga, what the fuck is up with you. You need to give me some of whatever you're smoking.

- Ø I told you, try pussy for a change.
- Ø Eat dick.
- Ø You see. You like that shit, and that OK with me. Just don't hit on me.
- Ø Yo Ozz. What the fuck is up with you?
- Ø I told you. Good Pussy all the time. Well Prince for me that works, maybe not for you. Try a guy.
- Ø Yo, get off that shit.

I was enjoying fucking with Prince and I did not know how to contain myself; my spirits where good. From what I gathered, Prince had some concerns. We were making no progress getting info on where the $6 container was. He seems to be carrying some other problem. What could it be? I did not know nor cared.

He drove me to my car, and I left through a different route. I thought it wise to learn about the area. Just in case. Yea! That's the ticket. Just in case.

The day was young. I called my girl, Abby.

- Ø Dad. I'm in West Palm Beach.
- Ø OK, Love you.
- Ø Love you too.

G was home watching TV. She pulled the covers off and invited me to rest near her. She was wearing my favorite… nothing. I dove in. Yea baby! I like it. I like it a lot. So far, her plan, whatever it was, was working well for me.

After a few hours of playing and relaxing I took out my laptop. More research. Edwin opened my eyes, or I should say; he brought something to my attention. I had the option of looking into it or disregarding it. It really wasn't much of a choice at this point. It started innocently for knowledge of the NETA, but in my quest for such, I've stumbled upon big things. I can't keep away anymore. Not that it's consuming me, for my priorities are straight, but it does occupy my time. And I might add in an 'illuminating' way. BTW, that's a hint. Here is another, May 1, 1776. I hope this doesn't get me killed. I started writing, I think, as therapy. Maybe it was to kill. To kill time that is. Maybe I really wanted to know why I did what I did. I starting by asking, what was the circumstance or circumstances that brought me to jail? I am still on that quest. I still have not figured it out. I still do not know. On the surface it seems it was because I bought drugs. But that is not the answer. There is something much, much deeper. In truth, I think it's more about love or perhaps the lack of it. I'm still not sure. Whatever the answer may be, I now find myself asking new questions. Questions that are not the scope of my original quest. Perhaps, after I find that answer, I can explore and/ or write about new revelations. I now find myself losing sleep about what I am uncovering. I've been able to keep my demon at bay, or maybe it's him that has chosen not to bother me. No matter, something else lurks in the dark. This does bother me. I will have to ask myself if I will become part of it or become an antagonist. Ok. Leave it alone Ozzie. Leave it alone.

It was now towards the end of April. The tax season in the car business was winding down. Soon it will slow again. The used car market in Florida spikes considerable in February. Many use their tax returns as down payments. I have done well for myself. My low overhead has allowed me to put some money aside. It's Tuesday evening and the garage door is open. I hope Tom stumbles in. It's time. Time to do the next arrest. For now, this is priority; my main focus. It was about 9pm when a white Chevy Cavalier pulled into Tom's driveway. I've seen the car before. It was the short guy, Mike, one of the guys that I met the previous week. Tom walked over with Mike.

- Ø Hi guys what's up?
- Ø Hey Ozzie.
- Ø What's up Ozzie?
- Ø You guys care for a beer?

I retrieve two beers from the fridge.

- Ø Mike. I'm glad you came over. My boy wants me to get three ounces if you can handle it.
- Ø Just say when.
- Ø Sure, but it might have to be when I am at work and not here. My girlfriend stays here a lot and I don't want her to know what I am doing. Besides I have to get the money and then make the delivery,
- Ø I'm ready for you. Just let me know the day before.

Tom had headed back to his garage. Mike finished a game and then took off. Yes, I was going to get another arrest in the bag.

The following day, I placed a call.

- Ø Jerry. How are you?
- Ø Well. What's up?
- Ø I got one lined up. Mike came to the house yesterday and said he will sell me whatever I needed. I just had to call him a day before.
- Ø Do you want to place a controlled call?

Ø No Jerry. We can kill two birds with one stone. Once I do this I am forced to move out. Give me a day or two so that I can set up the other guy as well. Should be on the same day, so that no one finds out, until it's too late.

Ø Good move Ozzie. Let's shoot for this Thursday or Friday.

Ø Will do, Jerry. I'll call you as soon as I reach him.

Several hours had passed before I sent the other guy, James, a text.

Ø Yo. It's Ozzie, Tom's friend. Can you get me a few things?

Ø I'll come see you tonight.

Ø OK. Garage door will be open. Just come straight in.

At gym I rushed my workout and headed to the Bat Mobile. OK, to the garage, my garage. James arrived half hour later.

Ø What's up James?

Ø Thanks for coming. I figured you did not want to discuss things on the phone. Care for a beer?

Ø No. My wife is in the car. We have to go pick up my son. He is at the sitter. I only have a few minutes.

Ø My boy called me. He wants me to bring him a few ounces. I'll know how much tomorrow. I did not want to involve Tom. Can you handle that?

Ø I got you. Just call me when you're ready.

Ø OK. Thanks.

Brief and to the point. James did not bother to stop in Toms' house. That worked well for me. The less Tom knows the better. My question now becomes, do I try for a third guy at the same time? Ok, thought about it. The bird in the hand. I had what seemed to be a sure thing. Best I make a run for it before it runs away from me. This evening, G was at here place. Time for a booty call. I had them lined up. But G was my favorite. Not only was sex great, she was also fun. There was always something to laugh at. Yesterday as we played, I had my way with her. One day while she was lying on the bed, I asked her to place her hands to her side. I'm doing an experiment, I said. Need your help with it. As she submitted I managed to wrap the quilt around her. Tight enough so she could not break free. Her arms could not be raised. Relax. She smiled and wondered what I was up too. I got off the bed and picked her up while still wrapped, and placed her on the floor. With that I started to roll her within the quilt. I managed to get my belt and tie it around her. Now she was in trouble. For I did to her what she hated most Keeping a firm grip on her I managed to get a hold of her bare feet. She knew it was coming and in anticipation started yelling. It was to no avail. For there was no one to rescue her. I then did it. Her outbursts were uncontrollable. As I tickled her feet she violently galloped, and tousled around. There was no escaping. She was at my mercy, and I was having my fun. After a moment it was time for the next foot. Again she buckled.

Ø I'm peeing. I'm peeing.

Ø Liar you are.

Ø Ozzie. Let me go.

G did in fact; release a minute amount of urine. Just enough to drive me crazy. I checked her, and licked her, followed by play time on the floor. Childish, one might say. But that was typical of pranks we played on each other. G was fun, lots of fun. Fuck it I said. With that I called her. Why did I need anyone else?

35 ARREST THREE AND FOUR

Thursday morning I called Jerry.

Ø Hey Ozzie.

Ø Jerry, I'm ready. We can get these two guys tomorrow.

Ø Do you have a plan?

Ø I think so. I have given it much though. From what I gather Mike should be second. Just a feeling.

Ø Let's call James and see if he can get you the things for tomorrow. Let's shoot for about 1-2. This will give us a few hours to book him and still have time for the other. Call James. Tell him you want three ounces. Say you will be driving from Miami and need to travel back. See if he can meet you around Hollywood.

Ø Ok. Do you want me to call now?

Ø Yes.

By now not only did I know the drill, I was comfortable with it.

Ø Hello.

Ø Hello. Who this?

Ø Hey James, it's Ozzie. You should have my name and number locked in. Can we meet up tomorrow?

Ø Sure. How much you need?

Ø Three ounces.

Ø What time.

Ø I will call you in the afternoon was I am sure. But I am thinking about 1. I have to run to Miami to pick up some money and then go back to make the drop. Can you meet me around Hollywood?

Ø Sure.

Ø What's the damage?

Ø $3300.

Ø Ok. But it has to be good at that price.

Ø You'll like it.

Ø Ok James. That's. I'll call you tomorrow. But just to be sure. You can get it, right.

Ø I already have it.

- Ø Great. I'll see you then.
- Ø Jerry, did you get that?
- Ø Got it. Good job. Let's go ahead and call Mike. Tell him the same but let's shoot to meet about 4.
- Ø Ok
- Ø Mike?
- Ø Yo, what up.
- Ø Hey Mike. Can you get me that for tomorrow?
- Ø Not a problem. How much you talking about?
- Ø Three ounces. I'll be ready about 4pm.
- Ø Just call me when you ready.
- Ø Hey Mike. I'll be driving up from Miami with the money and then need to drive back. Can you meet me around Hollywood?
- Ø Yea, just call me when you're ready.
- Ø Ok. But I need to be sure you will have it for tomorrow because I am responsible for the money.
- Ø I got you.
- Ø Ok.
- Ø Jerry, did you get that?
- Ø Yea. Good job! Be ready for my call in the afternoon. We will make another control call to confirm.
- Ø Ok. I'll be ready.

That evening after work, I rushed home. I knew I needed to get my item out. I called G and she offered to come and help. It was a big red pickup truck that I drove home from the lot. G was there when I arrived. I pulled into the garage as far in as I could, so as to hide from Tom. I was scared of being found out. His garage door was open as usual. Tom smoked weed every day and sometime he would just fall asleep for a little at about this time. I don't know if that was the case as I did not see him. In twenty minutes we loaded several item and departed to the storage unit. By now it was almost 9; Closing time. I knew we did not have time for another load. But then there wasn't much more, just the bed, some clothing, dishes and food. When I arrived Tom's garage door was closed. He was either sleeping or out getting food. For the next hour G and I packed some electronics in plastic container bins; about four in all. Included were cables, cable box, modem and several other items. Everything was unplugged and stored. There was nothing left to do. Tomorrow we would finish moving the remaining items. With that we showered, and played.

Friday morning was here. G offered to make some breakfast while I showered.

Before I headed to work we placed some bins in her car. I left before she did. She was to pack the food and take it to her house. The departure from her this morning was different. She hugged me and gave me a kiss.

Ø Be careful.

Ø I will. Don't worry about anything. Everything will be fine.

Her concerned with genuine. Once at work I reminded Ed that I was to leave early. He knew what I was doing and did not question.

Ø Just let me know when you're ready to go.

Again I found myself to be somewhat excited about the events that were to follow, but I was neither nervous nor anxious, more like relieved. Relieved in knowing I was achieving my goal; the goal to remain free. I thought about what I was doing, and for about 30 seconds felt bad. Bad for James, for he had a family. Oh well too bad. Someone turned me in, and I had a family. Fuck it. It's his time. Someone has to take my place, and I did not care who that was. That's it. That is the extent of my sympathy.

12 o'clock passed and Jerry had not called. Shall I call him? I think not. I'm sure he knows his job. Maybe he is planning the day. I'll just sit and wait some more. It was another hour before he called.

Ø Hey Jerry. I was starting to doubt if we were still on for today.

Ø We needed to plan.

Ø Yes I figured

Ø Let's go ahead and make a call to James. Tell him you are running late, but that you will be ready around three. Ask him again to meet you in Hollywood. Also confirm the amount and the price.

Ø Ok.

Ø James.

Ø Yo, what up?

Ø I'll be ready about three. Is that good for you.

Ø Just say when. I got to pick up my son by 4:30.

Ø Just to be sure you have 3 ounces right.

Ø Yes

Ø And its $3300 right?

Ø Yes.

Ø Okay got it I will call you in a little.

Ø Jerry did you get that?

- Ø Got it Ozzie. Let's go ahead and make a call to Mike. Tell him the same thing but make it a little later. Tell him you, about four.
- Ø Got it Jerry
- Ø Yo, Mike, Ozzie
- Ø You ready.
- Ø I'll be ready about 4 o'clock.
- Ø Okay just hit me up?
- Ø That's 3 ounces right?
- Ø Do you want more?
- Ø No three is good for now. And that is $3300 right.
- Ø That's the going price.
- Ø Okay Mike. I'll get you later. Remember I'll be coming up from Miami and then I'll have to drive back. So if you can meet me around Hollywood. That would really help me out.
- Ø Got it.
- Ø Okay Jerry. Did you get that?
- Ø Ozzie be ready. I'll call you in about one hour and tell you where to meet us.
- Ø Okay I'll wait for your call.

I knew I was in for a long day. Today lunch would be one of the fast food places. Because I ate well for the most part, a greasy burger every so often, I reasoned would be okay. And so it was. Biggest burger I could find, accompanied by the largest size French fries I could buy, and a large diet soda to wash it down. Several of these meals and I could kill myself, or should I say I could be killed. But I won't get into that now. After lunch I made it a point to use the restroom. Last thing I needed was to take a shit during a drug bust. Did I just say, shit? I could have been more polite, but today this was my demeanor. Shit, and fuck, those were the words for today.

Jerry finally called, just as I had finished. Shit I thought, was he watching me?

- Ø Ozzie meet me in 30 minutes just right off I-95 and Sterling Rd. There is a hotel there. Go to the back
- Ø Okay Jerry. See you shortly.

For the third time in as many arrests, I came in contact with the same group of detective. Football was in the air, literally. It came crashing onto my windshield. What the fuck. Is this payback? Can't be? I dismissed it. One of the officers pointed at a parking space. That was my cue to park. Joe, once again greeted me. We walked to the grass just a few feet away and he started to prep me for the microphone and the transmitter. As he did so one detective entered my vehicle checked it. Upon exiting proceeded to search the trunk.

All clear, he said.

Ø Where's Jerry?

Ø He will be here shortly.

Joe asked me to sit in my car and wait. Several minutes later Jerry arrived.

Ø Hi Ozzie. How are you? It's going to be a long day. Just make sure to follow our directions. Let's go ahead and make a controlled call to James. Put this microphone in your ear as you make the call. That will record it. Remember to tell him to meet you in Hollywood. You will call him back shortly. Ask him what's the quickest he can meet you?

Ø Hi James its Ozzie.

Ø Yo. You ready?

Ø I'm still in Miami James picking up some money. What's the quickest you can meet me in Hollywood.

Ø 45 minutes.

Ø Great ask perfect for me. I'll call you in about 30. I'll be traveling on 95 so maybe you can meet me on one of the exits.

Ø Okay, just let me know.

Jerry exited the vehicle and gave the command to move. All jumped in their vehicles and headed out. This time there seem to be a few more detectives than the previous. There were four female detectives. Twice as many as I said before. It seems that this was training for a few new detectives. I stood behind with Jerry and Joe. Jerry told me to relax. The meeting place was nearby. I was relaxed but I also wanted this day to be over. Jerry got a call on his walkie-talkie. Everyone is in place.

Ø Let's go Ozzie. Before we do let's make one last call. Tell him to meet you in the parking lot where the big fishing store is. Whatever you do, do not move from there. The units are in place. Try to get him to come in your car. This GPS will record audio and video, make sure it is on. Remember if you see a gun, make a remark as to what type of gun it is. If he pulls it out and tries to run say; hey don't shoot, just take the money. Do not try to fight. Once you see the drugs and give him the money say my buddy will like this. In the car off. If anything goes wrong, run away from the car as quickly as possible. Any questions?

Ø Now I think I got it by now. I'll be fine. I know what to do.

Ø Remember we can hear you, if there is anything you need to say just say it. If you feel anything is wrong, let us know.

Jerry instructed me to follow him. The ride was no more than 45 seconds. Before we arrived he already knew of where I was to park. He called me as we took off, giving me instructions along the way. I did as he said and parked. The parking space was among the furthest from the store. There were no vehicles within 15 to 20 feet from me in all directions. An 8 foot fence ran along the front of the car. It had a square perimeter of about 400 ft. In it were a few boats and trailers. I wondered if any of the detectives with there. At the far right of defense was a gate with a padlock on. That answered my question. Using my members I looked around for any of the detectives. I could not recognize any vehicles. Where the hell are these guys I thought?

Jerry instructed me to call James again, and check on his time of arrival.

Ø Hey James,

I gave him directions and instructions. He knew the vehicle I was driving for he had seen it parked in my driveway. Nonetheless I made sure to point it out.

Ø I'll be there in 15 minutes.

Ø Okay just parked near me when you get here.

It was 20 minutes when James called.

Ø Ozzie, I am across the street from you. You will have to drive over and meet me.

Ø James I'm sorry but I am not doing that. I don't know you and you don't know me. This is not my first time. Several years ago I was robbed at gunpoint, so I am not moving. Next time around I will meet you on your ground.

Ø Okay stay put. I'll be there soon.

I would imagine James was staking out the place. His few minutes turned into 10 minutes.

Ø Hello James. Where are you?

Ø I am in the parking lot walking. I cannot see you.

Ø Let me stand outside to see if I see you.

Ø Ozzie I don't see you.

Ø James I don't see you either. James can you see the front of the store.

Ø Yea, I see it.

Ø Okay look to the sun and walk towards it. If you look down, you will see a big fenced area with boats in it.

Ø Yea, I see the fence.

Ø My car is the only car parked against the fence. I am standing up looking for you.

Ø Okay I see you.

- Ø I don't see you.
- Ø Am wearing a black shirt.

Then I saw him and waved. He took notice and continued walking towards me.

- Ø Okay guys I see. Black man with dreads. Black shirt. About 100 feet away walking towards me. I'm going to sit and car and wait.

The communication system is a one-way system. I could not hear anything, but they could clearly hear me and any conversation within the car. I knew they were listening. James entered and sat on the passenger seat.

- Ø What's up James?
- Ø Yo, what up.
- Ø Thanks for meeting me. I was pressed for time.

James looked around as if he was nervous. He took notice of the GPS sitting on the dashboard. He made no attempt to examine it.

- Ø Do you have the stuff with you James?
- Ø Know I have it in the car. You have to follow me there. Do you have the money?
- Ø Of course I have the money. But I need to see the dope first.
- Ø Okay let me walk to the car and get it. I'll pull up right next to you. The car is at the other end of the parking lot; you should just drive me there.
- Ø James I much rather wait here. If everything goes well, there will be a lot more deals and I will come to you.
- Ø Okay wait here.

James exited walked to where he came from. Just to be sure everyone knew what was going on I said.

- Ø Okay guys. He's on his way to the vehicle to get the drugs.

Five minutes had passed and James had not returned. I tried calling him there was no answer. I wondered if he had been arrested. Suddenly Jerry calls

- Ø Ozzie this guy is leaving. Someone is driving him. Looks like a female. Do you think he has the drugs with him?
- Ø Jerry I'm sure he does. He must have been spooked.
- Ø Just sit tight.

That I did. 20 minutes went by. No one had approach. I did not notice any vehicles come and go. What could be going on? It was another 10 minutes when Joe came over to me.

- Ø Ozzie relax for now. Jerry and the team are on Interstate 95. There has been an accident.
- Ø Is anyone hurt?
- Ø Everyone is fine. I don't know all the details but they gave chase and tried to pull him over. He started to dump some of the drugs out the window; they did catch him with an amount. It will be a while before they get back here. Just relax.
- Ø Will this still count for me?
- Ø Yes, it's still a good arrest.

James somehow read the signs and knew something was wrong. Nonetheless, for him, it did not end well. For me it was great. All is well that ends well. After an hour of further waiting hunger set in. I asked Joe if I could get something to eat. He suggested I don't leave the parking lot, put did point out there was food in the store. The store was about 40,000 sq. ft. There was a restaurant in it. I asked how quickly they can make a sandwich. To my dismay, they did not prepare any take out. I had no time to sit and eat. I opted to get a soda at the front register. Along with that I picked up a small bag of popcorn and a candy bar, the one that says, "It really satisfies". For the moment it had to suffice. I sat in my car and devoured the popcorn first, then the candy bar. I was not satisfied. Still hungry but at least there were no hunger pain.

Joe had instructed me to meet him, where the unit was first station; where I meet them earlier in the day. Therefore I needed not leave the confinement of the parking lot, but rather just drive to the other end. A few the guys were throwing a football back and forth. Is that how they stayed in shape? It was undeniable many worked out. Some were enhanced, but I'm sure they were under medical supervision. Yea, that's the ticket. Joe did not work out. He was older than the others and seemed to be content with his donut belly. There was something charismatic about him. He walked over to me and asked if I was alright.

- Ø Other than being a little hungry, I'm fine.

Joe explained that the guys that stood behind were from the team in charge of my safety. I was taking a liking to donut Joe.

- Ø Is the microphone and transmitter still in place?
- Ø Yes. I have not touched it.
- Ø Make sure it's off for now. We will turn it on again when we need to.
- Ø OK.
- Ø Alright. Just sit tight for a little more.

It was now three. It seemed these guys could throw a football all day long. One guy walked to my car.

- Hi Ozzie. I am detective Gonzalez. Jerry is going to be tied up for a bit longer as he has to process the arrest.
- How did that go? Does it count for me?
- Sure. It was good for you. We gave chased on Interstate 95. His wife was driving. He dumped some drugs out the window, but later cooperated and admitted he did have three ounces. I think the wife had swiped the side of the car along the left lane wall traveling north. There were no guns in the car. Jerry might be able to tell you more later today. For now I want you to place a call to the gentleman. We need to know if that is still a go.
- Sure.
- I'll be back in a few and make that call.

Det. Gonzalez had me fooled for a minute. He stood about 6' 3". Well built, tall, lean and muscular. His eyes were light. His skin tone pale. Obviously he did not throw the football while in the sun. He looked more Anglo, but then Hispanics come in all shape and colors. Several minutes passed before he entered and sat in my car. We place a call to Mike.

- What up.
- Hey, it's Ozzie.
- You still good for today.
- I got you.
- I'm running late. I have to go to Miami and pick up the money. Then I'll come hit you. I'll call you in about an hour. Maybe we can meet up in Hollywood.
- Just call me when you're ready. I'll be waiting.
- Ok.

Gonzalez recorded the conversation. He exited and gave the thumb up to someone. It's a go. I also exited the car and just stood by. Donut Joe walked over.

- Ozzie. Det. Gonzalez will be in charge of this one. Jerry is going to be busy.
- Thanks for the info. Sit tight a little longer. The units have to be in place. Several of the guys are still at the arrest area.

Ismael called me as I waited.

- How are you?
- Ok. But I can't talk. I'm waiting for instructions from the police regarding the next arrest.
- Oh, how is that going.
- Can't talk about it this moment. We did an arrest earlier today and working on number two. Everything should be Ok. I'll call you today.
- By.

Conversation with Ismael were usually brief and to the point. He knows I was not one to talk much. G was off today, and I called her to give her some news.

- Ø Bicha!
- Ø Bicho!
- Ø Everything so far is good. The first arrest went down without a problem. The guy food off as he got scared, but was fallowed and taken down on 95. I still don't have all the details. Shortly we should be done with the next.
- Ø Okay, be careful.
- Ø Did you take the foods to your house?
- Ø Yes, I grabbed some things and brought them over.
- Ø Ok. I'll call you later.

Till now it did not occur to me that I had not made any sleeping arrangements for myself. I knew staying at my mother's would not be a problem, but I have yet to call her. I procrastinated as I have often done before. Why should today be any different? I'll stay with G for tonight and then will notify my mother tomorrow.

Det. Gonzalez came to me.

- Ø Ozzie. We are getting ready. Call and see what time he can meet us.

It was now past four.

- Ø Hey Mike.
- Ø Yo.
- Ø I'm leaving to pick up the money. How soon can you meet me?
- Ø I'm waiting for a friend. Give me an hour.
- Ø Ok.

I was beginning to bore, but I knew I need to stay focus. So, I just waited some more. Besides there was nothing I could do. Donut Joe came over to check on the equipment. It was fine. There seems to be some activities among the group. Det. Gonzalez had me place one more call.

- Ø Mike.
- Ø Yo
- Ø I'm on my way up. Meet me around Commercial and 95.

I'll be there in about 30 minutes.

Some of the guys already headed out. I was to follow Det. Gonzalez, north on 95 for several miles. On the exit to Commercial blvd. We headed west, and turned into a group of stores on the right side of the road. Most of the guys were there already. That was not to be the final meeting place. I wondered if they were trying to throw me off guard, or if they just weren't sure of the best spot. Some left their vehicles there, while they departed with someone else. We traveled back east, passed 95 and then into the parking lot of one of the big home improvement store. All the while never leaving Commercial Blvd. The parking lot was to the front of the store. From there one could easily see across Commercial Blvd. There was a donut store there. Coincidence, maybe. I was instructed to park just as soon as we turned in. It was the far end of the property, away from the entrance to the store. In all there were about nine detective vehicles scattered about. By now, I did not care how near of far they were from me. It seemed my arrest was being made without myself having to exchange money.

It was now past 5. I sat in my car and called Mike, making sure to put him on speaker so that the guys could hear him.

- Ø Where you at. I just got off on Commercial. Where the big home store is.
- Ø Ok. I'm coming soon.

Everyone was on alert. Twice I called Mike to get his eta.

- Ø I'm coming. I needed to pick up the stuff from my friends house. I'll be there soon.
- Ø What car are you driving?
- Ø White Chevy Cavalier.
- Ø Okay

All right guys. Did you get that? Look for a white Chevy Cavalier. Four doors if I remember correctly. They stop making that car years ago so it might be beat up.

I waited some more. It was now 6:30. Everyone seems to be getting restless. Not only was I, but now I was also hungry. Det. Gonzalez text me several time.

- Ø Ozzie, blow up his phone. Keep calling.

Several tries later Mike picked up the phone.

- Ø Yo, I'm coming.
- Ø You've been saying that for the past hour and a half. I am walking around with $3300 that belongs to someone else. If you were not coming through you should have just told me. I'm leaving. Don't bother coming. I got to get back to Miami.
- Ø No. Don't leave. I promise I'm less than five minutes away. I'm coming up on Commercial in a minute.
- Ø If you're not here soon, I'm getting the fuck out.

- Ø I got you.

I called Gonzalez.

- Ø Did you get that?
- Ø Yea. Nice.
- Ø Sit tight. Let me know if you see anything suspicious.
- Ø Ok.

Finally it seems this is going down. I now eagerly looked around as cars came and left the parking area. No white Chevy Cavalier around. He did say he was picking the drugs up from his friend. Could he be in that other vehicle?

Mike's five minutes turned into 15. I called several times and sent him several texts as well. His phone was off, not available. Could he have been in an accident? Could he have been pulled over with the drugs?

It was now past 7. The call was made to cancel. Now, I was a little embarrassed and disappointed. We all headed back to the previous stop on Commercial. The one we first went to. Once there the talk was of going home. Jerry came out of one of the cars.

- Ø Hi Ozzie. Sorry this one did not go well but at least you got the first one. That puts you at three.

As Jerry was talking to me, my phone rang.

- Ø Hey Jerry, It's Mike on the phone.

Jerry signal for all to quiet down.

- Ø Ozzie, see what he wants.
- Ø Yo.
- Ø Hey, I'm here.
- Ø Where is here?
- Ø Where you told me to meet you.
- Ø Well it's too bad. I left already. I'm heading south on 95.
- Ø Yo come back. I'll wait for you.
- Ø I'll call you in a minute.

Jerry asked the guys if they wanted to go back. To my surprise they all said yes. I guess they really like their work; must be the adrenalin rush. Immediately some vehicles took off. Jerry stayed behind with me and Gonzalez.

- Ø Ozzie. Call him back and tell him you will be there in 10 minutes. We have to let the guys fall in place.

Ø Hey. I'll be there in 10 minutes.

Ø Got u. I'll be here.

After a few more minutes, we took off. Jerry was in constant contact with the team. I followed one of the vehicles into the parking. He continued straight as I parked where I was originally. I looked around but could see no Chevy cavalier, nor white car for that matter. So I made another call.

Ø Yo Mike. Where are you?

Ø I'm across the street. Will be right there.

Ø Are you in your car?

Ø Yea.

Ø Okay.

I was able to see across the street. There were no white cars there. I gave him a few more minutes, and then called again.

Ø Hey what's up with you? I'm coming. Be there in a minute.

By now the sun had set. It was past 8. I knew Mike was now fucking with me, so did the cops.

Gonzalez called me again.

Ø Ozzie, make one final call. Tell him you are leaving. If he does not show in a few minutes, leave the parking lot and wait for us at the other location.

Ø Mike. I know you are fucking with me. I'm getting the fuck out of here.

Ø Waite one more minute.

As Mike spoke, so did someone else. Mike was not alone. Five minutes later I left the parking area as instructed. When I arrived, Jerry was there. How did he get there so fast?

Ø Ozzie. Come quick.

Ø My guys made an arrest. Call Mike now.

I did as Jerry said. Jerry was on the phone with someone else.

Ø Ozzie, call again.

And so I did.

Ø "It's ringing" Jerry said.

Ø What's the number?

Ø My number?

Ø No

Jerry lifted his finger for me to pause. He was speaking to the guy on the phone.

- Ø Ozzie, What the number on your phone.

Jerry repeated the number to the guy he was speaking.

- Ø Okay. That's him. We got him.
- Ø Ozzie, stay put. My guys were staking out the place. They apprehended two guys in a black car. Waite by your car. I'll come in a few.

I thought that was good news. I went to my car and waited for Jerry. As I sat there my eyes focused on something three parking spaces directly in front of me. It was a car which is rear facing me. I step out of my car to get a closer look. Holy shit! Fuck! Can't be so? Jerry noticed me. He was only about 15 ft away. Without saying one word I pointed forward. Jerry looked towards where I was pointing but did not pick up on it. I was in amazement. Holy shit! I said to myself. Can't be so? Although I was thinking, I could not speak. Jerry looked with amusement. I pointed again. Once again he looked.

- Ø What?
- Ø The car. That's the car. White Chevy Cavalier.
- Ø Ozzie. Don't go near it.

I walked to the side so as to get a side view. I've sold hundreds of cars if not thousands. I knew cars. Shit! That's a fucken white Chevy Cavalier. They stop making them over 10 years. What are the odds? I knew that was the car.

Jerry called me to him. He took out his phone and showed me a picture. A few of the detectives had left to the other locations. Something was going on.

- Ø Do you know this guy?
- Ø Nope. Never seen him.

A minute later Jerry shows me another picture.

- Ø How about this guy?
- Ø Yea. That's him. That's Mike. Still has the pimple on his forehead.
- Ø Are you sure?
- Ø Jerry. I'm sure. That's Mike. I never seen the other guy.
- Ø We are running the plates on the Cavalier.

Jerry got on the phone. "We have a positive ID."

- Ø Stay put Ozzie. It's looking good. Do not go by the Cavalier. Else they can say you put something in it.

Jerry's remarks did not occur to me, but it did make a lot of sense. These guys knew their stuff. Very quickly my level of respect for the police rose. Not that I did not respect them, but seeing how they operated gave me a different perspective.

Five minutes later, a bomb sniffing unit appeared. Well, it was a K9 unit. The car parked away from the Cavalier, and the police that was driving retrieved a dog from the back seat. It was a huge German Sheppard. The long hair type; as there are two. I also knew dogs. The handler walked the dog around the Cavalier. After sniffing around the trunk the dog sat. Once or twice it made an attempt to continue into the trunk. It was clear he was excited.

Jerry came to me,

Ø Ozzie. Go home. The dog has signaled that there are drugs in the trunk. The plates check out to Mike. More than likely he has the drugs there. The other unit has him in custody and will bring him here. We will take his car keys and confirm that he has access to the car. Looks really good for now. I'll call you in the morning.

Ø Okay Jerry.

Fuck. What are the chances of both the cops and the bad guy parking next to each other? I would have to say slim. There were hundreds of different places to park. Was it luck? Was it fate? The Gods were with me this day. I called G and told her I was coming to stay with her this evening. I let her know everything turned out well. It was now almost 10 pm. I knew I needed to get the rest of my things out of the house. I also knew the storage was closed. Fuck it. I'm hungry; starving. I'll get my shit tomorrow. It was now the next morning, Saturday. G woke up upon hearing me. I rested myself by her side and dozed off rather quickly. The morning was followed by a breakfast; shower and then we were both off to work. We still have not discussed where I was staying.

At work I made arrangements for a friend to give me a hand, retrieving my items left in the house. I could of managed alone but the king size mattress was cumbersome to retrieve alone. I've done it before but I was afraid to go there; Let alone spending time loading a mattress. Who knew what I could have encountered. Perhaps a man standing behind a gun. Nope. Not worth it. I'll use the help. Before entering my street I slowly drove by it, checking if anyone was lurking. I turned around and entered the cul-de-sac. Tom's garage door was closed. Perfect. Now let's be quick. G had left the place spotless. A TV stand, chair and bed set were all that remained. It took about 10 minutes to load. I checked to see if anything was left behind, and quietly departed. The trip to the storage was along the way to G's place. Being Saturday, it closed an hour earlier.

Ø G

- Ø Yes, bicho
- Ø The storage is closed.
- Ø Just bring the things over. I'll use your bed for the time being.
- Ø Ok.

I took the help back to the store and headed to Hollywood. G helped me swap out the bed as well as the TV stand and TV.

- Ø Tomorrow, I'll take these items to storage and will let my mother know that I will be staying with her for a little.
- Ø Don't be so foolish. You can just stay with me until you find a place.
- Ø Are you sure?
- Ø Sure.
- Ø Okay.

My intension was not that, to stay at her place, at least on the surface; else I probably would have made arrangements by now with my mother. Maybe, by default, I did choose. Well, I'll have playtime every day, plus a delicious meal. But more important, I'll have someone to hold at night. That evening after setting things in place we spoke a little. I was relieved the two arrests were behind me. That puts me at four. I don't think enough to get off entirely, but it was a good start. It was enough to maybe buy me more time, so as to get in some more arrest.

Sunday, my favorite, was once again upon us. It was the typical Sunday morning. However, we were both off from work and so about 12 we thought it best to take the things in the truck to the storage facility. Along the way back, I remembered that I was to go to the Vault. I decided to give Edwin a call. Perhaps we could talk some more. It would have been much easier for me to go with G. But I did not want to involve her. I told her I was going to call Edwin so that he could ride with me to the Vault. As we drove I placed a call.

- Ø Boriqua.
- Ø Que tal, Ozzie?
- Ø Well I'm going somewhere and want to know if you're up for a ride?
- Ø What do you have in mind?
- Ø I need to check out a place in Ft. Lauderdale. A storage place. Figured we could talk a little.
- Ø What time?
- Ø About 45 minutes. Meet me at 95 and Sheridan. By the hotel. You can ride with me.
- Ø Ok

Good, I said to G. She had heard me speak of him. She asked no questions. I did say we were going to check something out. She knew of the Vault and that Prince had something he was investigating. G knew I was never a drug dealer, nor did I do drugs. She never doubted or questioned me. Not that she was naive, for the contrary was true. She just gave me, and respected my space. What I shall temporarily now call hone, her place, was only minutes from where Edwin was to meet me. However she was closer to the beach, in the better part of town.

Ø I'm going to cook.
Ø Do you prefer I bring something?
Ø No. I don't want that food. I prefer my meals. I know what's in it?
Ø Okay, works for me.

I pulled to the house, dropped her off and proceed to the rendezvous. Edwin was there by the time I arrived. I parked near him and exited to meet him. He came over and we shook hands.

Ø Ozzie, you look good. You've been eating a lot.
Ø Yes, I've been sleeping and eating right. I have a Peruvian girl on a mission. She's trying to win me over through my stomach. Little does she know I'm on to her! But, for now, it works for me.
Ø So what are we doing?
Ø I need to open a safety box in a storage unit. I figured I bring you along so that we could talk.
Ø So you want to know more about the NETA.
Ø Edwin, I want to know more about a lot of things, and I want to know more of you. After all, you and I are going to Puerto Rico. It's part of an investigation into some of the things you spoke of and also as vacation.
Ø OK.
Ø So Edwin, how is it that you know so much.
Ø It's a long story.
Ø Humor me.
Ø What's that?
Ø Entertain me. Oh do I need to speak thug with you? Perhaps Ebonics, Oh Spanglish. Ok, I just messing with you. So tell me, how do you know so much?
Ø I'll tell you a little, but some things I can't talk about.
Ø Go.
Ø Ozzie. I am a NETA, because I was forced into it. Before I went to jail, I was a Freemason.

Ø Are you fucking with me Edwin?

Ø No it's true. My father was a high level Mason. He brought me in. My dad's family had money and influence. I was the black sheep and got into trouble. My cousin who was in Jail with me, the one I told you, that I saved his life was also a Freemason. His son, my cousin, in Ft. Lauderdale is a Mason.

Ø Why did you not say anything?

Ø It's not something we talk about.

Ø So that is why you know a lot of the history of Puerto Rico.

Ø In 1858, a Spanish boy by the name of Manuel Fernández-Juncos who became a Puerto Rican by adopting the island as his country came from Spain. He became a writer and a statesman, then later a Master Mason, 32° Scottish Rite Mason, and the founder in 1893 of Lodge Patria No. 61 in San Juan, Puerto Rico. He was also the Lodge's first Worshipful Master. He became one of the great heroes of Puerto Rico and a founder of Freemasonry in Puerto Rico. He wrote about newsletters on health, society and government. It was the only documents that stood up when the government, dominated by Madrid, hindered the economic and political progress of the island.

In 1887 during the tenure of Romualdo Palacios as Spain's Military Governor of Puerto Rico, all Masonic Lodges were closed by the governor and civil rights of the people were suspended. The Civil Guard was authorized to imprison and physically abuse Puerto Rican citizens. It's kind of what was happening in the jails when the NETA was formed. Any two or more persons meeting were subject to immediate arrest. This dark episode lasted almost a year until the Queen of Spain appointed a new governor. In the history of Puerto Rico, this year is often called "The Year of Terror." In 1897, the Spanish Government implemented an autonomous government for the colony of Puerto Rico.

This first self-governing cabinet was composed of local patriots such as Luis Muñoz-Rivera, and Manuel Fernández-Juncos, the latter as Secretary of the Treasury. So just like in the US. One of the first political members of Puerto Rico was a Mason. The next year, 1898, the Spanish-American War broke out, and The US Took over the island, putting in place its own military government. Some of its members were also Masons. The American Military Governor, requested its members to stay in order to form a bridge between the two governments. For the most part, the Americans didn't know the laws and customs of the people nor the Spanish language.

Ø Edwin, I had no clue you could speak this well. What the fuck. Oh. Let me reframe, for I am in the presence of a true scholar. Please, do pardon me?

Edwin smiled. It seemed we were both on the same page. Both able to adapt to situations as they presented themselves. Go on.

Ø Bro. Fernández-Juncos, seeing the Spanish language was in jeopardy, took over the task of adopting, translating, and writing books for use in the schools. Bro. Fernández-Juncos is considered a true Puerto Rican though he was born in Spain. His dedication to Puerto Rican culture and to the betterment of Puerto Rico was of extraordinary service in preserving the island's rich past and assuring its secure, prosperous future. This outstanding Freemason is also the author of the words of "La Borinqueña," Puerto Rico's national anthem.

Ø So, Puerto Rico's nation anthem was written by a Mason.

Ø Yes. Also the second most important avenue in San Juan is named after him, Manuel Fernández-Juncos Avenue. The first being Juan Ponce de León ave. Juan Ponce was the first governor. But freemasonry was started in 1885, by Don Santiago R. Palmer.

Ø So Bro. Fernández-Juncos was not the first?

Ø No.

Ø But was within the first few. Several foreign Masonic lodges took the task of setting up lodges in Puerto Rico. The first recorded lodge was in Mayaquez near San Juan, under Spain. There were lodges from France, Santo Domingo, Cuba and from Pennsylvania. Venezuela came in August 1863. So there were a few. Union Hermana was started in San German, Puerto Rico in July 8, 1866 under the charter of Santo Domingo Republic. By 1884 there were 14 legitimate lodges on the island. Today seven of the lodges are still active.

Ø Edwin. That's a lot of history.

Ø My father was the one that made me learn all this. My cousin in Ft. Lauderdale knows more than I do. You know Ozzie; I know a lot more about Puerto Rico than most people. The US has done a lot of bad things to our island and our people. But that's for some other day.

Ø Edwin, I started doing a little research into what you told me before. I came across a few disturbing things. Some of which are downright evil.

Ø Yes. They used us for many years as genie pigs. People's misconception of Puerto Rico is totally wrong. Its economy is classified by the World Bank as high and as the most competitive economy in Latin America. It's mostly driven by manufacturing and pharmaceuticals, textiles, petro chemicals and electronic. Followed by finance, insurance, real estate and tourism. Also, Puerto Rico has the second most competitive economy among Ibero-American states, surpassed only by Chile

Ø Don't tell me you are an expert on Central and South America also.

Ø Na. I just know of my island, many Masons in Puerto Rico are told of these things.

I was so captured by Edwin that I had not noticed I was now parked in front of The Vault. I knew there was something to this guy. Something different and real.

Ø Edwin we are here. Come with me. It will only be about 30 minutes then you could tell me more.

Ø Dale. (that's Spanish for lets go)

Ø Edwin, check out this girl. She's a fucken book. I met here before. She knows the whole brochure by heart. Look at that fucken ass on her.

Ø She strong.

I told her I had a container already and would like to lease a box.

Ø Yes, I remember you. You were here last month with some big guy.

I went ahead and leased a box. The fee was nominal and so I paid three months in advance; again without giving any personal information. As the lady took us up to the room where the small units were, we crossed paths with a male employee. Edwin made a gesture at him and he reciprocated. I figured he knew him, but I was not about to ask at the moment. The lady explained how to operate the electronic system so that we could get access to our box.

The room was about 30 ft. by 15. It seems that it was one of several similar rooms. It resembled a bank vault with many safety deposit boxes. The smallest was about 8 inches wide by 6 high. Not big at all. Some were about 15 inches by 12. We picked one 12 by 6. Document papers size. There was a camera in one end of the room. It was obvious this place was monitored. However that did not matter. The purpose of renting the box was to check out a different part of the building. Already, I saw problems. Two elevators transported people to and from the first and second floor. There is a third floor button on the elevator panel, but you need to insert a key to access it. The question now becomes. What's there?

There was not much to see from the customer's perspective; only a few cement walls leading to the elevator, which takes you to the second floor that opens onto three separate rooms with security boxes. Not good, I said, but at the very least I was getting a rough layout of the land. My mission so far was accomplished, that is, as far as leasing a box goes. I did not say much, but did take notice of the surrounding, looking for cracks in the wall, false ceilings, lighting, electrical outlets and the likes. That was just my usual self.

Ø Edwin lets go.

Ø Let's go.

Edwin did not ask me any questions about my being there at the Vault. I wanted to continue picking his brain. I started driving away but not paying attention, I found myself lost. Edwin knew the area and guided me out.

Ø Edwin, that guy you greeted; what was that about? Was he a Mason?

Ø Oh no Ozzie. He is not a Mason. One thing that we say is that you can know a Mason in the dark as well as the light. A blind man can tell you who are Masons, because of how we interact and how we greet one another. I've met Masons on the train, they were sitting down, and I went up and greeted them because of the way they sat and what they did when they were sitting. Two Masons could talk in front of you and you wouldn't even know what they were talking about.

Ø So Edwin, You said there were things you could not talk about. Can you at least give me an idea as to why?

Ø One thing many people get wrong about the Masons is that they think we don't believe in God and the Bible. The Compass is set literally on top of the Bible. It's set on a certain page, which I can't divulge. There is an oath we take on the Bible, like the Presidential oath, or the one you do in court. We are founded, for as much as you can say, on the Bible. I can't talk too much about the Masons because of that oath. Many things that the US has done to Puerto Rico are what I was talking about. It's just best to keep quiet and alive then be in the ground.

Ø Edwin. I'm still not getting it. What could be so bad? I did some research and have an idea, but I want to know more of whatever it is you know.

Ø Let's meet up some other time. I need to think about if I want to say more.

Ø Okay Edwin. I'm with you. Thanks for the history. I know you are holding on to the ugly parts. When you're ready.

We talked a little more about commonplace things. Nothing to note. As we were arriving to the parking lot, I saw him smile. I don't know what that was about. He did seem to like talking about the things he spoke of. He was fluent in his thoughts as if almost repeating things without giving it much thought. Once or twice he also held back.

Ø Edwin thanks for coming with me, and sharing your knowledge. I really enjoyed it. Let's meet up next week.

Ø Dale.

Ø Thanks again.

36 APRIL SHOWERS

While the saying might be true in the northern states it certainly was not in Florida. Our weather pattern is slightly different. For the Hurricane season stretches from June 1 to Nov. 30. So why bring it up? The saying, that is. April showers bring May flowers. Simple: to mark the passage of time. To let you, the readers, and those not so astute, know where we are at within the year. For I mention it before, April and tax season was coming to an end. Several more weeks have elapsed. It seem Prince has given up for now, or at the very least set it aside; the $6. project. Harold has not bothered to call neither. It is mid-April now. No showers here in Florida, just the occasional rain. I've spent the last 2 ½ weeks immersed at work. All the while I put on a few more pounds of solid muscle and now find myself to be in excellent shape. Once or twice I've looked through the classifieds for a place to rent; a place to call home. I have to say, the time I spent doing so was minimal, almost as if I did not care. Hey I was saving money, and enjoying time with the G.

Ed my boss seemed to be on the edge. Although his demeanor for the most part was pleasant, something seems to pester him; for now he was a little uptight. His girlfriend had visited several times behind closed doors. From where I sat the yelling was evident. Actually there were no attempts to conceal their dismay for one another. I just minded my business. Tax season had been good to Ed and I had been good to his business. His profits were the best he had ever had. Something however was wrong. That something affected me one day, ever so slightly.

- Ozzie, you have to wait a few days for your check.
- Okay Ed not a problem.

I did not think too much of it. In business things like that happen. During the day, two other fellow workers complained of the same. They lived paycheck to paycheck and made a stink about having to wait. As usual I didn't say much. I just minded my business. True to his word Ed make good several days later. To me it was a nonissue. I've been in business before and I was well aware that every so often a big unforeseen bill might arrive.

The next week was a repetition of the previous one. The Thugs had not called and Ed excuse himself for not paying me on time. Was this to become commonplace? Of course some of the workers were up in arms. There was nothing they could do but wait. Jerry had called throughout the month several times, checking in on me, asking if I had anything new. The answer was always the same, "no but I'm working on it." I did some more research on the topics Edwin spoke of. I started to notice that it was not the United

States doing alone that had performed transgressions against Puerto Rico. There seems to be something deeper; a group or groups, at work, with certain agendas. Once again I was becoming, "illuminated". What are you waiting for, I told you to look it up. Yes you the reader. You will enjoy this book even more. Go, and come back later. As you start typing your search, notice what pops up. Add to it an Italian flare. I'll leave it at that.

I was learning things, seeing things: things that were present and visible the entire time. Things we chose to ignore and or disbelief. Things that were hidden in plain sight. Again an oxymoron but nonetheless true. How can governments be involved in evil things? How can it be? Are they evil? Or maybe is it just me?

Janet the secretary found herself one day alone with me in the office. Her husband Miguel worked there as the Porter.

- Ø Ozzie. Do you know why Ed is having problems?
- Ø I have no idea. I hope it's a temporary thing.
- Ø Eight months ago he purchased a big house in Lighthouse Point. Right on the intercostal. He tore part of it down and rebuilt. His home theater alone cost him $80,000. His kitchen over 20. You know those two big Brazilians that come here every week?
- Ø The ones that go in the office with him and closed the door?
- Ø Yes those. They are part of the Brazilian mafia. Ed borrowed $300,000 for his house. Every week they come to pick up money. That is why he cannot pay us. Who knows what will happen when it totally slows down in September.
- Ø Janet thanks for letting me know. I knew his home was new to him, but I was not aware that he was heavily indebted. I know it's not our business but do you have any idea how much he owes?
- Ø No, but I know it's still a lot.
- Ø So you mean yes?
- Ø What do you mean?
- Ø Well I asked you if you have any idea. Janet, never mind. Thanks for the info; I can see the writing on the wall.

That explains a lot. I could care less about Ed and his problems. Or about the two big guys that come to collect. Ed's problem was not my problem. I had my own to worry about. Nonetheless I mentally started making a move. A few days later I prepared a resume. Having done financing with Ed has opened many doors. I now had direct contact with numerous subprime lenders and found myself looking through classified postings for subprime bank representatives. I stumbled upon two banks looking for reps both of which I was doing business with already. After a few phone calls I managed to secure two interviews, both with recommendations. The salary for one commenced at $110,000 and the other at 90,000. Looks good I thought. I have a good chance. Both require a phone interview before a physical interview. Within minutes of each phone conversation I was rejected… Bummer. These jobs required a clean background. I was now a felon, and I was going nowhere; At least not with these banks.

Well, there is always the six dollars deal with Prince. Sure. That thought lasted but only a minute. We get so tied up and consumed by trying to make a dollar that we forget what's really important. I was out of jail. I was free for now. I had my health and my sanity. I thought about all the things I had, and then about the things I did not. I became saddened. For I once had a loved one that I would never see again. All of a sudden my family became important once again. I thought of my children, and then I struggled to contain myself. Time to change the subject, before the subject changes me.

I am in Florida and not up North. I don't know if April has brought showers there. There is a saying, "when it rains it pours". That is certainly true of Florida… Sudden torrential downpours. It seems that was also true of Ed's business. Problems were pouring in quicker than Ed could resolve them. He seems to be drowning in a puddle he created. I've not been paid for two weeks. I am out of here. Between the two weeks and earn commissions for the month I am owed about $5000. I took a week off. I told Ed I would return only if he would pay me. It turns out he wouldn't call me; I had to call him, as well as my lawyer.

It's been quiet. The thugs were becoming a thing of the past. What a boring end. Of all the questions I started with I still have some unanswered. Is my quest over? Do I do more time in jail? I was not worried. The reason being I always manage to somehow pull through at the very last minute. I worked well under pressure. There are still many unresolved issues. I know I am not done. Something is missing; I just haven't figured it out yet. And then it hit me. Fuck, Holy shit! Fuck, fuck, fuck! Happy dance, happy dance. Holy shit, Holy shit! I got it. I think I got it. I fucken knew it, the answer was there. At that moment, I got sidetrack by his answer, for I had asked him the wrong question.

Its 2am. I still write at this time; I still stay up, although not with the frequency I used to. G tires me out at night. I never thought I would say that. But she does keep up. Sometimes I want more and sometimes it's she. That's when I'm able to sleep, after play. Tomorrow I will make a phone call. I will have answers. No way, I'm sleeping tonight. I better wake up G. I'm out of work and have time to kill.

37 MAY FLOWERS

If April showers bring May flowers, what does May bring? Here are some answers I found on the internet:

- Ø June flowers
- Ø The Pilgrims and turkey
- Ø Erosion
- Ø Flooding
- Ø beautiful marijuana plants
- Ø mud
- Ø mating season
- Ø Spring
- Ø $6,000,000 (my addition to the list)

Spring, It's on about May 21s. Ah, finally an acceptable answer. One I like. What is spring? Just another day that marks the passage of time. It's around the 20th of May. Called the equinox. There are two in one year. Sept 22 marks the other. The name "equinox" is derived from the Latin *aequus* (equal) and *nox* (night), because around the equinox, night and day is about equal length. The declination being 0. In December we find the winter solstice. The word *solstice* is derived from the Latin *sol* (sun) and *sistere* (to stand still), because at the solstices, the Sun stands still in declination, that is, the seasonal movement of the Sun's path (as seen from Earth) comes to a stop before reversing direction. For about three days it barely moves. For the religious, please take notice that Jesus birthday is placed on Dec 25. (The winter solstice) And Easter Sunday is designated in May (the equinox). All this is just food for thought, although at this moment, I have thoughts of food.

So what does this have to do with anything? Can you connect the dots? In the winter solstice, the sun does not move any further. On the third day it appears to move again. And so it indeed does, by 1 degree. Thus on the third day it raises or changes direction.

So what does this have to do with anything you ask? It's the mood I am in at present, besides being hungry. I am at ease, relaxed, pensive, and content, for I made a phone call and confirmed my hunch. My happy dance from two nights ago was not unfounded. I confirm that I have a reason to celebrate. I now know something. I have something my thug friend needs. It's big, and I'm going to run with it. Sometimes I never seize to amaze myself. That's why I don't worry too much, because at clutch time, I come through.

Can you say $6? Can you say $6,000,000? I figured it out. If Prince is true and the money does exist, I know how to get it. I'll give the guys a call and check to see what the heck is going on.

Ø Price. How are you?
Ø Hi Ozz. Was going to call you. It just that I've been busy; tax season.
Ø Tax season. You're an accountant now?
Ø No, never mind. What up?
Ø That's what I'm trying to find out. It seems you gave up.
Ø Not really, but I can't talk about it over the phone.
Ø Would you like to meet up?
Ø Good idea.
Ø Do you want to get the money?
Ø Off course.
Ø Well let's get it.
Ø That's the plan.
Ø That's your plan. Without much of a plan. I however, have the plan.
Ø What are you talking about?
Ø Can't talk over the phone.
Ø Yo Ozz. What are you saying?
Ø I'm saying. I CAN'T. TALK. OVER. THE. PHONE!
I'll call you in a day or two.
Ø Yo, you're giving me goose pimples.
Ø I'll call you in a day or two.
Ø Ok.

Its 2am and I find myself wide awake. Something peculiar, yet normal, is taking place. I've done it again, without intending. Is this what I am to be? An oxymoron, an intelligent idiot or a dumb genius. "The enlightened ignorant one". For again I find myself as such. How ironic; satirical perhaps, rhetorical or paradoxical. Which one am I? Who am I? What's becoming of me? For just a few days ago, I was cheerful and in good spirits. April showers bring May flowers. How lovely. That was my frame of mind. Now that I found a way in, a way into the Vault, I don't think I want it. I'm not afraid physically. I'm not afraid of dying, for that might relieve my pain. I'm becoming afraid mentally. Peculiar because I should not be afraid. Normal because I've lived it for several years. I am afraid. Afraid of finding within my hands something I never intended for. More blood money. One would think $6,000,000 would be enough. But it's not. No amount is. I should know. I've been there. The settlement had an undisclosed amount. By court order, I cannot reveal. The first digit being a one, closer to two, followed by six zeros. They gave me money, for a life. For little do they know I was to blame for that life. Yes, how ironic. Despite this, I can't find a way to walk away. Why not? What's compelling me to move forward? Because forward, I will move. Even though it might drive me to madness. But why? Is it my destiny? How do I keep my head straight? How do I fight this internal battle?

Twenty minutes have passed since I've typed a word. I've been somewhere else. Not sure where, but a thought has just come. Perhaps I am afraid this book might come to an end, and my evil friend the demon might return. Maybe this is therapy. Maybe I need help. I think, therefore I am. I need to get back to work. Need to distract my mind. Especially from all the new revelations. Edwin has opened my eye, but now I don't like what I see. Besides I think it's too late. 1776 set things in place that we, the average Joe, cannot overcome. I am not talking about the Declaration of Independence. This happened in Bavaria. Do I die trying to point things out, or do I just go along? Either way, you and I are fucked. Yes you, the average Joe. The people that have been asleep immersed in TV.

38 I'M ALL IN

Fuck it. I'm all in. There is no turning back. Deep down, I knew this would be the path. Have I chosen it, or has it chosen me? The last few nights I've done some soul searching. Can you say transcendental meditation? My thoughts have been clouded by too many different things at once. Too many revelations, too much knowledge. I had to make a decision, and that I did. Not through default. Not negatively. But instead positively. I've decided to throw everything aside for now and focus on one thing, $6,000,000. No sense trying to speak of those evil forces I have no control over. No sense wasting my time through default. Fuck my demon for the moment. I'll deal with him later. $6,000,000. Yea, that's the ticket. I know how to get it. Complicated but yet easy; here we go again. Okay, Okay. I'm all in. Physically and more importantly, mentally. Tomorrow, I will make some calls and formulate a plan. There is no turning back. No looking back. I'm in the here and now. Thanks dad. It was the use of the meditation class you made me take when I was 18 that has cleared my mind. Can I use it against, my demon? Oh, let's erase that for now. Only positive thoughts, I think therefore I am.

First on the agenda.

Three hours. That's how long it took to find a place to work. After my beautiful, sexy, fulfilling, delicious breakfast, I made some phone calls. The options for the day were about four. Cruisers Auto, in Davie, Florida; that's where I landed. To me it was a no brainer… Sundays off, and 10 to 6 during the week; More like banker's hour. I worked out a guarantee with Yesid the owner. Yesid did business the right way. Good cars, good prices, backed up by his word that he would take care of any problems. More importantly, I was allowed to do whatever I needed to do. That is, I had a place to work with the freedom of taking care of my personal business. Yesid and I had former acquaintances, and I came highly recommended. For me, the agreement was convenient for the time being. The move was more politically motivated; for I had to show the court I was in good standing.

Second on the agenda. Meet with Prince and discuss the logistics. Because of the knowledge I now had, I don't even think I needed him. One thing however was holding me back. Being resourceful I could probably figure it out, but then why get greedy. That's what gets people in trouble.

Third on the list. Get a hold of Howard and see if he is still involved in this, or at the very least, have some discussion with him. I don't think he is the type of man I would cross. Although it might not be apparent, we are somehow connected in this.

Forth was to meet with Edwin.

It is only after completion of these steps that I can formulate an intelligent, calculated plan. For I have a feeling there is more to Prince. I don't trust him and it's almost certainly a good thing. I rather feel this way up front and prepare for something to come, than to be taken totally off guard in a situation I can't control.

I decided to call Harold first;

- Ø Viejo que tal?
- Ø Hola Ozzie. Finally you called.
- Ø What do you mean finally, you have my number! Why didn't you call me?
- Ø Ozzie, I'm sorry. I misplaced your number after you left. I got a new phone and did not download my contacts. I spoke with Prince about three times. He said he gave you my number.
- Ø Harold, why did you not ask him for mine?
- Ø You know Ozzie. I don't know.
- Ø Hey Howard. So before anything else how have you been?
- Ø I've been ok, but I do need help with something. I'm a little stuck. But I don't want to talk on the phone.
- Ø Okay Harold. Today is Wednesday. How about I come see you Saturday evening after I get out of work. We can meet about 7. Have some more steaks ready. BTW, this is my cell. Make sure to store it.
- Ø Harold, before I go what's the deal with Prince.
- Ø Not on the phone Ozzie. Be careful what you say on the phone with him?
- Ø All right. See you Saturday.

So there is something going on with Prince. It could be anything. Why would he not want me to talk to Harold? Maybe he doesn't want to involve him thinking he can keep that portion of the alleged money. I'll wait till I meet with Harold. I'll give Prince a call and see what is going on.

- Ø Hello, Prince.
- Ø Hi Ozzie.
- Ø What's new?
- Ø Well I have been busy doing a few things, but it slowed down now and I think we should focus on getting my $6.

- Ø Yea $6. You'll be rich. BTW Prince, how is Harold?
- Ø I haven't spoken to him in a minute.
- Ø Oh well, I'll be free Sunday. Let's have a drink.
- Ø Sound good.
- Ø I'll call you Saturday.
- Ø Ok Ozz. Thanks for calling.

This is going to be fun. I was humored by Prince. If it's one thing I get off on, is playing the underdog. Letting people believe they have the upper hand, only to capitalize on their misinformation, or mistaken belief. It is because he is a con man, that I must think three of four moves deep. Ah, a new game of chess. Prince did not seem too excited about my prior call alluding to the money. Perhaps he was really busy, but busy doing what? I don't know. Or perhaps, there is no money. Again, I'm going with my instinct. Something is there. I know it.

39 THANK GOS IT'S FRIDAY

It was about 7:30pm, and I was thirty minutes into my traps and shoulder routine. The two ephedra and aspirin pills had kicked in and I was in my normal grove. The music coming in through my ear piece drowned out all external voices and commotions. By now, most of the 9-5 working class was done with their exercises. As I stood standing in front of the squat rack, I placed my left arm-rap around the bar which was resting on the rack's lowest position. That was followed with the right. Looking into the mirror I noticed two young guys doing squats adjacent to me. One of them reminded me of myself when young; the other looked like Ozzie Jr.; tall and lean, blond hair combed to the side and youthfulness written all over. I watched him as he went up and down; up and down with the barbell across his back. All of a sudden my phone rang. Today I was compelled to take a look to see who was it that was calling, as I don't normally answer phone calls while in the gym.

- Ø Hey dad.
- Ø Ozzie. What a surprise. You won't believe this but I am watching you right now.
- Ø So what am I doing dad.
- Ø You are doing squats, as if you don't know.
- Ø Well I watching you too dad.
- Ø So, you tell me, what am I doing?
- Ø You're in the gym, with your blue shirt on. Did you wash it?
- Ø Ozzie, if I didn't know any better, I would look around to see you, but you know I am usually at the gym at this time, also I always wear blue.
- Ø Yea dad. That one was simple.
- Ø So, what is new? Is everything Ok.
- Ø Yea dad. I just wanted to reach out to you. I've been thinking about you and of all those times you told me you loved me. So I want you to be at peace with yourself knowing it's Okay. I am currently away on a trip. I would like to see my family again.
- Ø Okay. I'll send you a ticket. I'll call you during the week to make arrangements. I'm in the middle of my workout.
- Ø Yes dad, I know.
- Ø You're scaring me Ozzie. Are you suddenly a father?

Ø On no dad. I'm fine. Just haven't heard from you. Love you.

Ø Love you too Ozz.

How weird, for me to be looking at some guy that looks just like my son and then he calls. What a coincidences. The gods are playing with me. Next thing I knew I found myself walking aimlessly through the gym. What was I up too? Did I fall and get hurt? Did some heavy weights fall on my head? I felt no pain, so I guess I must be alright. Water, yea, that's the ticket. I leaned over, pressed the lever and presto, delicious poisonous water; Courtesy of the US government. Chlorine, fluorine, d**ioxin**, and who knows what other poisons they've added. Nonetheless it was refreshing. What was all that about? Did I even finish my shrugs? Was I dreaming? Oh well, shoulder time.

Saturday at work was typical. The subprime used car customer is much easier than the new car customer. Those who can buy new cars tend to look down and treat sales people differently than those who have bad credit. The latter is humbler, and not as demanding. Either way, I am well versed with both, and if I have a say so in the matter, I won't sell new cars anymore. At 6 pm I bolted out and headed home to a quick, refreshing shower. Yes with chlorinated and fluorinated water. Although I was in a rush, I paused a moment while holding something. Something I used almost every day. Now that Edwin has opened my eyes, I see things differently; for I was blind, consumed by everyday ordinary things. I read the label. It was a long list, and so I reserved myself to take a second look into the products found in the shampoo I was using. I quickly made my way to Harold's house, knowing I had some research to do.

Ø Harold. How are you? It's nice to see you again.

Ø Hi Ozzie, come on in.

Ø Thank you. Where is the lovely wife?

Ø She is at her sister's house. She should be back a little later. Come; let's have a drink and talk.

Ø Do you still have my drink?

Ø But off course. No one here drinks that's.

Ø Well in that case, double it up. Light on the ice. Hey, I see you have the grill going.

Ø Yes, some steaks and vegetables.

Ø Great. So tell me Howard, what's the deal with Prince? I need to know a few things, as I know he is up to something. I don't know what it is, but I don't trust him. I feel funny telling you, because we are all supposed to be in on this together.

Ø Look Ozzie. I really do like you and I once again am grateful for your help in getting me out. What I am about to say is between you and I. Please do not let

Prince know I said this. As far as I know the money in the vault is real. Prince came to me and asked me if any of the members in The Latin King, could help him in getting the things out of the Vault. I on the other hand, needed help with some hacking into the police department so that I could somehow bring to light the fact that the police that arrested me was corrupt and planted those drugs. He then robbed me of my jewelry. In jail Prince and I made this agreement to work together. However, it has not turned out the way we expected. Being a member of The Latin Kings, there is no way I can snitch on people. It's not what we do. I made an agreement to get out thinking I could bring this corrupt cop to trial and be exonerated. I also thought we would be able to get the money. As it turns out, Prince says he can't find a way to know which container belongs to the man. On top of that, even if he knew which one it was, he is not sure how to get access to it. So it seems, I might have to do jail time and also that he won't get the money.

Ø Something still does not add up. However that does explain a few things. I myself had to find a way to save myself. I did make a few arrests hoping I could have a reduced sentence. Harold, I can't put my hands on it. But I know Prince is up to something else. He is not telling me anything. For that matter, he never told me you lost my number. It's as if he has to stay in control or maybe he is just used to lying and scamming.

Ø Ozzie. Again, this is between us. I trust you with this. You already know a few things about me, and I am comfortable with you.

Ø Waite Harold, before you begin. Do you really know drug cartels as you once said?

Ø Ozzie, everything I told you is true. Yes I have ties to drug cartels. I know the big guys personally. Turning them in would be a death sentence. I am stuck now. I relied too much on Prince and now think I made a bad move.

Ø So what is the deal with Prince?

Ø Prince thought he would already have access to the money. He was broke with high attorney's fee. His girlfriend spends a lot of money. I don't know why he keeps her around, but according to him she is dragging him down. His wife knows about her but because Prince supports her drug habit, she stays around. He did have some money before; maybe that's why she hangs in with him. Besides they have a son together. Prince has been working with the police to bring in an identity theft group. You know he was good at hacking and getting peoples info. Tax season has just passed. Prince was doing a great deal of income tax fraud. I know this for sure, because one of my Latin King members is in with him. I try to keep my distance, so that if he goes down, I won't be associated with him.

Ø You know Harold. I knew something was not right.

Ø Yes, I know you have good instinct. I picked that up about you in jail. I too am the same and felt comfortable with you.

Ø Is Princes' girl, in on the income tax fraud?

Ø As far as I know, she is his right hand. She helped recruit people to cash the income tax checks. The way it works is; they steal people's identity. From that they make up fraudulent w2 forms and then claim large returns. They set up different address to have the checks mailed to. No one place can receive more than five returns or a flag will go up. Once a check is sent, they make fake ids for the people that will cash the checks. They give those people a small amount and everyone is happy. In a two month period they can do over $300,000. One problem is that the more you make the more people you need to use, and therefore the greater chance of getting caught.

Ø So, the whole time, Prince is out helping the police get these income tax thieves, he is helping himself to a piece of the pie?

Ø Yes, but you did not hear that from me.

Ø So why would he not give me your number?

Ø I don't know. Maybe he just wanted to keep distance, knowing he might not be able to get the Vault money.

Ø Naa, Harold, that doesn't make sense.

Ø Let's eat.

Ø Yes. I'm a bit hungry. So Harold, what is your plan now?

Ø Not sure Ozzie. I need to come up with something. If I don't, I'm afraid I will end up putting a bullet in the head of that bastard cop.

Ø Harold, let's say for the sake of argument, that I was able to get into the Vault and get the money. What would Prince do? Would he get greedy and try to kill me?

Ø No. I don't think so. Prince actually does like you. He did mention that he owes you for getting him out.

Ø So what gives? Why don't I trust him?

Ø Well, maybe you picked up on the fact that he might not be able to pull through. He might be trying to save face. I don't know what to tell you. But I don't think you should worry about him doing anything to you at all.

Ø You know Harold. Because you say so, I believe you.

Ø Now, what do you need to do to clear your name?

Ø A miracle.

Ø Seek, and you shall find.

Ø Tell that to Prince.

Ø I will.

Ø So tell me Harold. What does Harold need?

Ø Ozzie. My group the Latin Kings is big, but we have no one in the Hollywood police department or Broward Sheriff's office that can get me info on this guy. The police have a brotherhood where they cover up for each other. Also, if you run a background search on them, it would raise a flag and they might come knocking on the door. Prince was supposed to get me this info, but he hasn't. I think the only thing he is good at is scamming people. This should have been easy for him, but it hasn't. I counted on him and I fucked up in doing so.

Ø Sorry to hear that Harold. I guess you and I fell in the same boat, with Prince being a fake captain and not knowing how to navigate.

Ø That's a way of putting it.

Ø So again, what does Harold need to save himself?

Ø I need an insider I think. Either an insider perhaps in internal affairs or someone within the force that knows of his bad doing.

Ø Harold, there are many good people and many good cops. I know Jerry is one of the good guys. There are also many bad people and many bad cops, including bad governments, bad politicians and especially bad, evil bankers. Of course there are always exceptions. There are brotherhood in all aspects and walks of life. It's going to be hard to get some inside help, unless you know and have an inside connection. So you either have to find an insider; through hook or crook, or set him up yourself.

Ø Hey, Ozzie. That's it.

Ø What is?

Ø Set him up.

Ø Hey, why didn't I think of that?

Ø You just did.

Ø Yes, it's a figure of speech.

Ø Ozzie, that's it. You're a genius.

Ø Yes, I know an ignorant genius.

Ø That doesn't make sense.

Ø Well Harold, I'm not too sure about that. It does sound like an oxymoron but is it really?

Ø What's that?

Ø An oxymoron is a figure of speech that has contradictory words. Such as, the dark light. In my case to be genius would be to have an I.Q. of about 160. However one can still be ignorant despite one's ability to reason. It's like most of America. We think we know what is going on because we follow news that is told to us by liars, from people with an agenda. We are asleep, or too stupid to see danger that is right in front of us.

Ø Ozzie, what happen to you?

Ø Edwin. That's what happened.

Ø What do you mean?

Ø Never mind Harold. It's a long story. BTW, Harold, have you asked Edwin for help.

Ø No. I don't think he can help me in the way that I need.

Ø How well do you know him Harold? Because he is a lot more resourceful than he appears to be!

Ø Well, I know him from the streets, and have done a few transactions, but we tend to keep to ourselves.

Ø Harold, again the steak was delicious. You must have marinated them for a while. Before I leave is there anything I can do for you.

Ø Well, help me plan to set up this bad cop somehow.

Ø Okay Harold. Send me his name. I'll see if I can help you in any way. BTW, Harold. Don't say anything to Prince of what we spoke off. I am going to confide something. I'm still looking into it, so don't ask me too much, but I can get the money from the Vault.

Ø You're joking.

Ø Well Harold. Let's just say, I found a way in and know something. I have to fine tune it. Best thing is it only requires three or four guys.

Ø Ozzie, are you for real?

Ø Harold lets meet up in a week or two. I'll know then for sure.

Ø Okay Ozzie. That's good news. I won't mention it to Prince yet. Let me know if you need anything from me.

Ø Will do. I'll call you soon.

As I left, I thought about all the things Harold mentioned about Prince. Deep, deep, way down, something is definitely wrong. I have a much better understanding of Prince, but my gut warns me. My success into the Vault is assured. I've thought it best I just play with Harold a little and not give him everything I knew; for knowledge is power, while ignorance is bliss. That's why there are so many happy people; oblivious, happy blissful people. In a way I felt bad for Harold. I'm beginning to believe that he was innocent as he first mentioned. He tried to get out proving that. His miscalculation of Prince has now left him with grim choices. Do I want to help Harold? I probably would if I could, but I have enough manure on my plate. Hey, I guess today I feel intellectual for I did not use the word shit. Oh, pardon me, I recant.

Sunday, thank God it's Sunday, Sunday, Sunday. Oh wrong song. Well anyhow it's my favorite once again. First on the, to-enjoy list, is G. Well you know the rest, so I'll spare you.

It was about 4 when I meet up with Prince at his house. His wife was not there but his girlfriend was. Just as she did last time, she made herself unavailable. No intro, no revealing herself, nada. No matter. I was not there to meet her, and truth is I didn't need to. This time Prince was a little more relaxed.

- Ø So Prince. What's new?
- Ø Man, I've been really busy working on a big take down with Jerry. That's why I have not called you.
- Ø Yea, Prince. I figured you would be really busy with Jerry. I too managed to do a few arrest.
- Ø Yea. We have an investigation going on but I can't talk about it.
- Ø Well I wish you luck. I didn't want to put any pressure on you, and that is why I've not bothered you. BTW, I'm curious Prince. What the hell is the name of the guy you are getting the $6,000,000 from?
- Ø I rather not say. If any type of info on him gets pulled, he will be notified.
- Ø I'm not looking to pull his credit. I'm just curios.
- Ø I'll get you that some other time, as he has been known to use aliases.
- Ø Prince if he does, you would have to know which one he uses, but you already know that because you hacked into his computer and manage to find a bill for the Vault.
- Ø Yea, Yea, so anyway, how have you been?
- Ø Just look at me.
- Ø Handsome, elegant, intelligent, sweet.
- Ø Yea Ozz, that's from Magilla Gorilla.
- Ø If the shoe fits, where it.
- Ø You know Ozz; every time I see you, you have more and more jokes.
- Ø Well, you were used to seeing the guy from jail. This is the other side.
- Ø True That.
- Ø So, I take it Prince, you are stuck and don't have a way to get into the Vault. But I do know it's because you have been working on other things, and have not had the time to dedicate to it. So when do you think you will have time?
- Ø I don't know. I have to get with Harold and see if he is available.
- Ø How is Howard?
- Ø Don't know Ozzie, Again I've been concentrating too much on taking down this group. Within the next few weeks, we can plan for the money.
- Ø What does he bring to the table?

Ø He knows people in his gang that might be able to help.

Ø Hey prince. If we did not need Howard, would you still include him?

Ø I don't know. What are you getting at?

Ø Just curious, let's say he can't help you out at all, but you knew you could get the money, would it be necessary to cut him a piece.

Ø Man, we made an agreement to get out of jail and help each other out.

Ø Let's assume that you can't help him and he can't help you, does the agreement still hold?

Ø What are you trying to do Ozz, put me on the spot?

Ø No not at all. I'm just making conversation. Here is a different scenario. Let's say you could not use Howard at all, because he has nothing to offer, but there was someone else that could. Someone that could guarantee the Vault. What would you do?

Ø In that case I would have to go with the new guy and split with him.

Ø So, what is the plan Prince?

Ø Again Ozz, I've been so busy, I haven't given it much thought. But I will be doing so now.

Ø Well, let me know when you want to get the money.

Ø Yesterday.

Ø Yesterday, I thought you have been too busy.

Ø I have.

Ø Oh, that's what I thought.

Ø What do you mean?

Ø Never mind Prince. Look, I can get the money.

Ø You mean we can get the money.

Ø Nope. I mean, I can get the money. I know that you are up shits creek. I know you don't have a fucken clue of where that container is within the Vault.

Ø And you do?

Ø Yeap.

Ø Sure you do Ozzie. And I'm an elf.

Ø You the biggest elf.

Ø Eat shit; are you going to start up with your jokes?

Ø Why not.

Ø So are you saying you can get in?

Ø Maybe yes, Maybe no.

Ø Come on Ozzie, stop playing with me.

Ø Okay. I'll stop playing. Because that's actually what I have been doing all along. So let me give it to you straight. I can get in, and I don't need you, and I don't need Howard. The only thing I really need from you is a name. I can get in myself.

Ø Tell me you are not fucking with me.

Ø Not fucking with you. I have someone. You need to cut him in as well as his man. I'm not looking for anything extra for myself.

Ø Ozzie, are you really serious.

Ø Prince. The game has changed a little. Sometimes I stay quiet and play the fool. Don't think I don't know you have been taking me for one.

Ø No Ozzie, don't think that way. I never took you for a fool, nor do I think you are anything near that. On the contrary, I know you are very smart and could help out. If what you are saying is true then that proves me right.

Ø Good choice of words Prince. It's what a con man does best, stroke peoples eagle. Let me ask you something. In jail you came to me with this proposal. You say you planted the seed, but did you really? Don't you think I read through you? I know when you lie, Prince. You have a dead giveaway that you are not even aware of. No matter. We are in the here and now. As of now, all you have is an idea. An idea that is dead in its tract. This place, the Vault, has proven to be too much security for you. I figured it out Prince. I have the answers, and the people to do it. I checked it twice and then one more time. I'm not talking caca. There are two people that are coming along. Two people, that's all we need. I don't care what you do with Howard. I don't care for more money. If you want this, then this is the only sure way. After we do this we depart as friends. Don't think for one minute that after we get this money you will dispose of me in any fashion.

Ø Yo Ozz, where are you coming from with this? If you don't trust me then don't come in.

Ø Prince, I don't trust you. You have lied to me a few times, and I don't care to discuss that. As of now, I am your only way to get what so much desire. I will take measures to prevent you from trying to get rid of me in any fashion. This is business. Let's keep it that way. Trust me Prince. The person involved belongs to two different organizations. I pledged my money to them if anything happens to me. If I don't get paid, you will have to pay them. They will take the bulk of it and make sure my daughter receives some. There is also a lawyer that will have a sealed document within his files. If I don't check in with him once a week he will open it up. There he will find details about you. Details you are not aware that I know off.

Ø Yo, I'm not liking this.

Ø Cut the shit Prince. I know all you want is to get your hands on that money. Speaking of which, there better be some money in there. The two guys coming in will harm you if there is nothing for them. I am in the clear. It all falls on you. This all needed to be said for me to go forward. I'm not a fool Prince. Remember I grew up in the streets of New York, by myself from the early age of 16. I can smell things a mile away. Before I go any further, you need to figure out what you are going to give these guys. If it's not enough, they won't join. Also, please know that we can probably do this without you, if you chose not to include us. So you really don't have much choice. We will talk again on Wednesday. I'll need some answers for them.

Ø Yo Ozz. I don't like you talking like that.

Ø Look Prince. You're a smart man. Don't let your emotions cloud you. If there is no money in the container, you better say so now. In which case, I will go in with them, and see what the hell is so valuable to you. We will take our chance and you won't be held accountable for anything. On the other hand, if there is something, then you better think of a number to throw at them. This is past you now. Again its business. A percentage of something is better than 100% of nothing.

Ø Wow. This all came from left field. Fuck it Ozz. If you really can get in, then let's do this.

Ø Think of a number for them. I have to report to them. I'll check in with you on Wednesday.

Ø How soon can we do this? Two to three weeks. It has to be well planned. Once you give me a number for them, I can start to set it up. Besides I have a hunch about something.

Ø What's that?

Ø Never mind. It doesn't have anything to do with this. If anything, it might help out Howard with his quest. OK Prince. I'm out for now. It's Sunday. I'm going fishing with my friend. Or I should say going swimming with my fish.

I left Prince home in a rush. His place gives me the creeps. Or as some of you white folks would say, the heebie-jeebies. "I came, I saw, I conquered. " I said what needed to be said, leaving no doubt in his mind that he would be mistaken if anything happens to me. As I started driving home I picked up the phone.

Ø Boriqua.

Ø Hola Ozzie. Que Tal?

Ø What's up Edwin? What are you up to?

Ø Chilling.

Ø Want to get a drink?

Ø Sure. Where?

Ø Hard rock. Same as last time. 45 minutes.

Ø OK. I'll see you soon.

I knew my friend G would be home waiting for me. Knowing her pretty well by now she probably has food prepared. It occurred to me that I should give her a ring and let her know I would be late. It also just occurred to me that I was answering to someone. I had gotten used to my independence and freedom. Both from jail and from humans, especially of the female species. Am I now afraid? Should I dump her? Not sure. Oh well. No rush. For the moment, it's working for me.

How nice, I managed to sit at the same table as I did when I was last here. It's a spot I like. Watching the girls go by is something I could never get tired of. I ordered a drink and sat back to do just that as I waited for Edwin.

- Ø Edwin, Que Tal?
- Ø Hola Ozzie. Dam you just get bigger every time I see you.
- Ø Yea, but I think this is at big as I want to get. Otherwise I'll start to get fat. I have to say, I feel great. So what's new?
- Ø Nothing much. Same old thing.
- Ø Well Edwin, I'm sure you know why I asked you to meet me.
- Ø Yes, I have a good idea.
- Ø Edwin before we get started on that, I have a question, well maybe more of a request. Edwin, what do you know about Howard and his release?
- Ø He does not tell me much. We have an agreement between his gang and my gang to keep our distance, but nothing prevents us from doing a transaction or making money. We are both loyal to our gang and he and I respect each other.
- Ø Edwin, Howard has a problem and I am wondering if somehow you could help me. Look at it more as a favor for me than for him. I trust you Edwin with this so please keep this between ourselves. Howard agreed to sign some papers in jail so that he can hit the streets. He said he was set up by the Hollywood police department. Now that he is out, he is stuck. He told the prosecutors that he knew some big drug cartels, but he had no intention of turning them in. He figured he would be able to get enough info on the cop so that he could be proven innocent. Prince was supposed to help Howard out with getting some info about that cop. Prince is also stuck and it's looking bad for Howard.
- Ø So Ozzie. What if I told you I could help? What would I get?
- Ø Wait, Edwin. Are you saying you can help?
- Ø Sure, I can. That one is easy also.
- Ø Edwin, what the fuck. Who the fuck are you?

Edwin laughed. Not a sarcastic laugh, but a confident, genuine laugh. I could not believe what I just heard. Edwin was the man. I was right about him. I knew it from the moment we first spoke. The big thing in a small package. Fuck, Fuck, Fuck, Once again, happy dance. We had two drinks that evening and discussed several things. I was in heaven. Oh wait, I don't believe in heaven. Okay, I was ecstatic, euphoric, elated, enchanted, and enraptured, but was not on ecstasy. Actually I never even tried it. Wow, look at that. Holy shit! A goddess. So there must be Gods. Wow, maybe I am in heaven. I'll believe if that's what it will take me to get her. Sure I'll be a traitor. She's fucken beautiful. I noticed Edwin smiling as I stood to salute her, for she was worthy. Before I could say one word, reality hit me. G, my friend showed up, as if to ruin my party. Not physically but worse, mentally. I was not in heaven. I was in the presence of mere mortals. Okay. For the brief 30 seconds it was wonderful. G? G? Why have thou forsaken me? You have delivered me out from within heaven and back to reality. What have you done to me? Normally, I would not give a shit. But this time I did. G was my friend, and companion, and I wasn't going to let her down. I will need to examine this relationship. I'm not giving my heart to anyone ever again. Despite the moment, I could not be in better spirits. For Edwin gave me reasons to rejoice. I guess the only thing left for today would be to have an orgasm. Well my turn to visit her. G, here I come.

This Sunday, turned out to be much better than I expected. It was now 2 am, and I was still wide awake. Tonight I was not haunted nor hiding nor running. Tonight I was at ease. Plans consumed me; or rather the formulating of plans consumed me. Plans of getting into the container within the Vault, and plans to help Howard with his dilemma. How could this be? I wonder if it were not for Edwin, would I be able to accomplish these two tasks. And so now, I seek an alternative solution. Why? Is it my ego? I have the answers I sought and needed, but then the answers were not a result of my own thinking; not attributed to my genius. But rather attributed and obtained through someone else. I guess this is how Christopher Columbus, Newton and Leonardo da Vinci, (who happened to get many of his ideas from his mentor), felt like. I think two geniuses were Einstein and Volta. Yes Volta, The one who created a source of free energy. An energy source kept hidden from us, the sleeping masses, by the mighty powers that be, i.e. the oil titans and bankers. An energy form suppressed because they could not put a meter on it. Free, that's no good. You can't make money if it's free. An energy source that has led to the creation of HAARP. It's just the same as we Americans believe. We think we are free, but little do we know that we are slaves, and zombies. Walking and working while asleep. For the moment we are born, we are promised and delivered to the bankers. That's the reason for our social security number. We are pledge as collateral. Collateral for the interest on the money we allow them to print. Pledge by an illegal act of congress that was never ratified. OK, Ozzie. Think straight. There is a task at hand. There are solutions. Formulate a good plan and then execute. Stroke your ego later with an alternative answer. Well let me stroke it just a little.

I'll say, "The Genius was is knowing that Edwin was different." Yea, that's the ticket. I like it. I like it a lot. For now it's a no brainer. Fuck it. Sleep, sleep, here I come.

40 HERE I COME

HERE I COME, walking down THE STREET. Getting the funniest looks, from everyone I meet. Hey, hey, I am dreaming; dreaming of 6 million dollars. Going to buy G a lot of flowers. Six million dollars to monkey around. Yeap, that's the ticket. It's the mood I'm in.

- Ø Howard
- Ø Ozzie, How are you.
- Ø I'm great Howard. And You?
- Ø I'm okay. Concerned a little, but Okay.
- Ø Howard, I solved your problem
- Ø What do you mean?
- Ø I found what you are looking for. I have your freedom.
- Ø Ozzie, don't fuck with me.
- Ø Howard. Listen to me. This is not a joke. Tonight I want you to kiss your beautiful wife, and tell her you are going to take her on a trip in a few months. Tell her there will be no jail time for you. Tell her your charges will be dropped, soon. Today is Monday, my squat routine day. I'll come visit you Wednesday. Make sure you still have some of my drink. Don't ask any questions. Your problems are solved.
- Ø Ozzie, I don't know what to say. Wow, I am in shock. Can you come see me tomorrow?
- Ø Howard tomorrow is my chest day. Wednesday I can take a break. Don't worry Howard. I kid you not. You have been delivered from evil.
- Ø You're preaching. I thought you did not believe.
- Ø I believe Howard. I believe I can't fly. I believe I can't touch the sky. I believe I'm not a fool. But I know you were on the verge of breaking down, through your silence you were so loud. I felt your pain Howard. Yes I can see it, and now with my friend there's nothing to it, for I know that I can do it. So I believe, yes I believe in me.
- Ø Ozzie stop. What song is that?
- Ø That's the Magilla Gorilla song.
- Ø No its not. What has gotten into you?

Ø I'm happy Howard. I'm happy for you. I did solve your problem. Wednesday we can start a plan.

Ø But Ozzie, HOW?

Ø Howard it's done. A done deal. Don't worry. I'll give you all the details. You just make sure those Cubin Cousins don't come near me. So do as I say. Eat, drink and be merry. Oh, one other thing, I might be able to do something with Prince. I might also need your back. I'll tell you Wednesday.

Ø Okay Ozzie. And thank you.

41 HERE I GO AGAIN

Here I go again. G has told me to be very careful about writing truths that I have known and that I have been discovering. There are a number of things that I have alluded to. Things that are not so obvious. Example 1776, and the Illuminati, I told you it was a hint. I also told you to look it up. NOW, (New World Order), Freemasonry, poison in the water. You, my readers, whom I do not know but somehow feel a connection with, are in serious danger. It is not my intention to start a panic, nor uproar. Truth is, you, the reader, either think, I am crazy, or stupid, and/or you just don't care. How can it be? Wake the fuck up?

It's been several days since I have spoken to Howard. It's been several days since I have spoken to Prince. It's been several days since I have spoken to Edwin. It's been several days since I wrote anything. It's been several days since I felt an urge to get the money. It's still going to happen. But why have I not done anything at all about anything? What is it? For starters, I did not feel any urge to do so. No motivation. Not because of lack of energy, but because of a lack of something. I haven't placed it yet. But something is happening to me. I am discovering and changing. Yes, once again I am changing. Not midlife crises, nor religion, nor a sense of needed to belong. I am now finding myself being confronted by a much, much bigger question. Much bigger problems. Problems I have absolutely no control of. My quest for a simple answer as to what are the events that landed me in jail has now taken a turn and shifted to something more profound. I am scared. Who am I? What should I now do? How shall I decide? That is now the question to be answered. Yes, I do need some mental help to get over the pain and agony I am so often confronted with. And I do intent in getting that help. But I am now confronted with a new question. How do I decide?

Today is Sunday. As usual, coffee, love, breakfast. Today, G asked to go to the beach.

- Ø Sure I said. It's just a few minutes away. Let me see you change into your skimpy sexy bikini.
- Ø Which one?
- Ø Try them both.
- Ø OK.

Ø The red one.

Ø Then red it is.

The beach was, well, the beach. Do I need to describe it? In Florida, it's pretty much all the same. Hollywood beach is very clean and has a large tourist population. The sun was sunny, there were some clouds, they were cloudy, and the beach was sandy. How's that for a description. Well if you haven't been to the beach, go find out for yourself. Once there I sat in my chair. It was flanked by a beach umbrella. I sat in its shade and did some people watching. G laid out her towel and stretched out to gather some rays.

Wow! What a sight. Look over there. There's, more; much more. How does this happen? Where am I? I think I need to head to South Beach to watch the pretty people. Or has society changed since I got locked up? I found myself doing people watching. I could not understand. How could these people allow their bodies to get so big? This by no means is an attempt to ridicule anyone. That is not my style. It was an honest observation. The percentage of overweight people was out of control. I am not talking of those who are twenty pounds over. We Americans are unfit. I know it's hard to stay in shape, especially as we get older. But it's something we could do if we really wanted to. Just stay away from the fast food restaurants that damage us. Tell them no, by not giving them your money.

That's when it hit me. It hit me hard. It put a fear in me. For I now have to take a stand. I am going to have to take a side. I do not know the answer of as yet. That is, I do not know which side to take. How do I decide? How do I decide? For my entire life I grew up being strong; both mentally and physically. I started lifting weights to put on a few pounds. It grew into a love; a love of life. I always sided with the just cause. I was always for the good. One day, while riding a subway in NY at the age of 16, I witness three guys pickpocket a lady. She had no idea of their doing. They exited upon the next stop and I followed. Why? I don't know. I wanted to get her wallet back. Staying several feet away I saw one of the guys hand over a knife to the other. That's when I pulled back. Is it worth it? Nope. That one was easy. I was not stupid. I hung back and waited for the next train. Anger raged throughout. I did not know this lady. Maybe to her it was not that important. Maybe her wallet was, but then she might think she just misplaced it: Never knowing that she had been robed in plain sight. Was it her fault? Her fault for being asleep? Or was it that she was hit upon by experts that gently robbed her? She was spared the pain. The anguish of knowing she had been duped. She was oblivious. This is the same exact position I know find myself in. Do I try to wake the sleeping masses, you my readers, or do I just say fuck it? It's hopeless? Who am I to try to save, the world? How shall I decide? Do I stay quiet and hope to make a few dollars from the sale of this book? Or do I take the chance of getting myself killed by those few elite whose purpose it is to depopulate the world: the ultimate aim of having a world with only 500,000,000 people. Yes it's true. Look up, The Georgia Guidestones. Most of you are thinking I have fallen off the deep end. It is because of that, that I have been very careful in what and how I reveal or mention things. As I looked into the small waves coming in and out, I thought about what a beautiful world we live in. I thought about the mountains and hills of Puerto Rico. I thought about how wonderful life is, and about how happy and healthy we really could be. And then, Bang.

It came to me. Maybe they are right. Maybe they do know better than we do. Maybe there are too many people in the world. We live in it and we destroy it. Like all living entity, it can repair and heal itself, but only to a certain degree. Too much damage and there will be irreparable harm. Yes. Maybe the powers that be do in fact have it right. There are too many people. Maybe the earth does need human intervention to protect it against them. You see my fellow humans. There is a plan: One which you are not privy to. You are collateral damage. There is a war going on, but once again I will leave it there; for I do not want to be silenced. And so, I now have to decide. Do I choose by default and do nothing. Just float away and mind my business. For you guys won't see it coming. Do I choose negatively, that is by saving myself and joining those powers that be, such as the military men. Or Do I try to save you, knowing it will get me nowhere. How do I decide?

42 THINGS ARE CONNECTED

It's true. Things are connected. We are somehow all connected; even if we chose to live disconnected.

It's still Sunday, early evening. G decided to make a quick healthy meal. I had not spoken to her about the people at the beach. Nor did I share with her my new dilemma. Instead of beaming documentaries to the TV, which I usually do, (as I refuse to watch regular TV), I connected my laptop's HDMI cable to the TV and searched the YouTube channels for topic of interest. Today, I wanted to see muscles. Why, I don't know, as it's not something I watch any more. Maybe to offset what I saw at the beach. After three or four clips I came across an interview with Dorian Yates.

Dorian Andrew Mientjez Yates (born 19 April 1962) is an English professional bodybuilder. He won the Mr. Olympia title six consecutive times from 1992 and holds the fourth-highest number of Mr. Olympia awards of all time. He is widely considered one of the top athletes in modern bodybuilding history.

The clip was more a documentary consisting of 1:52:58. Titled, **"Dorian Yates - Into The Shadow - REDUX | London Real"** Almost two hours, no, that's too long. Not into that. Not going to happen. Wrong! It did. I sat and watched. Why? I don't think there is anything in bodybuilding for me to learn. By now, I've read it all, tried it all, and do consider myself an expert. So why? Simple, you shall see. It's because things are connected. One hour and thirteen minutes into his interview he said so himself. This is his quote, "Things are connected". So you see it's true. Things are connected. He said so. I say so. I'll say it again, Things are connected. There. Try to follow and connect the dots once again. The following is taken from that documentary. These are not my words, nor is any part of this made up. Actually, if you haven't figured it out yet, everything in this book is real. This book is not fiction. Some people learn through repetition.

Things are connected, By Dorian Yates.

"Pineal gland

Let me go somewhere now with this. Because the pineal gland in the brain, a tiny gland in your brain, There is a concerted effort to stop that functioning in every body, because the powers that be, a small group of people that control the world and the nature of what we believe is reality, they know, this is like our antenna to touch our spirit world with the real reality. We now have pictures of the pineal gland that is now totally covered in calcium like deposits to stop it from functioning, and this is from the fluoride in the tap water. Not only is it stopping you from connecting with your higher self, it's also a poison. So, please don't drink the tap water.

Why do you think the powers that be are trying to suppress the function of the pineal gland?

Because if we all realize how powerful we are, we would not be so easy to control. If you are a conscious person, you are not going to go the other side of the world to kill people simply because you are getting paid. You're going to start questioning things. There is a concerted effort to dumb down the population. Everything you see on the TV is all bull shit. Who's fucking who? Who cares about that, how about the children that just got blown off in Afghanistan?

Everything that's presented through the media is accepted as truth. Take 9/11, Osama bin Laden did it., but if you look clearly it's all bull shit. There is no conspiracy theory, there is a conspiracy fact. If you look it up you could find it. If I said there was a cure for cancer, or in fact many cures for cancer, how would you feel about that. Because there are people out there getting cured from cancer. And the cancer industry is just that an industry. Why would you want to cure people? Because it's a business. Doc Rick Simpson in the states has proven to have cured literally thousands of people including terminally ill people. You can't patent the ingredients.

People's reality is feed to them through schools, religion and media and those are all controlled through organizations.

I looked up the pineal gland. This is what I found on Wikipedia;

The **pineal gland**, also known as the **pineal body**, **conarium** or **epiphysis cerebri**, is a small endocrine gland in the vertebrate brain. It produces the serotonin derivative melatonin, a hormone that affects the modulation of sleep patterns in the circadian rhythms and seasonal functions. Its shape resembles a tiny pine cone (hence its name), and it is located in the epithalamiums, near the centre of the brain, between the two hemispheres, tucked in a groove where the two rounded thalamic bodies join. The gland has been compared to the photoreceptive parietal eye present in the epithalamiums of some animal species, which is also called the pineal eye or the third eye. René Descartes believed it to be the "principal seat of the soul"

Another source states:

The pineal gland is responsible for your DNA system. It is referred to as being the seat of the Soul or the seat of consciousness. It is capable of making a compound called DMT. DMT is released from the pineal gland during extraordinary states such as time of death and the time of birth. This gland may be the mechanism from which we enter and leave our physical bodies. Research has been done on the affects of fluoride and the pineal gland. The soft tissue of the adult pineal gland had more fluoride than any other soft tissue in the body. The level of the fluoride is capable of inhibiting enzymes. The hard tissue of the pineal gland accumulates more fluoride than any other hard tissue in the body, including the teeth and bones.

Natural Entheogens (not for everyone): Ayahuasca, Psilocybin Mushrooms, Peyote, Changa, Cannabis, Salvia, DMT and more. A couple of months doing a number or all of the above will leave your pineal gland decalcified and detoxified in no time!

Look up, Doc. Rick Simpson as well as the Gerson Cancer Cure. If you don't, then I am correct when I say we Americans are sleeping. And we chose to remain that way.

Thank you, Mr. Yates. You had the courage to say so, as well as many others have. Some of whom have died unexpectedly. I don't want to be one of those. BUT, then there is a side to me that says. Fuck it. I'm on the fence for the moment. But I also feel connected with you Mr. Yates.

How do I respond? How shall I respond? Imagine all the sleeping military men, those from FEMA, ICE, Homeland Security and other agencies that will one day be forced to pull the trigger on us. How will they decide? And I thought my problem was bad. At least I don't have to pull the trigger. Unless of course in self-defense.

It's getting late. Tomorrow, I will set myself back on tract. Fuck it. At the very least, I am going to get that money, and I am going to help Howard, for we are connected.

The Devestating Effect of Fluoride on the Pineal Gland

Summation - **Fluoride & Pineal Gland:**

Up until the 1990s, no research had ever been conducted to determine the impact of fluoride on the pineal gland - a small gland located between the two hemispheres of the brain that regulates the production of the hormone melatonin. Melatonin is a hormone that helps regulate the onset of puberty and helps protect the body from cell damage caused by free radicals.

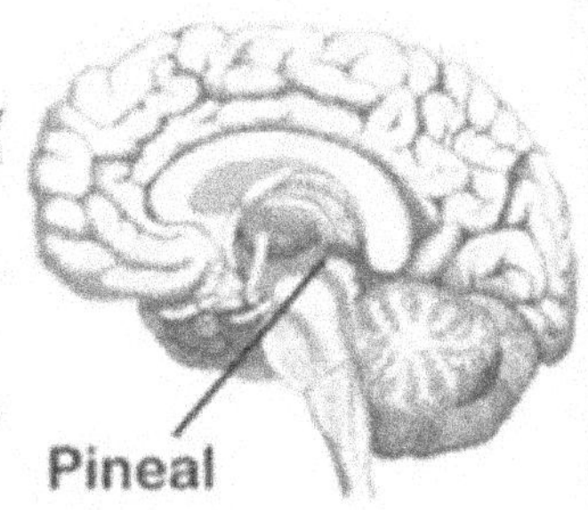

It is now known - thanks to the meticulous research of Dr. Jennifer Luke from the University of Surrey in England - that the pineal gland is the primary target of fluoride accumulation within the body.

The soft tissue of the adult pineal gland contains more fluoride than any other soft tissue in the body - a level of fluoride (~300 ppm) capable of inhibiting enzymes.

Quick Facts

More people drink fluoridated water in the United States than the rest of the world combined.

Heavy tea drinkers risk fluoride-induced bone disease.

97% of western Europe has rejected water fluoridation

Fluoride has been linked to male infertility.

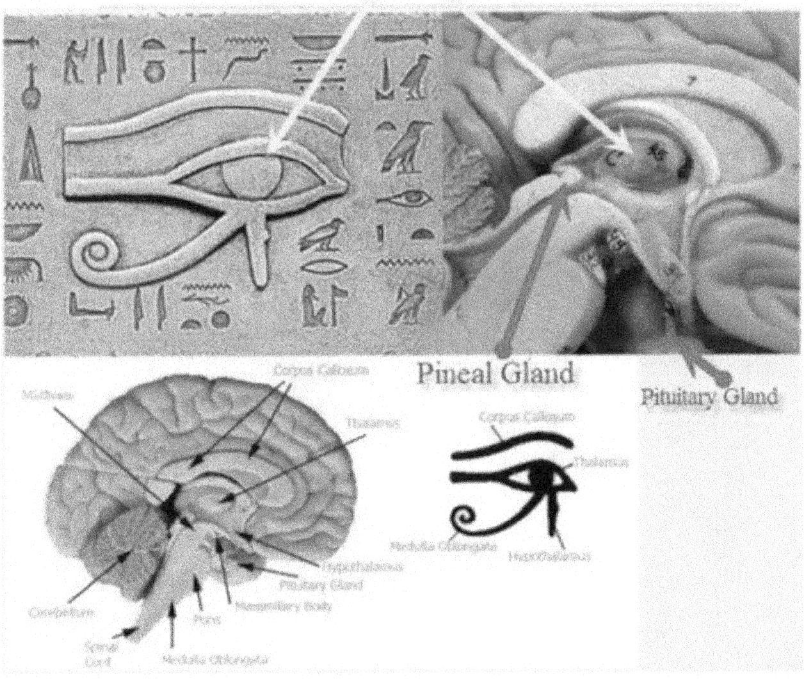

43 2ND SUNDAY, I'M BACK AGAIN

Its Sunday once again, early afternoon. The past week has brought me a fever and a mild flu which I seem to quickly put under control. Strengthening the immune system was the focus. I did some research into the best type of water to drink. Mind you, my research into what should be a quick and simple find usually turns out for me to be an undertaking. Hours of reading has led me to this simple conclusion. One I shall share with you, because, we are all connected in some way.

> Spring water is the best water to drink not minding where it comes from and where it is purchased. The second best drinking water is carbon water, which is basically tap water. However, caution should be taken when drinking due to possible contamination. Soften water whether it is softened by tablets, salt or potassium. Well water is not good in the United States as well as in many other places due to possible contamination as well.

> ***The best water to drink is usually plain spring water.*** *It does not matter if it comes in plastic bottles. Well, maybe just a little. You may be able to have it delivered in recycled plastic bottles, or you may find a local source at www.findaspring.com. The second best type of drinking water is usually carbon-only filtered tap water. Use the following cautions with tap water:*

> *A. Do not drink softened water, whether it is softened by salt tablets or potassium tablets.*

> *B. Be careful with well water. Most of it is not that good in the United States, and elsewhere.*

Distilled water. Distilled water has gone through a rigorous filtration process to strip it not only of contaminants, but any natural minerals as well. When water is distilled, by boiling it and condensing it, all solid matter is left except chemicals that were in the water.

Because it is devoid of minerals, distilled water grabs and holds onto minerals in the body, a process called chelation. Distilled water can be used for a few months to remove toxic metals and toxic chemicals from the body quite effectively. Drinking distilled water for longer than this, however, always results in vital mineral deficiencies.

Tap Water - Tap water contains heavy metals, fluoride, chlorine, medicines like antibiotics and antidepressants and hundreds of chemicals, many of which are not even measured or regulated. Fluoride causes many, many side effects, weakening bones and increasing your chance of developing osteoporosis and cancer, yet it's added to almost every municipal water supply in the country. Drink it if you dare.

The fluoride abomination. Although laws in America such as the Clean Water Act of 1974 prohibits adding any substance to drinking water except to make it safe, many communities in the USA and Great Britain, in particular, have been convinced by ignorant and corrupt health authorities to add fluorides to their drinking water. These chemicals are poisons, and are sold as rat poison, in fact.

Fluoride does not reduce tooth decay in most studies of it. Any health authority who reviews the data in an unbiased way would never recommend adding fluorides to drinking water. In fact, some medical studies show more tooth decay in fluoridated areas. All nations except the United States and some parts of Great Britain and Australia have given up the practice based on the research and on the principle of people's right to choose whether or not to have their water medicated. Adding fluoride has nothing to do with the safety of the water, and in fact makes it much more toxic.

Please, do not drink tap water. Do not let your children drink tap water. Do not let your children brush their teeth with fluoride toothpaste. Okay enough preaching.

Food for thought; these things I mention will be relevant as I go further into my book. There will be a quiz at the end of this chapter. This will go down on your permanent record. Sorry, folks, I can't help myself. I'm actually smiling as I write this. It's a quote from a teacher I had. Yes, I went to school. Thank you.

When I say we Americans have been sleeping. It's almost true. We are governed by a group of people with an agenda. We are not governed by the US Government; well we are to a degree; for the law makers are mere puppets. We are ruled and owned by the eliminators. And I tell you. We will be eliminated. This is how the true world map really looks like. Things are not really as we think they are. Truth be told, the average Joe doesn't have a clue.

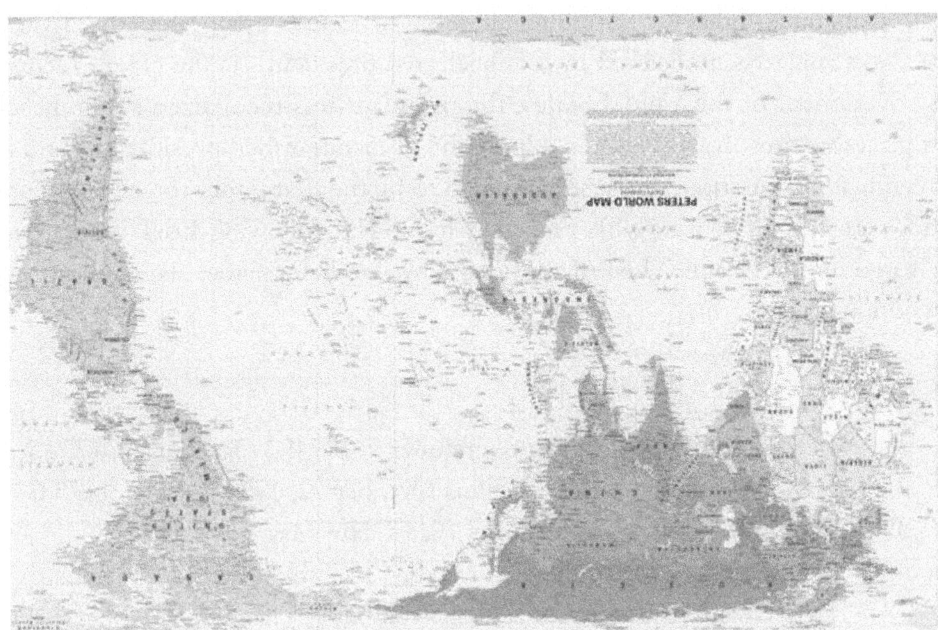

The opposite poles of two magnets attract. Therefore, when the red end of a magnet or compass is pointing north, it is because it is being attracted in that direction by the south end of another magnet (often colored blue) this is the imaginary magnet inside the Earth.

Mercator, the traditional world map, works for navigation because that projection preserves angles. That means, if you have to go from Hawaii to Australia, you can trace a straight line in the map and will correspond to the shortest trajectory on a globe. If you were using other projections like Peters, a shortest path in a globe would be a curve traced on the map.

Fuck, now that I am on it, here is some more food. Many people know this already.

Following is a list of previous president prior to George Washington.

"Who was the first president of the United States? Ask any school child and they will readily tell you "George Washington." And of course, they would be wrong at least technically. Washington was not inaugurated until April 30, 1789. And yet, the United States continually had functioning governments from as early as September 5, 1774 and operated as a confederated nation from as early as July 4, 1776. During that nearly fifteen year interval, Congress—first the Continental Congress and then later the Confederation Congress—was always moderated by a duly elected president. As the chief executive officer of the government of the United States, the president was recognized as the head of state. Washington was thus the fifteenth in a long line of distinguished presidents—and he led the seventeenth administration—he just happened to be the first under the current constitution. So who were the luminaries who preceded him? The following brief biographies profile these "forgotten presidents." List of presidents by numbers, name, state/colony, term start, term, end months in term;

1. Peyton Randolph Virginia September 5, 1774[a] October 22, 1774 2
2. Henry Middleton South Carolina October 22, 1774 May 10, 1775 6
3. Peyton Randolph Virginia May 10, 1775[b] May 24, 1775 <1
4. John Hancock Massachusetts May 24, 1775 October 29, 1777 29
5. Henry Laurens South Carolina November 1, 1777[c] December 9, 1778 13
6. John Jay New York December 10, 1778 September 28, 1779 10
7. Samuel Huntington Connecticut September 28, 1779 July 10, 1781[d] 21
8. Thomas McKean Delaware July 10, 1781 November 5, 1781 4
9. John Hanson Maryland November 5, 1781[e] November 4, 1782 12
10. Elias Boudinot New Jersey November 4, 1782 November 3, 1783 12
11. Thomas Mifflin Pennsylvania November 3, 1783[f] June 3, 1784 7
12. Richard Henry Lee Virginia November 30, 1784 November 4, 1785 11
13. John Hancock[g] Massachusetts November 23, 1785 June 5, 1786 6
14. Nathaniel Gorham Massachusetts June 6, 1786 November 3, 1786 5
15. Arthur St. Clair Pennsylvania February 2, 1787 November 4, 1787 10
16. Cyrus Griffin Virginia January 22, 1788 November 15, 1788[h] 10

Here is one for you black people. Obama was not the first black president of the US, BTW. There seems to be some conflicting report as to the correct number of presidents before Washington. Suffice it to say George Washington was not the first.

The following was taken from an article from Dick Gregory Global Watch:

"George Washington was not the first President of the United States. In fact, the first President of the United States was one John Hanson. Don't go checking the encyclopedia for this guy's name he is one of those great men that are lost to history. If you're extremely lucky, you may actually find a brief mention of his name. The new country was actually formed on March 1, 1781 with the adoption of The Articles of Confederation.

This document was actually proposed on June 11, 1776, but not agreed upon by Congress until November 15, 1777. Once the signing took place in 1781, a President was needed to run the country. John Hanson was chosen unanimously by Congress (which included George Washington). In fact, all the other potential candidates refused to run against him, as he was a major player in the revolution and an extremely influential member of Congress. He took office just as the Revolutionary War ended. Almost immediately, the troops demanded to be paid. As would be expected after any long war, there were no funds to meet the salaries. As a result, the soldiers threatened to overthrow the new government and put Washington on the throne as a monarch.

All the members of Congress ran for their lives, leaving Hanson as the only guy left running the government. He somehow managed to calm the troops down and hold the country together. If he had failed, the government would have fallen almost immediately and everyone would have been bowing to King Washington. In fact, Hanson sent 800 pounds of sterling silver by his brother Samuel Hanson to George Washington to provide the troops with shoes.

Hanson established the Great Seal of the United States, which all Presidents have since been required to use on all official documents.

President Hanson also established the first Treasury Department, the first Secretary of War, and the first Foreign Affairs Department.

Lastly, he declared that the fourth Thursday of every November was to be Thanksgiving Day, which is still true today. Six other presidents were elected after him Elias Boudinot (1783), Thomas Mifflin (1784), Richard Henry Lee (1785), Nathan Gorman (1786), Arthur St. Clair (1787), and Cyrus Griffin (1788) - all prior to Washington taking office.

So what happened?

Why don't we ever hear about the first seven Presidents of the United States?

It's quite simple: the Articles of Confederation didn't work well. The individual states had too much power and nothing could be agreed upon. A new doctrine needed to be written something we know as the Constitution.

And that leads us to the end of our story.

George Washington was definitely not the first President of the United States. He was the first President of the United States under the Constitution we follow today.

Okay, enough history. Just remember, all this will be important.

Anyway, getting back to my health. I managed to boost my immune system with oregano oil drops, and with virgin coconut oil. Both have extremely potent yeast and fungi fighting properties. All medium chain fatty acids found in coconut oil kill yeast, viruses and bacteria. Some probiotics were also in order to replace many good bacteria I lost a few years ago while taking antibiotics, and finally some vitamin c. Keep in mind that sickness comes when our immune system is down. So that which I have been taking is because of a lack thereof.

This past week I have had no rush, or desire to contact the thugs. They are waiting for me in eagerness. However, I am confronted with a much bigger task; that which I have previously mentioned. Things that might be beyond my control. I believe I have found an answer. Yes, it is possible to save the world from those who believe that we should be Illuminati, oh I meant eliminated. The question does still remain. Should I intervene? Should I get involved? Should I care? Yes, I have found a possible solution; one which will do me no good to discuss at this point in time. It will be a big undertaking; one which will require much thought and planning, with months or possible years in the making. I won't tell them, you know, the exterminators, about it at this writing. So now that I have it figured out, I must get back to the previous task; the money, the corrupt Hollywood cop. Then I will be off to Puerto Rico; as part of my solution might have some merit there. Edwin, of course, once again, a possible solution, I'll say no more. Money, here we come. Yea baby! I am back. That's the ticket, and I like it. I like it a lot.

44 MONDAY

Ø Hello Prince.

Ø Yo Ozzie. What the fuck have you been up to? I've been waiting for your call.

Ø I've been busy trying to save the world.

Ø What the fuck does that mean?

Ø Never mind Prince. Let's just say, I've been busy. But I'm ready now. Did you get a number for your savior?

Ø Yea, $250,000.

Ø You're joking right. This guy is the only way in. It's guaranteed and you want to throw less than 5%. Come on Prince, get real. I know they are not going to accept that. You don't have a choice in this matter. Up the number and give me a call when you get serious.

Ø Yo, Ozz. I have to try. Why give away money if you don't have to?

Ø I understand. Look Prince, I'll give it to you straight. Their number is $500,000. Take it or leave it. Just so you know Prince. Don't try to fuck them. It will be a big mistake. Theses cats are well connected.

Ø Okay Ozzie. Let's just get on with this.

Ø BTW Prince. Does your girlfriend know anything about this?

Ø Na. Besides she is out of the picture.

Ø So she dumped your ass?

Ø No. I dumped her. She was getting on my nerves. All she did was ask for money, but never did anything to earn it.

Ø So she did not work?

Ø Nope.

Ø I thought she was your girl. Your big love.

Ø Yea. But she was costing me too much. She just kept draining me.

Ø So she never helped you make any money or helped you hack into a system.

Ø Na. She was dumb. I had to let her go.

Ø Okay. Prince. So what you are saying is I don't have to worry about her finding out about this?

Ø Yea, Yea Ozzie. Everything between us is safe. Trust me she won't be around ever again. I made sure of that.

Ø So are you back with your wife?

Ø Well she won't be coming back neither. She left me for good.

- Ø So you are single now. I could just see you going on a big spending spree in a few weeks.
- Ø Let's hope so.
- Ø No Prince. There is no place for hope here. It's being planned and will happen. Hope is for those without resolution.
- Ø True That.
- Ø Yo Ozzie. We said a lot on the phone. What the fuck.
- Ø Yo, stop being paranoid. Besides Prince. I'm not too worried about being found out by the police.
- Ø Why?
- Ø Oh, let's just say, I know things. I have an inside in the police department.
- Ø What the fuck, Ozzie. What does that mean? We could be killed by those fuckers.
- Ø No. Not going to happen. I won't get into that now, but I can assure you, I am protected and safe.
- Ø Yo, let's meet in a day or two. I can't stand talking on the phone.
- Ø I'll call you in a few days.

Call to Edwin:

- Ø Hello Edwin.
- Ø Hola Ozzie. Que Tal?
- Ø Edwin. Meet me at the Hard Rock today about 8:30. Same place. I should be done with my exercises by then. If I am running late I'll call you.
- Ø Dale, Ozzie.
- Ø Okay. See you later.

Today was Monday, my leg day, which I happened to have done yesterday. So chest and triceps was the order. Despite being a little under the weather, I was strong. It's strange, because during sickness my energy level is not the same. No matter. I enjoyed myself as usual. The Hollywood gym I attend is only several minutes from the Seminole Casino. And I now wonder what will happen to them when the eliminators come. Will their land be taken away, just as ours will? Oh well. I really need to stop. Edwin, Edwin, what have you done to me? The atmosphere at the Casino is always the same; upbeat and exciting as well as being a beautiful place. Entertainment abounds. Ah, once again. The gods are with me. For the third straight visit, I find my all too familiar spot vacant. It was waiting for me. Shall I check the underside of the seat, to see if my name is inscribed? Maybe the Inca gods are watching or perhaps the Anunnaki. Yea, that's the ticket. Oh well, I shall not let them down, and so will sit in my reserved spot.

- Ø Edwin

Ø Hola Ozzie, Que Tal?

Ø What's up Edwin? Sorry I have not gotten back to you in a timely fashion.

Ø What's up with you talking that way?

Ø Oh, Shall I speak Ebonics

Ø What's that?

Ø Exactly.

Ø Ozzie, you look buffed.

Ø Yea, just had a good chest workout. So I'm a little pumped. It will reside soon. Anyway Edwin, I have a number for you. I spoke with Prince today. His number was a little low to start, but I took care of that. Its $500,000. That's for you to decide how you will split it with your source or partner.

Ø Damn, Ozzie. That's a lot of fucken money. Are you serious?

Ø Yes Edwin. I'm serious. It's real. I told Prince not to even consider thinking of crossing us. But Edwin, just so you know. I don't trust him. So we need to take measures to make sure we don't get fucked.

Ø Ozzie, $500,000. That's a half of million dollars.

Ø Yea, Edwin. That's right. Half a million dollars.

Ø Oh shit! I can buy me a nice house in Puerto Rico.

Ø You might be better off Edwin, buying a house in South America. Things are going to get bad here in the US, within a few years. The United States Dollar, or rather I should say the United States Ponzi scheme is coming to an end. The powers that be are going to arrest many people, throw them in FEMA camps indefinitely, and will keep their property. Or perhaps WW3 will be the excuse for the US to execute its own people. You know, just as they did with the World Trade Center.

Ø Damn Ozzie. You know more than I thought.

Ø Well Edwin, I knew a lot of things before meeting you. After we meet I became very curious as to a number of different topics. I also did a great deal of research into your brotherhood the Freemasons. I know you are not free to talk about certain things with non-members. And so out of respect, I won't ask you. But I did read up how you guys cover each other's back. Edwin, do you think I can join?

Ø Well Ozzie, if you ask me I have to bring it to the attention of the lodge. They will do an inquiry and make a determination.

Ø Edwin, don't go that far as of now. I am not sure what I want to do. I am on the fence on a number of things. I don't know which side to choose. Do I attempt to help the people and get fucked, or do I side with the powers that be and perhaps save myself. I know many of you Masons will help each other out. I came across a web site that showed the distress sign, but again, out of respect, I won't attempt to play that game.

Ø So Ozzie. Let's talk about my $500,000.

Ø Oh Sorry Edwin. As of late I find myself drifting off into different topics. So Prince wanted to up only $200,000. I knew how much money he is going after, and so I told him your minimum was $500,000. Now that I think about it, I might have been able to get you some more.

Ø Ozzie, I'm good with that. I will give my guy some money out of that.

Ø Yes, Edwin. That is for you to decide. The more you offer him the more he might actually want. Don't let him know how big of a score it really is. Whatever you decide just let me know so that I keep the story in line with you.

Ø OK. I will think about the amount and will let you know.

Ø You really don't have to if you don't want to Edwin. I'm not trying to get into your business. It's all up to you. Now what we really have to talk about is how we are going to deal with Prince if he gets stupid on us. Edwin, I'm with you on whatever we need to do. But if we need to get rid of him, I really don't want to know about it. I told him I was making plans in case he thought of doing anything stupid. He does not know who your connection is or how he is related to you. I just told him you are well connected by two different groups.

Ø Yea, that's right. With the money I am getting I will have a few NETA guys around as back up.

Ø Edwin. I don't want to die. Not that I am scared of dying, but because I have Abby, my daughter that still needs me.

Ø Ozzie. I know what you are saying. I have family too. Believe me, you are safe. You know, Howard also asked me to look after you.

Ø How and when?

Ø Well. I went to his house to do a deal with him. He is grateful that you put him in contact with his wife when they were both locked up, and he is also grateful for you getting him out of jail. He asked if I knew who the Cuban guys that put the hit on you are. I told him I did not know but that I would look into it. You know they have their own gang, mostly in Miami. They don't like to come up to Broward. They say Broward is the worst place in Florida to commit a crime. So they stay away. Unless there is a high level order. I'm thinking those two guys were just soldiers. Low level gangsters. Anyway, those two guys are still locked up. My nephew, who works for the Hollywood police department will let me know when they come out.

Ø Your Freemason nephew, whom you saved his father's life in Puerto Rico.

Ø Yeap. You got it.

Ø Damn, Edwin. You are the fucken man. So you have my back.

Ø Yeap.

Ø You are the fucken man. We have to get together again to make a plan as to getting into the Vault. You will need to open your own box. There are two scenarios that can play out here. One is, right from within the vault we can each store our money, and make a clean and free getaway. We can later go back and retrieve it when it is safe to do so. The other scenario is to depart with our money on the spot. However, we will need to make sure that no one tries to attack us. Again we have to be very careful of Prince.

Ø Okay Ozzie, we will visit the Vault during the week and I will rent a security box. At the same time I will have a word with Jimmy Aten.

Ø Jimmy Aten. That sounds white. I thought he was Puerto Rican.

Edwin looked at me and suddenly burst into laughter. The drink in his hand almost spilled. He set it on the table, looked at me again, and leaned forward in his chair laughing uncontrollably.

Ø What is that about Edwin?

Ø It's an inside joke Ozzie.

Ø So is Jimmy some type of God. Such as Aten Ra.

Ø Ozzie, its Amen Ra.

Ø Yes Edwin Amen Ra, The only god chosen by King Akhenaton to be the true God. For there was to be the only god, the sun. Its name was Ra. The full name being Amen Ra. Most Christians have no idea that every time they say Amen at the end of a player, they are paying homage to the Sun God, Amen Ra. The Pharos said, "When we pray to god we must pray through the son of god. Amen Ra, because he represented God." At the end of the prayer, they would say Amen. In the scripture Jesus said, if your eye be single, then there will be light in you. This single eye was the symbol of Amen RA. This eye was always within the circle, the sun. The eye of god. That image can be found on the back of the US dollar. But just so you know Edwin there seems to be some confusion as to whether they are both the same or not. Aten was associated often times with the sun God Ra. Ra was the ancient Egyptian solar deity and a major god in ancient Egyptian religion. Ra is depicted with a human body and a bird-like face, with Aten right above his head. It was believed that all forms of life were created by Ra. The Egyptians highly worshiped the sun, so it made sense for them to worship Ra as well.

Ø Ozzie, that's too much info. The only god I care about right now is in the Vault. I call him Money. Get with it. Where the hell did you get this entire god thing from?

Ø Edwin, I never told you, but I did study theology.

Ø No wonder. Fuck that shit. Say money, money, money.

Ø Money, money, money.

Ø You see, doesn't it feel good? Say it again.

Ø Money, money, money.

Ø Don't you feel good?

Ø Edwin, I'm not sure. I might not want this money. It will all depend. I am not sure I will keep it.

Ø Fuck Ozzie, give it to me.

Ø Edwin. I know what it's like to get money for someone's blood.

Ø Ozzie, brother, Keep it together. Let's get this and then you decide.

Ø Yes, Edwin it's going to happen. That I am sure of. Anyway, what the hell was so funny?

Ø Oh, my boys name is Jimmy. His last name is not Aten. Aten is NETA backwards. Some of us local boys will say Aten, if we think we are talking to a NETA.

Ø Yea Edwin but what about the other signs.

Ø Well it's the other signs that really tell us apart. But sometimes if we are not wearing the colors or the beads nor have a tattoo showing then we might say Aten.

Ø Okay. Edwin, can you say pineal eye or gland?

Ø What the fuck is that? Some type of penis.

Ø No I did not say the Washington Monument. Our eye into the world. Never mind Edwin. It's not important. Just don't drink tap water.

Ø What the fuck are you talking about?

Ø Nothing Edwin. Money, money, money.

Ø Ah, finally. That's what I'm talking about.

Ø Edwin lets meet Wednesday, to make more plans on the Vault. Now let's talk about helping Howard.

Ø Ok, Ozzie. That one is easy for me.

Ø Why is that?

Ø Look Ozzie I can't tell you much today. My nephew is a Freemason. So am I. Let me talk with him during the week and then we can form a plan.

Ø Okay Edwin. I am thinking we should do both things on the same day.

Ø Sounds good to me. But again, let's meet up again to discuss Howard, after I meet my nephew.

Ø Sound good. I think it's time for me to go fishing.

Ø Oh, you mean get laid.

Ø Yeap. You got it.

Ø Hey Ozzie. Does your friend know about this?

Ø Gissela?

Ø I guess. The one you call G.

Ø Edwin, she thinks I am planning and meeting you guys to get leads for arrest. I think she does have some idea, because once or twice I have spoken to Prince on the phone while she was present. And I think I might have given her some idea, that there might be something at the Vault worth investigating. But I never really told her about the money. She is a good girl, that is why I keep her around, but I think she is really the one that is keeping me around. I think she has a plan. Shit, I hope she doesn't know about the $6,000,000. Now I have to watch my back from her. Fuck Edwin. Should I be afraid?

Ø Oh well, sorry Ozzie. I didn't mean to scare you. But you know how these ladies can be.

Ø Yes I know Edwin. I guess I have to be a little cautious now with her. Well it's getting late and I need some. So let's talk in a day or two. Remember, I have to help Howard. If everything works out well for him, maybe I will throw you a little extra.

That evening I came home to G, but was not my usual self. She asked if everything was okay. Was I subconsciously being distant? I don't know. Sex was good, but my guard must be up again. I guess that's what she was picking up on.

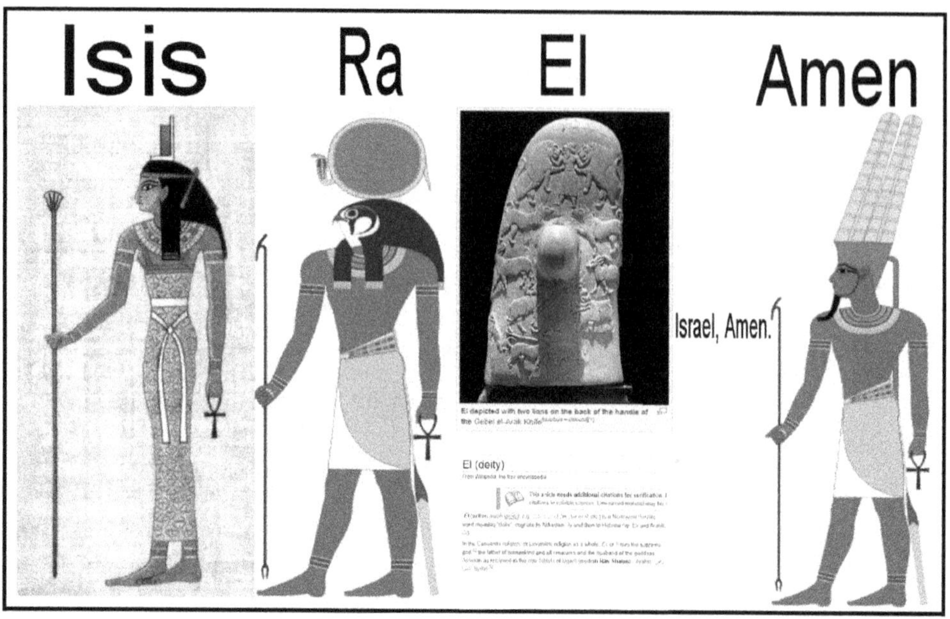
Isis
Ra
El
Amen
Israel, Amen.
El (deity)

ANNUIT CŒPTIS
MDCCLXXVI
NOVUS ORDO SECLORUM
THE GREAT SEAL

45 TUESDAY

Ø Hello Prince.

Ø Yo Ozzie, what up?

Ø Hey, do you want to meet up tomorrow?

Ø Sure. Where.

Ø Well depends on the time. I tell you what. Go to my job around 1 and we can talk for a little. It's Cruisers Auto in Davie, on SR7. As I have something to do after work.

Ø All right. I'll see you tomorrow. Is everything fine?

Ø Yes. We need to get money. I'll fill you in tomorrow.

Ø Got it. Buy.

Ø Buy.

It's been a while since I had spoken to Howard. I decided to give him a call for I failed to call him as I promised.

Ø Hello, Howard.

Ø Hola Ozzie. Como Estas?

Ø Toda Bien Howard. Listen, I am sorry I did not call you. I've been busy trying to save the world.

Ø The world. You are having a hard time saving yourself.

Ø Yes I know. One thing I can do is save your ass Howard. I needed to check with some other people so that I can start a plan for you. I already have something in mind, but might be a little complicated. However I will know more towards the end of this week. I know we will be able to put that guy away.

Ø What do you mean away? Everyone knows you can't kill a cop and get away with it.

Ø Howard, my plan is for him to want to kill himself; that is after we can show the things he has done to you. I don't want to say much more on the phone. I will visit you this weekend. I can't do anything yet, until I get word from an insider.

Ø You mean a cop?

Ø Yes Howard. A cop. Can't talk about it yet. Believe me, this weekend we will discuss more.

Ø Ozzie

Ø Yes.

Howard paused for a moment. As if not wanting to say what he was about to start.

His silence spoke loud. Something was wrong.

Ø Okay Howard. It's too late. Your silence started, now finish it with words. What's wrong?

Ø Look, I don't really want to scare you. But I think you should be careful with Prince.

Ø Go on.

Ø I told you my group is big. I have been keeping track of him and you. I know he has been talking to some Cubans in Miami. What about I am not sure. It could be about drugs or about tax fraud. I am not sure. But just be very careful. Sometimes the one that does you in is the one you would least expect.

Ø Fuck Howard. You know, I always get these bad vibes from him. At least I know when he is lying. I am scared now.

Ø Look, if you can get him in the Vault, then you are safe till then. Again Ozzie, I am not saying he has anything to do with you and the Cubans. My feeling the whole time is that he really does like you. It's probably nothing to worry about. Maybe I should not have scared you. I am probably wrong. I just want you to be safe.

Ø Howard. Have you heard anything about him leaving his girlfriend?

Ø No. I don't see why he would. She was the one that would put things together. She would get the people to cash in the checks. I think he needs her.

Ø Well, he said he left her. But then he also said or did his little lying sign. Something must be wrong.

Ø Ozzie, I will look into that. You can count on me.

Ø Fuck Howard. I'm scared. I'm Abby's dad. I can't leave her alone yet. BTW Howard. I don't like getting into people's business, but we are going to be able to get into the Vault. I'm meeting the insider tomorrow.

Ø Damn, another insider. Not a cop right.

Ø No cop. But I can't say at this time. I don't know what your agreement with Prince was and it's not my business. I did not ask him for anything extra. I'm to get one million. The insider will split $500,000. Between the two. I want you to hear it from my mouth, so that we can be clear.

Ø Thanks for the info. I'm going to have a few guys follow him around. I'll send someone to put a camera at his place so that I can watch. But you need to keep that hush.

Ø I promise Howard.

Ø Ozzie, go get your money. Make backup plans. If you want I can send a few guys to watch over you on that day.

Ø No Howard, I have that part covered already. I'll see you in a few days.

Ø Okay, Ozz. Please let me know ASAP.

Ø Will do Howard. Buy

Fuck, fuck, fuck! I did it again. Once again, I am getting closer to danger. I need a workout. Yea, that's the ticket.

Ah, it's been several hours since my conversation with Howard. My initial fear has subsided a bit; must be the endorphins. It seems to sooth me; calm me; almost as if it were some type of meditation. Perhaps it's a gateway for it; although I don't hold the position or make the universal sound, Om. Hey an Onomatopoeia, for you scholars.

So questions are, Was Howard doing a number on me? Was he trying for some reason to keep me in his pocket? Was he trying to make it seem that he was looking out for me, so that I would be compelled to help him? Did he really know something? Or worse, does he know more about Prince and the Cuban guys in Miami than he told me? Anything is possible. There is a lot of money involved. Men have killed for much less. Maybe he wants to protect me on that day so that he can rob me. Fuck, I don't trust anyone. I even doubt my friend G. What the fuck is her plan? What did Howard mean when he said he was keeping track of Prince and me? How shall I know? Oh… Edwin. Once again, Edwin. He is the answer. I do trust him beyond belief. Why, I hardly know him. But I can feel it. It's something I learned from my dad. I can feel when there is love. Problem is there seem to be hardly any of it in this world. Maybe the eliminators are right? Shit man. I'm doing it again; getting away, deeper than I should. Maybe I should clear my pineal gland and smoke some weed. But I don't have any; weed that is. Next option, Go and screw G. Yea. That's the ticket. I like it, I like it a lot.

46 WEDNESDAY

It was 11:40 am. The window by my desk overlooks the entrance where the cars come in. I have the vantage point of seeing people come in before my coworkers do. This morning a late model BMW pulled in. It looked familiar, and that's because it was. Prince exited the vehicle and came in. Yesid the owner was at action buying cars. Eddie who usually opens the business was out and about. That just left me and nosey secretary Luz. Prince came and sat by my desk. It was safe to talk there and so we did not have to go out. Prince as usual, dressed well.

- Ø What Up, Ozzie?
- Ø Hey Prince. Thanks for coming by.
- Ø This is a nice setup here.
- Ø Yea, I happen to like it a lot. Low key and a family atmosphere. It's why I decided to come here. Anyway. Let's get busy talking about some things. Before we start, have you heard from your girlfriend?
- Ø Oh No. I told you, she would not be coming back. She is out of the picture.
- Ø What did you do? Kill her?
- Ø Come on Ozzie. Are you serious?
- Ø Yea, I'm just fucking with you. So tell me, did you kill her?
- Ø No, not me. I would not do such a thing. Anyway, what does she have to do with us?
- Ø I'm curious as to how many people actually know about our adventure.
- Ø Not many. Just relax. She is away. Yea, Yea.

Oh fuck. There it is. Its Prince dead giveaway when lying. My heart started raising a little. Holy shit! Did he really eliminate her? I guess there is no way of telling. Just relax Ozzie. Keep composed. Stay focused. Maybe I am wrong. Maybe I am reading things wrong?

- Ø Yo Ozzie. What's wrong?
- Ø Oh nothing. I was just thinking of my daughter for a minute. Anyway Prince, the guys have agreed to do this. I am also going to help Howard. So later during the week, I should have a good time frame as to when we can execute the plan. There is something I need you to look into.
- Ø Sure, What?

Ø Do you remember when we were locked up and I showed you a newspaper article about some guy in Hollywood that was jamming the radio frequency of certain makes of automobile? He had a pirated radio station on the top floor of a tall building.

Ø Vaguely.

Ø Here is the article.

Ø Where did you get that from?

Ø That's the actual paper I showed you. When you approached me about the $6,000,000. My mind started working. You know what's funny Prince; or rather coincidental. On that very same page is an article about the Vault. Notice the date on the paper. It's from the Florida Sun Sentinel, Broward County Edition. The date is Sunday, December 20, 2012.

Ø Wow Ozzie. I did not realize it when you showed me that there was also a column on the Vault. Damn, what were you thinking?

Ø That's how I am Prince. I think in advance. Just like you need to in a game of chess. You don't make a move until you see the moves. That means several moves ahead. Just as well, I have a good plan for getting in. I've just been quiet about it; until I was sure I could put it together. Anyway, I need you to find this guy that was running the radio station.

Ø Why?

Ø I need him to jam the Hollywood Police station frequency.

Ø Why?

Ø Why? You have no clue. You have no idea. You have formulated no plan. Trust me. We will need this guy to buy time. I am going to do Howards Plan on the same day we do The Vault. As far as The Vault. I will have a second getaway car that will carry my loot as well as the other two guys. You need to figure out how you will depart with yours. Getting back to the Pirate, by tweaking the frequency slightly I can jam the Police frequency. I have someone that will help out with that. With an oscilloscope he will capture their frequency and then help the pirate retune. That is the best way to go. I am working on a backup plan to that. I will have a backup plan to everything.

Ø Damn Ozzie. You are for real. Fuck. I think this is really going to happen. I have to tell you, I was giving up on it.

Ø You know Prince, I always find a way. But I am stuck with something.

Ø What that?

Ø How do I save the world?

Ø What the fuck you talking about? Fuck the world. Save yourself. There are just a bunch of fucken idiots out there.

- Ø Yea Prince. I know. I'm just being philosophical.
- Ø Why? Are you going through midlife crises?
- Ø Not at all. It has to do with Edwin.
- Ø With Edwin? How is he by the way?
- Ø He is well. I'll tell you more about him as I need to. BTW Prince. Have you ever heard anything else about the Cuban cousins that put the hit on me?
- Ø Na. I think that's a dead issue.
- Ø Wow Prince. Nice choice of words. Makes me feel like I will be the dead issue.
- Ø Oh, I did not mean it that way.
- Ø Yes, I know what you meant.
- Ø So Ozzie. How soon do you think we can do this?
- Ø Two weeks at earliest if everything goes well. But I'm thinking more between three and four. No sense in rushing this and getting it wrong.
- Ø True That.
- Ø Okay. Anything you need to talk about.
- Ø Na, I'm good for the moment.
- Ø So then let's meet up this weekend.
- Ø You got it.

As soon as Prince left the office I sat back in my chair and asked. What the fuck are you getting into? I have no fear of breaking into the Vault. On the contrary, it's an adventure. My question is more as to, Who am I dealing with? The more I dealt with Prince the less I trusted him. His girlfriend came to mind. I wonder if he did dispose of her. Fuck, Fuck. My instincts are usually right. I don't know for sure, and I don't have much to go by. But I really, really wonder. Could he possibly have disposed of his wife also? Will he try to dispose of me? Should I dispose of him before he does me? Why do I have to think so much? Shit, I need a good workout, but it's not my day. This reminds me, I have to go with Edwin to the Vault.

Following is an Actual News report

Rogue radio station caused keyless entry systems to fail, left car owners locked out. By Chris Welch on December 28, 2012 06:43 pm Email 102**Comments** 16.

For months, frustrated car owners just couldn't explain it. As the Sun Sentinel explains, parking anywhere in the vicinity of the Hollywood Police Department would render their vehicle's keyless entry system useless. As more and more cars were towed away thanks to the baffling phenomenon, it was discovered that functionality returned once cars were a safe distance away from the police station. Rumors swirled as to what the cause could be, with one popular theory attributing the interference to a powerful antenna owned by police.

Authorities finally solved the mystery, however: beginning in August, a rogue radio station had been operating from the roof of a building just one block away from police headquarters. Aside from broadcasting Caribbean music 24 / 7 to those in range, the station was also blocking the signal between electronic key fobs and their designated vehicles. Cars from Lexus, Toyota, BMW, Ford, and others were impacted by the unauthorized frequency override, though police don't think whoever was behind the station realized the trouble it was causing. Even so, should they succeed in locating the person responsible for setting up the now-confiscated equipment; he or she could face a $10,000 fine from the FCC. The resolution is likely good news to local residents, some of whom were forced to dig out their car's manual to learn how to unlock their doors the old-fashioned way.

Still Wednesday. Meeting with Edwin. -

Ø Hello Edwin. It's Ozzie.

Ø Hola Ozzie. Que Tal?

Ø Edwin lets meet at the Vault at 6; 30. I work only about 15 minutes from there.

Ø Okay Ozzie. Do I need to bring anything?

Ø No. I will pay the bill. You need to get a box for yourself. Also go a little earlier and drive around so that you become familiar with the area. Is your contact going to be there?

Ø I think so.

Ø Ok. I'll see you then.

It was now only 1pm, my lunch time. Because of the research I have currently done, G and I have decided to take our own health into our own hands. First on the list was to eliminate corn for two reasons. One it has been genetically modified. This in itself is not a bad thing. The bad thing comes into play when it's been crossed with different cells of different species. Hum? Yes it's true, and it's been going on for years. Talking of food, hear is food for thought. It has been claimed by certain powers that be, that human origins was a cross between species; The Anunnaki being one. I'll leave this alone for the moment. Getting back to GMO, Farmers in the US that grow corn that has crossed pollinated with the GMO corn have to pay a penalty for using it. The powers that be have copy right laws on genetically modified foods. One strain called Starlink, was approved only for animal feed in the US, but was found in food, leading to a series of recalls starting in 2000.

The second reason is that the corn has been genetically modified to tolerate large amounts of poisonous pesticides. These pesticides actually find its way into our bodies. Hair analysis reveals trace elements of pesticides. Not only is corn grown to tolerate poisonous pesticides, but most food grow in the US have as well. Those poisons kill bacteria and other living organisms in the ground that produce micro nutrients. Most fruits and vegetables are striped from the macro nutrients they used to provide. Our bodies are now lacking these micro nutrients leading to many diseases. Where we once used to absorb micro nutrients, we are now actually absorbing poisons in the way of pesticides. It's gotten to the point where our bodies can no longer digest all the corn we eat. Have you ever recalled seeing undigested corn in you stools? Even cows that are corn feed can only survive on it for no more than eight months, they then start to develop cancers and ulcers. That's the time to harvest them. Look it up. Connect the dots. We are purposefully being eliminated by the powers that be. If the New World Order is going to eliminate me, it won't be through foods; Besides the Cubans might get me first. Anyway, I pulled out some delicious fish and asparagus… Delicious tasting asparagus, organically grown. It seems we have lost our pallet for natural tasty food. Tomatoes grown in the US have hardly any flavor. Our sense of smell is the first contributing factor in perceiving or detecting flavors. If it's bland, with no delicious order or taste, it's properly no good any more. I had my fill accompanied by delicious Florida Spring bottled water from Zephyrhills. Hay a free plug. But if it's good for you and me, I will say so. Just so you know, the plastic container we use for our bottled water is no way near as detrimental as drinking the wrong water.

Its 6: I meet Edwin at The Vault

Ø Hi Edwin, How are you?
Ø Que Tal? Todo Bien.
Ø Did you get a chance to drive around?
Ø Yea. I did. Not too many ways in to find this place.
Ø So you noticed. That could be a good thing or a bad thing.
Ø Ok. So let's do this.

Edwin walked in before me as if he knew what he was doing or going. He seemed to take charge and did not bother to wait for me. It reminded me of walking with my father as a child. He had a wide gap and I always found myself almost running after him. He could not hear, so yelling at him to slowdown was like talking on deft ears. Can you hear me dad? I somehow was amused as I followed along. Edwin quickly made his way to the office and greeted Jimmy Aten with their special hand shake. Aten or God was alone in the office with us.

Ø Yo Jimmy this is my brother Ozzie.
Ø Yo Ozzie was up?
Ø Hey Jimmy. Nice to meet you.

It was evident that Jimmy knew we were coming. In a rush he asked Edwin for the cash money for the three months of a box rental.

Ø Total is $55.

I pulled out the funds from my pocket and handed to him.

Ø Edwin, sign here, does not matter, you can put any signature.

Edwin scribbled down a signature. And with that Jimmy grasp the pad he was using and rushed us out the office. We headed out through which we came. Once there, in the lobby, instead of getting on the elevator to go up, Jimmy opened a door that required a special key. The movements were quick and deliberate. There was no time to ask questions. It felt like an adventure; as if I was being lead on a ride. Beyond that door was a small enclosed area maybe 10x10 feet with two more doors. These doors did not have any locks on them, just a simple doorknob to turn. Were they closed on the other side? Three seconds is all it took to answer that. Jimmy turned the doorknob to the left of where we were now standing. It gave way to a corridor about 50 feet long.

- Ø Guys this passage way is the area behind where the cars pull in to access their containers.

We continued walking the length of the corridor and at its end, opened another door and went through. Again it was unlocked. As if there was no reason for it to be.

- Ø Hurry, we are not supposed to be back here. I only have a few minutes before the girl comes back from her break. This is where the containers are stored. That big machine over there is a jack. There are three of them. It's all automated. Once you press your code and your thumbprint is verified, the computer tells the lift which container to bring to the waiting area. If there is a thumb print that is required, it's almost impossible to get the command to pick up your container without it.
- Ø Yes, but can't you override it from the office.
- Ø Yes, but only when the account is in default. Then we can send that container to an area where we will action it to the highest bidder. No one is allowed to enter the unit until it has been auctioned. So people will bid on containers without fully knowing what is inside. If the account is still good, then the workers cannot access the container. I can look up in the computer and know which storage container box is his, but to get in we would have to break into it from this back room. Depending on which day of the week it is, will determine how many engineers are working. Usually, there will be one guy back here taking care of any problem that might come. During lunch time there is no one. So if there is no finger, then the next step is for me to bring the box down and break into it from here. They will know it was an inside job. If you have a thumb print, then the box will be brought to the car area and you can take your time doing what you need to do. No one will have any idea.
- Ø Are you able to get us the code one needs to punch in?
- Ø Yes, I can get it. I am paying someone to do that for me. He is going to hack into the system when I tell him to. I know the passwords to get into our computer system. That one is not hard. Now let's get out of here and go to the storage box you rented.

Quickly and quietly we made our way back to the main corridor where the elevator was. Once there Jimmy seemed to relax. He took a deep breath and slowed down. As if to say, we were in the clear. The security box Edwin was given was in a different room next to mine. Everything else seemed equal. Jimmy gave instructions on how to access it and use it. Edwin chose to use his finger print as well as a code. After two practice runs he got the hang of it and we left. All the while my eyes were taking in the surrounding, trying to notice the unnoticeable. Or should I say the not so obvious? "Seek and you shall find" was a quote that I was always fond of. Nothing here seemed to be different than from the adjacent room where my box was. For a second I wondered if Prince has bothered to open a box. He did rent a container. Is that where he was to stash his loot? At this point it did not matter to me. His escape was not my concern. But wait, should I make it my concern? Maybe I do want to know how he is planning to make his escape. Maybe I will choose a different path than his. Ok So I shall ask him, just to be safe. Who would think this idea came to me as a result of simply looking for things that are not so obvious.

Edwin and I were out of there in 20 minutes. His practice run and signing up took the majority of that time. Sunset was present as we exited. I notice the beautiful sun rays hitting some of the clouds to the far west. Ozzie Jr. came to mind. For there is a beautiful picture of him, Nancy had taken while we were on a cruise ship. In it he was leaning over a banister; the water beneath him and the sunset behind. The sun rays reached for him, and then beyond.

- Ø Yo Ozzie. Let's go.
- Ø Do you want to meet at the Casino and talk or should we catch up tomorrow?
- Ø Tomorrow is fine with me.
- Ø Okay.

It took me about one minute to compose myself. There was something magical about those rays. They were talking to me, in some strange language I could not understand. Was I out of tune with nature? What is it? What are you trying to tell me? Then I caught myself. It started coming back. I started to panic as I recognized it. Darkness was befalling. I had not realized, as I have been so busy with things, that there once was a time when it was always dark and cloudy. Maybe I was healed. For without the need of a woman, or anyone else, I could see the beautiful sun as it revealed itself to me. I had failed to notice that I was now able to see night and day.

Everything was no longer a dark cloud. Was that what the sun was trying to tell me? Or perhaps show me? I'm getting scared. I can see him coming. Later on after those rays are gone, he is coming for me; my loyal friend, the demon. How do I escape him tonight?

Should I tell him to let me go? To go away and leave me alone. Was that what Ozzie wanted to talk to me about. After all, he was aware of my pain. Is it time to let go? Can I ever forgive myself? Maybe I will call him. Fuck. I know I won't sleep tonight. I better get drunk. It will relieve my pain; my pain of losing family. Fuck you demon. Fuck you. I think, therefore I am.

That evening upon entering home, I gave G my usual kiss, followed by a glass of Galliano… Plenty of it. G asked if I was alright. I said yes. But I was not. Deep, deep down inside, I was in pain. It's something I don't like to talk about. Little does she know about my internal pain and suffering. Tonight I was not going to let the demon confront me. I did not want to deal with him. One drink, was followed by another, and then another. My cheek started to numb a little and so did my other senses. Ah, that's the ticket. I feel no pain. Sleep. Sleep.

Thursday morning I awoke with my usual hard on. G was still in bed. I turned towards her and pressed myself against her. That's all I needed to do. She back up; with her left hand she grasped me and guided me in. After several minutes of play, a thought came. Although I was enjoying myself, last night came to mind. I don't remember what happened. As I thrust in and out her I thought about the finger. Neither my finger nor hers, but rather the finger of a man I did not even know. It threw me off for a minute. But all the while I was hard as a rock. She just kept moving to and fro, not knowing I had something on my mind. After we finished, I wrapped my arms and leg around her while still inside.

This morning Prince came to mind. Not him so much, but rather the fingerprint that we needed to make this break-in possible. I do not even know what to call this. Are we thieves, robbers, felons, or thugs? What am I? Who am I? What have I become. Fuck it, I will answer that later. The allure has overtaken me. It's not the money. It's something else. I knew I needed to talk to Prince. I need that fucken fingerprint. I also need to formulate plan two. That would be without the fingerprint.

- Ø Hey prince. How are you?
- Ø Yo Ozzie. I'm good. What Up?
- Ø We need to talk. Do you want to stop by my job or talk on the phone?
- Ø No phone. Let's meet after you get out.
- Ø Yo Prince. I'm going to the gym after work.
- Ø Fuck, Ozzie. How about after/ well Maybe, but it's easier if you just came by.
- Ø Okay. I'll see you in a few hours.

It was almost noon when Prince came by. The sun was overhead. Base on the shadows it cast I could give a good approximation of time. Why was he in so early? Anyway, it doesn't really matter. Prince pulled up and exited the car. There were two people in it. They seemed Hispanic. I tried to make them out but to no avail. From within my office it was difficult.

Ø Yo Prince. What up.
Ø Hey Ozzie. What up.
Ø Come let's walk outside and talk for a minute.
Ø Hey did you eat?
Ø I bring my lunch in. I don't do poisonous fast food any more.
Ø Damn, you have become psychotic? First you worry about saving the world, and now this. You need to chill.
Ø You need to wake up. Do you know why part of you is so heavy? It is because the foods you eat are laced with chemicals that make you crave for more.
Ø I'm just a big boy.
Ø Yea. A sleeping walking time bomb.
Ø Yo fuck you Ozz. What the fuck. I asked you a simple question.
Ø Yo Prince I answered negatively.
Ø What?
Ø Exactly. Look the reason I need to talk to you is because I need a finger.
Ø How is this one?
Ø Fuck you. Put that fat finger down, and shove it up your ass. Then tell me if you like it.
Ø Hey, you never know.
Ø Okay Prince. Let's get serious here.
Ø There are two scenarios that can play out. Apart from the actual finger, is to get a scan of the finger. That is the best solution. The other angle is to bring the container box down and then break into it from the ground. That will let the house know that an internal job was being performed. But worse yet, our plan could be foiled by those workers. It's a chance I rather not take.
Ø So you want me to cut off his finger.
Ø That's not what I said. I said I need his fingerprint. See if you can break into his house and get a fingerprint. You are resourceful. I'm sure you could manage that. Perhaps you can find a way to lift his print from a glass. How you accomplished that is up to you. Just get me a print. You said you had a contact in Israel that would be able to produce a duplicate finger mold from his scan. Just make it happen. I need it done within two weeks.

Ø Hey Ozzie, aren't we in this together? Sure. That's why I'm telling you what we need. If you don't want to just say so. My guys will go it alone. You opened up a can of worms. Some have slithered away and you can't put them back. If you can't do this let me know. I will get someone else to do it.

Ø Damn Ozzie, calm down. I think this is getting to your head.

Ø Getting to my head. Prince, it's been in my head for a while. Thanks to you. You are to blame. You put it there. You planted it. Now it's time to harvest. You can't stop it. I can't stop it. It needs to come out. So just get me a fucken fingerprint.

Ø Is that all you need?

Ø One other thing.

Ø I need to know what your escape plan is.

Ø Why?

Ø Simple Prince. So that I don't run into you. We need to know not only how to get in, but also how to get out.

Ø True that.

Ø Okay. We can talk in a few days. I'll give you the finger.

Ø Fingerprint Prince. Fingerprint.

Ø Okay Ozzie. Fingerprint.

Ø Okay Prince. Talk to you later.

I watched Prince as he walked over to his car. Although I did not ask about his friends, I was curious. Two young light skin guys. As he entered his car I caught the attention of one. Politely he nodded, acknowledging my presence, to which I reciprocated. Shit, if I did not know better, I would swear they were the two Cuban cousins. I knew the cousins were in jail as per Edwin. Could these be the guys Howard spoke of? Fuck! Could they be part of the cousins' gang, and Prince is going to deliver me to them after we do the heists? Well I don't know. Am I being paranoid, or just cautious? I rather err in favor of cautious than ignorance. Oh well! I need to contact Edwin again and see what is going on with his nephew, the Masonic Neta Aten.

Ø Hello Edwin.

Ø Hola Ozzie. Que Tal?

Ø Everything is good Edwin. I'm calling to see if we can meet tonight?

Ø No, not good. Let's do it tomorrow. Today I am meeting with my nephew.

Ø Oh good. I was curious to when that was going to happen. I need to give Howard some news.

Ø I'll call you tomorrow.

Ø Okay. (pause) Edwin.

Ø Yea. Never mind, it's not that important. Remind me to tell you tomorrow.

Ø Okay, Dale.

Ø Okay Edwin. Talk tomorrow.

Looking outside my office window, I noticed the sun just slight to the west. The light post in front of the property had cast a shadow of about three feet long towards the east. It was about three. Not because the shadow was three feet, that part was coincidental. Experience has taught me to tell time in this manner. Besides last time I checked which was about an hour ago, it was two. As soon as I tuned back in to my computer I noticed an email. It was from my lawyer.

Ozzie, please note that we have a court date in two and a half weeks. At which time the judge might set sentence. That is unless they give you another extension. I've not heard anything to the contrary. This is a mandatory appearance. Next week I will give you a call so that we can speak.

OH, Fuck! Just what I needed; talk about timing… Fuck! Its bad timing. Nonetheless, I took it as an opportunity and reminder to finish the harvest. Two and a half weeks to pick the crops to get the job done. Once again, the pressure was on. Why did I think my court date was next month? Because of that I had not rushed. Oh well. Let the games begin; Chess under the clock.

Ø Hello Prince.

Ø Yo what up?

Ø Prince, you better put a rush on things. I just found out I have two and half weeks for sentence.

Ø Shit Ozz. That's bad news.

Ø Tell me about it. Well at the very least we have a warning. Just make sure you get that for me. Or I am going to have to do plan two.

Ø Okay Ozz. I got you. I'll call my guys as soon as we hang up.

Ø Okay Prince. Will talk tomorrow.

47 FRIDAY

Ø Edwin

Ø Que Tal Ozzie?

Ø Edwin, where you able to meet your nephew?

Ø Yes.

Ø Good lets meet tonight and talk. I Received an email yesterday from my lawyer and I have two and a half weeks before I go to court for sentencing.

Ø Oh shit Ozzie. That might not be enough time for my nephew to help Howard.

Ø I was afraid of that Edwin. What time can you make it?

Ø Anytime is fine for me.

Ø 7; 30. Same place. Okay. I'll be there.

So my fellow readers. Here is a question for you. I am meeting Edwin at the Hard Rock Casino once more. Three Visits in a row I was able to sit in the same spot. Will it be four for four or has luck run out? Just think about it for a minute. Who has taken matrix mathematic? Ha? What? I did. So what are the odds? Will it be available, or has luck run out. I know the answer; because I am writing this after the fact. Ok. I'll give it to you later.

Ø Edwin, what's up?

Ø Hola Ozzie. Que Tal?

Ø Edwin let's get right down to it.

The waitress already knew my drink. She brought a glass of Galliano along with Edwin's drink. Good for her; an intelligent person in Florida. Not to mention fucken sexy. However, I for some reason can't seem to look at young girls as a sexual object. I guess it's because I have young daughters. I tend to see them all the same. Anyhow we did our cheers and continued with our talk. Ok so we were at the same place. But were we at the same seat?

Ø So Edwin is your nephew on board.

Ø Yes. He has to. Doesn't have much of a choice.

Ø Why is that?

Ø Because we are both Mason.

Ø And?

Ø Ozzie. The code within Masonry transcends everything else. We pledge to help and support each other in this brotherhood. It's a bond that is thicker than blood.

Ø Yes Edwin, but you are also family.

Ø If that was the case then he might have to say no. But from one Mason to another, he is obligated to help.

Ø Damn Edwin. That's some strong stuff. Does he feel any obligation to help you because you saved his father's life in jail?

Ø I did not bring that up, nor will I ever. There is a brotherhood among us that we all recognize and respect. We don't have to throw things in each other's face. Just the fact that we are Masons is good enough to help in any endeavors that are requested.

Ø So you are saying he is in.

Ø Yes. He will help me with anything I ask. Actually he is glad to help.

Ø Why is that?

Ø Well Ozzie. I should not tell you certain things because you are not a Mason, but I do feel a loving connection to you.

Ø You know Edwin. I feel it also. Maybe you are related to me.

Ø Nope. I would know. There are no giants in my family.

Ø I'm just tall, average by many people's standards.

Ø By my standard you are huge. Anyway Ozzie, My nephew is pleased to help. This bad cop has put away a few Mason. One or two that could have been innocent. There is an order, from a high level freemason, to investigate this bad cop.

Ø Why?

Ø Well there was this guy that was falsely accused of running a drug clinic. It was said that he had a pill mill.

Ø Edwin, Is this guy Balbi?

Ø Yea that's the guy. They say he was innocent and that he was set up by this cop. The Freemasons put up $250,000 for his defense. Some investigation on their part has shown that he was innocent.

Ø Edwin, we were in jail with Balbi. Some people did tell me he was innocent. But in jail or for that matter even out of jail, you never know what to believe.

Ø Ozzie, I know we were in jail with Balbi. There were other Masons in there also.

Ø Wow. So why did Jerry ask me to keep an eye on him?

Ø What do you mean?

Ø Edwin, Jerry, my arresting officer ask me to keep my eyes and ears open as to Balbi. He asked me to call him if I heard any info. Why would Jerry care?

Ø Ozzie, Jerry is a Mason.

Ø Holy shit, Edwin. You are fucken kidding me, right?

Ø No Ozzie. I don't play with things like that.

Ø Jerry is a fucken Mason. Your nephew is a Mason. The judges are all Mason, and they have to protect and help each other out no matter if right or wrong.

Ø That's it Ozzie. You got it right.

Ø So it's not about right and wrong. That's just an illusion. It's about who you know and what brotherhood you belong too. One hand covers the other.

Ø Yes that's how the real world works. Why do you think, I got out of jail so quickly?

Ø I don't know. I thought your crime was a minor thing.

Ø No Ozzie, it was bigger than minor. They just gave me different charges.

Ø Okay, Edwin, I want in.

Ø It's not that simple. You need to clear a thing or two first.

Ø Yes I know. But that for the future. We need to finish what we started here. So Edwin, Does Jerry know anything about helping Howard?

Ø I don't know. He works for the Broward Sherriff's office. My nephew works for the Hollywood police department. I'm sure they might know each other but I don't think Jerry knows about him helping Howard.

Ø Do you think we can do this within the next two weeks?

Ø I'm not sure. That's really pushing it.

Ø Edwin, I have to be in court in two and half weeks. I need to get all this done within this time frame. Especially the Vault.

Ø Again, I am not sure. First we have a plan for someone to break into the bad cops' house.

Ø Damn, that is dangerous.

Ø There will be an undercover cop within the area watching.

Ø What are you talking about?

Ø My nephew knows that the jewelry stolen from Howard is in his house of this cop. Don't ask how he got that info. It's there. The first part of the plan is to break into the house and document the robbery. The whole time recording it. Howard will be allowed to keep his jewelry, but it might be needed down the road as evidence. He is not allowed to take anything else out of the house. As part of his defense if anything goes wrong down the line, he can claim that through an informant he became aware of his jewelry being there and he simply went in to retrieve what belongs to him. If he takes anything else that does not belong to him then it will be considered as stealing. There are terms for each scenario. If it does not get video recorded then things change if it has to go to court. You need to talk to Howard and let him know that a few of his boys have to do this. They should cover their faces and make sure they don't show it on the video. Howard has to let me know when it's going to happen because there will be a cop that is going to video tape them from outside. No arrest will be made, and the guys will be allowed to do this. The next step after that is to set up the bad cop in a sting operation and show that he does in fact tamper with evidence. After date we can formulate another plan. Several of the good cops can't stand this guy. They know he has done bad things, as so they will look the other way. There are about eight Mason cops in the Hollywood Police department that will look the other way.

Ø Edwin, are you sure about this?

Ø Ozzie. It's not my plan. It's what my nephew suggested to do. All I can tell you is that Howard's guys won't be arrested.

Ø Edwin, don't you think it would be better if they gave the jewelry as evidence against this bad cop,

Ø Problem is Ozzie that internal affairs will not allow a scandal like this to break free. They might cover it up.

Ø This is planned by my nephew. It's as good as it's going to get for now. I trust him. So let's do it this way.

Ø Ok Edwin. At the very least it's a plan. However I don't like doing things until I have a good grip on how it's going to play out. I think what I am saying is I would like to know more as to how your nephew sees this playing out.

Ø Ozzie, I know you like to be in charge of what you do. But just go along. It's a good thing.

Ø Okay Edwin, I trust you. So how quickly can we get started?

Ø That is up to Howard. When his guys are ready, I will give him the address of the bad cop. It has to be during the day, when he is working.

Ø Okay, I'll get with Howard later or in the morning.

Ø Now how about the Vault.

Ø Well, are you going to be able to get the fingerprint?

Ø I asked Prince for it. I think I need to get on his back about it. Also let's talk about plan two just in case he can't come through. BTW Edwin. Last time we spoke I was going to mention something to you.

Ø Oh yea, I was supposed to ask you about that.

Ø Yes you were. But we have been busy with the other plan. So here it goes.

Ø When Prince came to see me there were two Spanish looking young guys in the back seat. Howard had mentioned that Prince was visiting and doing some business with them. I'm curious if you know anything about them. More important Edwin, I want to know if they have any relation to the Cuban cousins in jail.

Ø I don't know Ozzie. I will ask my Nephew about that. Last I heard they were still locked up. So it has to be someone else. I'll see what I can find out.

Ø Thanks. Now we also have to make a plan for dealing with Prince, should he decide to do something stupid after the Vault job.

Ø Do you want to get rid of him?

Ø Do you mean get rid of him for good. Six feet under.

Ø Yea.

Ø Fuck Edwin. No. That would be dumb. There is no statute of limitation for a murder. So anytime during your life you could be charged. With the robbery it's only seven years. I don't want to be looking over my back my entire life. It's not worth it. No amount of money is. Now, if he gets stupid, and pulls a gun then I would not think twice about it. Shit, I won't even think once. I would just fire away just as I would with anyone who tries to hurt me. As of now, I don't trust him. We need to make a plan just in case. I am going to mislead him. However I think we should have a few of your ATEN gods on the lookout.

Ø Okay, I will take care of that. I got that covered. I will let you meet with them just so they and you know who is who.

Ø That sounds good to me. Next thing is to make the plan with no fingerprint.

Ø Do you want me to get his finger?

Ø You mean fingerprint.

Ø No I mean finger.

Ø Man, what is it with you guys? It seems everyone wants a finger. It's not just a matter of the print. We have to get it to a specialist to replicate it.

Ø Ozzie, my nephew can get that done for me.

Ø Yes Edwin. But at what cost? I'm trying to keep this under the radar. Oh, a palindrome.

Ø What's that?

Ø A palindrome, it's a word that is spelled the same backwards. But in reality radar is an acronym. Mom, dad, kayak, racecar, are palindromes.

Ø Oh I see. Anyway you're funny Ozzie. You come out with some crazy shit.

Ø Okay, sorry. Back to the finger. I think it might be best to let Prince handle this one. This way you and I stay out of that.

Ø Okay.

Ø So to recap Edwin. We need to make a plan to get in and be able to take our time using the finger print. We need to make a plan to break into the container if there is no finger. We need to make plans for our escape. And we need to make plans for any trouble we might encounter during the escape. That included Prince getting stupid and trying to hold us up. And also, if for any reason, the police are on our tail during the escape.

Ø So when do you want to meet again.

Ø Real soon, Edwin, We need to rush this.

Ø Remember Prince still needs to get the pirate radio guy to jam the frequency.

Ø What's that about?

Ø When I was in jail with Prince, a newspaper article came out about some rogue radio station operating under a frequency that was causing the door remotes of cars to fail. Once the vehicle was out of range it would work as usual. I asked Prince to find this guy, so that he could jam the Hollywood police stations frequency. It's just to buy a few extra minutes. Just in case.

Ø Do you really need to do that?

Ø I don't know. Maybe I am too imaginative. But I think in jamming the frequency it might make it a little more difficult to communicate between the cops and the station. They might have to switch to cell phone making the entire process slower for them. Howard will create a diversion for us by confronting the bad cop on the street. The focus is going to be over there away from the Vault. During that time they won't care about someone breaking into a box, when there is an issue going on at the same time that might involve the life of a cop.

Ø Oh that's fucken good Ozzie. I like that a lot.

Ø Yea, Edwin, I too think it's a good plan.

Ø What does Prince say about that?

Ø Prince was a lost puppy. He did not know how to get in. Once I took charge and made him understand he just went along with the plan.

Ø So he is a follower.

Ø I'm not going that far. He is not to be taken lightly. He can turn out to be the devil in disguise.

Ø I hear what you are saying.

Ø Okay it's getting late. Let's get the fuck out. I need to go fishing.

Ø Damn, you are a horny man.

Ø Na, I don't see it that way. I am a healthy, energetic man. My body is not as toxic as others. I've worked out all my life and for the most part ate well also. So, I'm healthy. Many people let their bodies go to waste, by concentrating on the wrong things in life. Like over eating poisonous fast foods, laced with toxic chemicals designed to make you hungry so that you can eat more. Others have been poisoned by the water they drink.

Ø Okay, Okay Ozzie, stop. You're going off a little.

Ø Okay Edwin. But you started. You said I was a horny man. I was defending my position. It's not me that is over aggressive; it's that everyone else is sedated. That's what the fluoride in the water does. It's been proven. And it's why it's there. To turn us into sleeping monkeys, doing as we are told.

Ø Ozzie, I got it.

Ø Okay. I'm going fishing. Or if you want it in plain English. I going to fuck. BTW fuck is an acronym, means, 'Fornication under Consent of the King.'

Ø What the fuck?

Ø I bet you did not know that. Fuck no.

Ø In colonial time, which was after the original meaning, people would be charged with, 'For Unlawful Carnal Knowledge'; police shortened it by writing FUCK.

Ø Anyway, enough history. I'm going to fornicate. Yea baby. I like it.

Ø Oh Edwin, BTW, do you believe the gods are with us?

Ø You're not talking about my friends the NETA.

Ø No, I'm talking higher powers that be.

Ø I thought you don't believe.

Ø I don't believe in Gods, but maybe the Anunnaki have brought us here. What the fuck is that?

Ø Nothing Edwin. I'm just fucking with you. The reason I ask is, have you stop to consider the odds of us sitting in this same place for the fourth time in a row.

Ø Not really.

Ø Well for a place that is usually crowed, the odds are high.

Ø Hey Ozzie, now that you mention it. Maybe the gods are with us. You know what I think Ozzie. It's your destiny.

Ø Funny thing Edwin. That's what I've been saying all along. I have a new destiny that was bestowed upon me. Surely it's coincidental, but then again. It's the gods. The coincidental gods.

Ø Okay Ozzie. Let me get out of here before you come up with some more crazy shit.

Ok. Fuck it. Fuck off. Fuck you. G, I'm coming.

Ø Ozzie. Estas loco.

G must have heard my conversation and so I was in trouble; for she was naked in bed watching TV. Next to the bed was a glass of wine. Looking at the bottle on the table revealed how much she drank. Wine and Feta cheese turns her into a wild woman. She looked at me and smiled. That was all I needed, however I knew I needed to pace myself, because in that condition the only word she knows is, more, more. So more it was. Two hours of more. Yes, it's true. But who am I to complain.

It was Saturday; a typical one. I had made arrangements earlier with Howard to meet in the evening. I decided to bring a bottle of Merlot. I was once again greeted by his beautiful wife Jackie.

Ø Hi Jackie. How are you? You look beautiful as usual.

Ø Why, thank you, Ozzie. Come on in

Jackie escorted me to the patio where Howard was relaxing. It's refreshing scenery. A gentle breeze blew by; Boats going to and fro, as the sun was setting.

Ø Howard, what's up?

Ø Hola Ozzie. Glad to see you again.

Howard had my Galliano already out. He retrieved some ice from the chest and placed some in a cup.

Ø Delicious Howard. I don't know what it is about this drink, but I can't get enough of it.

Ø I can see. Come, let's sit.

Ø Howard. I have some really good news for you. First off, I want you to know that you have to trust me. There are some things that I need you to do that might seem a little suspicious. I promise you. If you do what I say, you will have your freedom.

Ø Ozzie, I believe you.

Ø Good, because it's important. I would never cross you Howard. You need to know that.

Ø I have that feeling about you. You always seem real. Anyway go on.

Ø The cop that fucked you over is a corrupt cop. There are some good cops that know about his dealings. They tolerate him because of the brotherhood. But there are other powers that are higher than him or his brotherhood that he has also fucked over. These are a group of influential people. There is an insider that belongs to this higher power. He is going to help you. They want to put this bad cop away because it will vindicate some members of that higher power group. In a way you are lucky that they want to expose him. They are going to help you. Listen to them and you will have your freedom.

Ø What group is this?

Ø The Freemasons. The bad cop has put away a few Masons. They claim two of those that were put away were innocent. You know one of them. He was in jail with us.

Ø Who is that?

Ø Balbi.

Ø Balbi. I use to sit with him often.

Ø Yes I know that.

Ø Wow, Ozzie. I remember him telling me he was framed, but you know in jail everyone says they are innocent. Except for you. You never hid what you did.

Ø What difference would it make? I had no one there that new me from outside. Besides I think you get more respect that way.

Ø I think you are right.

Ø So Balbi is a Mason, and his fellow Masons are looking out for him.

Ø Yes, don't you remember the story that they put up $250,000. For his defense.

Ø Yes I did hear that. So Ozzie, We are getting inside help from a Hollywood police officer that is a Mason.

Ø Yes you got it.

Ø And you are sure that I won't be framed?

Ø Yes I am sure. They need you and you need them. So here is the plan. At least the first part of the plan. We will see how the second part plays out.

Ø Go on.

Ø You are going to send your guys to the house of the bad cops and break in. You can be there if you like. It's up to you. It will be during the hours he is working. No one will be in the house. Your guys will go in with their face covered. They need to have a video recorder, and every move must be recorded. They are only allowed to retrieve your jewelry and nothing else. Otherwise they will be charged with burglary, and so will you. If you don't record it with a tape that is clear, you will be charged. You are to keep a copy and hand over the original. Your guys will be watched as they break in and will be recorded. That's the reason for the mask. They don't care who goes in. Just that it's done as they say and it's documented. You will be allowed to take your jewelry home and keep it. Or you can put it in the mail, and mail it to yourself as if it were from an anonymous person. Can you handle that Howard? What I mean is can your guys get it right.

Ø Ozzie, I think I might want to be there.

Ø Again that's up to you. When you have your guys ready they will give me the address. It will be on the same day. If not, you will be charged.

Ø Got it.

Ø After you do this there will be a plan to have him rob someone. That will also be recorded. And from there two different things can play out. One… they will let you confront him with the evidence. It will be somewhere that will be well lit and also where it can be recorded and documented. All they want him to do is to confess or at least be able to show that he is corrupt. Every person he arrested will then be let go without charges, including Balbi and you. They are not doing this for you. They are doing it for Balbi, and also for someone else who asked for help in this matter. That person happens to be another Mason. You just landed across my path at the right time. You know Howard, on December 12, when I was supposed to leave, and there was a gas leak at the jail, that made us turn back. You told me on that day, that it was not my turn to leave yet. You said something or someone was missing. Someone I needed to meet before I left.

Ø Yes, I remember that day, but I don't remember who that person was.

Ø Well it's not important at this moment, but you were right. Destiny had not fulfilled itself yet. I was not supposed to leave on that day. Not only was it part of my destiny, but also part of yours.

Ø So that person is helping.

Ø Well yes. But I won't reveal names at this time. What matters is that we are here, and for some reason we are all connected.

Ø Seem true.

Ø Howard you need to get your guys together and work on this quickly. I have to be in court in two and half weeks and I want this done before my sentence. I don't want to leave anything to chance. We don't have much time. How much time do you need?

Ø Three days. Set it up for three days, I will be ready.

Ø Okay. We will take it one step at the time. BTW, did you find out anything about Prince and the two guys he is with?

Ø You know, I think I saw them in his car when he came over to talk to me.

Ø Ozzie, those guys are Cuban, and they belong to a Cuban gang. I don't know if they are related to the cousins in any way. I do know those two are doing some type of deal in Miami. I think they might be in with him on the tax fraud. So far that all I could get. Two of my guys followed him all day. The guys do live in Miami. You need to be careful with Prince. It's probably nothing at this time, but don't let your guards down. I will talk to him and let him know not to fuck with you or we will come after him.

Ø Thank you Howard. Have you heard from his girlfriend?

Ø No she seems to have disappeared. Maybe she left to another state.

Ø Do you think he could have killed her?

Ø I don't know. Anything is possible.

Ø He says his wife is also gone.

Ø Hum. Can't tell. Just be careful. Watch your back. I told you I can have a few guys watch over you.

Ø Howard, I think I have that covered. But if I feel I need to I will ask you. BTW, we have a plan to jam the police frequency when you confront the cop. But we will talk about that further down the road. For now let's make this break-in right.

Ø Okay, Ozzie. Let's eat a little. Monday, I will tell you when we will be ready to go.

Ø Okay. Let's eat.

Howard was soft spoken and polite. Contrary to what one expect from such a high level gang member. It's what age brings and does to us. But, it's also accompanied by wisdom, which takes years to accumulate. He seemed to have been content with our progress but also a little anxious to move ahead. I ate quickly; had my fill and departed. There are many things that need to get handled before the big day. In my mind, Prince was the weakest link. I knew I needed to stay on top of him and check his progress. I think I should have Edwin's guys on standby, in the event Prince can't get the fingerprint.

48 SUNDAY-MONDAY-TUESDAY

- Ø Hey Prince, what's up?
- Ø Hey Ozzie. What's up?
- Ø Any progress on the fingerprint.
- Ø No, not yet. My boys are on notice. Sometime during the week we will Go in the house and pick up a print.
- Ø Okay Prince. Just remember, you can't take too long. I have to be in court in two weeks. BTW, Prince. Can you send me the man's address? If in a few days you can't get it then I will send some guys to do it.
- Ø Yo Ozzie, I told you, I got this. This is easy for me. Just need a day or two and it will get done.
- Ø Okay Prince. But if you don't have it by Wednesday, please let me get the info.
- Ø Okay. That's fair.
- Ø Have you been able to contact the radio pirate guy?
- Ø No, not yet. But on Monday I should have that info. A hacker friend of mine is looking into this.
- Ø I'll give you a call on Monday evening.
- Ø Ok Ozzie.

At this point, I did not place much credibility on Prince. I knew that I would have to take some action if I could not get the info I needed from him. Edwin was always ready to participate and he was much more resourceful. For the moment all I could do was relax and enjoy my time off.

Monday.

- Ø Ozzie, Que Tal?
- Ø Hey Howard. What up?
- Ø Ozzie. I am ready.
- Ø Damn Howard. You are not playing.
- Ø I told you three days, but I could have been ready in hours. I have my guys in place. But Ozzie, I need to be 100% sure that they will not be arrested.

Ø Howard, I understand your concern. This is being setup in part by a cop that is very dear to Edwin. He is our inside man. Believe me Howard; we will not let you down.

Ø You know Ozzie. I wondered if Edwin was the inside help, but I did not want to push it. I feel much better knowing this. Shit, I might even go in myself.

Ø Whatever you decide to do you will be safe. This is not a setup. I would never do that nor would Edwin. He was promised that everything would be according to how it was planned.

Ø Good Ozzie. You have no idea what a relief it is to hear that.

Ø I can imagine. Anyway Howard, I will call the contact and let them know you are ready.

Ø As soon as I get a reply from them I will give you the info. They might need a day or two. So let's see which day it will fall on.

Ø Okay, Ozzie. I'll be waiting. And once again, thank you.

Calling Edwin.

Ø Edwin.

Ø Hola Ozzie.

Ø Edwin, I got a call from Howard. He is ready. Let your nephew know. Any day is good. The sooner the better.

Ø Okay Ozzie. I'll call him and will get back with you later. BTW, any word on the fingerprint.

Ø No, not yet. I spoke to Prince about it yesterday. He said he would give me a ring today. Trust me Edwin. If I don't have it in a few days, then we will send your boys for it.

Ø Okay Ozzie. Later.

The day was coming to an end. It was already evening and I have not heard from Prince. Time is of essence and I don't have the luxury of waiting.

Ø Prince, What's Up.

Ø Hi Ozzie. Was going to call you. Keep in mind I don't like this phone shit. Anyway. I got a number for the radio guy. Tomorrow I will pass by. I'm not talking any more on the phone.

Ø Okay. I'll see you tomorrow.

Tuesday.

Prince came by my office. This time he was alone. The car was left running as if he would only be a minute or two. From my vantage point I saw him pull in and so I proceeded to meet him outside. Quick he was. He handed me a small piece of paper. It had two names, numbers and address.

Ø What's this?

Ø It's what you asked me for. The first one is the pirate radio guy. Don't call him yet. I have someone who will contract him. I'm trying to keep distance between myself and him, as well as any other person that we might need. The other number is the name and address of the finger guy. He is currently in town and not up North. I should have the print by Wednesday or Thursday at the latest. Then we can get it to my friend in Israel. I sent him an encrypted message. There are two ways to go. One way is better. If I lift a print, I can send him the glass or object, containing the print. The other is to send him a scan. Although it usually works, it's not 100%. The only sure way is to get the actual finger and press it onto a clay mold and then send it to him.

Ø Okay prince. Nice work. I doubted you would get this in within time. Good news. Please let me know how it goes.

Ø I got you Ozzie. Got to run.

Ø Okay Prince. Talk to you later.

Ø Later.

Calling Edwin.

Ø Edwin, Que Tal?

Ø What up Ozzie.

Ø Edwin. Let's meet. I have some info. I'll be done at the gym in Hollywood about 8.

Ø Ozzie, at the same place.

Ø No. Meet me at the gym. It will only be a few minutes. I have a paper to give you. It has an address.

My workout was refreshing as always. Must be the chemical release that produces a natural high. Edwin was punctual.

Ø Edwin. Hi.

Ø Hola Ozzie.

Ø Thanks for meeting her Edwin. I was not up to going to the casino. Maybe I'm afraid my seat will be taken and luck has run out.

Ø Na.

Ø Yea, I know, I really just pressed for time today. Anyway, here is a number with for finger print guy. Prince brought it to me today. He said he has it planned out for the next day or two. So wait till Thursday, if we don't have anything then maybe you can send you boys over.

Ø How is everything else coming?

Ø Well Howard is ready; which is the other reason I wanted to talk to you. He is ready with his boys on standby. I just need to give him the address and a further detail your nephew might have.

Ø Ok. I will call him tonight and let him know that Howard is ready. I'll call you tomorrow and let you what he says.

Ø Okay Edwin. Also, I think we should have a few of your guys stationed around The Vault when we go in. I don't trust prince. I need to be ready in case he tries anything stupid. I will pay your boys a few dollars for that. You and I already planned two different escapes, but we need to make sure Prince does not interfere with it.

Ø Okay. I will get a few guys to watch over us. Also, I think, I will have a guy or two, follow him around to the finger guys house. As soon as you know when he is going in to get the prints, let me know. I know his two big friends drive around in a black Chrysler 300, with big rims.

Ø Figures. You know how many people get pulled over for riding in that car, especially with rims. Racial profiling.

Ø Yea, I know. That's why I drive a simple car that no one notices. Don't need to bring any attention to myself.

Ø So Edwin, Let me know as soon as you know, the address for Howard.

Ø Sure. I'll have it tomorrow. I'll call you. Anything else.

Ø Na. Well, maybe. Prince got a hold of the info for the radio pirate guy. I think he is having one of his boys, contact him. I'll let you know, how that goes.

Ø Okay Ozzie. Don't forget to let me know when Prince is going to the finger guy.

Ø Will do.

Ø Okay Ozzie. Talk to you later.

Ø Okay Edwin. Ciao.

Later that evening Edwin called. I was already in bed, enjoying my time with G.

Ø Hello, Edwin?

Ø Hola Ozzie. I spoke to my nephew. He said to tell Howard to be ready on Thursday about 12. I will call you with the address. Howard will have one hour after that to get in and out. Everything must be done as told. Remember he has to video record every step. No blackout. The tape must be unbroken without any gap. He can make a copy, but they want the original one. They can only take Howard's jewelry and nothing more. Otherwise they will be arrested. There will be a white van on the block that will record you guys going in and out. They have to go the same way they came in.

Ø Got it Edwin. I will call him in the morning and let him know.

Ø Okay. I will call you Thursday with the address; he is getting only one chance. If he misses it, it's too bad.

Ø I'll let him know Edwin.

Ø Ok, good night Ozzie.

Ø Good night Edwin.

For me the evening was still young. G asked if everything was okay. I said yes. She also asked me if I would like some coffee. Yummy, I said. With that she got up and made some for the both of us. Pita chips are what she accompanies it with. Yes it has some gluten, but it's a small treat for her. I sat in the chair and turned the TV on. Shit, things are finally starting to move fast. Maybe I would get all this done by my next court date. The coffee over stimulated me. I started to think too much. I tried to formulate too much. Am I under pressure? Well it's okay. I thieve on it. G knew my mind was going. She did not say or ask anything. Being a woman she usually tries to reach her daily ritual of 5000 words. However, the average words spoken by a woman on any day is 7000. With me, I stay well below the average for a man of about 2500. I wonder if my thoughts count. Nope they don't. Just imagine if a woman's thoughts were counted.

Things like, does he think I'm fat? Is my hair done right? Am I going to get my period this week? Oh No. I hope I don't have it while having sex. Yes, just imagine. I can see why dad used to say it was a blessing being death. Anyway. I'm thinking too much, and it's getting late. Sometimes that brings me a visitor I care not for. So, let me finish my coffee and relax in G's arm. I'll call Howard in the morning and let him know.

Wednesday.

Ø Good morning Howard, How are you?

Ø Hi Ozzie. Glad to hear from you.

Ø Howard, I got a call late last night. You need to be ready tomorrow, about noon. They said you only have one shot. At about 12, I will get a call. I will be given the address of the bad cop that has your jewelry. From the time they call me you will have one hour to get in and out. No more, no less. Everything must be done as they say. There will be a white van parked down the street from the house. You guys will be watched and recorded. Make sure you have your mask on. Also make sure the tag on the car you use does not belong to any of you guys. From the moment you approach the block you are to start recording. As they say, it must be a continuous recording without any pause. You have one day to get me the original recording. You can make all the copies you want. Remember you are only to take what is yours; else they will come looking for you. The cop that is doing this knows this is for you, but they are really doing it to help out someone else. So they are allowing this.

Ø I got it Ozzie. You said that already.

Ø Yes, but I need to repeat it because it's very important we do it their way.

Ø Don't you worry about anything.

Ø I'm not worried about myself Howard. I don't want you to get this wrong, and then they come looking for you. Who know what can happen.

Ø I know. There will be bloodshed

Ø Howard. Stop and think. First these calls are all recorded and stored. Be careful what you say.

Ø Okay Ozzie. You are right. My guys will be ready. I will wait for your call.

Ø Okay Howard. I'll call you tomorrow.

Ø Okay Ozzie.

Howard scared me for a moment. Once again it brought to mind how anything could go wrong at any time. It would seem that everything we do is a gamble. Some are calculated and are a better bet than those that are not thought out. Sometimes, shit just happens. At this point, I'm not going to worry about it. Especially since it's something I have no control off.

Several hours later, Prince called.

Ø Ozzie, what's up?

Ø What's up Prince?

Ø Tomorrow, my friend will go get prints.

Ø Great news. What about the radio guy. I believe that's covered. I will know more in another day or two.

Ø Okay. So please call me tomorrow and let me know that everything worked out.

Ø I got you.

Ø Okay Prince. Talk to you tomorrow.

Things are moving along. Instinct told me to call Edwin and so I did.

Ø Edwin, how are you.

Ø Hola Ozzie, Que Tal?

Ø Edwin, I just got a call from Prince. He said he will get the prints tomorrow. He did not say what time, but I guess it will be afternoon or evening. I also spoke with Howard and he is ready. I pointed out everything he needed to do as you said.

- Ø Great Ozzie. I will call you as soon I get the call and you can give it to him. Remember to call him without wasting any time. I'll keep an eye on Prince for tomorrow.
- Ø What does that mean? Are you Amen Ra.?
- Ø No Ozzie. I'm not the ever seeing eye. I am saying that I know where he lives and who his guys are. I had my nephew get me all that info. I have a few of the Aten guys keeping an eye out.
- Ø So it's true.
- Ø What. You and the Aten, watchful eye.
- Ø Oh, I get it.
- Ø Okay Edwin, let's talk tomorrow. I'll call Howard as soon as I get your call.
- Ø Okay Ozzie.

Thursday morning.

G awoke by backing up into me. It seems I am always ready at a moment's notice, for I quickly responded with my own little nudge. She was off today and so decided to make us breakfast after some love. From the looks of it, one would never think I had so many things on my mind. For I knew it would be Howards day. Some form of redemption for him. However the bigger picture was soon to follow. I went about my daily business as usual. This morning I tried not to think about Howard too much. After all, he was a grown man who happens to have traveled through life this far without getting himself killed. What's the worst that could happen to him anyway? He could die. Would that be the worst? For some, dying is an escape. I think the worst that could happen to him is to spend the rest of his life in jail. Oh let me not forget. He could lose his son or daughter. Yea, that would really be terrible. I should know. Anyway, it was 12:14 pm when the call from Edwin came. Edwin gave me an address. The town was only 15 minutes away. I asked no questions. Just said thanks, and with that called Howard.

- Ø Howard.
- Ø Yes Ozzie, do you have an address.
- Ø Yes, write this down. Remember you now have less than one hour to get in and out.
- Ø Thank you Ozzie.

- Ø Sure. Good luck.

The call to Howard took less than one minute. He was matter of fact and quick. I gave him the info and then managed to forget about him for the rest of the day. As the evening went by I thought about Prince. However I made no attempts to call anyone. I'll just get the details tomorrow. It was now 6 pm. Gym time. Let the games begin.

Friday - Information time.

It was now Friday. As I made my way to my office, Eddie asked me if I heard the news.

- Ø No, Eddie. I don't listen to the lying news or watch that stuff anymore. I don't even watch regular TV.
- Ø Why is that?
- Ø Well for starters. CNN is owned by Ted Turner. He was quoted as saying that he believes the world's population should be reduced to 500,000 inhabitants. He wants you and me dead. His news team is a cover for the New World Order, and more importantly the bankers. Everything about it is bogus. It's all propaganda.
- Ø You're joking.
- Ø No Eddie, I'm not. You were in the intelligence business. You should know better. I'm sure you just don't talk about things like that. Anyway it's true. Just look it up. It's all there, if you chose to see it. So what's this news you are talking about.
- Ø A home invasion last night in Ft. Lauderdale.
- Ø So what's big about that? Shit like that happens every day. Did they rape and kill a 90 year old lady?
- Ø Oh no. They broke into some high profile stock brokers home and cut his finger off.
- Ø You're joking.
- Ø No it's in the news. Just stay watching the TV. It will come back on.
- Ø So what's the big deal about that?
- Ø They stole $100,000 in cash that was in a safe and then they cut the home owners finger off.
- Ø That's funny. You know when they cut the finger off it usually denotes that person has been stealing.
- Ø Yea, that's why the police are saying, the Mafia must be involved. The home owner reported two black guys and two Mexicans.
- Ø That doesn't sound like Mafia to me.
- Ø Well, it could be the Mexican mafia. Might be connected to drugs.
- Ø Eddie was anyone killed?
- Ø No, but shots were fired.
- Ø So what else is new?

Ø That's it. If this guy was not such a big broker, it would not have made the news.

Ø Well, he properly got what he deserves.

Fuck! Prince did it. I knew this was his doing. So now he has a finger plus $100,000. Fuck, do I want any of this. If we break into the vault and use that finger then it will connect us to that man. Fuck, fuck! I better call him and find out what went wrong.

Ø Hello Prince.

Ø Ozzie, don't say one word. I'll meet you later tonight. I'm not talking on the phone any more.

Ø Are, you good.

Ø Yea, Yea.

Ø Okay.

Fuck! Prince and his telltale signs of lying. "Yea, Yea!" It's his kiss of death. I'll have to wait till tonight to find out what happened. Let me see if I can get a hold of Howard.

Ø Hello Howard.

Ø Hi Ozzie. Things went okay yesterday. But I have to say, I took more things than I was supposed to.

Ø Fuck Howard. That's no good.

Ø Yes, I know. But this is good stuff. You need to come and take a look.

Ø Howard, do you have a copy.

Ø Yes.

Ø Listen, I'll be there in an hour.

Ø Okay, Ozzie. I'll be here. Jackie is out; I'll leave the front door open for you. Should I fix you something?

Ø No Howard. I have to run back to work. I'm only taking off an hour or two.

Ø Okay.

Fuck, Fuck some more! Now I have to worry about Howard getting into trouble with Edwin's Nephew. The instructions were clear. What could have been so important that he was compelled to take? BTW, was he himself there? Oh well. Fuck it. I'm not going to jump to conclusions. I'll soon find out. I told Eddie I would be stepping out for an hour or two.

Ø Are you coming back before Yesid arrives?

Ø I don't know. He is at actions. I might. But either way, I'll be back. If he asks you, tell him I went to find the guys finger.

Ø Oh, that's funny.

Ø Little do you know Eddie?

Ø What?

Ø Never mind. Got to run.

Howard was less than 20 minutes away. As he said, the front door was open. I made my way to the patio.

Ø Howard, how are you?

Ø Ozzie. Thank you. Things went just as you said.

There was a white van several houses down from the address you gave me. I could see there was someone in it.

Ø So you went there yourself.

Ø Yes. I'm glad I did.

Ø Fuck Howard. I hope you don't get in trouble for this. Howard, wait a minute. I'm getting a call from Edwin.

Ø Tell him to come here.

Ø Now.

Ø Yes now.

Ø I want to thank him.

Ø Edwin, can you come over to Howard's house now?

Ø No Ozzie I can't at the moment. I'll see you later today. I'm running around doing a few important things.

Ø Okay, Edwin. I'll see you later.

Ø Howard, Edwin is tied up for the moment. He won't be able to come now.

Ø Okay, so as I was saying, I decided to go myself with two boys. As we canvassed the place we did see a white van parked several houses away. There was a person inside but not on the driver's seat. Anyway we knew we were being photographed. As we drove around I recorded the van as it sat. After circling twice we parked in the driveway and looked around the property. There was a side door, which led to the garage. One of the guys broke one of the four squared glass. From there he reached in and unlatched the lock. We were surprised there was no alarm. The camera guy recording the entry as we were told. Once in the garage we opened a door that led to the foyer. Looking around we could see that the bedrooms were to one side of the house, so we headed in that direction. The camera guy walked first followed by me and then the other. They belong to my crew.

The second door we opened was the master bedroom. The camera guy made sure to scan first before we entered. From where we stood, I could see some jewelry on the dresser. We walked over to it but it was not my stuff. We did not even touch it. Before we open any of the dresser doors we went to the closet and poked around. There was a safe in it. By the looks of it, it must have weighed over two hundred pounds. It stood about five feet high. It was the type that holds guns and rifles. It was locked and my thought was "fuck, what to do now?" We were not prepared to move that out by ourselves. For a moment I thought about burning down the house. I decided to look through the draws without making a huge mess, even thought I knew we only had a short period to get out. One of my guys looked under the bed and found some plastic containers. I got on my knees to pull some of them out. The first container we opened had some documents in it as well as jewelry. Again none was mine, so I pushed it out of the way after placing the lid back on. The second container also had some documents as well as jewelry. I also pushed it to the side. The third container had some things I was familiar with. Holy shit! I said. There was my stuff. My Latin King gold chain, my ring, my watch and my bracelets. The camera was recording the entire time. Wait till you see a copy of it. The expression of my face was funny. I had my mouth open in disbelief. I took the container and held on to it as I stood up. I started to head out of the room when an idea came to me. Without saying one word I placed the container on the bed and got on my knees again. There were about three more containers left. I was curious as to who else items where in there. The next container I pulled out also had some documents in it, and a bag which was marked Broward County Evidence Department. There were also some numbers on the bag. In it was a kilo of cocaine. It was clear this item was taken from the evidence department. I figured I might as well check the other two. The next had some sex toys items which we recorded. The last container had some newspaper clippings, as well as some documents and a ring. The newspaper clippings caught my attention because in it was a photo of him, the cop, doing an arrest. The person with the handcuffs was someone I know. Immediately I realized that I was looking at evidence that could put this guy away, so I decided to take all the bins as evidence.

Ø Yea, Howard. But you were told not to touch anything else.

Ø Yes Ozzie. I know that. But here was the opportunity I was waiting for. I knew this was it. This was my escape. Even if they come and arrest me now, the evidence will still set me free. Don't you see; my freedom was staring me in the face? What would you have done?

Ø Good point Howard. Maybe I would have done the same.

Ø Come Ozzie. Let me show you something.

Ø Oh fuck Howard. I am not sure I want to know. Come let me get it, so you can see for yourself.

Ø See what?

Ø The person in the newspaper clipping.

I followed Howard to a room. It was his home office. There on the desk were some small plastic containers. I was certain they were the ones taken from the house. Howard opened the top container and pulled out the picture. Holly shit. I recognized the man in the picture immediately. There was no mistake. Howard was right. His freedom was in the containers. I looked at him without saying one world. He looked at me and smiled. I also smiled. Thirty seconds passed without one word being spoken. I looked in the container. There was a ring in it. The markings on the ring were clear, for in the center of the gold ring was a compass and square. This ring belonged to a Freemason. I looked at Howard again and smiled.

Ø Jackpot Howard.

Harold smiled some more and lifted his hand for a high five.

Ø You were right. Waite till Edwin finds out. Everyone is going to love us. Howard, you fucken lucked out big time. This might be the evidence needed to set you and him free.

Howard continued smiling. No words came out. He was redeemed and was relishing it. I looked at it one more time. Howard picked up the ring and pointed to the engraving on the inside. There was a name. Again I looked at him in disbelief. He continued to smile. I leaned over for a second and stood upright. Howard placed the ring on my palm to hold. I was not sure I wanted to get my prints on it. But by this time it would probably be a moot point as to any negative consequences.

Ø What are you going to do with all this evidence?

Ø There is a young news reported that is coming over later to recover the items. I know her dad as he was a long time member of my group. The media is going to have a field day with this. I also made a copy of the tape we recorded.

Ø Howard, why don't you just give all the items to Edwin's nephew? After all, this is kind of his doing.

Ø Are you loco Ozzie? First, this will save him from letting the other police know that he turned in one of their own. Second, I know that the reporter will air this. That has been arranged already. There will be no cover-up with her. This is my freedom we are talking about, as well as a few others. It's perfect. His corruption will be noted and perhaps all those he falsely imprisoned will be vindicated. This is bigger than me now. This is my break. I'm not taking any chances. I am a free man.

Ø Yea Howard. But didn't you still want to confront him.

Ø For sure. I want to break the news to him, as well as his face. I have a plan for doing so. Maybe Howard's nephew can help me with that.

Ø Well, I will talk to Edwin tonight and will discuss it. Remember I need to take the original tape to him.

Ø Yes. I have that ready as well as several copies. I even set one to my lawyer.

Ø Howard, are you sure you don't want to turn over that evidence to Edwin's nephew.

Ø Ozzie, I am sure. That is not the best thing to do. I don't care if I get arrested again. My lawyer will have me out within hours. No, No! I'm not making that mistake. It's already settled. The news reporter will have it soon.

Ø Okay. BTW, what was in the other containers?

Ø There were some documents and jewelry. I'm sure the owners of that jewelry are also innocent people he robbed or got arrested.

Ø Fuck Howard. This worked out better than you could have hoped for.

Ø Yes Ozzie. I was right about you the whole time. I knew you were a good man that could somehow help.

Ø Howard, you know if it were not for Edwin, this would not have happened.

Ø Ozzie, you are wrong.

Ø What do you mean Howard?

Ø You are underestimating yourself by saying that. Sure, in this case, Edwin helped out. But, I know that if Edwin were not in the picture, somehow you would have found another way. But here is what you don't know. That other way that was supposed to happened, never did, because you found a better way of doing it. Do you understand what I am saying?

Ø I think so. You are saying that I found a better way, than the alternative way, that did not need to come to light because Edwin was surely a better way.

Ø Yes, that is what I am saying. You see Ozzie. On December 12, when you were supposed to have left jail for home, there was a gas leak in the construction of the adjacent court. You remained in jail and meet Edwin that day. That was your destiny. You did not know it at the time but you went with the flow. Your gut feelings told you there was something good in all that happened that day. You stuck with your instincts and made a friend out of Edwin. You did so subconsciously. You were in tune with your destiny and picked up on it. You then followed through. Somehow you knew. Just like you knew that the alternative way to accomplish the same thing was not as good as this one. Surely, you would have found that other way. So don't cut yourself short by saying it was Edwin's doing. It was your fate, your destiny, your wisdom, your instinct that has landed us here. The very first time I spoke to you in jail, I sensed something good about you. You have this positive energy that carries and transcend.

Ø Wow Howard. That's profound. I never really thought about it that way. I do know about myself that I always manage to pull things through at the end. I guess that's why I really don't worry much. But I think because of that I tend to wait for things to long, or rather put things off. Once or twice, it has gotten me in trouble.

Ø Sure it has, maybe once or twice. But on the other hand, all the other times, it has gotten you out of trouble from bigger problems. Those far outweighing your once or twice troubled times.

Ø Well tell me then, why did I end up in jail? Why did I not find a better way?

Ø Ozzie, Perhaps jail was the better way. Maybe you were supposed to go through this. This is still unfolding. See where it takes you. Again, perhaps this was the better way, the best path, for what is to come in your future. Life is showing you something. Take the time to figure it out.

Ø Howard, I started writing a book, to kill time at night. To escape from a demon that pops up anytime he wants to. One that follows me around. Anything can trigger his visit. I don't know how to shake him off. In the book I ask myself, what are the circumstances that have led me to jail?

Ø Maybe jail offered you the time to write and evaluate yourself. In finding the answer, you will be able to let go of him and him of you. But before that happens, you need to let go of a few things yourself. You see Ozzie. I know who you are. I know what happened to you and your family. I know why the demon follows you. But I can't give you the answer. You must find that out by yourself. You must then forgive yourself, and you must let go. Only then will your demon release you.

Ø Damn, Howard. You're a philosopher.

Ø Let's just say wise.

Ø Okay Howard. Thanks for your kind words. I need to get out of here. I can't wait to let Edwin and Prince know of your fortunate finding. Let's talk in a day or two so we can make plans for your confrontation with the bad cop.

Ø Yes. I already have a plan, but maybe yours might be safer or better. Let's see how Edwin's nephew wants to handle it. I'm sure his buddy will be ecstatic knowing that he will be set free from jail.

Ø Yes, it's a good thing for all.

Ø Okay Ozzie. Let's get going. Thank you. Let's talk in a day or two.

Ø Okay Howard. Let me know if anything new comes up.

Ø Surely.

I quickly left Howards place and raced to work. For a moment I felt like a defeated man. Why was I not yet able to free myself of my demon? I know Howard saw the look in my eye. One that was trying to contain tears. Despite all this I was happy for Howard, as I knew his troubles were over. How he wants to handle his aggression towards the cops is something to think about. Will he get in trouble in his attempt to get even? Well, more important, I have some excellent news for Edwin and his nephew. Looks like this event might actually set his Mason buddy free. I find myself a little excited and must contain myself. In a few minutes I will be at work and will call Prince. I need to know how the finger drama played out. This will give me two stories to tell Edwin.

Upon arriving at work I noticed things to be the same. My brief departure was not even noticed. Eddie asked a question.

- Ø Did you find the finger?
- Ø No, not yet. But I know where it's at.

Eddie laughed as if he inferred it was up someone's ass. I went back to my desk and it was business as usual. It would be four pm when I got the next call. It was Prince. He wanted to meet me at the casino. We made arrangements as to where to meet. No, it was not the same bar that Edwin and I meet. I did not want Prince bad karma to interfere with my luck at that table. We had agreed to meet at the inside bar where we had done so before.

- Ø Hey Prince, how are you?
- Ø Yo, what up Ozz?
- Ø Hey let's get a drink before you start. I want to know all the details.
- Ø Okay Ozz, but it isn't pretty.

I had Prince wait several minutes before he would go on. I knew I needed a drink for this one and so I ordered my usual, and he did as well.

- Ø Okay Prince, start from the beginning. Don't leave anything out.
- Ø Yo Ozz, I'm not sure where to start.
- Ø First of all, Where you there.
- Ø No. But I think I should have been. Anyway, two of my boys have been staking out the place for a few nights so as to get an idea of fingerless arrival schedule. For three straight nights in a row he showed up at nine. He would park his car in front of the garage and enter through the front door. So my boys decided to go in about 7pm. When they arrived, there was no car in the front, so they parked in the space and walked to the side. They then broke in through a side window. Both entered through the window and one went to the kitchen and the other went to open the front door so they could easily run out if they needed to. They quickly opened every door and made sure no one was home. They then went to the kitchen and started to collect some used glass cups and plates. There was also a cup of wine and a wine bottle that had been used. One of the guys said he saw prints on the bottle and wine glass. As they started to gather it, Fingerless crept up on them with a shotgun. They clearly knew what it was by the cocking sound it made. The voice followed, "any little move and I will blow your head off. " They

said they were cornered in the kitchen with no way out. One guy had a gun on him but did not dare reach for it. He said he knew this guy was serious. So they put their hands up in the air. A center island stood between both and Fingerless.

Ø Yea Prince but up to this point he is not fingerless.

Ø Wait, you said you want all the details, or do you want to tell the story?

Ø Go on.

Ø So both of my guys had their hands up and Fingerless started asking questions. My guy with the gun said he was going to make a quick move when the time was right, so they waited for the right moment. Fingerless was smart and said I know you guys have guns. If you try to make a move we are all going to die. He told them to one at a time slowly reach for their gun with the left hand and place it on the ground. The first guy did so and the other said he was not armed. He lifted his shirt and spun around. For some reason his gun was in his ankle. Fingerless had an evil look in his eyes and my guys told me they knew this was not going to end well. It was a crazy look one of them had seen before. All of a sudden there was a small distraction by the window in which they came in through. Fingerless stepped back a few feet while still pointing the shotgun at the guys. He glanced over to the window but only saw the cat go by. One of the guys said the cat knew someone was near the window because it had his back arched and hairs raised. Fingerless took two steps into the kitchen, and then that's when everything happened. The guy with the gun reached down for his ankle and that's when the shotgun went off. One or two pellets pierced my boys arm and he froze. He placed his right hand over his left triceps where blood was pouring out. He then applied some pressure. Fingerless pointed the gun at the other guy as if to shoot him also. His finger started to pull on the trigger. Out of nowhere a short Hispanic guy clobbers Fingerless on the head with the butt of a large gun. Fingerless drops to the ground and was struck again. A second Hispanic pointed his gun at my boys. He pointed at the gun on the floor and told my boy to pick it up. He said someone sent them to check up on things. The same guy that spoke told my boys to collect the glass items with the fingerprints, but to stay back away from him and his partner. That same guy pulled an object out of his pocket. A small black rectangular box. He dropped to his knees and grabbed Fingerless hand. He then started to take each finger and press it against a clay material. It was clearly designed for the purpose of gathering fingerprints. They took all ten prints. Then he pulled out another box that had ink on it and pressed it against the fingers. He then pressed each finger onto a cardboard paper. He also did the same for all the fingers. At this point my boys had dropped their hands down but were watching what was going on.

The second Mexican guy was still pointing his gun at my boys. Fingerless started to come around and so they struck him for the third time with the gun. This time blood poured out from the scull. My guy swore they killed him. The same guy that took the prints put the two boxes away as well as the paper prints and then pulled out a long sharp hunting knife. Without saying one world he stretched Fingerless hand on the marble floor. He curled all the fingers back except for the pointing finger. After tying a rope tightly around the wrist he proceeded to pressed the knife on the middle of the finger. He then took his gun, turned it around and raised it as high as he could. With force he banged the butt onto the knife and the finger separated from the hand. He put the finger in a small plastic bag which he also had in his pocket. He stood up and then put it in his pocket. Without turning their backs to my guys they headed out through the front door and left. My guys grabbed the items and ran out the front door also.

Ø Prince you are joking right.

Ø No Ozzie. I swear, it true. My guys would not lie to me. I believe what they said.

Ø So where is the finger?

Ø I don't know. I thought you send these guys in.

Ø Not me Prince. I had told Edwin about it, but I did not tell him to go in and do anything. Let me give him a call. BTW, what happened to the $100,000?

Ø What $100,000. As far as I know there was no money. Where did you get such an idea from?

Ø It was in the news?

Ø What news?

Ø The TV news. What other news do you think?

Ø Ozzie, you mean to say that this made it to the news.

Ø Yea. Where the fuck have you been?

Ø Yo, this only happened last night. I don't wake up early and watch the news. Holy fuck. What else did they say?

Ø There were two black guys, which we know who they are, and two Mexicans.

Ø Ozzie, the guys had bandannas on. I think one of my guys said it had red, white and blue. So they must have been American.

Ø Damn Prince. I thought you knew more.

Ø What do you mean?

Ø Never mind. So were they Hispanic or Americans. I'm not sure. I was not there.

Ø So, who took the money?

Ø They did. That's why they heard a noise in the room. Yea, Yea. They took it.

Ø Prince. I know you well. Was there money taken or not?

Ø I don't fucken know. Besides what the fuck does it matter? You are going to help me steal millions. To add to that you had a guy cut and takes his finger. Why the fuck do you care about it?

Ø Yea, you are right. What the fuck difference does it make? However Prince, please keep in mind that that money might be traceable once it's found on the wrong hands.

Ø Yo, get off that shit. You are as guilty as anyone else.

Ø Prince. I was not there. I did not partake in any money and I did not send anyone. So who has the finger?

Ø I don't fucken know. Call your boy Edwin. I'm sure it must be him.

Ø Hold on let me try his number.

By now I was in some mild form of shock. I've actually experienced once before. This was however not nearly as intense. But it seemed I was now doing things without thinking. I don't know how I managed to dial Edwin's number. I do have him in my contact list with his name clearly marked. His phone rang but there was no response, it went straight to voicemail. I left him a message and then sent him a text.

Ø Prince. I can't get in contact with him at the moment. This is strange, because it has not happened before. He is always quick to answer, even if to say he can't talk. You don't know anything about where he might be?

Ø Come on Ozzie. What the fuck are you saying? How the fuck would I know where he is?

Ø Well, Prince, he did not tell me he was doing anything. So I don't know it is him that has the finger. Are you sure you don't have it?

Ø Yo, I don't need this bull shit. Are you trying to say I have the finger?

Ø Prince, I don't fucken know what is going on. If it were someone else that did not answer maybe I would not find it strange that he is not answering.

Ø Look, I don't know who the fuck was in the house and took the finger. I'm sure it was him. Yea, yea. It has to be.

Ø Prince, that double yea, yea, you saying it only makes me doubt you more.

Ø Yo, fuck you Ozzie.

Ø I don't need this shit.

Ø Prince. Maybe you got rid of him after you got the finger, so that you won't have to pay him. So now that you have the finger and the prints you can go it alone.

Ø Ozzie, fuck you! I don't need this fucken crap.

Without notice a security guard had made his way to us. He asked if everything was Okay and if so to please tone it down. Prince and I decided to take this outside. We walked towards the center of a courtyard and proceeded.

Ø Ozzie. I'm upset. If you think I would do that then you don't need to be with me.

Ø Prince, are you trying to say, I'm not involved in this anymore.

Ø Look, I'm not saying that. You are insinuating too many things. Some of which is some fucked up shit.

Ø Prince, I've been around the block a few times. I'm not naive. I don't trust my own mother, do you think I should trust anyone?

Ø Okay, I get your point. But it's fucked up. I don't know where the finger is. Who has it, or who took it. I don't know anything about $100,000. And I don't know where your boy Edwin is. I'm going to get the fuck out, and when you hear from him you fucken let me know what's up.

Ø Okay. Let's leave it at that and call it a night. We will talk tomorrow.

Ø Not on the phone. Everything gets recorded, whether you believe it or not. Every fucken cell phone call, every email, gets recorded. Remember that.

Ø Okay. I got it. You say it all the time.

Ø That's because I know for sure. Believe me I know.

Ø Okay, okay. I got it.

Ø Peace, out.

Much to my surprise, Prince seemed to be a little upset by my innuendos. This time I was not sure if he was lying. He did say his "yea, yea, I'm lying "words, but his demeanor told otherwise. So now I don't know what to make off all this. Edwin needs to contact me to clear this up. Else, I would have to think Prince did a number on him. As I walked to my car, I thought about what a mess it might be if Edwin does not surface. Prince is surely capable of doing anything for money. It now seems I am too. But then, am I doing this for the money? If not, then why? Why don't I just stop and call it a day. Let me put an end to this before it's too late. But how do I? How do I contain myself? Can I reframe? I feel compelled to do this. Underneath there is something deeper and more meaningful. I know it. I just can't see it. Can I continue if Edwin is no longer around? Or has fate come to an end? Is this saga over for me? Shit. I need answers. I hope my friend is still alive. If he is not, I will revenge his death. Prince, you mother fucker. I'm coming for you. If I don't hear from Edwin tomorrow I will go to the Vault and visit his buddy. I better have a double drink at home and find a way to sleep. Edwin, if you are dead, please don't send your demon to me. One is already too many.

Saturday.

Saturday morning I awoke with anticipation; for I was eager to contact my buddy

Edwin, but I did not want to seem desperate. I do believe in giving people their time and space. Surely I thought Edwin would contact me during the day. I had my breakfast as usual and proceeded to work. At about three I decided to call Edwin. Once again the call went straight to voicemail. Could he have lost his phone? It's possible. After all, they do break easily and are often stolen. A little later I decided to call Howard.

Ø Hi Howard.

Ø Hola Ozzie.

Ø Howard, I'm sorry to bother you, but I am curious if you have heard from Edwin.

Ø No, why? Did you not speak to him yesterday evening?

Ø No Howard. Last I spoke to him was from your house when I called him to come over. He said he would call me later on, but I have not heard from him yet.

Ø Well Ozzie. He is a grown man. It could be anything. He knows how to deal with trouble so I would not worry about him too much.

Ø Howard, I usually don't worry about anything. However, I had a long talk with Prince, and it has me a little worried. While I was talking with him I tried to reach Edwin but his phone went to voicemail. I sent him a text also but got no respond.

Ø So what about the talk with Prince has you worried?

Ø Howard, Prince sent two guys to the house of the man we are taking the $6,000,000 from. Things went a little wrong and he said that two Mexicans went in and saved his boys from trouble. He thinks Edwin was involved. There was some money that was reported by the media as being stolen. Prince also said he knows nothing about that money nor who the Mexican guys are. Supposedly the Mexicans took prints and also cut one finger off.

Ø Are you serious Ozzie?

Ø Howard, I think Prince might have something to do with Edwin's disappearance. It is out of place for Edwin not to call me or answer his phone. BTW, Howard. I have to ask just to be sure. Was it your guys that went in?

Ø Oh no, Ozzie. I did not even know that was happening. I was too involved in my own situation. So why do you think Prince would get rid of Edwin.

Ø For starters, Prince had lost control of the plan. I told him that Edwin and I were going in with or without his help. I also told him that we did not even need him. I think he was a little upset about that. Second, after having a set of fingerprints, he might have felt that he had no use for Edwin anymore and would rather keep that money to himself. Maybe I'm reaching to far Howard but it seems something Prince would do. So, I truly am concerned.

Ø Ozzie, If Edwin is out of the picture, what will you do?

Ø I don't know yet. I haven't given it much thought. I will probably get the money and then kill Prince, and keep it all.

Ø Are you capable of that?

Ø I'm not sure Howard. I haven't given it much thought as I said before. Maybe if Prince did get rid of Edwin, I will split Prince's money amongst Edwin's family.

Ø You know Ozzie. That I believe about you. Don't worry about Prince. Look, if Edwin is gone, I will send my boys to help you. I will take care of Prince. All you have to do is say so. I will do whatever you ask of me.

Ø Thank you Howard. But all I really want for the moment is to find Edwin.

Ø I will make a call in a few minutes. I will find him. For now try to relax. Remember there is still unfinished business you need to do. Maybe this might be your alternative plan.

Ø No Howard. It's a plan I don't want. Not if it means Edwin is dead.

Ø Ozzie, people die all the time. Once one is dead, then he is dead. Life for us on Earth continues. Besides, I'm sure Edwin is somewhere.

Ø Howard, are you suggesting Edwin is alive?

Ø Oh, no, I don't know where he is. I'm saying he is probably okay. Give him a little more time. I'm sure he is ok. In any event, as I said, I will have some guys look for him.

Ø Thank you Howard. Let me know as soon as you do.

Ø You let me know also if you hear from him.

I continued my work till six and still had not heard anything, so I decided to release some stress by going to the gym. It always does the job. I don't know how I do it, but it always works. Later that evening, I relaxed at home with the help of a drink. I tried to keep my mind occupied as I did not want to awake my demon.

Sunday morning G asked to go to the beach. I thought it was a good idea, even though it's something I don't normally do. Of course I had my phone with me, and as I did my people watching while sitting under the umbrella, I awaited for it to ring. All morning and afternoon my phone never rang. Not a big deal. I prefer it that way. Contact with no one. I like it. I was able to relax as I told myself I knew Edwin would be ok and would soon call. Maybe he got locked up again. I'll check back later at night if I hear nothing.

As I took in the breeze I started to think about the New World Order. Not that I wanted to, but then life as we know it is on the line. I thought about their plan to make one central world government. I thought about the chaos that is going to happen in the US within the next few years. Hitler and the Holocaust came to mind. That was all planned as everything else in this world has been, and yes by the same families with the same objectives. I thought about how people gave up their rights and guns during the Holocaust so that they could be protected.

It's a funny thing that this is exactly what is going on in the US. First the powers that be took out a new insurance policy on the Twin Towers. Then one week later they took them down as well as building 7. Building 7 was not hit by anything except a little debris from the towers; Nothing major, however on the word of one man, the owner, his exact words being "I gave the order to pull it", and voila, it magically fell. Such power. Anyway, after Sept.11; many new executive orders were passed. They want to take our guns away from us so that we can't defend ourselves and our constitution. People who believe there are evil forces are misled. Sure, there are evil forces. But it's not the Taliban, or Al Qaeda, which was made up for this event, or Osama Bin Laden. It's the guys you least expect. The people who control us and the nation. The people who tell the President what and how to do things. They have done an excellent job of nearly completing their goal. These people believe that too many inhabitants will suck up the Earths oxygen and make the place inhabitable. That's what scares them. That's the reason for a reduction in population. That's the reason to suppress cancer cures. That's why doctors are forbidden to talk about those things. That's why the cure for diabetes is also hidden. That's the reason for FEMA concentration camps, which by the way have begun to operate. Yes it's true. The process has already started. Look it up. I'm not making this up.

Here is a copy and paste from, (http://humansarefree.com/2013/10/fema-camp-round-up-has-begun-homeless_7.html)

In August, according to MSN, the Columbia City Council unanimously approved the plan, creating special police patrols that would enforce "quality of life" laws involving loitering, public urination and other crimes not necessarily restricted to the homeless population.

Those officers would then offer the homeless a choice:

Go to jail for their homelessness or be shuffled to a 240-bed, 24-hour shelter on the outskirts of town, which they wouldn't be allowed to easily leave. (Fema: http://humansarefree.com/2013/10/fema-camp-round-up-has-begun-homeless_7.html#sthash.6ptmwKr3.dpuf).

According to the Activist Post ,the Columbia South Carolina plan is already complete with an urgent Emergency Homeless Response report. And that report includes information about hauling the homeless away in transport vans to an already stationed shelter with workers, phone number for townspeople to report "the person in need," an officer stationed to control foot traffic, public feeding moved there, more foot patrol officers for the city to keep out the homeless – oh, and the homeless can't walk off the premises!

The government wants to take our freedoms and guns away. They say it's for our own protection, but it's all lies. Just like Obama care. First He said we could keep our existing plan. Three times he said so. In the plan one is asked if they have ever had any mental problems or sickness. One is also asked upon a visit to the doctor, if there are any guns in the house. If the answer is yes, the doctors must file and register that report. When shit hits the fan; they will come looking for you first. They will call you a terrorist. Under new executive orders they can imprison you in the FEMA camp without a trial. You and I are fucked. We need to wake up, because what happened in the Holocaust is exactly what is starting to happen here. In all this, Jerry, came to mind again. For I know he is a good man, just like myself and countless other people and law enforcement officers. Will Jerry and his team allow another Holocaust or will they disobey Federal orders that have no jurisdiction over state laws and help save us. To all you Jerry's out there.

What will you do? Our fate in part is in your hands. Remember they will start with the sick and homeless. This is now a crime. Then they will go after people like me who speak out. Then they will go after the Christians, and all other believers; the gullible people, the weak. After we are gone, you Jerry's will also be expendables. The Masons might express their distress signal and might be spared. Jerry's, don't be their pawns. Fuck them. Will you help them kill us? Our will you fight for the oath you took?

Fuck! No more beach for me. My problem at the moment is not that I know and think about these things. My problem is that I have the balls to write about it. Will it get me killed? Fuck it! If it helps save my children and others, than yes. I'm not going to participate by default in the new Holocaust that is coming to us. Nope. I rather die fighting. Yea! That's the ticket. Fuck I'm going home. So with that in mind I have a riddle. Figure it out, (a Columbian Enterprise to Endeavor for the Discover of Atlantis and all Challenges shall be destroyed. No man has ever ascended higher than 300 miles). I'll post a website with the answer. I'm hungry and horny.

It's now Monday, 4pm. G tired me out last night; which was good. I fell asleep early. All day today I waited for a call from any of the thugs. But there was none. Time seems to be running out. In a week I have to be in court. I don't know what the outcome will be, so I better finish this. I'll give it till tomorrow and will call the guys. I'll also set up a plan tonight to continue with the $6,000,000 deal. I'll try to formulate plan B and plan C. I decided I'm going through with this. I knew it all along. I'll see what tomorrow brings.

Tuesday.

Once again it's about four. Last night I formulated different plans for the money. There are plans that still involve Edwin and plans that don't involve him. For the most part Howard is safe. As well as someone Jerry told me to keep an eye out for. In a few days I will call him and let him know. At the moment I don't know the best way to proceed. I need to somehow get a hold of Edwin's nephew at the police department.

- Ø Hi Howard.
- Ø Hola Ozzie. Any word from Edwin.
- Ø No Howard. I was hoping you had some news. I checked the jail but he has not been arrested. So, it is starting to look bad.
- Ø Ozzie, I don't have any news either. I sent two guys around his home, but they have not seen him or his family. I have to say I am now a little worried. Do you want me to send my boys after Prince? I am sure they will make him talk.
- Ø I don't know Howard. My gut feeling is to give it another day or two. I have made some plans to get the money with Prince, but now that I think about it. I

should just go and get it myself without him. Edwin has an insider that is a NETA. I'll go and visit him today. I'll see what could be done. If I need to do this with Prince, then I will get the money and you can do whatever you need to do after he has walked away. I think I might also want some protection. It's better if he knows that I do have back up. This will keep him from trying something stupid. I'll call Prince in a little bit and see what is going on.

Ø Okay Ozzie. Be careful, and keep me posted. I'll make my own plans for the confrontation with the bad cop.

Ø Howard. I had a plan to do both at the same time. Don't do anything until I get back with you in a day or two. I have someone who will jam the police frequency radio.

Ø Okay Ozzie. I will wait for you.

As the work day came to an end, I decided to call Prince. How much he would discuss over the phone was debatable, but I still needed to communicate.

Ø Hello Prince.

Ø Hi Ozzie, What up? Have you heard from your boy Edwin?

Ø No, nothing at all. I call Howard and asked him if he knew anything. He sent two boys by his house but they could not find him. I also checked the jail. He has not been incarcerated.

Ø Damn Ozzie, that's fucked up. I'm sure he has the finger.

Ø What makes you so sure?

Ø Look Ozzie, How many people did you give fingerless address to? Wait scratch that. Ozzie. I don't want to talk on the phone.

Ø Prince, if someone is on to us then we are already fucked. Maybe someone is on to you, and that's why you are so scared.

Ø Ozzie. I don't know where Edwin is. That's all I can say. If you want to talk more than we can meet up. And yes. I have been working with Jerry on some arrest and I am concerned my phone might be tapped.

Ø Okay Prince, say no more. Let's meet tomorrow.

Ø Okay. Just let me know.

That evening after work I decided to go to the Vault and see if I could make contact with Edwin's guy, Jimmy. My first stop was to the office to see if he was there. Since I did not see him I decided to play it off and visit my security box. As I walked out of the elevator I caught up with him as he was entering with some guest he was showing around. I stopped him for a second and asked for his number. He knew who I was and kindly gave it to me. I also asked if he had heard from Edwin and he said no. With that I went about my business after letting him know I would call him within the next day. I proceeded to my box; opened it, looked at the emptiness within and then closed it and headed out and to the gym. Upon my arrival at home G asked if I was alright. She must have picked up on my concern I might have had for Edwin. I assured her things were ok and went about my usual business.

So far, for the past few nights I have tried not to think about Edwin too much. I am now starting to find it a harder task. I manage to focus on the money and am trying not to let things bring me down. Sooner or later, there will be answers. At the end, everything comes out. If he is dead, than there is nothing I can do about it. If Prince had anything to do with it, then I will avenge. Fuck! Its 2am; I better get some sleep.

Ø Hi Ozzie.

Ø Hi dad.

Ø Come give me a hug and a kiss.

Ø I can't dad.

Ø Why not?

Ø I'll tell you some other time.

Ø You fucker.

Ø No dad, you fucker.

Ø You know Ozzie. I always found that funny about you. I remember the first time I told you, "fuck you". Your response was, "No dad, fuck you" You caught me off guard and we just stared at each other and then burst into laughter.

Ø I do remember that dad. We were on a trip with Justin and we were all in the rest room at one of the truck stops.

Ø That's right. So Ozzie. What brings you here?

Ø Dad, I did not come to you, you came to me.

Ø Oh yea. I did. I was thinking of you. I never called you back from a few weeks ago.

Ø So is this your call back?

Ø I don't Ozzie. I don't know. I always think about you. I love you.

Ø Dad, you tell me that all the time. So what else is new?

Ø I don't know Ozzie. I was thinking about a friend who is now missing and I wondered if he was with you.

Ø Are you crazy dad? Why would your friend be with me?

Ø Yea, Ozzie, never mind. I don't know what I was thinking. Maybe I wasn't thinking. Maybe this just came to me.

Ø Well dad, your friend is not with me. You will find him soon.

Ø Are you sure Ozzie?

- Ø Yes dad. I am sure.
- Ø Okay. You're a Vargas. I believe you.
- Ø BTW dad. I'm glad you called. I miss you also.
- Ø I miss you too Ozzie. More than you will ever know.
- Ø No dad. I do know. I can feel you.
- Ø Ozzie, so many things in my life remind me of you. It's hard going through life without you. You sister Jenelle is also away as well as your brother Christian. I miss all you guys.
- Ø Dad, I know.
- Ø So listen Ozzie, I have some unfinished business here. I've been working on a few things and now have a deadline that might come before I can complete it.
- Ø Ah, don't worry dad. That's not like you. You'll get it done. You're a Vargas.
- Ø Thank you little fucker.
- Ø Thank you fucker dad, besides I've grown to 6 feet. Not that little fucker anymore.
- Ø Ok, big fucker… Ozzie!
- Ø Yes dad.
- Ø I need to get healed.
- Ø Dad. I know. I've seen you suffer. It's okay. What happened in the past is not your fault. Things just happen. Let it go dad. Let it go. It's Okay. Call me when you finish your goal. We will take a trip together. Love you dad.
- Ø Love you Ozzie.

Wednesday.

At about three I decided to call on Edwin's Neta guy from the Vault.

- Ø Hello Jimmy.
- Ø Yes.
- Ø Jimmy this is Ozzie. I am Edwin's friend. You gave me your number last night.
- Ø Oh yes. How are you Ozzie?
- Ø Jimmy, Have you seen or heard from Edwin?
- Ø No. I've been waiting for him to call me. Last conversation was over a week ago. He was going to get a fingerprint replica.
- Ø So, since that conversation you have had any contact with him.
- Ø Nope.
- Ø Do you have any idea where he might be?
- Ø Nope. What is going on? Have you tried the jail?

- Ø Yes I did. He is not there.
- Ø Is he alive?
- Ø Jimmy, I don't know. I don't want to talk on the phone. Can we meet tonight?
- Ø Yes, but it will have to be after 9. That's when I get off.
- Ø Okay, what area are you in?
- Ø Hollywood.
- Ø Great. The casino at 9:30. The inside bar.
- Ø Okay. I'll be there.

Jimmy Aten was punctual. We greeted each other with a hand shake and ordered a drink. It was the same area that I often met with Prince. The place is always full of people and a lot of activity. Seven or eight TV's are always on covering the sport action. For a moment a thought came to mind. Does Jimmy have the finger? Was he with Edwin at the house? If not, was he at the house without Edwin and decided to take the finger and go into the Vault without us? Fuck. Now I am scared again. Or I should say apprehensive. Okay relax, Ozzie. These thoughts are actually good. Trust no one, fear no one.

Ø Jimmy thanks for meeting me here. I have a few important things I need to know. First, Edwin is missing. I have no idea where he might be. I've checked with some friends I know. One of those friends in a top leader of the Latin Kings. I'm not saying this to alarm you. This friend of mine is also a friend of Edwin. We have a few guys out on the streets trying to find him. Do you know anything about his where about? Has he said anything to you that might give you a clue as to his presence?

Ø No. The only time I spoke with him was last week. He told me he was going to be able to get the fingerprint we needed. He did not say how or when. I have been waiting for him since. I tried to call him but it would go straight to voicemail. I have no clue where he is. I hope he comes up soon. I could have a few NETA guys look for him. My cousin is good with things like that. He is also a member. Will this put an end to the job?

Ø I don't know Jimmy. In part it depends on some info I need from you.

Ø I was counting on some money from that to buy my daughter a nice gift for her birthday.

Ø Well, let's see what we can do. Let's say, the finger shows up or the prints. What else would one need to access the container?

Ø Well, for sure we need to know which box belongs to him. There are a few ways the systems verifies that the person is the owner of the container. In this case the fingerprint is needed because I am assuming he picked that option along with his password. We don't need a password. In my case, I need to know which box is his. I can figure that out a few ways. One way is to know the registered name of the box owner. It could be an alias or actual name. The second way is to know the account number of the box holder. With that info I can go in the system and get the container number. The container number itself is another way. In this case, at the moment I don't know anything. So even if the fingerprint shows up, I can't access the container without knowing which one it is. There are thousands of containers there.

Ø So for sure we need either an account number, or container box number to call it.

Ø Yes. Do you have that info?

Ø No. Shit. There is only one guy that has it. That's Prince. He is the one that told us about what is in it.

Ø Does he know the security code that the man punches into the keypad to bring up his box?

Ø I don't know. I don't think so. I do know he does have the account holder invoice.

Ø Well, with that info I can access the box number, but he won't be able to pull it from the keypad. There are security measures in place to prevent against things like that. With that info and the finger, I can get you in.

Ø So if he had the prints and the account holder's info he would not be able to call the box down and open it.

Ø Correct. I would be able to do it from the office, but no one else from the outside.

Ø So, it seems that even if I did not have the prints and no further info, you nor I could get in.

Ø That's right. If Prince has the info, then we can know which box it is. I can get in by breaking into the box without the fingerprint, but no one else would be able to.

Ø So I need Prince at this point?

Ø It looks that way. His info is more important than the actual print.

Ø So Jimmy. I just want to be very clear. Let's say either you or Edwin had the finger, but did not have any other info, you would not be able to access the container.

Ø That's right. It's the container number itself, which is important.

Ø Okay Jimmy, please do not take what I am about to say the wrong way. Let's say you yourself had the finger. OR you knew Edwin had it. It would do you no good to get rid of Edwin because you still need missing info.

Ø That's correct Ozzie. I see where you are going with this. Believe me; I have no idea where Edwin is. The finger by itself does us no good. However if your friend Prince knew the security code to call the container and then verified the fingerprint then he could access the container without needing anyone.

Ø So if Prince has the security code and the prints then he would have a motive to get rid of Edwin? This way he could go in all by himself and not have to share any of the money with anyone.

Ø That is true Ozzie. However if he does not have the exact security code then he will need me to access the container number. This means that you and Edwin are still involved.

Ø Okay. So now I just have to find out how much info Prince actually has. I know he has someone in Israel that would make him a replica fingerprint from the items he got out of the house. I will meet with him tomorrow and try to wrap this up. I think we should make preliminary plans to do this next week. I have to go to court Friday next week and I need to finish this by then. Also, I might need a few of your boys to back us up on the day we do this. I don't trust Prince.

Ø That's not a problem. Just let me know. What about the money?

Ø Well, what was your agreement with Edwin?

Ø He promised me $100,000.

Ø Okay Jimmy. You will get your $100,000. If Edwin is not around, I will give his portion to his family.

Ø Okay Ozzie. Thank you. I'm in with you. If Prince got rid of Edwin then you know as a member of the NETA, I have to do him in.

Ø Jimmy, you do what you need to do. Just make sure it does not tie back to me.

Ø Okay. I will have a few high members look into this.

Ø Jimmy, give it a few days before you let anyone know what is going on. If Edwin pops up then it would be a moot point.

Ø What's that?

Ø Moot point means, it doesn't matter anymore because of the circumstance.

Ø Oh, okay.

Ø Well Jimmy. I need to get going. I'll call you after I speak with Prince tomorrow.

Ø Okay Ozzie. So long.

Fuck. All this is leading to Prince. Is he going to try to get into the box without including us? If so, he is a dead man. Shit, I better call him and figure this out.

Ø Hello Prince.

Ø Yo Ozzie. What's up?

Ø Prince any sign of Edwin?

Ø No. Shit is he still missing?

Ø Yes he is.

Ø Fuck. That's not good.

Ø Prince, can you meet me at work tomorrow for about 15 minutes.

Ø Sure. It would have to be about one.

Ø Okay. I'll see you tomorrow.

As I continued home, I am starting to seriously believe Prince has done a number on Edwin. But what good would that do? It doesn't make too much sense. After I speak with him tomorrow I will call his nephew at the police station. Well if I do, might that put an end to the money? Okay, I need to relax and let the answers come. My priority at the moment is to get the money.

Thursday.

One o'clock seemed much longer than normal. I have to say that as next week is approaching, coupled with Edwin's disappearance, I am beginning to get a little uneasy. I am not scared, spooked, nor am I shaken; it takes a great deal to rattle me. However something is starting to irritate me. Maybe it's the not knowing part. Anyway, Prince should be here soon. Maybe I'll get some answers; if not now, then later. They will come. They always do. One just has to be in-tune to pick them up.

Ø Hey Prince. Thanks for coming over. It makes it easier for me.

Ø Sure Ozz, not a problem. So what's new?

Ø For starters, Edwin is still Missing.

Ø Something must be wrong. Will this set the job off for a while? I can use the money now.

Ø I am not sure Prince. Let's see if we can figure this out.

Ø Ozzie did you check the obituary or check with the state for dead people?

Ø No, but I will. Prince. I am running out of time. I only have seven days to do this as I have to be in court next Friday. If we are still doing this within that time frame then we need to get some things worked out.

Ø So what is the plan?

Ø I have met with Edwin's insider. He is good to go, with or with Edwin. What have you been able to accomplish as far as getting the replica fingerprint.

Ø Ozzie, I had a scan of the prints sent to my buddy in Israel. I also sent him the items that contained the prints.

Ø How long before you get the replica?

Ø Not sure. I will call him later today and see at what stage he is in. I don't even know if he has received it yet. I sent it out express so he should have received it. I spoke with him two days ago. He is going to rush it out to me.

Ø Do you think you will have it by Tuesday or Wednesday? I'm thinking Wednesday might be a good day to do this.

Ø I think I should have it by them, let's make plans to do this Wednesday. Tuesday, I will give you the info to give your insider so that he can find out which is the container.

Ø Prince, maybe you should give it to me a little sooner. Perhaps Monday. This way we have ample time to find the correct box.

Ø Okay Ozz. I'll give it to you Monday. I'll call the pirate guy and have him ready for Wednesday.

Ø Oh, how is that coming along?

Ø I told you I got this. Everything is in place. He has a contact in the same building that will let him do his thing for a few hours and of course a few dollars.

Ø Will he be able to jam the police frequency?

Ø That's the whole purpose. Or else he will not get paid.

Ø Prince. We need to be sure. You can't leave it to chance. Ether he can or he is not sure, which is unacceptable. He has to do a test run. Edwin's friend has an oscilloscope which can determine the correct frequency.

Ø Can we borrow it to be on the safe side?

Ø I don't have his number or correct name. Edwin has that info. You will need to get one and you will need to make sure this happens. If not it might create problems.

Ø Okay. I will buy one tomorrow to be on the safe side.

Ø Prince Tomorrow is Friday. We have to have everything ready by Tuesday. This guy has to do a test run by then.

Ø Alright Ozzie. I'll make sure that happens. I need to see it in operation.

Ø Prince that building has a radio antenna used for broadcasting.

Ø Yea, it does. That's how he was able to play his music.

Ø Ok. Because you need a strong antenna to cover a wide area of Hollywood. At least the east section of it.

Ø I think that area is covered.

Ø Well Prince. I did some research on the frequency. Hollywood is a big area. They have two different frequencies they use. One is the 145.000 range and the other is between the 443.000 and 445. You really need the oscilloscope to get the precise reading then you need a frequency jammer to send out to that frequency.

Edwin's contact was also going to help out with that. But it seems we might have to go it alone.

- Ø Ozzie, tomorrow I will get all the items I need. Remember I was in the hacking business. I know people that will tell me what I need to know. And more important I know they will be hush about it.
- Ø Okay. Also please know that the police have a backup plan for things like this. So they might easily switch frequency. You will have to get their alternative frequency. It might take them 15 minutes to figure out their frequency is under attack.
- Ø I got this. Don't worry. Leave it up to me. Your job is to get in and out of the Vault safely with the money.
- Ø True. So I will meet again with the insider and set the plan for Wednesday. I think we should meet again Saturday.
- Ø I will make sure we do a test run of the jammer on Monday. And I will also give you fingerless info to give to the insider.
- Ø BTW Prince. Edwin's people need to get paid what was promised. Its $500,000. If Edwin does not show up, then I will give his part to his family. Prince. I have to warn you, if there is no money and or if you don't pay them, they will kill you.
- Ø Shit Ozzie there is no need to go there. There is plenty of money. I'm sure Edwin will turn up by then and then you can apologize to me. Their money as well as yours is good. I give you my word on that. Yea, yea, don't worry about anything.
- Ø Well I just did. Thanks for the warning.
- Ø What are you saying?
- Ø Never mind, Prince, Never mind.
- Ø Ok. I got to go. We will meet on Saturday, and then Monday also.
- Ø Sounds like a plan Prince.

Shit! I fucken thought Prince might be up to no good. Once again he mentioned his I'm lying words. Fuck. This guy has no intention of paying them. I fucken know it. I better check with Howard for extra backup; backup to the backup. Yea, that's the ticket. Let's see if this fucker is smarter than I am. I am going to have a surprise for him. On second thought I better get with Howard right away.

- Ø Hello Howard.
- Ø Hi Ozzie.
- Ø Howard. I need to talk. Can I come by this evening about 8?
- Ø Sure Ozzie. I'll get you your drink.
- Ø That would be great. See you later.

Ø Okay Ozzie.

Fuck Prince. I need to Plan for the worst. And I'm going to do so.

Promptly at 6 I left work and headed to the gym. Shrugs and shoulders were the order of the day. By 7:20 I was done. Howard's place was about 20 minutes away. Right about 8 I arrived at his door. His wife Jackie greeted me in. Howard was in what seems to be his usual spot. That is in the back patio overlook the river. The Galliano was already on the table. Jackie must have prepared some great food as a wonderful aroma filled the air.

Ø Hello Howard.

Ø Hola Ozzie. How are you?

Ø I am concerned a little Howard. There is still no sign of Edwin. I met with Prince today and I have a feeling he does not plan on paying Edwin's accomplice if Edwin is not around.

Ø Did he say that?

Ø No on the contrary he said he would pay them. His actions and body language told differently. For he said his famous Yea, Yea words. He subconsciously says those words when he is indeed lying. I met with Edwin's inside contact and I promised him he would get paid. He is to get $1,000,000. If Prince does fuck up in any way, then I will pay him from my own money. But Howard, Edwin's contact did say that if Prince did do away with Edwin then he would be forced, out of respect to the NETA, to kill Prince. That I am not concerned about. However, I do think, Edwin's family should get Edwin's money.

Ø Yes, Ozzie. You're a good man. I think you are right. So what would you like for me to do?

Ø Edwin's insider will have a few boys looking out for us on the day of the robbery. We have that tentatively set for Wednesday as I have to be in court on Friday. I am sure Prince knows we will have a few of Edwin's boys looking out. So if he is going to do anything, it will be with that in mind. I need a few of your guys to stand back at a distance and watch for Prince's boys to make a move on Edwin's guys. If they do try something stupid then your guys will surprise Prince's boys and rob them. I don't care what you do with the money, I just need to be sure I have what was promised to me and also that Edwin and his guys get their $500,000. The rest is up to you. I plan on taking my share up front. I will synchronize our watches and have walkie-talkies available. Also, I am going to buy several heavy duty backpacks in two different colors. Some black which will contain only my money and the other blue which will contain Edwin's money. All the backpacks will have miniature GPS embedded in them. I will also give some to Prince, this way we can trace his if the need arises. I will know the location of each bag. I need you to have a guy escort me around as soon I depart the building. Once I make the call to your guy, he will meet me in the front of the building. He is to be armed. I trust in you Howard and feel safe telling you this.

Ø Yes Ozzie. I owe you the rest of my life. You have saved me from damnation in jail. No one would believe me. I am a free man because of you. Don't you ever worry about me doing you in.

Ø I don't Howard. Anyway, I'm not sure how Edwin's insider will hide his money. He will have a few of his boys waiting outside. How he does so is not my concern. I plan to split the money right on the spot. That's what the backpacks are for. I told Prince to find his own means of departing with his money. I am not sure of how he plans to do so but I suspect he will put his portion in the backpacks and drive off with it, as his car will be in the loading area. Only thing is the surveillance cameras will record it so I have to find a way of deactivating them. I will work that out with Edwin's guy. I would assume it gets digitally recorded onto a hard disk. Your guys are to stay back and just observe Prince's boys. I'm sure he will have one or two cars watching us and what goes on. I don't want them to know they are being watched. If Edwin does not show up by then, maybe you can hijack Prince's guys and take his money or you can do whatever you like. Besides, Edwin's inside guy thinks Prince might have killed him, if so; Prince is a dead man anyway. However I do think it best that whatever happens to Prince does not do so on the same day, as I could easily be connected to him. I suggest you take the money if you want until Edwin's shows up. If he doesn't then let's let the NETA's do him in.

Ø Okay Ozzie. I understand what you want. We should meet again before Wednesday. I will introduce you to one of my guys that will escort you to the safety box. I will also have a few guys do some surveillance from now and especially on Wednesday. Now let's talk a little about some radio frequency jammer you had mentioned.

Ø Yes Howard. I was hoping Edwin's nephew could help us through with this one. But we might be on our own. At the very least you need do nothing. Your freedom is already won.

Ø Yes Ozzie. But I swore I would avenge his actions.

Ø Howard, you can't kill a cop. They will come after you and all this will be for nothing.

Ø He will suffer much more if we can get a conviction against him. You have enough info to make that happen. BTW, I sent the tape to Edwin's nephew. I have not had any feedback. You need to be careful how you go forward. Let's plan something for Wednesday also. Prince has it set up for some pirate radio guy to air some music at the same frequency the Hollywood police department uses. That will jam their frequency. This will start just as we are about to do our thing. We should plan for you to meet the bad cop at the same time. I will come up with a plan by Sunday. I need some time to think about it. I know you don't need me for this Howard, but give me a chance. I don't want you to get too caught up in your emotions and fuck things up for yourself?

Ø Okay Ozzie. I will let you come up with a plan. But keep in mind, I already do have one. It was something I was going to do anyway.

Ø Fair enough Howard. Let's meet Sunday or Monday at the latest.

With that, I departed. I had consumed two drinks by then and as always they were delicious. I was not in the mood to eat. All I wanted to do was, go home and start thinking about my next move. I need to come up with a third alternative plan, just in case, the NETA boys and Howards boys get silly on me. But what that plan should, as of now, I have no idea. So back to the drawing board. Time is of essence and there is no time to wait. Tomorrow I shall buy the backpacks and take them to my friend to get chipped. That evening I arrived home and did nothing. Why? I don't know. In part I was still concerned about Edwin. But deep inside, I felt at ease; I guess it was because of the conversation I had with my son Ozzie. I took what Howard told me last week to heart. Ozzie is trying to tell me something and I feel it. Maybe I am being cured. It still early to tell, but I do feel relieved. Well it's time for some loving. Oh G, come to me. Yea! That's the ticket. The rest will come. It always does.

Friday, Friday, Friday, hey put a smile on your face, things are coming your way. Okay, okay. I'm in a good fucken mood. Sometimes you feel like a nut, sometimes you don't. Ozzie Vargas has balls and my girls don't. Okay. I can't contain myself. G what did you do to me last. Today I will think things through and tomorrow get with the thugs and finalize. Why this way? I don't fucken know. I'm just going with the flow.

Saturday morning was the same as usual. My good spirits and positive well-being were at a high. I seem to have gained some positive energy, although I am very positive and confident to begin with. Yesterday I picked 8 backpacks and took them to an acquaintance so that they could be outfitted with trackers.

Ø Hello Prince

Ø Hi Ozzie.

Ø Hey Prince, can you come around today for about 15 minutes.

Ø Not till this evening.

Ø Yo, I'll give you a good carwash. Free.

Ø Okay what time. About 6. That's when I close.

Ø Yea, that's a good time. Okay but don't be late or the detail guy will leave.

Ø I'll be there.

Ø Great see you then.

After I called Prince, I went to the rear of the dealership. Danny, an Afro American with dreadlocks, was detailing cars. This guy loved playing with cars. Last week he drove in to work in his 30 year old Buick. The car sat on 28 inch rims. It had been fully customized. There must have been 30 speakers in the car. It was a traveling nightclub. Anyway, I asked him if he could install a tracker in Prince's car as well as do a quick wash. His response was a polite yes.

Prince showed up at 5:45. I think he really wanted to get his car detailed. Little did he know what I was up to? The tracking system is the same used by the banks to tract their vehicles when the loan goes bad. It's a live 24 hour system. You can log in to the account and do a live surveillance on the vehicle.

Ø Hi Prince. Thanks again for meeting me. Let me take your car to the back. Waite here for me. It will only take a brief moment.

I quickly took the car to Danny. He had the tracker on hand.

Ø Okay Prince. We need to talk a little. How is the radio guy coming along?

Ø That is set up already. Today he took his equipment to the building. I bought the oscilloscope and a friend of mine showed me and him how to work it. Monday we will do a test run at about 1. First some music will play for about 30 minutes, and then they will briefly jam the frequency. So far, that seems to be on target.

Ø Great. One thing less for me to worry about. Now, do you know the best way to deactivate the surveillance system at the Vault?

Ø I will look into it. I did not give that any thought, let me get back to you on that. Monday we can meet again. So what is the plan for Wednesday?

Ø I bought some heavy duty backpacks. They will be able to handle the weight of the gold bars.

Ø Oh good. I was going to pick some up.

Ø No need to. I already have them. I'll bring them to you on Monday. I have about four for you.

Ø That should be good enough.

Ø Tomorrow go to the Vault and take items to the box you rented. It will give you a reason for visiting on Wednesday. We will say if need be that somehow or another, the wrong container was brought to you.

Ø Yes. I will do that tomorrow for sure. What else?

Ø Have you received the fingerprint replica?

- Ø No not yet. My boy emailed me. I should have it by Monday or Tuesday.
- Ø Okay. If we don't have them, we will switch to plan B, which will be treacherous. That rout will show that this was an inside job. We will then have to justify our actions.
- Ø I'm certain I will have them by then.
- Ø Okay. I'm counting on you. BTW, Prince, what is your escape route?
- Ø I will bring my car to the loading dock. I'll place the gold and the bonds in the backpacks and throw them in my trunk.
- Ø What happens if the police come by or we need to call them?
- Ø I did not think about that. Maybe I can throw it in the trunk of my boy's car.
- Ø Do you trust him? Why don't you give it to your girlfriend?
- Ø I told you she is out of the picture.
- Ø Okay. You do what you need to. As for me, I will have a friend meet me and then he will help me carry my part to his trunk. We will leave together from there.
- Ø Okay. I might do the same.
- Ø So Prince. Let's meet again Monday night. Call me during the day as the radio guy does his thing. I need confirmation.
- Ø Okay Ozzie.
- Ø Let me see if your car is ready.

I went to the back and checked with Danny. He had already tested the tracker and it did indeed show its location. I thanked Danny and took the car to Prince.

- Ø Here you are Prince.
- Ø Nice job.
- Ø That's what I say.
- Ø Okay Ozzie. Talk to you later.

It seemed things were on target. Howards issue still needed to be resolved, but it was not that important as he was in the clear already. I still needed to fine tune the details of our job. As of yet there still has been no mention of Edwin.

Sunday. G wanted to go to the beach today. I was not sure. I still needed to get with Howard. I still needed to formulate his plan. Should I stay or should I go now? If I go there will be trouble. If I stay it will be double. Yea! If I go, I will relax and the fucken New World Order will come to mind. If I don't then G might not be too happy. Let me see, Eenie Meenie Miney Moe catch a- Okay I'll stop. The original version was not tiger. That's just a rhyme for a racist word. So, what the fuck should I do?

I hope I am not getting used to going to the beach. The atmosphere here was the same as usual. We are not in the hurricane season yet. So for the most part it's sunny. I should go to the Miami Beach where many of the girls are topless. Why I stay up here is more a matter of convenience. It's just minutes away. Hence I find myself staring at fat Canadian snowbirds. Many of the men think it's fashionable to wear a thong with their big bellies hanging over. It's not just the Canadians that are heavy. Those that are here are mostly the retired. I guess they are entitled to gain a few pounds. Anyway today two beautiful Brazilian girls came to rest just 10 feet in front of my chair. What a treat. I don't know how they manage to cover up their big delicious ass with a shoe string. I'm not complaining. It was a beautiful sight.

After about 20 minutes I started to doze off. New World Order started to come to mind again. I tried to change focus to Howard. Tomorrow will be Monday and I need to get with him about a plan; thing is I don't have one. I really haven't given it any thought, almost as If I don't care. My attitude is the same I've carried most of my life. Something will materialize as it always does. My gut feeling is to leave it alone and not worry. As if I know that there is a solution that has already been developed and I am not privy to it yet. Maybe Howards' case will also turn out to be a moot point. I decided not to stress about it. My children came to mind also, which I sometimes try not to think about. Not that I don't like to think about them but when I do my demon friend comes along for the ride. Today was different. Ozzie's words were comforting. I started to think about him and Jenelle when they were toddles. I thought about my two grandchildren. Surely I need to visit them. It's too bad they don't know who I am. Anyway, I find myself at ease thinking about my love ones today. I hope things turn out well on Wednesday and I don't die. Besides, I know I can't or won't. Abby still needs me around. So, why is it that I am so confident? Have I thought things out enough? Perhaps. Damn. Those two Brazilian look good. Damn, I had not noticed but G looks good also. Maybe I should go home now with her and tap that ass. Fuck this beach thing.

Monday.

My energy level has been higher than normal the last week or two. My morning stiffness found its self-pressing against G. Was it the visuals from yesterday. Was it G herself or was I just being my normal self. After we played for a while she asked if I would like breakfast. But off course, I replied. She has my breakfast recipe down packed.

At work, I found myself with anticipation, a good positive feeling. Did I know something I did not know? Ha, what? Never mind. Better yet. Was I anticipating something? Perhaps. I just did not know what. At about 11, the mail came as usual. There was a small package. I was the recipient. Eddie who normally gathers the mail called to me. Ozzie, there is something for you. Nonchalantly I retrieved the package and set it on my desk. Twenty minutes passed before I decided to open it. There was no return address on it. I figured it was some advertisement junk mail. Anyway I proceeded to open it. Inside the postal package was a small black plastic container. It was about four inches long by two inches wide and high. A clear tape wrapped around it. The box contained a black plastic bag, with an item within. I picked up the item and took it out from within the plastic. Holly shit! Holly shit! Holly shit! I could not believe what I was holding. This can't be. No fucken way. I examined it again and there was no mistaking what it was. Happy dance, happy dance. Yea, that's the ticket. I like it. I like it a lot. The Anunnaki Gods are with me. Okay, the gods are with me. Okay, the good forces are with me. Okay something good here.

This was no coincidence. There are only two people that could have sent me this. Well maybe three. Prince was one of them. But that thought lasted less than a fraction of a second. Neither he nor his guy would send this to me. If anything he would want it for himself. The second person could only be Edwin and or his nephew. But how? It's perfect, done by a professional. I'm sure it will work. Fuck, Edwin must be alive. He must be around. There is no other way for this to have happened. So my friend Edwin, where are you? Why have thou forsaken me? Okay, you religious people don't get carried away. I'm not mocking you. Fuck, I am ecstatic. Flabbergasted! Shit, Edwin, where are you. I fucken know you are not dead. You fucker, where the fuck could you possibly be? There was no note attached with the item; Nada, nothing to indicate who sent it. The item itself revealed its sender. So again, Edwin, where are you? Have you chosen to sit back and let me go forward without you? Will I ever hear from you again? This is definitely not the work of Howard. There are no other possibilities. It took me about an hour to settle down and let it sink in. I am on my way. $6,000,000, here I come. Ain't no stopping us now, we're on the move. Ain't no stopping us now we're in the groove. I ain't going let nothing stand in my way. No, no! This is a done deal. The gods have spoken. Faith had spoken. Destiny has spoken. Time to call Prince.

Ø Hello prince.

Ø Yo Ozzie, What's up?

Ø Any news from your Israeli guy.

Ø Yes, he did mail me the replica, but I have not received it yet.

Ø Are you sure he sent it?

Ø Yes. If he said he sent it, then he sent it. That was on Sat. I will have it by tomorrow.

Ø Prince, I doubt it. That is coming from another country. It can get held in customs.

Ø I'm not worried Ozzie. I know we will have it. Ok. BTW, did he mail it to your place?

Ø Yes, where else would he do so?

Ø Just asking. So anyway Prince. I think we might have to do plan b as far as the Vault is concerned. Edwin's guy knows how to easily break into it. He has been studying it for the past week. BTW, if you don't pay him, you will die.

Ø What the Fuck Ozzie. Look first we are saying too much on the phone. Second I told you he was getting his money.

Ø Prince, I'm just relaying a message. Don't fuck with him or Edwin. They will come after you.

Ø So where is Edwin?

Ø I don't know Prince. But deep down I have a feeling he will surface. When I don't know.

Ø So have you heard from him?

Ø No

Ø So why that feeling.

Ø Don't know. It's just a feeling. What can I say?

Ø Say, what you are not saying?

Ø Okay, I am saying I don't know.

Ø BTW, is the test run from the radio guy still on target?

Ø Yes, I was going to call you. It should be in about half hour. I need to get back to him. We have someone checking the frequency. I'll send you a text in a little. I'll tell you where to tune your radio to hear him.

Ø Okay Prince. I'll be waiting. We will have to meet tomorrow with Edwin's contact. I'll call you later on and tell you where. We need a good hour to discuss things.

Ø Okay Ozzie. Let me get back with these guys now.

So far, things are looking good. Really, really good; this in turn scares me, for it's easy to get cocky and over confident. So let me be cautious, and keep my feet planted on solid ground. So far, I just need to plan for Howard. But I don't know why I still draw a blank. Fuck it! I'm following my instincts again.

At once I received a text from Prince. "Test run in five minutes." He also instructed me to tune to a certain frequency. It was broadcasting Haitian music. All of sudden a small crackling pop appears for about two minutes. I don't know what that was. Could it be the jamming? Not sure. I am not tuned into the police frequency. I'll need to check with Prince later for confirmation. Several minutes past again before the next text message came in; jamming was successful. Call you later. Splendid, how much better could things get?

Monday was squats day. No way was I not doing them. At 7 I found myself staring in the mirror with the bar across my back. The gym was quite crowded. I guess many people don't go to the gym on the weekend. Today the weights felt lighter, or shall I say, I felt stronger. It all goes hand in hand, a feeling of well-being; means that the mind is right. The body is not toxic and is rested, and overall health is good. As I finished my routine a call came in.

- Ø Hello
- Ø Hello, Ozzie.
- Ø Yes, this is Edwin.
- Ø Am I dreaming?
- Ø No this is Edwin.
- Ø You don't sound like Edwin. This is a joke.
- Ø Ozzie. I'm recovering. I was in a coma for a few days.
- Ø So where do you know me from?
- Ø I did not lose my memory. We met in Jail. Through Howard.
- Ø Edwin is this really you? or are we both dead.
- Ø No Boricua
- Ø Oh say that again. That sounds like you.
- Ø Bori, que tal?
- Ø Fuck, Edwin, this is you. Holy shit! Fuck! What happened?
- Ø Long story. I'll give you just a brief version. You might not even believe this. It turns out that word got out to the police that Howard robbed and that I was responsible for the robbery. I don't know how he knew, but he did. He thought I was the one that broke in. So that night I was supposed to call you back, after I had met up with my nephew and given him the tape, this cop confronted me. I was in a car with my cousin and we got pulled over on a quiet street. My cousin was handcuffed and then hit with a stick on the head. He fell to the ground and passed out. The cop aimed his gun at me and asked for his items back. He said he knew it was me that broke in. I told him I didn't know what he was talking about. He said if I did not talk he was going to kill me. I told him to fuck himself and that's when he shot me. The first bullet went through my shoulder. He asked me again and again I told him fuck you. That's when he fired again. This time I was struck in the chest. I fell to the ground and hit my head on the curb. That's all I remember. My nephew told me the rest.
- Ø So tell me Edwin.
- Ø Well after the first shot, someone called the police saying a police officer was in trouble. So a swarm of cop cars showed up within minutes. The house in front of

where this took place had a video camera recording the driveway. My nephew also showed up at the scene. He said there was a gun in my hand, and that gave the cop a reason to fire on me.

My nephew later that day went back to the house and retrieved the recording. In it you could clearly see that he took a gun out of his ankle and placed it in my hand. The police captain that was on hand at the time, thought it was a justifiable shooting. My cousin has that tape and has not shown it to anyone yet. I was in the hospital under a coma for several days. The doctors said they induced it to help save my life. The entire time I was there I was under arrest with an officer present. It took about three days for them to realize what had happened. My cousin is well respected and told them that I was innocent and that the bad cop had planted the gun. I still needed to go to a hearing with my lawyer to set bail. I'm lucky to be alive. This guy shot to kill me. I don't know why he didn't put a bullet through my head. But anyway I am home free for the moment.

Ø Fuck Edwin. I'm glad you are alive. I was worried about you and had the NETA's and the Latin Kings search for you.

Ø For real Ozzie.

Ø Yes Edwin. Ask Howard. He sent his boys to find you. We thought Prince killed you and we had plans for him to die. I'm so glad. Now we don't have to kill him, but more important you're alive. Your boy Jimmy was making plans to kill Prince in the event you would not appear. So what is the plan for the bad cop?

Ø Let's meet tomorrow in the day and talk about that. Call Howard and tell him my nephew has put a plan in place. He has a lot of pictures and evidence against him.

Ø Well Edwin. I have made plans to get the money this Wednesday. Things are in place. Can we squeeze Howards plan in for the same day about 12 or 1?

Ø Ozzie, I will meet with my nephew and get back to you tomorrow.

Ø Edwin, if you are not up to it you don't have to go to the Vault. Your money is still good.

Ø Let's see how I feel. I am walking around in a sling. The bullets went through me. I have exit and entrance wounds. I suffer much internal and external bleeding. My energy is still a little low. I don't know how many transfusions I had, but I was told there were many. If I don't go in with you, I will have my cousin or someone drive me around and watch you.

Ø Edwin. Let's meet tomorrow. I have to meet with Prince and you're inside guy to finalize the plan. Also, I need to call Howard tonight and get back to him, as I told him I would formulate a plan.

Ø Tell Howard, the plan is made already. We will give him the details tomorrow provided my nephew okay's it. I will try to set it up the same hour. This is my new number Ozzie. I don't know what happened to my other phone. I need to nape a little. I'm tired. Tomorrow we will meet.

Ø Okay Edwin. Thank you. Get well. Don't worry about your money.

Ø Okay, thank you Ozzie.

Somehow I found myself within my car. I guess I made my way there while being amazed by Edwin's call. There I sat for a moment in disbelieve. My friend Edwin was alive. What a relief. My focus now started to shift towards the bad cop. Does this guy know anything about me? He tried to kill Edwin. Will he try to kill me? I think it's a stretch. But, one can never be too careful. I started to get a little upset at this guy, but it's not my problem to deal with. Fuck, wait till Howard finds out. With that in mind, I better give him a call.

Ø Hello Howard.

Ø Hola Ozzie.

Ø Howard. You won't believe what I just found out. I myself am having a hard time believing it.

Ø Tell me Ozzie. Que Paso?

Ø Edwin Called me.

Ø Oh Ozzie. That's good news. How is he?

Ø He is week, recovering from two bullet wounds.

Ø No Ozzie.

Ø What happened?

Ø This is the part you won't believe.

Ø The cop that you robbed. Thought that Edwin was the guy that broke in.

Ø How?

Ø Howard. He is a cop. I'm sure he has his sources.

Ø Do you think Edwin was framed?

Ø Howard, I did not think about that. I don't see how. The only other person that knew about this was his cousin, and surely he would not do Edwin like that. So it must be that through some work, he suspected Edwin. Anyway, he pulled him and his cousin over. Handcuffed his cousin and beat him up. Then he pulled a gun and shot Edwin. He wanted to get his belongings back.

Ø You mean the things he stole from others.

Ø Yes, that. So Edwin fell and other cops showed up. He placed a handgun in Edwin's hand and claimed self-defense. The other cops upon seeing the gun thought it was a justifiable shooting. Edwin spent several days in the hospital in a coma while under arrest. He is home now. He will let me know about a plan for you and the cop. I think they really want him now. So don't do anything for the moment Howard. I told Edwin of my plan to do this Wednesday. I need for his nephew to give the okay. As soon as I hear from him I will call you.

Ø Ozzie, this is incredible. I'm going to kill this fucken cop.

Ø Howard, relax. Don't let him off so easily. Make him suffer. In jail that is.

Ø Those friends of him will let him get away with everything.

Ø No Howard. Edwin's friends are freemasons. They are stronger. Edwin is really connected in this way. Not to mention his other group of friends. Relax knowing that this guy will be brought to justice. I have an idea. I will check with Edwin first before I share it.

Ø Wow, Ozzie. This is incredible. You were right. This is hard to believe. Tell me. How will Edwin prove that the gun was placed in his hand?

Ø That's easy Howard. It happened in front of a house that had a surveillance camera facing the front of the house. His nephew has that proof. It's just a matter of time before this gets to court.

Ø Okay Ozzie. You are the man. I'll wait for you, but please let me know immediately.

Ø Will do Howard.

Next Call Prince.

Ø Hello Prince.

Ø Hello Ozzie, What's up?

Ø Prince, I have to apologize to you. Edwin just called. He was in the hospital. Guess who put him there?

Ø Howard.

Ø No.

Ø Your mama.

Ø No asshole. Your mama.

Ø Okay. Ozz, what happened?

Ø The police that arrested Howard thought Edwin robbed him and so he tried to kill Edwin. Shot him twice and then put a handgun in his hand. Police came to the scene and said it was a justified shooting. However his nephew has evidence of what really happened.

Ø Damn Ozz, that's some fucked up shit.

Ø Yea, Edwin was in an induced coma for a few days. As well as under arrest. He had to go to court and set bail. He's home now.

Ø Great news Ozzie. Will he be there Wednesday?

Ø Not sure. At the very least he will be watching with a few of his boys.

Ø Good. So everything is still on.

Ø Yes. We have a plan for Howard also. I need to be 100% sure about the radio guy.

Ø That's done already. My friend and I tested everything. All is on target. Don't want to say much more.

Ø Okay Prince. Let's meet tomorrow to go over everything.

Ø Okay Ozzie. Let me know.

Ø Sure.

Wow, what a day. What turn of events! Hearing from Edwin had certainly been the highlight of the past few days. The box I received being the second. Tomorrow will be a busy day; as I need to meet with everyone and get the plans down packed. There will be no room for error. That is because plans for errors also need to be completed. Will I sleep tonight or will my mind be thinking late into the night as it has often done?

Tuesday, the day before.

This morning I had a hard time getting up. Why? Obviously I was up late last night. Longer than I had hoped for. Nonetheless I accomplished what needed to be done. Last night I laid myself down. G's warm body pressed against me, I laid there in bed staring towards the ceiling thinking about the events to unfold. She gently placed her head on my chest and started to caress me. What followed was a bit strange for I was thinking about the events to come. About setting a strategic plan and about properly executing it. As I did I realized that I had been holding her and caressing her scalp, just like my father used to do when he put me to sleep. What a wonderful feeling I was experiencing, all the while I was thinking of what needed to be done on Wednesday. Well I was able to accomplish both things. Talk about multi task. To be fair, I did spend much time awake after she dozed off.

By 10:30 I had arrived at work. I Told Yecid I would not be working tomorrow as I had personal things to do. He did not ask any questions and gave me the thumbs up. My plan was set for the most part. I needed to get together with the thugs and cover the plan. Howards plan was being worked out by Edwin's nephew. It was now 1 and I was still awaiting confirmation. Finally about three the call came.

Ø Hello,

Ø Hola Ozzie, Como estas?

Ø Good Edwin. So do we have a go for Howard tomorrow?

Ø Yes. Let's meet in a little. There are a number of details for him. I have them written down and Howard has to follow them completely.

- Ø Edwin, shall we meet at his house?
- Ø Sure, call him and let me know.
- Ø Okay, I have an idea. Let me just see if we can all meet in his house this evening. I'll call you in a little.

Calling Howard back:

- Ø Hello Howard.
- Ø Hola Ozzie.
- Ø Howard. I spoke with Edwin. There is a plan set up for tomorrow. I'm not sure as of yet what it is. Edwin needs to meet me. I'm wondering if it okay for us to meet at your place.
- Ø Sure, Ozzie. What time.
- Ø Somewhere after 5. BTW Howard, Edwin and I have to meet with Prince and with Edwin's boy Jimmy to discuss the job on Wednesday. Can we all meet at your place after we finish our talk with Edwin?
- Ø Sure Ozzie. I don't mind. It might be a good thing.
- Ø Okay. I'll see you this afternoon. I'll call you when on my way. Thank you Howard.
- Ø Your welcomed Ozzie.

With that I called Edwin and confirmed. The plan is to meet at Howard's house one hour before Prince and Jimmy come over. I followed that with a call to Prince and then to Jimmy. To play it safe I asked Prince and Jimmy to meet up at 7 pm. This would allow for Howard, Edwin and I to freely talk. At work, I made arrangement to depart at 5. As I left I called Edwin and Howard to inform them that I was on my way.

Shortly after 5, I arrived at Howard's house. The front door was unlocked and after several knocks I made my way in. It seems Jackie was not around, and Howard did not hear me as he was in the patio. Howard greeted me with a hug and expressed his gratitude for helping him. First thing on the menu was to pour the Galliano. Ah, what a treat. I like it, I like it a lot. I was in good spirits as so was Howard. Howard asked what was in the black backpack I was carrying. The one I was keeping for me. I reached in and pulled out a walkie-talkie, or as the sophisticated prefer, two-way-radio. They were powerful enough to cover 10 miles. "This is for you Howard" All of us will have one. I rented eight. I need to return them in a few days. You can give one to your boy so that you guys can communicate with each other, as well as with us. They are tuned to the same frequency. I'll go over the use of it later when the others arrived.

Edwin appeared about ten minutes later. Wow, I said. You look fucked up. Edwin was emaciated. Surely he lost 15 pounds or so. His frame was not large to begin with. It was evident he was still in distress, as he walked with a slight limp into the room. His movements were slow. I greeted him with a hug and so did Howard. Despite his condition Edwin was smiling. It was a sinister look: perhaps mischievous, as if he was up to something. We quickly sat at the patio table overlooking the river. Edwin had visited before and was familiar with the layout. As he made himself comfortable in the chair, Howard handed him a drink. Edwin proceeded to tell us the events of his shooting. Howard seemed to get a little angered. I think he was reliving his own beat down by the bad cop. Edwin did not show any signs of anger or frustration. There must have been something he knew that hasn't been revealed to us yet. He was calm and again smiled.

After he finished his story he pulled out a paper from his pants back pocket. It was folded four times. He started to tell us about the plan for tomorrow. His nephew had dictated to Edwin when and where to meet the bad cop. The event was to take place at about 12:30 on the East side of Hollywood. That's perfect I said. It falls within the area covered by the jamming frequency. Edwin made it clear to Howard that the instructions needed to be followed as stated to avoid putting anyone in danger. By the look on Howards face it was clear that he was not thrilled with the plan, or at the very least. He was expecting something else. After Edwin explained the plan Howard took the paper from him. He took a good look at it, folded it and placed it in his pocket. He looked at Edwin and nodded yes. Showing he would comply.

Howard had some meat on the grill and retrieved it. As Edwin and I made small talk, Howard placed the plate on the table accompanied by some cooked yams. A second round of Galliano flowed. As we ate we started talking about our plan; the $6,000,000. I expressed to both that I was very uneasy and suspicious about Prince. I made it clear we needed to have a plan in the event he would try to cross us. Edwin and Howard were in agreement. We decided to implement a plan as well as a backup plan in the event Prince Suspicions were realized.

Howard promised several guys at our disposal. Edwin seemed to have his own backup plan as well. He also was to have a few of his guys on the lookout. During this discussion, I revealed the tracker placed in Prince's car. Howard brought out his laptop upon my request and within minutes, we were able to tract Prince. He was on interstate 595 heading east. If he was indeed heading to us then it should take him about 10 minutes to arrive. I gave Edwin and Howard the info needed to track Prince, just in case it was necessary to do so. They seemed a little amused watching Princes' live movements. I also revealed the backpacks with the trackers. In the event Prince did not pay up, or if he was to be followed, the bags with the money could be traced. Howard seemed a little amused by the technology. He thought my idea genius. To me, it was a no-brainer. I would think most people would come up with something similar. Knowing Prince was soon to arrive we finalized the plans for our survival and protection.

The trusted tracking tracker truly traced thoroughly. Hey, how about that. Prince arrived as expected as per the tracker. Howard answered the door and escorted him in. Edwin stood up and embraced Prince. Prince took notice of Edwin's condition. I shook hands with Prince and we all sat. Howard quickly offered a drink to which Prince accepted. Edwin told a shorten version of his mishap. Prince once again was dressed in fine clothing. He looked around at the surrounding and seemed to have enjoyed the view. He asked Howard if he could pull out a cigar, to which Howard consented. Prince leaned back in his chair and puffed away. Was he nervous? I wasn't sure. Several minutes passes before the next knock on the door. Again Howard opened and greeted Jimmy. After a brief intro, they proceeded to the patio. Jimmy looked around taking in the beautiful house. We all stood to greet Jimmy. He gravitated to Edwin first. They did some special handshake and hug. Jimmy also took notice of Edwin's condition although he did not comment on it. I shook Jimmy's hand and then Edwin introduced him to Prince. Prince towered over Jimmy. Again, Howard pulled a drink, as well as horderves. We all sat together at the round table in what looked like a scene from Goodfellas. I found myself taking charge and going over all the details. There were things that Prince did not need to know; so I only expressed that which I wanted him to know, do, or say.

Before we knew it, 10pm was fast approaching. Jackie made her presence know as she walked into the kitchen. Quickly and quietly she proceeded about her business. The guys did not ask who she was and no other mention of her was made. We continued on and once again went over the plan. Each of us had a paper with a few instructions; as to when, where, who and how. I also went over plan b, should there be a change. I then handed each a radio, and explained how to use it. For I few minutes we tested them; but it was more like play. Right about 10:15 we stood up to stretch and depart. Each of us placed our paper in our pocket and carried the radio. The last thing left was to synchronize our watches, that we did and then marched on out. Edwin stayed behind and conversed some more with Howard. I was not concerned at all about that. I felt safe with them and trusted both. However, I still did come up with a quick escape plan from them if need be. As we departed we spoke for a few minutes on the radio as a test. Each of us was tuned in and each spoke.

When I arrived home, G was watching a YouTube documentary on giants. Both she and I are taken by documentaries that are produced outside the lies of big production companies. You know what's funny? Sometimes these big block-buster movies, actually tell us about the NOW, and plans for our elimination and suppression, and we think it's just fantasy. How they must mock us. Saying, "You know, we show these idiots what we are going to do to them and the laugh." Okay, it's not the time to go there.

I leaned over to kiss her and she pulled me onto her. Hum. Does she know I am getting money tomorrow? Has she been spying on me? If so, will she steal from me? Is this part of her plan? Damn, I'm thinking too much, but it has served me well over the years. Am I panicked? Tomorrow is a big day. I need to be clear minded and relax. Perhaps some meditation is in order.

49 THE BIG DAY

Last night I made a few phone calls. In part they were loving departure calls; goodbye calls in essence. I called my children and told them I loved them. I also sent my dad an email, expressing the same. That's it. Those are the only important people in my life. No brothers, sisters, family or friends. How sad in a way. It's part of how I grew up; in a dysfunctional family, lacking love. At least on my end. I can't speak for my siblings. For some were treated much different than I. Also in part, I am and have been a loner. Is it my genetic character? Perhaps. Anyway, after my calls I went over the plans; all the plans. I tried to envision things that might go wrong and how to handle them. Mentally I am ready; G however has me scared a bit. Why, I don't know. I haven't figured it out yet. She knows more than she claims.

At 10 am, my alarm on my wrist watch went on. With that I turned on the radio and said "hello gentleman, Ozzie, out" it was immediately followed by Prince, then Edwin, Howard, Jimmy, and two other guys. One was Howard's boy and the other Edwin's. We each said the same words interjecting our name. No other words were spoken. With that I shut the radio off and waited till 11am for the next alarm call. What followed was a repeat of that which occurred at 10. G was home at the time and found it amusing that I was playing with 2 way radios. Again she knew something was going on, but asked no questions.

The Vault was only 15 minutes away from my house. I needed to be patient; time was going by slower than normal. It was time to get dressed; dark jeans and shoes, as well as a black long sleeve shirt. I placed the black hat by my car keys so as not to forget. My backpacks were already in my car as well as some emergency items, such as a rope, duct tape, a knife, and tools. I did not have the luxury of legally being able to carry a gun. That was reserved for Edwin and his boy. At 11:30 the watch went off again. I turned my radio on and waited for Jimmy, who was at work. "Camera deactivated". Bingo was my reply. Prince also commented Bingo, as well as Edwin. This time the radio was to remain on. As I gathered my keys, phone, and hat, G came over and gave me a hug and kiss. "Be careful" she said. I looked at her for a few seconds and replied "I will", I'll call you later. There was something different about this departure. Was it that I was too caught up in the feelings associated with what I was about to do? Or was it something different. This girl was smart. I know her type, the quiet one that is capable of just about anything. I did not make plans to protect myself against her. What was I thinking?

I left home and in about 15 minutes arrived at the designated destination. It was one long block away from the Vault. It was the same place I met Prince last time we were together. Once there I picked up the phone and called Edwin.

- Ø Edwin, are you going in or waiting outside.
- Ø I feel good today. Waite for me. I'll be there in a few minutes.
- Ø How about your backup boys, are they in place.
- Ø Yes Ozzie. One is already there watching you.
- Ø Great Edwin, see you in a few.

Both Edwin and Prince arrived at the same time. Edwin stationed his car adjacent to mine. I exited my car and greeted him. His attire was the same as mine. It's what we all agreed on. After our greet, I retrieved my backpacks and items I had gathered. I walked over to Prince's car and he released the trunk lid. His backpacks were also there, as well as other items. Quickly I scanned the trunk for guns. I saw none. I placed my items within and then climbed onto the front seat as Edwin found his way to the rear. It was a little comical I thought for us to be dressed the same. So far, everything was on target. We sat in the car and talked a little. The entire time my eyes canvassed the area looking for any suspicious vehicle. I knew Prince had his boys around, but I could not see them. I wasn't worried too much as Edwin's boys were watching us; Howard had two guys watching Edwin's boys as well as Prince. Where there too many people involved in this? If so, how much did they know? For its very easy to get greedy, however plans were already in place. There was no time to second guess.

We needed to wait till 12 to enter the loading dock of the Vault. Howards escaped was to begin at 12"30. Would we be finished by then? It depends. For a few minutes we made some chat.

- Ø Prince, I am sure you were not able to get the replica prints.
- Ø No Ozzie. I know you figured that out. I know you are working on an alternative plan.
- Ø What makes you believe that?
- Ø Come on Ozzie. Be real. You would not be here calm if you were not ready.
- Ø Well, you have a point.
- Ø So what is your plan?
- Ø I'll tell you as soon as we get started.

I did not feel comfortable revealing to Prince my exact plan. He had a good idea, but I had misled him somewhat. Besides I was not sure if his buddies could listen in to what we were saying. Could his car have an audible device? I looked back at Edwin. He winked at me, as if acknowledging my actions. He said nothing. He just stood there and smiled; No sign of fear or concerned. I looked at him for a moment and he smiled some more. What is it? I thought? What does this guy know? What is he so happy about? All of a sudden our wrist watch all went off at exactly the same time. Wow, I said, how's that for precision? We each turned it off. That was the signal, time for us to enter.

Prince drove up to loading dock number 2 as Jimmy suggested. Once inside I looked for a small Puerto Rican flag. There it was, on the right hand corner of the area of the floor. It was Jimmy's sign that everything so far was okay. I went to the truck which was now wide open and looked through my backpacks. The second one I looked into contained what I was looking for. I reached in and grabbed a small plastic container. As I pulled it out I walked over to Prince who was now standing by the touch pad by the elevator door. There I set the backpack down and opened the box. Edwin smiled at me upon seeing it.

- Ø Edwin, the moment I saw this I knew you were alive.
- Ø Well Ozzie. I could have died, but you would have still received it. I gave it to my nephew and he followed through with it. He is the one that mailed it to you.
- Ø Fuck Edwin. So he knows what we are doing.

Edwin smiled again. I knew it was okay. He and his nephew had a strong bond. Prince just stood there and watched. I proceeded to open the box and took the plastic filled bag out. I set the box down and lifted the bag as to show Prince. I paused for a moment as if to say. This is it. My lips however were silent. I pulled the item out and showed it to Prince.

- Ø Fuck Ozzie. Nice work. Damn.

I could see the hairs on his neck stand straight. He cuffed his right hand and placed it against his mouth. Then he blew into his hand. He reached out and took the replica finger. For a brief moment he just stared at it. All three of us made eye contact and smiled. Edwin was infectious. Prince let out a sigh. With that he punched in the containers number and then pressed the replica on the scanner. The green light on the board lit and we smiled some more. We waited for a minute and then two. It seemed like an eternity. No container came. Edwin called to Jimmy.

- Ø Boriqua, hay un problema?
- Ø I'm working on it. When I deactivated the cameras, something happened within the computer and now the elevators are not working. Give me a minute or two.

Fuck I exclaimed.

- Ø Edwin, ask him if the box is on the ground floor or up high.

The reply came back that it was stack one container high, so that it's now sitting on another. Edwin and Jimmy and I had made provisions to break into the container from within the interior of the storage. However the plan was for Jimmy to have made sure the box was sitting on the ground. We would now have to survey the surrounding area to see how we could access it. Prince made his way to the front seat of the car as if in disbelief. He was not sure how to proceed. The look of defeat betrayed his calmness. Edwin looked at me again and continued to smile. He must be on some sedatives or uppers. This guy is feeling good, no matter what goes on. Five minutes had gone by and there was no sign of movement or Jimmy. Edwin checked in with Jimmy one more time. The answer was the same. "Working on it"

12:30 was almost upon us. Howard's plan was soon to take place. I asked Prince about the Pirate radio guy. He waved for me to come to him. As I did he turned the car volume up. Music was playing.

- Ø That's the station. In a few minutes the jamming will begin. What the fuck is going on?
- Ø It seemed Jimmy deactivated the surveillance system and now the elevators are not working. He says he is working on it.

Several more minutes passed. Once again our watches went off in synchronization. Its Howard's time. My guess is that he is positioned in place and things going according to plan, as no abort signals were heard.

Prince received a call. All I could make out was not yet. That however was enough to know that his boys were curious to know what was going on. We should have been out by now. I looked over at Edwin, but all he did was smile. Some fucken happy pill he must be on.

- Ø Edwin. I have an idea. Tell jimmy to turn off the main power switch.

Edwin called to Jimmy on the radio and re-laid the message. Jimmy responded

- Ø OK. It will take me a minute. I need to get to the back of the building.

I picked up my radio,

- Ø Jimmy
- Ø Yes. When you get to the back of the building let me know before you throw the switch.
- Ø Okay

I waited for a minute and then two. Jimmy came on

- Ø Bori. I'm at the switch.

Ø Okay Jimmy. Throw the switch and leave it off. Let's see if the backup generator will kick in and reset things.

Jimmy threw the switch. For a split second the light blinked off and then back on. It was clear the generator was on. I was surprised at how quickly it activated. I summoned Prince to the control board. On my command he entered the container number and followed with the replica fingerprint. Once again the green light came on. I wasn't sure what to expect and just waited by the elevator. No noise was heard from beyond. One minute turned into two and then three. After about five minutes it was clear it was not going to work. Maybe that will be enough power to reset everything. Let me know as soon as you do.

Ø Jimmy

Ø Yes

Ø Let's try this one more time. Throw the power back on. Stay back there until I tell you to leave.

Ø Okay

It took Jimmy about two minutes to throw the power back on. Prince and I stool by the elevator. We then heard something different but not from where we were hoping. The music that he had playing in the background muted and some strange noise was flowing. Prince and I looked at each other and knew what was happening. The frequency was being jammed. If we were to take advantage of it we would have to get going anytime soon. Two minutes after the power switched on I told Prince to try one more time. Jimmy was still waiting in the rear of the building. Prince entered the codes for third time and again followed with the replica scan. It was thirty seconds before we could hear something. It was not from his car radio. It was not the walkie-talkies. It was not Jimmy, Edwin Prince nor I. It was not a voice, but instead a sound from behind the elevator door. It was mechanical. Something is going on. We could hear something approaching the elevator door. Could it be the police and we have been discovered? Could all this have been a setup?

Ø Jimmy

Ø Yes. Run upstairs and if the system is operating, turn the cameras off again. Make sure two minutes pass between now and then.

Jimmy did as I said. I was taking notice of the clock. I fully expected for the container to be at the door by now. But, it was not.

Ø Jimmy, wait a minute. The container has not arrived.

Ø Oh sorry too late. I just shut the cameras off.

Fuck, I said out loud. I looked back at Edwin. He looked up at me and slightly raised his head and brought it back down. The entire time he remained smiling. I knew by now he was medicated. No one else could act that way. As I turned towards Prince, the elevator door started to open.

Holy shit, holy cow! Prince and I looked at each other without moving. It surely was a container and it wasn't ours. The box was large with many things in it. The lighting was dim. Prince walked to his car and brought out a powerful flashlight. I did not dare enter. Fuck I thought, if this thing is a trap, then let him go first. Prince stepped in and looked around. I am not sure if I was expecting something to happen. I took a step forward and then two. As I looked around I noticed a few tables with items on them. Everything was covered with linen sheets. You would think we would be frantic looking around, but we were not. On the contrary we were calm and took our time. After all, no one knew we were there. Towards the end of the container were two structures; also covered.

Prince and I started to remove all the linen covers. I pulled the covers off the tall structures and noticed they were two different glass shelved curios. The items within were wrapped in plastic. I opened one of the curios and picked up an item. It had some weight to it but not the kind I was there for. I placed it down and looked around some more. They seem to be some fragile pottery or similar. I placed it back and continued looking about the container. Prince found his way to a metal cabinet about four feet high. There were about six metal sliding doors, the kind that pulls out. He opened the top drawer and scrutinized it for a moment. "Hey" he whispered to me. I took a peak. That peak lead to a few blow stare. Was I seeing things? For we were staring at a finger. It was dried but not decomposed. Attached around it was a ring.

- Ø Prince. Tell me you are fucking with me. Tell me that is the finger that was cut off, and you just put it there.
- Ø No Ozzie. That is not the same finger.

Holy shit! What the fuck was a finger with a ring on it doing in a drawer? Underneath the finger was an envelope of legal size. Prince closed the drawer and opened the next; I stood by his side. This drawer was more frightening than the first. It contained some jewelry, as well as another finger. What the fuck? Prince reaction was the same. Underneath the jewelry were some photos. Prince picked one up. It was a photo of a young girl. In it she was tied up and naked. I pointed to the jewelry the girl was wearing in the photo. Holy fuck. Holy shit! What the fuck? It's the same jewelry. This was too weird. My hair started to rise. We were looking at something evil. Prince placed the picture in the drawer, closed it and opened the top drawer again. This time he pulled out the envelope avoiding coming in contact with the finger. There were pictures in the envelope. Again it was a young lady tied up. She was in her underwear. We tried to see if she was wearing a ring in the picture but her hands were not exposed. Prince placed the pictures in the envelope, closed the drawer and reached for the third drawer.

This one had some small panties in it. From the looks of it, it appeared to be that of a child. No finger or bones in this one. There was an envelope. Prince picked it up and opened it. There was something within as well as photos. The pictures revealed a child, a naked child, no more than four feet tall. Hands and feet tied together. This was a little too much. I thought of my children for a second. I managed to compose myself. As he was going to place the photos back he noticed something in the envelope. He opened the envelope and poured the contents out. It was a lock of hair. It was clear Prince and I was looking at a serial killer. Did I care to see more? Yes and no. Curiosity got the best of me, and so it seems of Prince himself. We were supposed to be looking for gold and bearer bonds. Instead we found ourselves captured by what was in front of us. Without any questions or comments, Prince went for the fourth drawer. Fuck! No more. What the fuck is going on? This is too much for me. One more finger. No jewelry this time. Another envelope with photos. You would be right to assume of a tied naked person; this one also a child. However this one was younger than the rest. My anger started to turn to a smile. Why? I looked back for Edwin. He had not entered the Vault. What the fuck? No way. I hit Prince in the arm to get his attention. Edwin was standing in the entrance. His smile never left him. Both his arms were to his side. In the right was an object. It was clear.

- Ø Edwin what the fuck?

He raised his hand up and pointed at me. I ducked down and away. His smile never changed.

- Ø Edwin
- Ø Que Bori.
- Ø Put that gun down. What is wrong with you?
- Ø I don't know. I feel anxious.
- Ø Edwin are you on medication?
- Ø Si Bori.
- Ø Fuck Edwin. Point the gun down.
- Ø Okay Bori.

I made my way to him and asked him for the gun. He just looked at me and smiled.

- Ø Edwin, give me the gun.

Without hesitation he handed the gun to me. I took it gently and placed it on my waist. I walked him to the back seat of the car and left him there.

Ø Edwin. Listen, your medication has you fucked up. Do not move from here. Call out if you need me.

Ø Okay, Bori.

Shit. Now I have a new problem. I need to go back inside the container strapped with a gun. Will Prince clobber me from behind and then try to kill me with the gun? Fuck, Ozzie. Stop panicking. I made my way back to Prince. He was all smiles.

Ø No way Prince.

His big smile told it all. I could see nothing, but I knew. He found what he was looking for.

Ø Where is it?

He reached down in front of the cabinet before him. It was not the same as the metal one. He pointed at a drawer and smiled some more. Okay, I'll bite. As I opened the door, Prince's flashlight revealed the contents. It was yellow shinny bars. Gold Bars. Holy cow! Holy cow! Holy cow!

Ø You were fucken right. How many?

Ø A lot. It's about what I expected.

Ø What about the bonds?

Ø Let's keep looking.

I reached in and picked one up. It was just as heavy as I expected. The backpack I purchased was the right ones for this job. I placed the bar back in and stood up. Prince was busy looking around for the bonds. I decided to take a closer look at the contents within the curio. I opened the cabinet door and took out the first item I had touched. Carefully I unwrapped the item. The light was dim and so I stepped outside the container. Fuck. Fuck. This gets better. It can't be I thought. I knew what I was looking at. I've seen it in my research. Well not an actual one, but pictures of it. This could be more valuable than the gold. The object was a Sumerian cuneiform tablet. At least I hope it's real. If so, this is really jackpot. The object was about two inches by two inches. I had no fucken clue as to what was written on it. But I knew it was important.

The Sumerians were one of the greatest civilizations that ever lived. The Sumerians invented the wheel, agriculture, the arch, the plow, irrigation and many other innovations. The place is often referred to as the Cradle of Civilization. It's where the story of Adam and Eve came from. Yes Adam and Eve, Hybrid human and Anunnaki. What? Never mind. The Sumerians developed the earliest known writing system - a pictographic writing system known as cuneiform script. They also developed the first mathematics on a base of 60. It's where we get 60 second in a minute, 60 minutes in an hour and 360 degrees.

Who was this man with this item? Could he be a member of the elite? The small percentage of the world's wealth holder? Illuminati perhaps? All of a sudden fear struck. Fuck. We must be messing with the wrong person. If I take this stuff, I might have to hide the rest of my life. Is this my destiny? Is this what I went to jail for? Is this why I met Edwin? Oh well. Fuck! Let me see what I can find. Am I to liberate these artifacts? Give them back to humanity.

I went back in, this time with a backpack. I carefully wrapped the tablet and set it on the glass. I did not want to place heavy bars on top of it. I then unwrapped another item. Wow, jackpot again. Fuck. This is too good to be true; a clay cone of about 8 inches tall. What the fuck was written or depicted on it was beyond me. If this is real and not a replica, man oh man, I'm in the money. I wonder if Prince has any clue at what the fuck I was seeing. I hope not. I shall keep these.

Further figures revealed to be pottery, statues and artifacts from antiquity. Question is, how much can I carry away? Fuck the gold! Well maybe not. This place is jackpot, big time jackpot. How do we get away with all this? Prince and I had already figured out how many pieces of gold bars Edwin and I was to get. I went to the trunk and retrieved all the bags, both his and mine. I placed them on the floor and continued looking around. On the bottom shelve of the curio were some envelopes. I took a look hoping it was the bonds, but there were none. Instead, there were some documents, old documents. One read classified. No bonds however, most of the money promised by Prince was in the forms of bonds. Could he have found them as I was attending to Edwin? If so, did he hide them somewhere? More than fifteen minutes had passed since we entered the container. Prince kept looking around. I don't know what he had discovered as I was well occupied with the objects in the curio. Standing a few feet from me he swung his arm wide. Bang, right on my shoulder. What the Fuck? Was this his attack? Nope. Not to be, at least not yet. He had not bothered to turn around or look sideways. Surely he grabbed my attention. I stood near him and looked at what he was reading. Bang there it was; U.S. bearer bonds. "Mother Fucker" I said out loud. Prince laughed. Jackpot again! Prince had been true to his word so far. Question now is do I pull out the gun on him and kill him before he tries to kill me or do I just go along. I reached into my waist. He noticed what I was doing and he stood straight. In a split second I continued reaching down and scratched my balls. We both laughed. The look on his face was funny.

- Ø Prince. First thing first. Let's put Edwin's share in a backpack and get that out of the way.

He handed me a note and one bar of gold.

- Ø Prince that's more than you said. Ozzie. There is more money here than I thought. Just take it and shut the fuck up.

We then figured out how many bars of gold I was to take. Prince handed me a few bars and several bonds. The Bonds alone totaled almost two million dollars. With the bars it exceeded two million dollars. I distributed the bars evenly among the bags, except for one, so as to make them manageable. With that I placed the squared tablet in the empty bag as well as the clay cylinder, followed by the documents, into the empty bag.

- Ø Prince. I am going to take these things up to a security box.
- Ø When did you get a box? I thought you were going to leave in my car with your bags and then I was to drive you to your car.
- Ø Yes Prince. That was the plan. This morning I decided to change it as I have now come across something I want to do.
- Ø What is that?
- Ø I'll tell you in a few. Wait for me here as I go up. It will only be a minute.

As I was about to pick up the radio to summons Jerry; a distress call came over it. "Shots fired. Shots fired." There was no mistake it was Howard's voice. I asked if he was okay. There was no reply.

Howard. Howard. Please reply. But there was none.

- Ø Edwin, check to see if Howard is okay.

Edwin tried to reach out but there was no response. Edwin called Howard directly at the cell phone. Again, no answer. Fuck, Howard is dead. I thought about Prince or his friends doing me in.

- Ø Jimmy. Come down and get us.
- Ø Ok.

Prince wondered how Jimmy was going to let us up. Part of our plan was for him to open the side door near the elevator door and walk us to the main elevator that would carry us upstairs to the smaller security boxes. Within a minute Jimmy was among us. As per our plan he turned and inserted a key; on the panel we punched our info, and turned the key 90 degrees. He then turned back and pulled the key out; Unbenounced to Prince, he was now unable to leave. He was held captive until Jimmy reversed the action. Jimmy escorted both me and Edwin, who still had his smile. Jimmy asked him if he was okay. I interjected that he was medicated, on a high of some sort pain killers for sure. We found our way to the main elevator and proceeded up. Edwin and I both deposited the contents of the backpack into the boxes. With that we headed back down.

Ø Jimmy. I need a favor.

Ø Yes.

Ø When we get back down, Take Edwin to his car which is parked right next to mine. You will ride to the car with Prince. Make sure he leaves safely with his backpack. You will get your money later. So far things are good. As soon as Edwin leaves, bring my car into the bay. I will remain here. I am going to call a cop I know to show him some items in there.

Ø Why?

Ø Jimmy. There are things in there you don't want to see. I know that part of the NETA code is to despise rapist. The man who owes that box is a serial rapist and killer. This might put him away for good and so maybe he won't come looking for us. Surely he is a man of means. It will be harder for him to investigate this from within jail.

Ø Okay Ozzie.

Ø Jimmy be careful out there. I don't trust Prince. Although I have to say till now he Has come through.

Ø Okay. Don't worry. Edwin has a guy that has been canvassing the area looking for trouble. So far I have not heard a word.

By the time we arrived back at the loading bay, Prince had gathered what he was to take. I had three empty backpacks and decided to fill them with whatever I could. I walked into the container, found my way to the curio and started to fill the bags with items that were still wrapped. Once the bags were filled I told jimmy to make sure he puts them in Edwin's car.

Ø Edwin, are you okay.

Ø Yes, don't worry Ozzie. I'm happy and good. I need more of these pills.

Ø Edwin, go home and make sure these bags are safe. Please don't open them. I'll come looking for them later.

Ø Sure Ozzie.

Ø Also Edwin. Once you are safe and home, find out about Howard. I will call you within an hour or two.

Ø Jimmy. As soon as you bring my car in the bay. Close the door, and go about your business. A cop might come knocking. Please don't worry. He is not here for you. I know this cop. If he asks to let him in, bring him to me. Act as if you don't know me and are not aware of anything that has happened. I suspect more cops will be coming thereafter.

Ø Guys do not attempt to call me. Clear you text messages and clear you call history as we spoke off. Remember the secret word we spoke off in the event one of us cracks down and needs to talk. If in the future anyone of us is questioned, they will come up with any and all kinds of lies.

Jimmy reversed his prior actions at the control board. With that he hit the override button and the bay door opened. The container door was not affected. After about four or five minutes, jimmy pulls into the bay with my car. I had already removed my black shirt and hat. It was in the backpack. Jimmy assured me that Edwin was on his way home. With that he left me to my own.

- Ø Hello, Jerry.
- Ø Ozzie, what's up?
- Ø Jerry. I am at a storage unit in Ft. Lauderdale. It's called the Vault. Jerry, I don't care what you are doing right now but you better get over here. It seems that I called my container to retrieve some items and the wrong unit was brought to me. The unit I am standing in now has body parts.
- Ø You mean actual human being body parts?
- Ø Yes Jerry. Fingers, bones, and pictures of young people and children tied up.
- Ø Ozzie. You're not kidding, are you?
- Ø Jerry. You know me better than that. This is some real freaky shit. You better bring a forensic team with you.
- Ø Okay, you are at the Vault by the airport?
- Ø Yes.
- Ø In a storage bay?
- Ø Yes. But I don't think I can let you in for fear that the container might close on me.
- Ø Okay, secure it. I will be there in ten minutes. Make sure to jam the door.
- Ø Okay. Come in the front. They will let you in. I am at bay number two.

For the next few minutes I sat in my car. Then a thought occurred. Holy shit! I have the gun on me, also, what about all the foot prints on the ground. I had given the two way radio to Edwin. It was now in the backpack. I picked up my phone and dialed Jerry.

- Ø Yes Ozzie.
- Ø Jerry you need to hurry. The police are on their way. I need to get rid of Edwin's gun and I also need a mop.
- Ø A mop. What for?
- Ø There are some foot prints that are not mine. Surely these cops will pick up on that.
- Ø Okay, give me a minute.

Fuck I said. I did it again. I opened up a can of worms.

Within a minute Jimmy was at the door. He let himself in and handed me a dust mop. Jimmy had a hand held walkie-talkie that pertained to the facility. He was called to the front desk. I handed him the gun, and quickly dusted the visible prints on the floor. The dust mop managed to do the trick. However before I could put it away, Jimmy started walking in with Jerry. I quickly picked up the flag and threw the mop against the corner. I placed the flag in my pocket just as Jerry walked in.

- Ø Jerry
- Ø Ozzie. Are you okay.
- Ø I'm a little disturbed.

Jerry asked Jimmy to excuse himself. I was not sure if Jimmy still had the gun on him or not.

- Ø So let's take a look.
- Ø Jerry not me. I don't want to go in there again. Open up that metal cabinet and look inside.

Jerry stared at me for a moment. His buddy cop had found his way to us. Again, Jimmy had escorted him in.

Jerry introduced us and then turned to look at the cabinet. His buddy cop stood outside the unit near me. Jerry opened the drawer and looked in. He took out a pen from his pocket and started to probe or move the object he was looking at.

- Ø Jerry, open the envelope and notice the ring finger of the girl in the picture.

Jerry did so, and immediately told his partner. "Looks like we have a serial killer here" That was news to my ears. It was my plan for calling him out. I instructed Jerry to open the other drawers. One by one he did. He stepped out of the container and called for a forensic unit to come. Jerry started to ask me a lot of questions. I knew that he had trust in me. He pulled me away from his partner and asked me if I knew anything about this.

"No Jerry" I replied.

- Ø Ozzie, this might be just what you needed. Surely this is going to look very good in the eyes of the prosecutor.
- Ø Jerry, I have some other great news for you.
- Ø What?
- Ø You know the Brazilian guy you asked me to keep an eye out for when I was in jail.
- Ø The pill guy.
- Ø Yes Jerry, that one. Balbi.

Ø Yes

Ø Well Jerry, I have proof he is innocent.

Ø How so.

Ø Jerry. Howard, has uncovered evidence that will set them both free.

Ø How do you know this Ozzie?

Ø Well, I had some help from within the Hollywood police department. There is a cop in there that is the nephew of a Freemason friend of mine. His name is Edwin and was in jail with me. Howard was innocent and told you he had big cartel people to turn in. However he just wanted to get a chance to prove his freedom. So he asked if I could help him. I had no clue as to how but then my friend mentioned his nephew working in the police department. This cop knew of many bad things that Howard arresting officer had committed. There were numerous cops that also were aware but would not speak. Edwin's nephew provided Howard with a plan. Howard broke into the house and found the evidence he was looking for. He took the evidence and recorded the entire event. Part of the evidence were newspaper clippings of the arrest, it was contained in a bin located under the mattress. Along the newspaper clippings was a ring. I saw the ring. It had a compass and square on its face. Balbi's name was inscribed within.

Ø Ozzie. You should have reported this to me sooner.

Ø Jerry, it was not my scheme. It was the doing of other cops. I was instructed to follow directions. Which I did. You are the first person I tell this too.

Ø Where is the evidence?

Ø According to Howard, he had a newspaper reporter pick it up and expose the bad cop. That should have happened yesterday or today.

Ø Ozzie, I am going to have to bring you in. I don't know what the judge might do.

Ø Jerry is that really necessary. You told me to look out for Balbi and I did. I gave you what you needed. Your fellow Mason is now to be a free man.

Ø Yes, that is true.

Jerry proceeded to ask several more questions. He was interrogating me. I played dumb as if not knowing what he was doing. After 15 minutes, Jerry called the station to find out how long it would be before the forensic team arrived. The reply was, "shots were fired in Hollywood involving a police officer". Based on the code, it sounded bad. Jerry was in disbelief, seems like a fellow officer was down. But if that involves Howard, might he also be dead? I needed to keep my composure. I could not let Jerry put these events together.

Jerry spoke to his partner.

- Hey, there is a man down in Hollywood. It looks like it's going to be a long day. A second forensic team needs to be dispatched here. Looks like the first one is involve at the other scene.

Jerry's partner started to look around the container some more. He walked over to the curio and picked up an item. He noticed that some items were recently moved. Shit not good. I continued with my ignorant ploy. I asked Jerry if I could make a phone call, to which he agreed.

I decided to call Edwin.

- Edwin.
- Ozzie, are you okay.
- Yes, are you?
- Yes, I am home, a car followed us for a few blocks but then some other car crashed into it. I did not stop to find out. I knew I was being followed. I think it might have been Prince Boys.
- Edwin. I am with Jerry. I think he wants to take me in. I don't know why. Can you have your cousin call me? I want him to talk to Jerry.
- Okay Ozzie. I'll do that right now.

Edwin hung up and no sooner than I could put my phone down it rung. I was not familiar with the number. I answered.

- Ozzie.
- Yes.
- This is Edwin's nephew. Is Jerry there with you?
- Yes.
- Let me speak to him.

I handed the phone to Jerry and told him it was Edwin's nephew. Jerry took the phone and started conversing. As he did, he looked up at me several times. I thought for sure he was upset. Jerry walked into the container as to keep me from listening. Several minutes later he handed me the phone and smiled. I was bewildered. What was he told?

- Ozzie, I need you to give a statement about what happened here. There seems to be an event in Hollywood that might be related to Howard. I have confirmation of Balbi being innocent. It's going to be a long night for us. If you know anything about the event in Hollywood, do not speak of it. I will contact you tomorrow and will send someone to pick you up. Make sure you are available. Only speak of how you came across this container by accident. There is an internal investigation going on regarding the cop involved. He has been shot. It is believed Howard was involved.

Ø Jerry did you know that Howard also has evidence of this guy stealing things from the crime lab.

Ø Yes. I was just made aware of everything Howard uncovered. I wonder if the radio going down a while ago had anything to do with that.

Ø What radio Jerry?

Ø Oh disregard. Has nothing to do with you. And that is how we will keep it. I am going to write a few things down. You are never to mention to anyone anything you might know about today's event other than what transpired here. That is you came to your box and this one popped up. When you noticed some of the items you called me. You got that.

Ø Got it Jerry.

Ø Okay. Go home and wait for my call tomorrow. You have court on Friday. I will make a special call to the prosecutor tomorrow to discuss your case. I am not sure if I need to be present on Friday. Tomorrow we will talk.

Ø Okay Jerry. I am going straight home and await your call.

With that I tried to leave but the bay door would not open. I pressed the intercom on the panel and told them I needed to leave. A woman replied, "Just a minute. I will send someone down." In a minute or two Jimmy showed up.

Ø Yes. How can I help?

Ø I need to leave but it seems I can't because that other door is open.

Ø Oh that is not a problem.

Jimmy inserted the key and soon the gate lifted. We made sure to make no friendly gestures. I pulled out of there as quickly as I could.

Now that I was out in the open I was a target. I looked around as I left. It was only three and I was starving. I had not realized so until now. I looked in all directions as I left. No cars were in the immediate vicinity. That is, no moving vehicles. Was I also going to be followed? Will someone crash into me? I peeled out of the area, watching for cops as I sped down the road. I decided to take a different path home. Just in case I was followed. I drove by the airport for ten minutes and then headed west on I 595. I pulled out the highway after making sure I wasn't being followed. Shit I thought could I possibly have a tracker on my car? In which case I don't need to be followed? Will G kill me and try to steal my money? Fuck, I'm thinking too much again. For the most part, I was home free. Free from doing years in jail and free, having escaped this episode unscathed.

I pulled into a fast food burger place, the ones that will kill you if you eat too many. I was hungry. I did not care. Burger here I come. If it could speak "I'm certain it would reply, "Death, here I come". Anyway the burger was satisfying. I'm sure it will send me to the rest room sooner than later. It's what happens when your body is not used to poisonous foods. You get the runs in an effort to eliminate them.

After the burger I called G and told her I was on the way home. I also called Edwin. He had not heard from Howard or about the incident. I also tried calling Howard, but there was to be no answer. If by tonight I do not hear from him then I might pay a visit to his wife. For now I just need to go home and have a drink. Perhaps a good workout followed by a good fuck. Can you say endorphins? Ah, I like it. I like it a lot.

For the next few hours I just sat in my chair and relaxed. Although I was calm I had numerous thoughts. Is Howard dead? I then thought about how Edwin had disappeared for a few days. I knew it was a matter of time before I would find out about Howard. Like myself, these guys were survivors. I'm sure he will be okay. My thoughts then shifted to the items in the curio. One would think that I would be contemplating my money. But that was not the case, for I was now in possession of what appears to be very important artifacts. It has brought to mind, things I had learned in life, and has made me consider all the lies we have been taught in school. For example, although ideas about the origin of the world abounds, we are encouraged to choose between two prevailing beliefs. One is creation. The other is the Darwinian theory of evolution. To me neither makes sense. For those who are Christians, your religion is a conglomerate of many pagan religions; mainly Mithraism.

Mithraism was a mystery religion based on the worship of the god Mithras. Mithras was born on Dec 25, from a Virgin birth. Had 12 followers, performed miracles, and rose from the dead. From Mithraism we get the wedding ring; it symbolizes the hallo, or corona of the sun. Mithraism is recognized as having pronounced astrological elements, but the details are debated. Mithraism proceeded Christianity by 1000 years; and ran side by side with Christianity for a few hundred years. Pope Leo the great in the 5th century commanded that his Christian subject stop worshiping the sun. Everything attributed to Jesus Christ was actually already in existence in the form of Mithra. Do the homework. Why is it that the Christian symbol is a fish?

Well since you asked, it's because Christianity had to do with the coming of the new era in the Zodiac, or more accurate in the Precession. Precession refers to the gradual shift in the orientation of Earth's axis of rotation, which, like a wobbling top, traces out a pair of cones joined at their apices in a cycle of approximately 26,000 years. Therefore Christianity marked the transition time between Aries, designated by the ram, and Pieces, symbolized by a fish. Incidentally the Mayan calendar accurately calculated time until 2012 and went no further, not that that was to be the end of the world, but rather the beginning of the new age; a new Zodiac sign to come. That being the age of Aquarius. It's the period we are currently in; that is, we are in transition between the two. There is no consensus on its exact beginning. There are twelve Zodiac signs in a Precession cycle.

The new cycle is represented by the number 13, and is a favorite number of the Freemason and NOW. The number denotes a rebirth or new beginning. Hence we find 13 steps in the pyramid on the US dollar. There were 13 original colonies. The eagle, if we can call it that as some claim it to be a phoenix, holds 13 arrows on the dollar. 13 illuminated stars on the Dollar, 13 stripes on our flag. Get the picture. Because of debts attributed to the Civil War, US became a creation, and a territory of the Bankers, Freemasons and the New World Order. This was a strategic move by foreign interests (international bankers) who were intent upon gaining a stranglehold on the coffers and neck of America. Congress cut a deal with the international bankers (specifically Rothschild of London) to incur a debt to said bankers. The corporation, owned by foreign interests, moved in and shoved the original Constitution into a dustbin. The US is now a corporation owned by them.

There are 2 United States, one formed in 1787, which consist of the several sovereign states of the union, and another separate and different one formed in 1871, which only controls the District of Columbia and its territories. The District of Columbia was itself the corporation, and still is today. Those territories it holds are Puerto Rico, Guam, and the Virgin Islands. The terms UNITED STATES and/or United States of America and/ or United States Government are all a private corporation, even with registered trademark. The date was February 21, 1871 and the Forty-First Congress was in session. Look up, "Acts of the Forty-First Congress," Section 34, Session III, chapters 61 and 62. On this date in the history of our nation, Congress passed an Act titled: "An Act to Provide a Government for the District of Columbia." This is also known as the "Act of 1871. The original Constitution for the United States (1788) was defaced, in effect vandalized and sabotage when the title was capitalized and the word "for" was changed to "of" in the title:

THE CONSTITUTION OF THE UNITED STATES OF AMERICA (1871) is the constitution of the INCORPORATED UNITED STATES OF AMERICA. It operates in an economic capacity and has been used to fool the People into thinking it governs the Republic. It does not! This act was unconstitutional. Little do we Americans know? I wonder if this is why I don't speak much. I'm not making this up, and, I am not picking on the Christians either. I talk more about Christianity because I know about it in depth, for I was raised in the Christian tradition.

By the same token there are numerous holes in Darwinism. For the most part, apes and primates do indeed have a different structure than humans. You will argue, Da, that's why we are different, we evolved from them. I say we did not. Apes are five times stronger than humans. Has anyone ever wondered why we have hard time digesting wheat? Why does our skin burn in the sun, unlike apes? Just as a side note. Darwin's father was a high level Freemason; as well as was many of his friends. However I could find no proof that Charles Darwin himself was one. Charles Darwin was well into eugenics and bloodline breeding. The Darwin's and Wedgwood have intermarried for several generations. That's the top Freemason way (the Rothschild's even married their sisters). Thus, Charles Darwin chose to marry his cousin, Emma Wedgwood. His grandson wrote a book, "The Next Million Years" by Darwin's grandson, Charles Galton Darwin (1887-1962) it is supposed to be a NWO blueprint. By heredity and upbringing, C G Darwin was himself a prime example of good breeding: like many of his illustrious forebears, he achieved intellectual eminence and was a striking demonstration that 'like begets like'. He was a committed eugenist, involved with the Eugenics Society for over thirty years, and served as its president for six years. So what does Darwin and his family have to do with Freemasonry? I say the theory was maliciously introduced as a cover-up. But a cover-up to what? Well it goes deeper than I will mention now. Hint; has to do with bloodlines and the gods. Connect the dots. Anyway, I'll stop here. It's not the scope of this book to discuss that in detail. Perhaps, a follow up? Maybe.

Here is something really crazy to considerer. Ancient people often spoke about Giants. We do in fact have documented and irrefutable proof of giants. We have the bones; some as tall as thirty feet. There are many. Not just one. So why is it that we believe what we believe? I'll tell you why. Simply, it's what we have been taught. We buy all the bullshit that is given to us. We are taught from an early age to get in a straight line in school, keep quiet and not to cause any trouble. Speaking of giants, which are mentioned in the bible, it also speaks of fallen angles having sex with our women. What could this mean? Look up the book of Enoch and learn something. There is one thousand times the evidence for alien intervention in our past and present than there is for any God. Actually, I know of no irrefutable evidence for the existence of God. Therefore to say there is one thousand times the evidence is misleading, for zero multiplied by one thousand still equals zero. Let me state a fact. There is no provable evidence for god, period. I think I need to define god here. If you consider god to be a living physical form or entity from the heavens above that has periodically visited us then I will buy that. When I say there is no God, I am referring to the biblical one. Could perhaps those we called god be aliens? Are we?

Never mind, I'm going to far here. The artifacts I took might be invaluable and have made me think about that I just spoke of. Have I been chosen for something?

Okay. I need to stop and call Edwin.

Ø Edwin
Ø Hola Ozzie.
Ø Edwin, let's go for a ride. I'll pick you up in an hour.
Ø OK.

Edwin did not ask any questions. G did not ask any questions either. I don't know what she was expecting, or if she was indeed expecting anything. She usually waits for me to tell her whatever it is I might want to say. G knew I had to be in court Friday and so I was doing work to help myself.

At about 7pm I arrived at Edwin's house.

Ø Hi Edwin.
Ø Hey Ozzie.
Ø Edwin how are you feeling.
Ø Man, I am feeling good. I took to many pills this morning. I felt good but I was also dazed.
Ø Yes, I would say that.
Ø You know for a second you scared the shit out of me.
Ø Oh, sorry Ozzie. I was not going to hurt you. The gun was on my side and was bothering me. So I pulled it out.
Ø Pulled it out. You fucken pointed it at me.
Ø Really, I don't remember that. I just remember you sitting me in the back of the car.
Ø Shit Edwin, You were fucked up. All you did the entire day was smile, smile and smile.
Ø For real.
Ø What, you don't remember?
Ø I remember everything except for pointing a gun at you. I have your backpacks upstairs. Do you want them now?
Ø No, after Friday. I have to make sure Jerry does not come to my house tomorrow. I might come tomorrow and pick them up and take it to storage. It all depends. I have to work around Jerry's call.
Ø Okay. So where are we going.

Ø Looking for Howard. Let's pass by his house. BTW Edwin, what was that about a crash?

Ø Jimmy put your bags in my trunk. Then he took your car. As I pulled out I noticed a car down the road do the same. It was not one of my guys. I then remembered I did not have my gun. I made a few turns on purpose to check if also would turn. The car followed me for a few blocks. It started to speed up to me and that's when the crash happened. A different car came behind it and hit it hard in the rear. I don't know what happened after that as I left. I know my guys were not involved at all.

Ø Perhaps it was Howard's guys.

Ø Howard's guy?

Ø Yes. I asked him to watch over us because I did not trust Prince. When we speak to Howard maybe he can confirm.

Ø So are we going now to Howard's house?

Ø Edwin, call your nephew. Ask if he knows about Howard.

Edwin did as I requested. As he spoke to his nephew he looked up at me. Edwin was not happy. By the looks of it, it seems Howard was dead. Fuck I thought. I told him to play it safe? What could he have done?

Ø Ozzie. Howard is in the hospital.

Ø Which one?

Ø Broward medical.

Ø Let's go. No wait. My nephew says the place is teaming with cops interviewing him. There are also news reporters around.

Ø He is not dead, right? Otherwise he would be in the morgue.

Ø No he is not dead. But the police is.

Ø The bad cop?

Ø Yes

Ø Fuck, did Howard kill him.

Ø I don't know what is going on. My nephew is not saying much. There is a cover-up I think and they are not sure how to handle it.

Ø Cover-up? How the fuck? So we don't know if Howard killed him or not?

Ø No. Is he under arrest?

Ø Not sure. All I know he is the hospital. They have been questioning him all day. Then he can't be that serious.

Ø I don't know Ozzie.

Ø Well if we go to the hospital and we can see him then he is not under arrest.

Ø Do you think we will be tied to him if we show up?

Ø Edwin, we already are tied into him. Your nephew is involved.

Ø No Ozzie. He is not involved in the shooting. He just helped expose the truth.

Ø Sure Edwin, but in uncovering the truth, we are to be found. The job we did today might not be tied to Howard, but we are, and not in a bad way. If anything, we were assisting the police in justice. Besides we were able to free their Freemason friend Balbi. I don't see a problem in showing up.

Ø Okay, fuck it. Let's go. So Ozzie, when can we take the money out?

Ø Edwin, I think we should wait a few days. The gold needs to be melted down into smaller units. That will make it untraceable. The bonds will take a few days also to get handled correctly. Prince knows how to dispose of them or rather cash them in. Monday or Tuesday we will work on that and find a way to have some cash. BTW Edwin, the bags you have at home have valuable things in them. Please make sure they are safe and do not break.

Ø Break. Is it glass?

Ø No, mostly pottery.

Ø Okay.

As I drove to the hospital I wondered about Howard. I thought about Edwin and about myself. For in a way we are all warriors and survivors. We have managed to stay alive in a tough word. We have encountered grave situations and have survived them. It's more than I can say for many people who cave in when problems arises. How many of us will be able to make it when the New World Order starts killing us in the FEMA camps. Who will survive? Fuck. Let me not start.

Two different news vans were stationed in front of the hospital, as well as two police cars. Was Howard under arrest? Shit, it's not looking good. We made our way to the third floor where Howard was. The room was secured and people were going in and out. Some were nurse and doctors. Not sure who the others were. All of a sudden Edwin calls out.

Ø Bori,

Some guys with a police badge turned and acknowledge Edwin. Edwin walked over and greeted him with a hug and a kiss. It was his nephew. Edwin introduced us and we shook hands. I thanked him for his help, without saying much else; after all, there were people walking around the corridor. A police officer stood standing outside the room we wanted to visit. It was Howard's room. Edwin's nephew escorted us pass the police officer and into the room. Jackie was sitting on the bed next to Howard. She stood up to greet Edwin and I. We both walked over and embraced her. Howard was on the bed wide awake smiling at us. A nurse was to his side taking some readings. After a minute or two she was done and departed. Edwin and I greeted Howard with a handshake. Edwin's nephew excused himself. It looks like his work was done there. He did not say if he would return. We did not ask him anything. As he walked out he closed the door behind him and we were free to talk.

- Ø Howard, how are you?

Howard grabbed his gown around the neck area and pulled it to the side exposing his chest.

- Ø Fuck Howard, that's a big black and blue. What the fuck is that.
- Ø I was shot.
- Ø Howard. That's just a black and blue. No laceration. What gives?

Howard speech was a little slurred. I'm sure he was on some medication, most probably, pain killers. Aside from that he seemed coherent and okay.

- Ø So tell me what happened.
- Ø At 12 I meet with Edwin's Nephew. The plan was to sit in front of a coffee shop in Hollywood. The cop was tipped that I was the one that broke in his house and not Edwin. Several cops were surveying the scene. I was to be approached by him and then I was to give him a video tablet with the recording I did of the break in. That video also had the recording gathered from the house where he shot Edwin. Edwin's nephew had placed a recorder on me and all he wanted was a confession. Then they were to move me out of the way; to put me out of harm's way. However, I had my own plan, as so that's why I got into trouble. After sitting at the place for about 10 minutes, a police car pulled up behind me. He exited his vehicle and approached me; I knew who he was for I instantly remembered him. The punch in the face and the beat down he gave me came to mind. I told him: "fuck you" and I gave him the finger. I then took off in my car knowing he would follow. I drove for about four blocks and then turned into a narrow street where two of my boys were stationed. As soon we drove in, a garbage truck that was already waiting for us blocked the entrance to the street. Police cars were following but could not penetrate around the truck. My guy ran out of the truck with the keys into a waiting car. They followed us for a few more blocks.

  Going on the tip you gave me, I knew the police frequency was being jammed, so there was a delay in communicating. I drove several more blocks and stopped in the middle of a parking lot. The police behind me hit my car in the rear. I slowly walked out of my car. By now he and his partner had their guns drawn on me. Both were standing behind the front open door in a crotched position. As I stood up with my hands in the air a few of my boys drove up and surrounded them.

They did not flinch. He continued pointing his gun on me the entire time. He then said, 'Today you are going to die.' I told him, "Today we are both going to die". He instructed my guys to put their guns down, but they did not listen. I was still recording audio. One of my guys had a video camera and also recorded the events. I told the cop that before he shoots me I wanted him to see something. I told him I have a video player and needed him to see it. I put one hand in my car and reached for it. I slowly pulled out a 7 inch tablet and played a clip of us breaking in his home. That was followed with another clip which was prepared by the news reporter I had contacted. It told of a corrupt cop that falsely accused innocent people of crimes. This cop would rob them and arrest them. Finally the next clip was of the shooting involving Edwin. It showed how he placed a gun in Edwin's hand. This cop knew he was in big trouble. By now his face was pale. The sirens in the background were fast approaching. I could hear many cop cars heading towards us. I don't know if the jammer worked or not. If it did, it surely gave us the brief time to get away and to expose him.

Police cars started showing up faster than I could count. All of a sudden my guys were surrounded. It was a tense moment. I had guns pointed at me. The bad cop had guns pointed at him. And my guys had guns pointed at them. I had told my guys not to shoot any cop other than the bad one if need be. I thought for sure my boys were going to kill him. Edwin's nephew had arrived at the scene. He was with some other officer. Both stood behind watching from a distance. All of a sudden a shot rang out. I ducked down as I did not have a gun. I fell to the ground and noticed a heavy pain in my chest. I thought I was going to die. I knew I had been hit. Time passed slow as I remembered saying I was going to die. But it was only seconds between that and a second shot. Two shoots, that all that was fired. I was still down on the ground in front of my car. I could not see if anyone was hurt. Everything went silence for a moment. The approaching siren was all you could here. There was not one sound within twenty feet.

I wondered what was going on but the pain in my chest prevented me from getting up. Truth is I was safer on the ground. I rolled over about three feet and was now able to see down the side of the car. On the floor was a body with blood pouring out the head. You could see a huge opening on the scull. It was clear he was dead. Part of his brain was on the ground. Blood was all over the outside door of his car. Two detectives made their way past my guys and looked over the scene. He shot himself one told the other.

A loud voice in the background commanded for every one of my guys to put their guns down and leave the area. I thought that was strange. It's as if they did not want any witness. One of my boys looked over at me and with a hand gesture asked if I wanted them to go. I nodded my head for them to do so. My guys left except for one. He was a young brave one. He came over to help me up but stopped as a police pointed a gun to his head. "Get out of here now why you still have a chance. Do not talk to the media or we will all come looking for all you guys. We have you car plates. We already know who all you are. I nodded for him to leave. I did not care if they were going to kill me. To me justice had come. This mother fucker got what he deserved. I was either a free man or a dead man. Within minutes a police helicopter appeared. Several minutes later the news media came. The police put me in the ambulance and brought me here. Edwin's nephew drove with me in the ambulance and told me what I needed to say. They are going to try to downplay this as much as possible. He assured me that I was free.

Ø So why is there a police outside?

Ø It's just a precaution. I will be home tomorrow or might be released a little later. It depends on how I feel and how my heart monitor readings go. Edwin's nephew called Jackie and told her I was here in the hospital. She has been here for most of the day. Some officer came by and told me my boys are to keep hush. If they do, they will stay out of trouble.

Ø So they are trying to do damage control?

Ø It looks that way.

Ø Are you in pain Howard?

Ø Not so much Ozzie. This does not compare to the beating handed to me by that mother fucker. I am glad that mother fucker is dead. When I am able I am going to his grave and piss on him. I will do so every year.

Ø Okay Howard. Relax. Don't get your heart rate to high or they won't let you go.

Ø That's not for them to decide. I can leave if I want to. I'm just making sure I'll be good.

Ø Well Howard. I'm glad you are OK, except of course for that bruise. BTW what were you wearing?

Ø I was given a bullet proof vest by Edwin's Nephew.

Ø Fuck Howard. To think, you could have perished today.

Ø What can I say? I'm alive. Fuck that mother fucker.

Ø Yes you are, and so are we. I don't want to say much, but things went really well today for us. We got what we were looking for and then some.

Ø Oh Ozzie. I'm glad for you. Just watch your back now.

Ø I intend to Howard. I have court Friday, I hope all goes well.

Ø I'm sure it will. Edwin's nephew mentioned he spoke to Jerry. Jerry knows that we have evidence that Balbi is innocent. You will be fine.

Ø Well Howard. I think we should get going. You need a little rest.

Ø Yes, it's been a long day, but I am still a little fired up.

Ø I will check in with you tomorrow. Do you have your phone?

Ø Yes. The police had it for a little bit but returned it to Jackie. I think it might be off.

Ø We tried to contact you and were concerned because of the news that shots had been fired. Anyway, be well Howard.

Ø Thank you Ozzie. Talk soon.

Ø Yes.

Edwin and I exchanged hugs as we left. Outside the room the police was still standing guard. No news media people were there. I don't know if they were following this story or something else. I did not care either. I wanted to go home and relax. The day was surely long. Edwin himself needed a rest. We spoke some more as I drove him home.

Once home I had a drink and sat in my couch for a little. G came over and planted a long kiss. She reached for my hand and led me to bed. She then took my shoes off and turned the TV on. What could she want? What does she know? I'm still baffled. I'm still trying to figure her out. Does she have a motive?

Thursday.

Thursday morning I woke rather early. I don't recall falling asleep or removing my cloths. Hum, what else could she have done? I felt no pain so I must be alright. Actually I felt great today. I spent most of my work day awaiting Jerry's call. The call finally came around 4.

Ø Hello

Ø Ozzie

Ø Yes, Jerry.

Ø Are you available?

Ø Well, I'm at work at the moment but if need be I will leave.

Ø No, not necessary. What time do you get off?

Ø I close at about 6:30.

Ø I am sending someone to meet with you. This person is with a special agency. Do not be afraid of him. He will ask you some questions and will also ask for your cooperation in a matter of interest. If you choose to cooperate with him then I will be in court with you tomorrow and will make sure you are freed. If you choose not to then you will have to see what the judge is going to decide. Is that clear?

Ø Yes, Jerry. But I think it might be somewhat unfair.

Ø Ozzie, do not say anything at this time. Wait for him and he will explain. He might be accompanied. You have some information he needs, which you are not aware of. They will be in contact with me tonight. Do as they say. I will see you in court tomorrow.

Ø Okay Jerry. BTW, any info on the man that owned the container.

Ø He is in custody. I cannot talk about that at this time.

How strange. What do I know or have that they need from me? What is going on? I wondered if Jerry knew or knows about the items that were missing. Was this man coming for it? Was I expected to turn in Edwin and Prince? For the next two hours or so I thought about endless possibilities and raised numerous questions. I guess I just needed to hear what he or they had to say and wanted. At 6 I told Eddie to leave. I told him I would lock up. By then Yesid had left. Eddie waited about 15 minutes after 6 then took off. The place was mine now to talk freely with my visitor. At 6:30 as promised a black unmarked police car pulled in. There was someone else with the driver. Both men exited the car and looked around as if they might have been followed. Oh shit! I said. Not a good sign. These guys have come to kill me. Maybe they were part of the Illuminati or elite banker team; maybe they would avenge the robbery. There was no place to hide within the office. It was pointless, besides Jerry said not to be afraid.

I greeted them at the door and invited them in. Both men were tall and lean. There was something strange about their appearance. I could not place it. For starter both seemed to be redbone. That is a biracial person consisting of a black and white parent, nothing odd in that off itself; for its rater common in today's world. I think it was more the color of the skin. I was good at guessing where people where from, but these two guys were clearly different, perhaps a burn victim with pink pale skin. They were not albinos for there was pigment in the hair and eyebrows. One of the two had bright blue piercing eyes. Almost like aqua color, but leaning more toward the blue. I've seen these eyes before on someone else. I have to say I was captured by them. Not by the man himself but by the pupil. It seemed to oscillate between round and vertical to some degree. Some strange deformity I thought, but then what about his partner? He also had a similar characteristic. Could they be brothers? I was not sure. Both wore a black suit as if going to a funeral. Mine perhaps? Where they the angle of death or the devil of life. Huh. Never mind.

Ø Hello gentleman, I am Ozzie.

Ø Yes Ozzie we know who you are. We need to talk to you about a few things. Are we alone?

Ø Yes we are. We shan't be bothered. It's safe to talk here. Jerry mentioned you would be coming to visit me. So officers, what can I do for you?

Ø Ozzie. You have been recommended to us.

Ø For?

Ø More important is by whom. We will get to the "for" later. The person that recommended you is Edwin.

Ø Edwin?

Ø Yes Edwin? We are brothers of the same fraternity.

Ø Do you mean Freemasons?

Ø Yes. That's right. He did say you were very smart and had a heighten awareness of people's feelings and intentions. You did something yesterday that has been brought to our attention. It is why we are here. Edwin has chosen you to work with us in this matter. To learn and be a part of us if you so desire. Edwin has a great deal of knowledge of what goes on in the world and how the world really works. But there are far greater things he does not know. Things that are only revealed to very few people. However to receive this knowledge there are things that will be asked of you to prove your worthiness and your commitment to us. How far you go, how much you learn will be up to you.

Ø Guys, I think I need to sit for a moment.

Ø Yes, let's have a seat. Ozzie, we know all about the container you were in yesterday. We know how you got in. We know who you were with. We are here requesting something. You have the option of refusal. However it might result in your death. Others will surely come looking for it. For you have disturbed many from the underground and many from far away. If you choose to cooperate you will be protected. You will learn of those things you have been seeking answers to. You will be illuminated.

Ø Is that a reference to the Illuminati?

Ø Perhaps. Maybe even deeper. Again it's up to you.

Ø What is it that you require of me?

Ø There were two Sumerian sculptures in the container. Sculptures that are not of this world. Both have opposite and equal powers. While in the presence of each other, there forces are in balanced and equilibrium. Hence they cancel each other and thus remain dormant. You managed to separate those sculptures. One is sitting in the Broward county evidence department, and the other is in your possession. There can be grave worldwide consequences because of this. Not just within this world but also abroad. The man that held on to these sculptures was aware of its powers. He was a man of knowledge. That power has now shifted. The bearer of the sculptures will also have good fortune and wealth. Because it is you that has separated them, it is you that needs to join them. Our request is for to hand over the sculpture you have, or prove your worthiness and commitment to us by retrieving the one in the evidence department and joining both together in a ritual. You must give your decision tomorrow to Jerry in court. The judge will hear you in a separate chamber. She is a member of the Easter Star. She will do as Jerry says, for Jerry is also a Freemason. If you choose to join the sculptures together you will have the option of placing them where ever you choose. Keep in mind that those two sculptures when combined with other artifacts you left behind, contain the hidden origin of humans. You have a few clay tablets that give the Sumerian account of Adam and Eve. That explanation and knowledge will be further reviled to you. Please be sure to safeguard them.

Ø Gentlemen. Can you guarantee that I will live if I agree to your request?

Ø Yes. You will have immense, knowledge and understanding of the world and of mankind, as well as a deep understanding of creatures that are not of this world.

Ø Okay gentlemen I will report to Jerry tomorrow that I will assist and do anything necessary to fix that which I have disturbed.

Ø Thank you. Please remember that you are bound to your word by death. You will have your freedom tomorrow if you agree. However if you go back on your word, death will come to you and all those you love. We will never speak of this day again. As of tomorrow we will only be concerned about the future and not about your past actions. Learning about your future requires learning about your human origin, whatever that may be. That is a gift I promise you will have. You are never to speak to anyone about what was spoken of today. There is no second chance if you err. You will be picked up next week and will begin an initiation ritual for the joining of the sculptures and for the knowledge you will uncover.

Ø Okay. I fully understand. Again, it's a little hard to believe, but I do understand, as well will I comply.

With that both men stood up. What happened next is something I will never mention for fear of being called a lunatic. Surely people will think that I made this up and no one will ever believe. One of the two looked at me, his pupil close completely for a second. They closed vertically as that of a cat and then opened to a round position. I was mesmerized by them. I had not noticed that he had shrunk down to just under my height and now was looking up at me. I realized where I had seen those eyes before. There was no mistaking it. Those are the same eyes Jerry has. There are in fact Jerry's eyes. Is this Jerry himself? Within a second the pupils closed again in the same vertical position and he now stood tall looking down at me. I was frozen. This was no normal mortal. I don't know who or what I was looking at. All I am sure of is that some transformation took place right before me. As if he was telling me or showing me something. They say actions speak louder than words: and so that was his intention. To show me by action that his words were real. That he was real. I am not crazy. I did not have any medication, drugs, drinks, or hallucinogens. This person or thing in front of me cannot be human. Both men walked away without looking back or saying goodbye. They had spoken, I heard them clearly.

For the next half hour I just sat at my desk. I knew what had happened. I knew I witness something extraordinary. Reality started hitting me, and a new reality has struck. Through Edwin I started doing research. I uncovered many things that were always there but yet chose to ignore, both out of ignorance and disbelief. My quest for knowledge and truth has brought me here. How much will I uncover? How much will I learn? Question is do I want to uncover the truth? The answer is indubitably yes. There is no second guessing myself. I want to know as much as I can. This is my destiny. I now know it. Edwin, Howard, Prince, as well as everyone and everything that has brought me to this point is all part of me getting there.

That evening I skipped the gym. I went home and sat in my couch. G looked several times at me and asked if I was okay. Does she play a role in any of this? Would I dare to mention what I witness? Well, I was instructed not to. So that's moot. Besides she would not believe me. No one would. So, here I sit, allowing time to pass so to absorb it all. Life has forever changed for me. I was too busy blaming the New World Order, the elite bankers, and the Illuminati for things that are happening in this world. Today, I have reason to believe that there are stronger forces and beings that might be the cause of our problems. It's premature to start postulating. As of now I only have a glimpse. For Edwin has helped to open my eye. Today I start to open the other. Will I see the future? Will I see with my pineal eye? Will I see the past?

50 SENTENCING

The day has finally arrived. This morning my alarm went off at 7. I had a tough time getting up as my thoughts last night consumed me; So much so that it was about 3am when I finally succumbed. I thought about today despite not begin afraid. More than anything I was fascinated and mesmerized by what I saw. By the two men, if you can call them that, who visited me. Edwin was right. Edwin was always right. I do have a heighten awareness of people and of their disposition, intention, demeanor, honesty and fallaciousness. I am able to pick up vibes that might or might not be obvious to others. I know what I witness yesterday. There is no mistaking it. Those guys were not your average human being. I can't place it yet. I can't place them, that is, who they are or where they are from. Something has brought me here; to this here and now. Could this be what Howard referred to when he said my destiny is still unfolding. I would certainly say so. I have much more unanswered questions now than ever before. It seems the more I learn, the more I am aware of how much I don't know. And to think, I am in tune with myself and others. At least I perceive myself to be. Blissful are those who are ignorant. The saying is true. No need for cliché.

G awoke with me and we showered together. No time for playing this morning. The last thing I needed was to be late. Although the courthouse is only 15 minutes away, I needed to provide ample time for parking and the security check point. 8:30 is the time the lawyer told me to be there. I thought it a bit early, but then I am at the mercy of others. G and I made our way to the third floor courtroom. Once there we quietly sat. From our seats we had a good vantage position to the prisoners. All had their hands shackled to their waist.

I remembered being there numerous times. It's very easy to look at these people sitting there and dismiss them as bad evil people. I have to say that I know for certain that among them one is innocent. The biggest crime is being poor and not having bail money and or a good attorney. Not to say that the court itself doesn't have them, that is good attorneys. On the contrary, the court has excellent lawyers that later move on to the private sector. Problem is these lawyers are over burden with cases. Anyway my eyes took to one Spanish guy. He was in the mid 40s. For about a year and a half he has been in the Broward jail awaiting trial I guess. I remembered talking with him once or twice when I was in. He was quivering; the freezing waiting area as well as courtroom temperature giving him the chills. G leaned over and asked if I saw my attorney. That quickly shifted the focus on me. No, I replied. It was still early and many lawyers and the judge herself were not present. I sent Jerry a text letting him know, I was in court and willing to cooperate with the men who visited me. "Will be there soon" was his response.

I sat quietly but not nervously, true to my natural way of being. I was cool, calm and collected. I actually felt worse for the freezing prisoners than for myself. Actually, I did not even feel bad for myself. You see, being there was just a part of my journey through life. An experience that helps complete me till the day I die. It is all a part of me. It's part of my journey. I always say it's not the destination but rather the journey that matters. It's living in the moment. It's living. Living in a world we know very little off; a world full of corporate lies and deceit. Being in this predicament has brought me knew knowledge, and with knowledge comes power. For knowledge is powerful. There is something out there in this world I have no knowledge of but suspect does exit. I'm not talking about a God, or spirits. I'm talking about a something that is on this world but not of this world. Or perhaps that which we consider to be aliens have always been here and never left. Anyway, whatever it is I am not privy to. But I can feel it. I saw a glimpse yesterday, and I want to see more. Where will that take me, I don't know. Where ever it does take me, I am going.

"All rise, this court is now in session" that was the bailiff's intro to the judge. She took a quick glance around the court room before she sat. She acknowledges the lawyers and clerks. One by one, cases were called, some lasting only minutes, either for an adjournment or a set-off. Others took several minutes as they were mostly pleadings, and not actual trials. My lawyer came in about 8:45. She made her way to the states desk and then looked around. She glanced at and acknowledged me. Several minutes later she pulled me outside the room and said the judge will be ready for us at about 11. I was to be sentenced behind closed doors. Those door being a smaller room adjacent to the main courtroom. All I could do was wait. G and I decided to visit the cafeteria; a coffee and something light. We killed about an hour there and then made our way back to the courtroom, with about 15 minutes to spare. G and I sat in the same spot. By now most of the prisoners were already gone and thus the seats vacant. Jerry had not arrived yet; still I was not concerned. For I have made a pact for my freedom; a pact with whom? Two men who were not human? Perhaps one was Jerry himself. Was it the devil himself?

At 10 minutes to 11, the bailiff called over to me and asked me to follow him. G was allowed to join me. He escorted us along the side of the courtroom into a smaller area. My lawyer followed. Several minutes later Jerry made his way in the room followed by the prosecutor. The moment has arrived. I was asked to sit at a desk alongside my Lawyer. The prosecutor sat at a desk several feet away; both being equidistant to the judge. G was told to sit in the back. Jerry made his way to me and shook my hand. I stared into his blue eyes. Other than the color I could find nothing out of the ordinary.

Ø Jerry. I agreed to work with the men that visited me.

Ø Yes, I am aware. You are not to mention them ever again. Neither to me nor anyone else. Do not mention anything about sculptures. As far as Wednesday was concerned, you called for your box and a different one came. You looked inside an immediately called me when you saw the human remains. You will get credit for that. I will be explaining to the judge why you should be freed. The prosecutor has already made that recommendation. Answer any questions the judge might ask you keeping in mind what you and I discussed. Don't say anything more than you have to.

Ø Got it Jerry.

For the minute or two Jerry spoke to me I continued looking into his eyes. I was looking for something. If Jerry was hiding something, it did not betray him. Oh well. Maybe I'm thinking too much. Was I? I found myself second guessing. Something was amidst. I fucken know it. Not anything bad or evil, just different. Right at 11 a side door opened. It was the judge. She had access through her own chamber. She acknowledged my presence and we all stood. She then sat to look over some documents. We mimicked her and also sat. After reading some formalities to me she asked if I understood, to which I replied yes.

Ø In the matter pertaining to Ozzie Vargas the state finds that it is satisfied with the cooperation Mr. Vargas has rendered and assisted in. Further a recommendation of time served as well as one year probation is to be administered. However it is up to the judge to administer the sentencing. Before I do so is there anything anyone would like to say.

Jerry spoke on my behalf and expressed he was satisfied with the work and assistance I had furnished. Jerry told of the cases I had assisted in and of how I gave testimony on a different case regarding two Cousins that had committed an armed robbery. The judge for some reason argued that five cases were not what she considered substantial assistance. Holy cow! Is she going to throw the book at me? I thought things were already arranged. Did I mix up the signs?

Ø Mr. Vargas is there anything you would like to say on your behalf?

Ø No Judge.

Ø I am curious Mr. Vargas as to why you decided to buy a half a kilo of cocaine with intent to sell.

I now found myself backed into a corner. Was all this necessary? Have I not a deal with Jerry and those other men. They said I would be protected, so what was it they meant? All of a sudden I found myself with the possibility of doing a long time. I thought about Abby and my children, especially Ozzie. I know why I did what I did. But I did not want to reveal it. I did not want to cry, especially in front of an audience.

Ø No judge. I have nothing to say.

Jerry asked for a moment and pulled me aside as if he were my lawyer.

Ø Ozzie. Do as I say. There is something more important that awaits you. You need to speak up and get the judge emotionally involved. The state and I have an agreement, but it has to be approved by the judge. This is not the time to be quiet. Say your piece now; else men will come looking for you.

I looked at Jerry as I tried to contain myself. I knew what was coming. I turned to the judge and exclaimed,

Ø Judge, I would like to say something.

Ø Go on Mr. Vargas. I looked straight at the judge. Our eyes locked on each other. I grinned as if to bite my tongue. For about a minute I just stood there looking at her. I wanted to say something but no words came out.

Ø Mr. Vargas, are you okay, do you need a moment.

My eyes were watery, although the tears did not come. A good job I did of containing them. I took a deep breath and started.

Ø Judge, I was the second born son to my parents. As a child I was very attached to my loving dad. He was deaf and quiet for the most part. By quiet I mean reserved. Somewhat like me. My father was a good man, a good human and a great dad. Although he could hear me and though he did not say much, there was a great deal of love between us. Words needed not be spoken. Being in his presence was all I needed to feel safe, happy and loved. My mother however was a nightmare. All I remember as a child was constantly being hit and punished. When I say hit what I really mean are extreme beatings involving whips, belt, electrical extension cords, sticks and the like. Weapons that left wilts and bruises on the body. She vented her anger and disdain for us. We were the recipients of her hatred. One which she displayed with a vengeance. Not once did my mother ever say the words, "I love you". It's as if it was impossible for her. I don't know what happened in her life that has created such a person. When I was about 8 my parents divorced. For the first time in my life I was removed from the only person I loved, and from the only person that loved me. I was in NY and he left to Puerto Rico. We were told that he was on business, instead of being told the truth. It was harder seeing my mother go on dates under this condition. Life went on and I grew up not knowing what it was like to be loved by a woman. My aunt Sheila filled that void a little but I don't know if it's the same or not. As a teenager I was stoic, and non empathetic. My brother

Ismael always told me I had a heart of stone. No emotions of the heart. I made the best of things for myself and at the age of 16 decided to emancipate myself. That I did. I rented a studio apartment with my brother Ismael for $50, per week. My mother always told the excuse that I left because I did not want to wash dishes. How foolish for people to believe such. Truth is, she and my step dad were always fighting because of us, and so I convinced my brother that it was best for all of us to separate. I think that might have saved their marriage. The only good thing I can say about my mother was that she always feed me, even after we left the house.

Somewhere about the time before we emancipated, my brother introduced me to some girls that lived in our neighborhood. That is when something happened to me that I had never experienced before. In retrospect I knew what it was but at the time I did not know what I was feeling. How could I? I never knew what love was. I befriended this girl and never really made an advance on her. How could I? How could I take a chance at loosing something that was magical? Her presence was enough for me. There was something there. As it was with my dad, it was with her. No words needed to be spoken. Two or three years later she took to a different country, to study abroad. I was now removed again from someone I loved. I was a very sexually active young man in my days. Women were no more than sexual outlets, to play with, to enjoy time with, but not to love. No, no, my brother was right; I had a heart of stone. It was closed off to everyone.

At about the age of 24 I married and had a daughter. It was the best day of my life and I still remember it clearly. Love finally succumbed to me. Jenelle was the love of my life, my girl, my daughter. The following year was followed with the second most important day of my life. Ozzie was born. By then I had a beautiful family, a business and a three story house in New York. But it was not to last. Two years later their mother, Maria, and I separated. For the third time in my life I was removed from the only peopled I loved. Not the mother but my children. Maria gave me an extremely hard time over visitation; many a times she would deny them their right to visit their dad, and I hated her for that. To this day it has affected Jenelle. When my daughter Abby was born I was afraid to carry her. I felt guilty for not being around Jenelle and Ozzie. I was afraid to open my heart to anyone again, but Abby's smiles prevailed. I also had a wonderful son in New York, Christian whom I did not see much.

For a number of years I was a happy man. That was until September 9, 2006.

For about the next minute I said nothing. I was frozen. I did not want to cry. The judge never took her eyes off me. She knew I was in distress. A tear finally came and I could not move. Not even to wipe it from my cheek. The judge asked the bailiff to get me some water. But I could not drink. I did not want to continue. I did not want to cry.

Ø Judge, I need help.

Ø What kind of help do you need?

Ø Since that day, September 9, 2006 I have been living with pain and guilt. I don't know how to shake off a demon that follows me around for what I did. I need someone or some help so that I may overcome this. I have been living in darkness for years.

Ø What is it that you did Mr. Vargas?

Ø I killed my son Ozzie.

I sat down for a minute, reliving the events of his death. Because I needed help I tried to contain myself so that maybe I could get that help. I needed to go on. But for another minute just sat. Time was passing slowly and I wanted to die. I wanted to relief myself of the guilt I carried. I looked at the bailiff for a second. I looked at his gun and he took notice.

Ø Mr. Vargas. I can see you are in pain. I need to know how you killed your son.

At this point my lawyer leaned into me and said I need to be very careful of what I said, as I could be prosecuted for murder. Without thinking I pulled my arm up and slowly moved her away. Again I made eye contact with the judge. There was not a sound to be heard in the court room. I somehow needed to continue.

Ø Judge, my son was a wonderful young man. He was tall and good looking. A leader and class valedictorian. School was about to end for the summer. On September 9, 2006, he went on a religious retreat with his mom and other family members. The place had a camp ground with a zip line ride over a lake. Ozzie decided to go on the ride and so was given a harness. The attendee improperly strapped him and upon take-off he fell 49 feet on to a gravel pavement. His cousin said he tried to get up but could not. His fingers were broken and facing backwards. He had a broken leg through which you could see the bone. His ribs punctured an organ and he also had a fracture on his skull. His mother was summoned to his side. As he spoke blood poured out his mouth. He knew he was dying. One of his last words were," Mom save me, I don't want to die." He was pronounced dead at the hospital.

Ø Mr. Vargas, were you there?

Ø No judge.

Ø Then how is it that you say you killed him?

For about another minute I paused. I was not hysterical. I was kind of quiet, tears flowing slowly. My breath was deep. The judge by now also had watery eyes.

Ø Judge. It's my fault he is dead. I was not around to protect him. To keep him out of danger. If I would have never divorced his mother, things would have been different. Circumstance would have been different. He would have been somewhere else. I was weak when I was young. I had an affair. It's my entire fault. No one else is to blame. I carry this guilt everywhere I go. For the next few years all I could see was a dark cloud. Even on the sunniest days. I was a walking zombie. I would look at street poles and determine its height. Then I would imagine Ozzie falling from it. Once I almost jumped out of my second floor window. Not so much so because I wanted to die, but because I could not stop thinking about 49 feet. Everywhere I looked, everywhere I turned, and all I saw was a pole 49 feet tall. I could not escape it. I cried for years.

After a few years, I was at home resting. It was a Saturday. The mail came in and Nancy my wife said I had a letter. It was from a Jackie. I asked her to open and read it to me. The only thing it said was, "Hello Ozzie. This is Jackie, your longtime friend from the Bronx. I'm sorry about the loss of your son. If you need to reach out you can call me at Jackson Memorial Hospital."

I knew who it was. It was her, (the girl). The only girl I had ever loved when I was young. Surely I loved my wife Nancy, but Jackie, the girl was my first true and only love. It was a magical friendship I could never explain. All the years I never mentioned Jackie to Nancy. But she knew she opened that letter. There was no indication of the sort in the note that revealed our friendship. But Nancy knew. She commented "Ozzie, please don't go there". I explained who Jackie was. Because we were both married at the time, Jackie and I decided that the only way to be friends was to introduce each other's family; and that we did. Several months later we both asked for a divorce as it seemed we were destined for it anyway.

Jackie and I dated thereafter and I felt alive again. I was no longer haunted by my demon. Yes I still cried every so often, but further apart in between. I was now able to see the sun. Life was good again. Two years later the award money I had received as a settlement started to dry. Purposely I blew through the money trying to get away. Truth is I wanted no part of it, the money that is. It was blood money. How could I live with that? As soon as the funds started to dry so did my relationship with Jackie. I took to the road and started doing road tent sales in different states. That's when I met Dustin. He offered to go into business with me in Miami, not a drug business. I thought this was a good way to win my girl back, "the girl". But again, it was not meant to be. Dustin had asked a favor of me. At first I said I could not help. After A month he asked again and so I contacted someone I thought might be able to help. It was an older man I had known for a few years. At first he also said no.

One month later he called me and asked if I still wanted help. I said I needed to make a phone call as that which was requested was for someone else. With that Dustin handed me some money so that I could get what he wanted. I had not given the negative consequences of my actions much thought. I was not aware of the severe penalty. Had I, I would not have proceeded. Anyway I meet with some guy my friend introduced me to. He wanted me to purchase an amount larger than I wanted. One half a kilo was the agreement I followed through the deal all along thinking I would get my girl back. As soon as I exited his vehicle I was confronted with people screaming at me. It was chaos. At least that's how I perceived it. All I noticed was a woman in black pointing a gun at me. I clearly noticed her finger on the trigger. Once on the ground I realized my life had change forever. I disgraced myself and my family. People I had known all my life would now turn their back to me. Even the girl; Jackie, turned her back on me, telling my brother I was never to talk to her again. I went down the wrong path. It seems that with her I was chasing waterfalls.

Today I stand in front of you in shame and disgrace. However I still have a much bigger problem. Bigger than any punishment you could hand me. I am still to blame for the death of my son. That, it seems, will never go away. That demon is a part of my life. I don't know how to shake him off. It's hard living life this way. I started to write a book in jail to help me keep my mind busy. I could not sleep. My demon was loyal and visited often. I don't know if writing was therapeutic or an escape from my demon. Whatever sentence you hand me will never be greater than the burden I carry.

My tears had subsided by then. It appears I had given them to the judge. I looked around the room. My lawyer also shed a tear or two. Jerry who had been by my side the entire time was quiet. He made eye contact and nodded in acknowledgement. There was something strange about how he looked at me. I was not sure if I was seeing things. He had the same eyes I saw in the man that visited me a day or two ago. I was confused. Who had whose eyes? For a split second, his eyes changed. The pupil, I thought closed vertically. I cleared my eyes and took a second look. They now were normal. WTF?

The judge said she needed some time and asked the prosecutor, Jerry and my lawyer to meet with her. 15 minutes later she came back with her decision.

- Mr. Vargas. It is the courts desire to issue you one year probation. As well you are to report to a grief doctor that will be paid for by the state. It has been brought to my attention that you have agreed to help out Jerry in a matter not to be mentioned. Please report to him instead of your probation officer. We are deviating a little here from regular protocol. Are you in agreement with this Mr. Vargas?
- Yes Judge.

With that I felt a sigh of relief. A grief doctor. Maybe he will help relive me of my demon. I looked back at G. She too had a tear in her eye. I stared at her. She at me. It was a moment. Something deep just transpired. I could not figure it out but it felt special.

Half an hour later, I was walking as a free man towards my car. Probation I said. Not bad. I should be able to stay out. It was a happy moment.

Later that evening I frequented the gym as usual, more positive energy. Yea, that's what I needed. While there a call came in.

- Ø Hello Ozzie.
- Ø Hey Prince.
- Ø So what's the word?
- Ø It's all good. One year probation.
- Ø Is that all?
- Ø That's it.
- Ø Damn Ozzie, that's good news.
- Ø Yes it's good. Turned out well.
- Ø Ozzie, tomorrow night I am meeting in Miami with a friend. Come with and celebrate.
- Ø Sounds like a good plan to me. We will confirm a little on in the day.
- Ø Great. Make sure you go Ozzie. I have someone I like to meet.
- Ø Should I bring G.?
- Ø Na, don't bring sand to the beach.
- Ø Prince, I'm not looking to meet anyone.
- Ø It's a friend of mine. Just go. You will have a good time.
- Ø Okay, I'll be there.

51 A NEW BEGINING

Saturday I set out for work. One would think that I would want to celebrate and perhaps take a few days off. Well my celebration will come at night. I was sitting with a security box with over two million dollars. Why go to work? Well to throw off the police in the event I would be a suspect in the robbery. Although I don't know what difference it would make as those two men who visited me as well as Jerry knew about it. So have I escaped that crime? Not sure. Only the future will tell. Maybe it's just because of my working habit that I was to go to work. No matter. In a few weeks I will go to Puerto Rico with Edwin and follow up on some of his stories. It seems I am fascinated and captivated by them. I do need permission from Jerry, my probation office to go. Why this deviation in probation? I don't know what the protocol is. It seems there are more people involved in this than I am aware off. Those ancient statues and artifacts must also have something to do with this deviation. Am I holding on to more power than I am aware of? What might happen if I join the two statues and hold on to them? Will I have magical powers, like the owner of building 7 of the world trade center: On his wish, the building came down. Might I be illuminated? Will I learn of things that I don't know existed? Who knows? All I can say is that I am on a new journey; a new destination perhaps, a quest for knowledge. Not the so called knowledge told and fed to us by the government, but instead knowledge based on actual truths and facts. This is my new adventure, my new mission. One I am excited to begin soon.

That evening I set out to meet with Prince in Miami. Mary Brickell Village was the destination. There are several eateries as well as clubs. The area is well lit with an evening population that is greater than that found during the day. As the sun sets it comes alive. There you will find music playing outside a coffee house. Across the street, the noise of numerous people conversing as they sit down on the street tables of a Mexican Restaurant; a popular club to be found on the upstairs level. I arrived about 9 and handed the keys to the valet. I then found a table at the sidewalk of the restaurant. Prince called and said he would be there in 15 minutes. I sipped my drink and did some people watching. Beautiful looking people abound. Most of who happened to be physically fit. Prince arrived and was accompanied by a male. As they walked over to me I thought the face familiar. Prince as always was well dressed. As they were about 10 feet away I recognized the man. It was one I initially feared while in jail.

- Ø Monsalvo?
- Ø Horsey.
- Ø Hey how are you. What a surprise. What the hell are you doing with Prince?
- Ø We've kept in touch. Out to celebrate today. I heard you got probation. Good for you.

Monsalvo was the Colombian thug that was placed in my room at Paul Ryan detention. He is the gentleman I thought was there to harm me, instead I misjudged him. That's not like me to do; misjudging someone. Anyway, I gave him a good look over and figured since he was a friend of Prince he was alright. We all shook hands and he and I made small talk as Prince ordered a drink. For the next thirty minutes we enjoyed the atmosphere and drinks. Prince did not mention anything, nor did I about our past adventure at The Vault. A call came to him; it was his friend who I was too meet.

- Ø Ozzie, in about 10 minutes lets head out to a place right around the corner. We will meet up with a friend or two and then hit a club on the beach.
- Ø Ok.

I was game. However I wished my friend G was with me. I did not second guess Prince. As far as I was concerned my troubles were behind and a new page in life was turning. Prince described the place we were headed too. I knew of it as I used to frequent the area prior to getting into trouble. Prince paid the tab in cash and we heading out. We were already on the sidewalk near the corner; all we really needed to do was walk about half a city block around the corner to the destination. As I hit the corner I received a phone call. I noticed the number and thought how strange. What the hell would he want at this time?

- Ø Hello
- Ø Hello Ozzie
- Ø Hi Jerry. Isn't it too soon to report to you?
- Ø Ozzie, I need your help with something urgent.
- Ø Yes Jerry, what would that be?
- Ø Listen Ozzie, I know it's late, but I have been trying to track down Prince all day.
- Ø Jerry, I'm with him now.
- Ø Does he know you are talking to me?
- Ø No Jerry.
- Ø Listen do not say a word. This is a very serious matter. I need to know where you are at, but you need to make sure he is not aware of this conversation.
- Ø You know Jerry I have placed a tracker in his vehicle. I can tell you how to access it.

Ø Ozzie I need to know your exact location.

As Jerry spoke to me Prince looked around. He glanced at me and I signal for them to continue on as I would only be a minute. Monsalvo was near him and seemed not to have a care in the world about anything. They made their way towards me and I told them to go ahead as I would walk behind them. I told Jerry were we were and where we were going.

Ø Ozzie, I have been looking for Prince since this morning. He is wanted for murder.

Ø Jerry, tell me this is a joke.

Ø Ozzie, this is no joke. We received a call from the state for his arrest. He paid someone ten thousand dollars several weeks ago to dispose of his female friend and his wife. That man is already in custody and cooperating with us.

Ø Shit Jerry. What shall I do?

Ø Don't do anything. I am going to make a call to Miami and have him detained for us.

Jerry spoke some more and gave me instructions not to leave the area as that would tip Prince off. It was to be only a matter of minutes before the police would come. Jerry put me on hold as he placed a call. I continued to follow Prince by about 30 feet. He looked back to make sure I was behind him. He did not seem to be concerned at all about my call. I guess he had no idea of what was going on. About 400 feet down the block two gentleman approached. I tried to keep my distance as I figured they were going to make an arrest. These two guys were short in stature and did not fill the bill of a police. That's because they weren't. Both Prince and Monsalvo greeted them with a hand shake. Surely these were the guys I was to meet. Prince waved for me to speed up. The entire time I had the phone to my ear awaiting instruction from Jerry. I walked over to them so as not to be rude; the intension being to say hi and then fall back a little. By the time I realized who they were we were all at arm's length. I did not reach out my hand. I was startled. Now I was petrified. One of the two Spanish looking guys had a big scar on the forehead. It was unmistakable. I was looking at the Cuban cousins.

There was no time to think. No time to react. Surely I could have outrun them, but I now found myself surrounded by all. I looked at Prince and said you mother fucker. By the time I turned back to the scarred man, it was too late for me. The gun he had pointed at me fired. It made its mark. Before I could hit the ground I was shot again. I did not know where. All I could hear were police sirens. Where they the men Jerry called to apprehend Prince? No matter, I felt no pain. I knew I was on the ground in a pile of blood. I found myself gasping for air. Is this what Ozzie felt? I just laid there paralyzed, not being able to feel my body. I was not dead, but I knew I was dying. As I opened my eyes I could see a bright light shining. Was it a flashlight? The light got a little brighter. I did not know where I was or where I was going. I was confused. The light faded and I could hear voices. I was being carried away. But to where? I had no clue. Several times the light would approach me followed by a sudden jerk. What are they doing to me? Why don't they just leave me alone? It's been a long day. I think I need to relax and sleep. But how can I? I am not home. Where is G? These people keep waking me. How rude of them. I want to sleep. I want to walk over and explore the light. And so I said fuck it. I'm going over to it. I need to know what is there. Could this have anything to do with the two men that visited me a few days ago?

- Ø Hello dad.
- Ø Hi Ozzie. I missed you and came over to join you.

Ozzie was accompanied by other people I had known from the past, but have not seen in a long time. I smiled as I walked by them, as I wanted to great Ozzie first. He reached his arms out to me and gave me a hug. For a long minute I embraced him. No words were spoken. I just held on not wanting to let go. I was not going to let go of my son again.

- Ø Dad
- Ø Yes Ozzie.
- Ø Let go. You need to let go.

I released Ozzie from my firm grip and smiled. I was not sure where I was, but it was peaceful. The atmosphere was quiet and people could not be heard. That is except for Ozzie.

- Ø So dad, it's been a few years. You look good.
- Ø You have not changed one bit Ozzie. You look just the same as I last saw you.
- Ø Dad. I have been watching you from afar. I have seen your pain and suffering. I want you to know that what happened to me is not your fault. The same was going to happen even if you were with me all along. It was my destiny dad. There was no changing it. Maybe I would have left in a different manor. Who know dad? I know you love me and I know you have always done so. I am supposed to be here. But not you dad. This is only a visit to let you know that your actions are forgiven, whatever you feel those actions might be. You need to go back and live life. A happy one. I am fine here and I like it here.
- Ø Ozzie, I don't want to go back.
- Ø Dad, you have to. Listen dad, someone is calling you. Listen.

I did as he said. There was a faint voice calling me. I did not want to pay attention. I did not want to answer.

- Ø Dad, listen again. You are not supposed to stay here. Listen to the call. Listen to me. Go back and live. You are forgiven. Now go back and forgive yourself. Your friend that has been following will do so no more.
- Ø But Ozzie,
- Ø No dad. You must hurry. You don't have much time. You will be stuck if you don't leave now. Listen to Abby's call. She needs you dad, more than I do.

From a distance I could hear Abby calling. I knew she was in distress, but I did not want to abandon Ozzie again. Suddenly I found myself in the center of a tunnel, being able to see only in one direction. Everything around me was twirling. That is, the circular walls if you can call it that. Were they walls? I have no way of knowing, for once again the only direction to see, the only direction to go was ahead. But where was ahead; for I found myself looking forward. Forward was not only ahead it was also up. My neck was tilted slightly upwards; not completely up. I was not walking a steep angle. For that matter I was not even walking. So what was going on? How was I moving ahead? Looking back was not an option. Let alone turning around. Where am I? Who am I? I was being lead; for I did not move of my own free will. I did not make that decision to move forwards through the twirling circular walls. I was just moving. Looking ahead I cannot see my legs as that would force me to look down. Where was down? For I was not standing on solid ground. I did not feel heavy. All I could do was continue ahead. There was nothing to think about except to continue moving through the tunnel I know found myself in. There were people waiting for me at its end. At least that is the feeling I was getting. I can't see anything except a long narrow path. Nothing to suggest there are others at its end. However I know what waits. I know there will be people there, but I can't make out whom. Am I dead? Am I alive, or is this simply my consciousness leaving my physical body and traveling somewhere? Am I actually moving ahead through the tunnel or am I still, and the tunnel is moving away behind me as its entrance moves towards me? There are not only people at the end, but also answers. Perhaps enlightenment. Will Jerry's friends dressed in black be there? Have they sent me on a new journey? Are they trying to show me something? One thing I can say is that despite not knowing where I am going, I am not afraid. Who waits for me at the other side? Is it Ozzie again? Is it Abby? It's not death, for where I am now, death does not exist. I was promised knowledge and immortality by the two guys in black that visited me. Could that be where I am going? Could they have lied? Is it the powers of the statues they spoke of which is now guiding me forwards? What about Edwin. Where is he? I was to go on a fact finding trip to Puerto Rico with him. Wow. I find myself starting to think about things. Can I slow down this trip through this tunnel? It seems I don't have that power yet. But what has made me choose these words. To say I don't have that power yet. Am I to have it? Power… For I was also promised power. Before I could reach the end I felt it. It was a sharp pain, a sharp jerk. These guys won't let me sleep. I was enjoying my sleep. Am I dreaming?

ABOUT THE AUTHOR

Ozzie Vargas is the creator of *"Am I Dreaming".*

Written in two parts; the first within the confinement of jail and the other while out on bail. Am I dreaming is the first novel in a trilogy, with parts two and three soon to be released. Having been emancipated at the early age of 16 has prepared him for the encounter which he writes about. Contrary to many living on the streets of New York, he was well educated; having spent time at NYU and Fordham University. In 2006 a sudden death of a loved one initiated a spiral that culminated into this book. Written with a flare of a gangster, mix with that of a college degree, Ozzie Vargas writes a tale of true events; Event which seem to be stranger than fiction, but nonetheless true. His writing appeals to and addresses a wide audience.

Ozzie Vargas , at first a profoundly honest man, influenced by a lack of love, writes a story of love, loss, heroism, honor, cunning, survival and ultimately, hope. Hope that he can somehow influence the outcome of a devious plan set in motion by an elite group.

www.ingramcontent.com/pod-product-compliance
Lightning Source LLC
Chambersburg PA
CBHW081939110426
42744CB00032B/1920
9780692287552